THE COMMODORES

CLASSICS OF NAVAL LITERATURE
JACK SWEETMAN, SERIES EDITOR

The purpose of this series is to make available attractive new editions of classic works of naval history, biography, and fiction. In addition to the complete original text, each volume will feature an introduction and, when appropriate, notes by an expert in the field. The series will include, among others, the following titles:

The Commodores

By Leonard F. Guttridge and Jay D. Smith
With an introduction by James C. Bradford

NAVAL INSTITUTE PRESS
Annapolis, Maryland

This book was originally published
in 1969 by Harper & Row.

Copyright © 1969
by Leonard F. Guttridge and Jay D. Smith

Library of Congress Cataloging in Publication Data
Guttridge, Leonard F.
  The commodores.

  Bibliography: p.
  1. United States.   Navy—History—19th century.
2. United States—History, Naval—To 1900.
I. Smith, Jay, D. II. Bradford, James C. III. Title.
VA56.G8 1984   359'.00973   84-18906
ISBN 0-87021-133-1

Printed in the United States of America

CONTENTS

ACKNOWLEDGMENTS

CHRISTOPHER MCKEE took time from his work on a social history of the early naval officer corps to read and comment on this introduction, which benefited from his suggestions. Leonard Guttridge furnished additional information on a number of points, particularly in regard to the way in which he and the late Jay D. Smith collaborated to produce the book. The contributors to *Makers of the American Naval Tradition: Command under Sail* provided me with a broad perspective from which to assess *The Commodores*. Few of these scholars will agree with everything in this introduction, but all improved it. It has been a pleasure to work with series editor Jack Sweetman and with the Naval Institute. To my wife Judy, I offer my fondest thanks for her cheerful patience and willing assumption of virtually all domestic chores. Without her support I would accomplish much less.

INTRODUCTION

THE GRADE OF ADMIRAL was not introduced into the United States Navy until 1862. Until then, a robust, republican prejudice against a word popularly associated with Old World aristocracy meant that the highest rank to which an American naval officer could aspire was captain. An officer serving in command of a squadron or station did, however, rate the *title* and the swallow-tailed pennant of a commodore. Thus, the leading figures of the sailing navy, the men with whom the history of the U.S. Navy begins, were commodores. By the end of the War of 1812, the last major conflict fought under canvas, their exploits had made them idols of the new nation. So deep was the commodores' imprint upon the American consciousness that many of their names—Preble, Decatur, Perry, Porter, Macdonough, Bainbridge, Rodgers, and others—remain familiar even today. But if the names are known, the men who bore them have become heroic stick-figures, dimly perceived through the patriotic mists of time. In this book, Leonard F. Guttridge and Jay D. Smith bring *The Commodores* vividly to life, and historian and general reader alike will enjoy renewing acquaintance with the commanders of the young American navy.

The U.S. Navy was launched as the Age of Sail was reaching its highest level of military development. During the Wars of the French Revolution and Empire, European nations were expanding their sea services into true navies organized into fleets with administrative hierarchies. Navies began to play key roles in national strategies, and the naval forces of the European powers were more closely balanced than they would ever be again. The Royal Navy was the world's preeminent service, but France, Spain, the Netherlands, and Russia all maintained powerful fleets capable of mounting serious challenges to Britain's power. Other nations, such as Sweden, Denmark, Turkey, Portugal, and the Kingdom of the Two Sicilies, had navies which could contest control of their coastal waters. Even Austria and the Barbary States had respectable forces.[1] It was primarily to deal with the last of these, the Barbary States, that the United States established its navy in 1794. Within twenty years, the fledgling navy would also enter wars against France and Great Britain, the world's two greatest naval powers.

To many Americans, it seemed foolhardy to compete with such vastly superior opponents, but the U.S. Navy managed to inflict more damage than it received. It was a heroic age, when men like Stephen Decatur, Edward Preble, Oliver Hazard Perry, and Thomas Macdonough triumphed in hard-fought battles like those at Plattsburg and Put-in-Bay.

Following the War of 1812, the Era of Good Feeling brought an upsurge of American patriotism. The navy, which had provided most of the victories in the war, basked in its new-found glory. Writers chronicled its successes and ignored its failures, and the nation worshipped a new pantheon of heroes.

The last decades of the Age of Sail coincided also with the beginning of the Romantic Age in the United States. "Romantics" rebelled against the lifeless logic of the preceding Age of Reason and placed greater value on intuition and feeling than on education and reason. Men of action were preferred to men of contemplation. The Romantic movement began in Europe during the 1780s but did not reach the United States for over a quarter of a century. Its arrival coincided with the passing of the Revolutionary generation—John Quincy Adams was the last president to wear a wig and dress in kneebreeches—and the rise of Jacksonian Democracy with its self-confidence, optimism, and faith in the common man and in the future of the United States.

All facets of American culture, including literature, were influenced by Romanticism, which brought with it a renewed interest in literary uses of the nation's history. James Fenimore Cooper was particularly important in marking the literary transition from Rationalism to

---

1. Otto von Pivka, *Navies of the Napoleonic Era* (Newton Abbot, England, 1980) is a well-illustrated and spritely written survey of the men, ships, and battles of the era.

Romanticism. He was the only American novelist before 1830 to make successful use of the nation's heritage. Equally significant, he was the first American novelist to enjoy great popularity abroad. Cooper drew upon his two years as a midshipman in the navy not only for his eleven sea novels but also for his two-volume study, *The History of the Navy of the United States of America* (1839), and for his *Lives of Distinguished American Naval Officers* (1846). Cooper's works set the themes—operations and great leaders—that would dominate American naval history for the remainder of the nineteenth century.[2] Typical of the genre is John Ledyard Denison's *A Pictorial History of the Navy of the United States . . . with a Particular Account of all the Most Celebrated Naval Battles . . .* (1860). Its opening paragraph represents the tone of works of this period:

> There is no species of historical writing more generally interesting, we had almost said, more certainly useful, than that which records the heroic deeds, and commemorates the exalted virtues of that hardy and chivalrous race of men "whose home is on the deep."[3]

The Civil War, which swept in so many changes, brought no broadening of the tone and focus of nineteenth-century naval histories. Few general works were published, and those on the Confederate and Union navies continued to stress battles and leaders. For a quarter of a century following the conflict, both the navy and the writing of its history declined.

At the turn of the century, a resurgence of interest in the navy and its past led to a new generation of naval history. The Spanish-American War, America's new overseas empire, and the Anglo-German naval race all attracted readers to naval subjects. History was emerging as a separate academic discipline at the same time, but most academic historians ignored the navy, and the writing of naval history remained the province of journalists, naval officers, and literary gentlemen. Works such as Edgar S. Maclay's two-volume *A History of the U.S. Navy from 1775–1898* and John R. Spears's five-volume *History of Our Navy: From Its Origins to the Present Day, 1775–1898* were well received.

The most famous of the gentleman writers was Theodore Roosevelt, whose two-volume *The Naval War of 1812* (1882) remains a standard

2. Russel B. Nye summarized Cooper's impact on fiction but does not mention his naval histories in *The Cultural Life of the New Nation* (New York, 1960), 255, and *Society and Culture in American, 1830–1860* (New York, 1974), 91–94.

3. John Ledyard Denison, *A Pictorial History of the Navy of the United States* (Cincinnati, 1860), 1.

secondary work.[4] The other standard history of the sailing navy dating from this period is by Alfred Thayer Mahan, the sailor-scholar who stressed the value of studying naval history for the "lessons learned." The first of Mahan's trilogy, *The Influence of Sea Power Upon History, 1660–1783* (1890), deals almost exclusively with Britain and France; the second, *The Influence of Sea Power Upon the French Revolution and Empire, 1793–1812* (1892), includes some material on the Quasi-War; the final section, *Sea Power in Its Relation to the War of 1812* (1905), discusses extensively the young American navy. Mahan's volumes mark a transition in naval historiography. Like the nineteenth-century writers, Mahan devoted most of his attention to operations and battles. But also like his contemporary progressive historians, he sought to glean lessons from the past and to use history to influence current policy.

Nevertheless, the clash of battle, the heroics of individuals, and the glamour of operations in exotic places continued to fascinate most naval history authors. The title of George F. Gibb's 1900 book, *Pike and Cutlass: Hero Tales of Our Navy*, indicates the contents of most products of the era. Certainly in a class above these was the work of Gardner W. Allen, who wrote operational histories of the American Revolution (1913), the Quasi-War (1909), and the Barbary Wars (1905). One exception to the predominant focus on operations was provided by Charles O. Paullin, who wrote *Diplomatic Negotiations of American Naval Officers, 1778–1883* (1912) and a series of articles on naval administration published in the U.S. Naval Institute *Proceedings*.

When academics began after the First World War to write about naval topics, the focus was often wider but the results fairly dry. Harold and Margaret Sprout's two-volume survey of the rise of American naval power and George T. Davis's study of the link between public opinion and naval appropriations were important works for scholars but certainly not attractive to a wide audience.[5] Even at mid-century little had changed and most naval histories continued to concentrate on operations and, to a lesser degree, on administration and policy.

Naval biography, almost a separate genre, followed a similar pattern. Until the early twentieth century, virtually all naval biographies

4. Theodore Roosevelt, *The Naval War of 1812*, 2 vols., went through three editions between 1882 and 1910.

5. Harold and Margaret Sprout, *The Rise of American Naval Power, 1776–1918* (Princeton, 1939); George T. Davis, *A Navy Second to None: The Development of Modern American Naval Policy* (New York, 1940).

were eulogistic narratives of operations commanded by heroes. Alexander Slidell Mackenzie's early biographies of Stephen Decatur and Oliver Hazard Perry were notable exceptions. Many officers were the subject of a single biography and a few, such as John Paul Jones and Oliver Hazard Perry, received multiple treatments. There were also a few collective biographies but most of these mixed officers from the American, British, and even a few other navies. Little attempt was made to draw parallels between the individual subjects. Alfred Thayer Mahan attempted to extract lessons from the lives of officers in the Royal Navy, and two Naval Academy instructors, Professor Carroll Storrs Alden and Commander Ralph Earle, sketched the lives of thirteen American officers in the "hope that the youths studying to become officers [at the Naval Academy] will by means of this book be led to realize more fully their debt to the great men who have preceded them in the Service." Both works consisted of laudatory vignettes showing men of ability and courage triumphing over great odds.[6]

At mid-century Fletcher Pratt, a prolific author of books in various fields ranging from criminology to cooking, published *Preble's Boys: Commodore Preble and the Birth of American Sea Power*, one of the most widely read and influential books on naval history since those of Alfred Thayer Mahan. Pratt had earlier written several other books on the navy. He appears to have begun work on a biography of Preble in the 1930s, when he published an article on him in the U.S. Naval Institute *Proceedings*. Either in studying Preble's life or in searching for characteristics shared by the officer corps in the War of 1812, Pratt came to the conclusion that Preble was the dominating figure who shaped a generation of young officers and laid the foundations of the U.S. Navy. In *Preble's Boys*, he limned a portrait of the commodore and fifteen officers who served under him in the Mediterranean and who went on to command American forces in all except one of the major victories in the War of 1812.[7] It was Preble's leadership, training, and example, Pratt argued, that gave these men the abilities needed to lead the tiny American navy to a series of triumphs over the formidable Royal Navy. To Pratt, the officers of 1812 were a band of brothers, united by Preble just as Horatio Nelson had united the Royal Navy officers who served

6. Alfred Thayer Mahan, *Types of Naval Officers Drawn from the History of the British Navy* (London, 1904); Carroll Storrs Alden and Ralph Earle, *Makers of Naval Tradition* (Boston, 1925).

7. The exception was Oliver Hazard Perry's victory at the Battle of Lake Erie.

with him. He treated his subjects as demi-gods, with few if any faults. This interpretation continues to influence the popular view of the early navy to the present day. Even many historians who have questioned Pratt's facts and his treatments of individual officers have accepted his band-of-brothers thesis.[8]

The view of the officer corps that Guttridge and Smith present in *The Commodores* stands in sharp contrast to the fraternity portrayed by Pratt. Guttridge and Smith did not consciously set out to write revisionist history, and, indeed, they do not mention Pratt's work in the text or list it in their bibliography. The challenge they pose to Pratt's view is implicit rather than explicit.[9]

When *The Commodores* was published in 1969, most historical journals failed to take notice. *The American Historical Review* and the *Journal of American History*, both of which publish notices of books they do not fully review, did not even list *The Commodores*. When *The Commodores* was published in Britain the following year with the subtitle *The Drama of a Navy under Sail*, its reception was similar. Even the reviewer for the *Mariner's Mirror* simply summarized its contents, saying nothing about its analysis. The only professional history journal in the United States to assess *The Commodores* was the *American Neptune*. Reviewer Christopher McKee, although recognizing the book's virtues and conceding that "specialists cannot ignore" it, questioned the authors' "highly personal interpretation of the men."

McKee made no mention of *The Commodores* in the Edward Preble biography he published in 1972. A decade later, McKee, while not retreating from his position in the *American Neptune* review, acknowledged that *The Commodores* has heavily influenced scholarship on the early U.S. Navy:

> The influence of *The Commodores* is paradoxical: it received no attention
> in the book review section of any major scholarly journal at the time of
> its publication, . . . yet its judgments can be found blended into the

---

8. Fletcher Pratt, *Preble's Boys: Commander Preble and the Birth of American Sea Power* (New York, 1950). For a recent analysis of Preble's thesis, particularly with regard to the age and prior service of the "Boys," see Christopher McKee, "Edward Preble and the 'Boys': The Officer Corps of 1812 Revisited" in James C. Bradford, ed., *Makers of the American Naval Tradition: Command under Sail*, forthcoming.

9. Two other classic works of naval biography might be noted: Eugene S. Ferguson, *Truxton of the Constellation* (Baltimore, 1956), and Samuel Eliot Morison, *John Paul Jones: A Sailor's Biography* (Boston, 1959). Both subjects predated Preble and neither author addressed Pratt's work.

texts of many [subsequent works on naval history], and it is repeatedly cited in their notes. So far no scholar has systematically challenged . . . Guttridge and Smith on sources, methods, or conclusions.[10]

Eminent naval historian David F. Long also makes no mention of Guttridge and Smith in his biography of David Porter (1970) but a decade later, in his biography of William Bainbridge, he praises Guttridge and Smith saying that "I and all others attempting to rewrite early naval biography are eternally in their debt."[11]

Perhaps it was *The Commodores*'s omission of footnotes or the authors' lack of academic affiliations that led review editors to assume the book was a popular work by amateurs and without merit for scholars. Guttridge and Smith's method of citing sources—a general four-page bibliographical note and a two-page listing of other works which were "seen or consulted"—is similar to that employed by Samuel Eliot Morison in his biography of John Paul Jones. Admiral Morison was, however, a well-established academic by the time he employed such methods. Neither Guttridge nor Smith had completed college or had much in common with other naval historical writers. Furthermore, both were air force, not navy, veterans; Guttridge served in the Royal Air Force during World War Two, and Smith was still in the U.S. Air Force when he began the book.

Smith grew up in Harrisburg, Pennsylvania; Guttridge in Cardiff, Wales. They met in Washington, D.C., when Smith was stationed there and Guttridge was working as the librarian at the Indian Embassy. Both wrote articles for magazines in their spare time and had an interest in jazz. This led to their first collaboration, *Jack Teagarden: Story of a Jazz Maverick*, which was published in 1960. The following year Guttridge left the Indian Embassy to write professionally. During the 1950s and 1960s, he contributed scores of articles to popular magazines. Smith was again stationed in the Washington area at this time. His wife worked at the National Archives, and one day she came upon a body of material on the early navy that had not been used by historians. These papers served as the basis for an article on James Barron and the *Chesapeake–Leonard* incident that Smith wrote for the Naval Institute *Proceedings* in 1967.

10. The review is in the *American Neptune* 30 (January 1970), 73–75; McKee's later comment in Robin Higham and Donald J. Mrozek, eds., *A Guide to the Sources of United States Military History: Supplement I* (Hamden, Conn., 1981), 34.

11. David F. Long, *Ready to Hazard: A Biography of Commodore William Bainbridge, 1774–1833* (Hanover, N.H., 1981), 318.

Smith shared his discovery with Guttridge, and the two began planning a book. Guttridge originally proposed writing a collective biography of Stephen Decatur, James Barron, Jesse Elliot, and William Bainbridge. After a Boston publisher rejected this proposal, he wrote to Harper & Row in New York, where Marion S. ("Buzz") Wyeth, Jr., suggested broadening the work to include all the sailing navy. The authors readily agreed and began work. When Smith, still in the air force, was transferred to Spain, the research and writing was assumed by Guttridge, who forwarded his drafts and other materials to Smith, who suggested alternatives. Guttridge, at least, was familiar with *Preble's Boys*, but the authors let the documents, not secondary histories, lead them. Evidence suggested, for example, that the Barron–Decatur duel was "almost a setup for murder." The "evidence [also made it] irresistible to write the [chapter on the Algerine war of 1815] from the perspective of the Bainbridge–Decatur feud."[12] Both authors were interested in historical mysteries, and Guttridge in particular was interested in interpersonal relationships. "Power struggles of whatever description—between individuals in a mutually tight spot—intrigue me," he once wrote, "and my love of the same took over in *The Commodores*."[13]

This is perhaps a bit hyperbolic, but it indicates something of the flavor of the work. For a century, naval histories were concerned almost exclusively with the description of operations and with a search for lessons. The work of Guttridge and Smith was different. Nowhere do they state a thesis or identify lessons to be learned from the early navy, though they do in a few cases draw parallels between the early nineteenth and mid-twentieth centuries, such as their reference to institutional resistance to new technology.

The genesis of *The Commodores* helps explain its nature. The first third is a general history presented from a biographical perspective of the first decade of "The U.S. Navy in the Age of Sail." (This subtitle appeared on the dust jacket but not on the title page.) A shift in emphasis follows and the next six chapters, 9 through 14, focus on one event, the *Chesapeake–Leopard* affair, and its aftermath. Six chapters then survey the naval aspects of the War of 1812, followed by individual chapters examining the Mediterranean War of 1815 and the Decatur–Barron duel. The two concluding chapters trace the decline

---

12. Telephone conversation with the editor, 3 January 1984.
13. *Contemporary Authors*, vols. 85–88, 232.

of the sailing navy from the 1820s to the destruction of the last of the great sailing warships during the Civil War.

The first eight chapters provide the best-available brief overview of the U.S. Navy's nascent years. They are not simply descriptive but contain a great number of insights, often stated in a single sentence. One such is their pithy summary of Thomas Jefferson's naval policy: "Jefferson's lifelong notion of a navy was as a hastily cut switch with which to chastise barbaric primitives, never as a permanent and expensive sword to be brandished at civilized Europeans." This is more sophisticated than characterizations found in other books of the time and anticipated by a decade the division of opinion Craig Symonds presents in *Navalists and Antinavalists.*[14] Symonds identifies two groups on the congressional level, those he terms the "navalists," who wanted a large navy capable of competing with those of the European powers, and the "antinavalists," who preferred a navy capable only of defending the American coast and protecting American commerce from pirates and lesser nations like the Barbary States. Guttridge and Smith foreshadowed this interpretation, calling Symonds's antinavalists "the Republican gunboat bloc," but also identified a third group, "the Anti-Navy faction," which they believe opposed building a navy of any kind. Other of the authors' strengths are equally evident in this section. It is filled with sketches of secondary characters and revealing anecdotes which give life to all their subjects.

Guttridge and Smith do not indulge in hero worship. The success of Thomas Truxtun is related, but so too are the failures of John Barry and Samuel Nicholson. Guttridge and Smith bring out the officers' individual personalities. Where Fletcher Pratt is readable but rather simplistic, Guttridge and Smith are readable and as subtle and complex as one wants to make them. Their writing is clear, understandable, and exciting, even to the reader who brings no knowledge of naval history to the book. Seasoned naval historians will find the narrative peppered with flashes of insight and telling facts. The authors' willingness to speculate and even at times to leap to debatable conclusions sometimes alarms, but more often challenges, historians. In the case of William Bainbridge, for example, they conclude that "in his early naval service at least, that period when, in the glibness of some historians, he was simply 'a child of misfortune,' it is as much miscalculation and uncer-

14. Craig Symonds, *Navalists and Antinavalists: The Naval Policy Debate in the United States, 1785–1827* (Newark, Del., 1980).

tainty as bad luck that precipitated disaster and left him prey to the only thing that he mortally feared: the censure of his countrymen."

Chapters 9 through 14 contain the most complete account in print of the *Chesapeake–Leopard* affair and its aftermath. In assessing the period as a whole, Burton Spivak's *Jefferson's English Crisis: Commerce, Embargo, and the Republican Revolution* (1979) shows that President Jefferson was far more hawkish than Guttridge and Smith portray him and argues that Jefferson considered the Embargo Act a preparatory step toward war rather than a substitute for it, but none of the authors' other major judgments have been questioned by later writers. Their discussion of the courts-martial of Commodore James Barron and Captain Charles Gordon cuts through the mass of material to the key points. It is here that they begin to draw together the dynamics of the interpersonal relationships of the commodores which they had explored earlier.

The animosity that the presiding officer, John Rodgers, evinced toward Barron dated from their service together in the Mediterranean in 1805 and 1806 when Barron's ailing elder brother clung to control of the squadron until peace was at hand, thereby denying Rodgers the opportunity for combat command. The authors take no side in the earlier quarrel but clearly imply that Rodgers should have sought to be excused from serving on the court, as did Stephen Decatur, because of prejudice. Their characterization of Rodgers is certainly defendable, though their contention that the entire court-martial was unique is questionable. The statement that "it was the only occasion in American naval history on which a commanding officer was formally charged with failure to prepare against expected attack" is technically true, but the last clause of their following sentence, "The court of inquiry ordered by the Navy Department to investigate the Pearl Harbor disaster of 1941 produced not dissimilar accusations against an admiral, but he escaped court-martial," ignores the fact that Admiral Husband Kimmel actively sought a court-martial for a decade after the Japanese attack. At the very time they were writing, another episode was taking place which would produce similar charges. On 23 January 1968, the USS *Pueblo* was fired upon by North Korean gunboats while in international waters, its captain and crew taken prisoner and held captive for eleven months. Shortly after his release the commanding officer, Commander Lloyd M. Bucher, was tried for "permitting his ship to be seized while he had the power to resist."

To say, as Guttridge and Smith do, that Barron's court-martial was "marked by prejudice and duplicity" is fairly accurate. The Navy's disciplinary system was clearly oriented more toward maintaining order and discipline than guaranteeing justice for individuals. In no way, though, is *The Commodores* a partisan defense of James Barron. An article on the Decatur–Barron duel by the British naval novelist C. S. Forester in the October 1964 issue of *American Heritage* is much more favorable to Barron and contains one particularly strong point in his favor which Guttridge and Smith do not include in their work. Forester asks how anyone could expect Barron to anticipate an actual attack by the *Leopard*. "British ships had been known, only too often, to fire into neutral merchant ships that were slow in obeying signals . . . but it was still inconceivable that *Leopard* would actually fire into *Chesapeake*. Barron may well have thought that the reply that he sent was a formal refusal to a formal demand, setting up a situation that the diplomats could argue about later. . . . Then, the unbelievable happened; *Leopard* . . . fired her broadside." Guttridge and Smith do not go so far as Forester to absolve Barron of culpability, but they do conclude that Captain Gordon was equally to blame. Forester calls Barron's suspension from the navy without pay for five years "a savage sentence and a terrible humiliation," but Guttridge and Smith pass no judgment on the court's punishment. Instead, they write that "one does not need to criticize either the judgment or the penalty in Barron's case to question whether Charles Gordon was so much less reprehensible that the court would scout his proven guilt, deliberately seek the softest punishment it could find for him, and announce that it had done so as if in public apology for having accused him in the first place." Thus, what to Forester is clearly a miscarriage of justice is to Guttridge and Smith more a case of unequal justice. Their conclusion that Captain Gordon was at least as guilty as Barron but that he escaped harsh punishment through the influence of his kinsman, Secretary of the Treasury Albert Gallatin, appears well-founded.

Chapters 15 through 20 recount the chief naval events of the War of 1812. The graphic account of Isaac Hull's escape in the *Constitution* from an entire British squadron by a remarkable feat of seamanship compares favorably with the description by Forester in his popular history, *The Age of Fighting Sail: The Story of the Navy War of 1812* (1957). As usual, Guttridge and Smith focus on personalities, demonstrating that during America's second war with Britain the "senior officers" of the U.S. Navy were "not altogether the heroic automata that two generations of juvenile romanticism has made them to appear but a company of proud and seasoned mariners with fiercely individual traits, whose patriotic incentives were sometimes hard to distinguish from glittering dreams of prize money."

Chapter 21, on the Algerine War of 1815, is the most provocative and perhaps the best in the book. At the start of the War of 1812 the Dey of Algiers had begun to prey upon American merchantmen. When the war ended and American trade returned to the Mediterranean, such behavior could not be tolerated by patriotic Americans at an hour when "the victories of the naval war, not the defeats and misfired plans" of the land war were "predominant in the popular mind." The time had come to chastise the heathen and to do so the two largest American squadrons yet formed were ordered to sea. One was to be commanded by William Bainbridge, the senior commodore on sea duty, and the other by Stephen Decatur, recently released from British captivity following his loss of the *President*.

As always, Guttridge and Smith focus on the personalities involved rather than on the operations they conducted or the ships they commanded. In most histories this minor conflict is simply a matter of vastly superior forces exacting justice from a far weaker opponent, but in *The Commodores* the conflict is not between Algiers and the United States but between Decatur and Bainbridge, two "commodores deeply entrapped in rivalry, the one pitiless and confident, the other sullen and embittered as he trailed far behind Decatur's wake with the consolation prize of the second squadron." To Decatur the chastening of Algiers was secondary to his drive to atone for the surrender of the *President* and "to satisfy the world of his untarnished renown." To Bainbridge return to the Mediterranean meant the opportunity to wipe away the humiliation heaped upon him by the Dey of Algiers, who had forced Bainbridge to carry his tribute to Constantinople. It also meant the opportunity to avenge his loss of the *Philadelphia* to the Bashaw of Tripoli. With Guttridge and Smith's retelling, the usually mundane becomes high drama. Stephen Decatur's dash becomes "ruthlessness," and the writers endorse Bainbridge's belief that he was a "victim of fraud hatched at home which deprived him of unique rights to glory in the Mediterranean." Not all readers will agree with these forthright assessments—Bainbridge must, for example, share some of the blame for his failure to put to sea from Boston as quickly as Decatur cleared New York. Even if he had been told that the squadron in New York would be ready for sea sooner than the one in Boston, it is doubtful that he would have refused command of the first American ship-of-the-line to be ordered to war, and that ship, the *Independence*, was fitting out in Boston. There was no way for Bainbridge to foresee that Decatur would have such instant success as to deprive him, the senior officer, of the opportunity to take a glorious part in the campaign against Barbary.

The Decatur–Barron duel is an oft-told tale. Both men had, and continue to have, their partisans, although Decatur has always had more. Guttridge and Smith present one of the more balanced assessments of the episode. Barron's second, Jesse Elliott, was a key figure. Other historians have theorized that when Oliver Hazard Perry died, Elliott transferred his hatred for his old commander on Lake Erie to Decatur and that the arrangements he proposed for the duel, especially the distance of eight instead of the usual ten or twelve paces, were calculated to ensure Decatur's death. Guttridge and Smith concur in this but go further. It was "almost a set up for murder," Guttridge recently stated.[15] In *The Commodores* he and Smith are a bit milder, but to a greater degree than previous writers they implicate Bainbridge whose "true motives can only be surmised. . . . The terms he had hatched with Elliott . . . hardly encouraged humane gallantry from the man he was supposed to represent." Neither second fulfilled his duty to seek accommodation and avoid the duel; the authors suggest that this was because both wished to see Decatur dead and neither cared whether Barron lived or died. Many will take issue with this view of Bainbridge. In his definitive recent biography of Bainbridge, David F. Long reviews the evidence for both interpretations and closes his assessment of the charges of Bainbridge's "complicity in Decatur's death" by saying that "perhaps the most useful verdict might be that pronounced in some Scottish trials—'not proven.'"[16]

Guttridge and Smith so fill their history of the sailing navy with tales of personal animosity and petty rivalry that interpersonal tensions seem almost central to the nature of the institution. The emphasis is highly questionable, but Guttridge and Smith find good and bad in virtually all their subjects; they even defend Jesse Elliot against charges of cowardice by citing his foray from Black Rock as evidence of a measure of courage. The sole exception is John Rodgers. In no instance do they single him out for extended criticism but the entire book is laced with statements critical of his conduct, enough so that K. Jack

15. Telephone conversation with the editor, 3 January 1984.
16. Long, *Ready to Hazard*, 246.

Bauer has recently referred to *The Commodores* as "an anti-Rodgers collective biography."[17]

While Guttridge and Smith are bold in many of their judgments, they do leave unanswered several questions. Although their assessment of William Bainbridge is well balanced, the reader still wonders how the man who surrendered the first two U.S. Navy ships to enemies and allowed a foreign potentate to impress a third managed to avoid dismissal from the service. At the time even Bainbridge wrote, "misfortune has attended my naval life—Guadeloupe and Algiers have witnessed part of it but Tripoli strikes the death blow to my future prospects." Similarly, one wonders when reading *The Commodores* how a service so racked by factionalism, jealousy, and feuds could have achieved as much as it did—or for that matter even function. Again, one of the book's chief strengths is that it raises new questions for scholars. No historian of the field can ignore it.

Near the end of the book Guttridge and Smith correctly conclude that the memory of the commodores "began immediately to undergo a unique romanticizing process [which] led to a comparative scarcity of intelligent literature about the Navy under sail and what seems even more of an injustice to the captains and commodores, a perversion of the subject into patriotic juvenilia and superpatriotic myth." Their work helped redirect naval historiography from this path for both the layman and the scholar. *The Commodores* is, above all else, a superb example of serious history with great general appeal. By individualizing the officers and perceptively analyzing their characters, it makes them human.

The original edition of *The Commodores* contained some typographical and other errors that have been silently corrected here. The interpretations remain those of the authors; indeed, it is worth noting that in the fifteen years since *The Commodores* first appeared there have been biographies of a number of the individuals who figure prominently in its pages, but few of Guttridge and Smith's views have been called into serious question. There are areas where different conclusions can be supported from the record; the most important of these have generally been discussed in this introduction. To go beyond this would be to cavil. Guttridge and Smith are sometimes controversial, but they are never boring. So too were their subjects, and the commo-

17. K. Jack Bauer, "John Rodgers: The Stalwart Conservative" in Bradford, *Command under Sail*.

dores would have respected the authors' willingness to draw conclusions and boldly state positions, even if they would not have always agreed.

JAMES C. BRADFORD

THE COMMODORES

Acknowledgments

THE AUTHORS are grateful for the patient assistance and unfailing courtesy shown them by the staffs of the New York Public Library; the Enoch Pratt Library of Baltimore; the Museum and Library, United States Naval Academy; the Manuscript Division, Library of Congress; the Naval History Division, National Archives of the United States; and the Navy Department Library. Particular thanks are due to the Director of Naval History, Ernest M. Eller, Rear Admiral, USN (Ret.).

A debt of appreciation is owed to the staffs of libraries and historical societies from Maine to the University of Virginia and from Maryland to the Henry Huntington Library, San Marino, California, for making available their valuable collections.

Many private individuals in widely varied stations of life, unaware of each other's existence but having in common the distinction of descent from closely associated commodores and captains, volunteered their own unique help. They include Mr. C. T. Gordon of Tellico Plains, Tennessee, who owns the specially designed sofa made for the enfeebled Captain Charles Gordon on the *Constellation*; Mrs. William Machold of Wayne, Pennsylvania, descended from Commodore Decatur's sister; and two proud defenders of an ill-starred commodore, Miss Anne W. Marr and Mrs. James Barron, both of Norfolk. A kind gesture came from the late Mr. Upton Sinclair, great grandson of the Lieutenant (later Commodore) Arthur Sinclair who recruited for the *Chesapeake* in 1807.

Finally, the authors acknowledge with deep gratitude the patience and guidance of Mr. M. S. Wyeth of Harper & Row.

1

A Prefatory Note on Rank

In February 1799 the United States Congress provided that all naval vessels of twenty or more guns were to be commanded by captains, those of eighteen or less by lieutenants or masters-commandant. Strict adherence to this rule was not always practicable. The rank of master-commandant (abolished long before the Civil War) fell between those of captain and lieutenant, and corresponded to the rank of lieutenant colonel in the Army. A captain, or more rarely a master-commandant, who had commanded a company of ships was privileged to call himself a commodore. His identifying symbols were a silver star on each strap of his epaulet and a broad, forked pendant flown at the main truck of his ship. They could also betoken jealousy and friction. Commodore was not a commissioned rank but a courtesy title which implied prestige rather than prowess and whose only emolument was vanity.

CHAPTER ONE

Talk of a Fleet

IN THE HEADY republican atmosphere following the Revolution, it was at first a matter of little concern that elimination of England's rule had removed as well the protection of her fleet. Few Americans perceived the relevance of sea power to their free republic. Even these could recall the Continental Navy, for all its weaknesses, as evidence that the new nation could in crisis improvise a naval force and thus did not require a standing one. Permanent armies and navies were, in the popular view, the playthings of tyrants, the ornaments of that very system which Americans had just so violently repudiated. Therefore, in the summer of 1785 no one mourned the sale of the frigate *Alliance*, the last surviving vessel of that scratch fleet ordained by General Washington, and when eight weeks later Algerian pirates carried off twenty-three American seamen it was ransom for their recovery, not measures to resist more outrages, that engaged the attention of Congress.

The greed and capriciousness of the Dey of Algiers, who ruled the most powerful of the Barbary Coast States, foredoomed his captives to long enslavement, and to a term of futility and humiliation those authorized to bargain for their release. After months of unpromising negotiations with the Dey, two of America's representatives in Europe exchanged views on how best to deal with him. Writing from his post in London to Thomas Jefferson in Paris, John Adams could see no immediate solution other than surrender; prolonged negotiations would simply promote greedier demands. And for America to

3

wage war was out of the question—unless, Adams added, the south-
ern states could be persuaded to it, in which case, he felt confident,
there would be no objection from Pennsylvania northward. On his
part, Jefferson unhesitatingly favored a fight. As the French foreign
minister had put it to him, the only agents likely to impress the
Algerian were money and fear. Jefferson was aware that while America had little enough of the one, she had no present means at all of
instilling the other. Nevertheless, force was his choice: war against
Algiers, more just and honorable a course than submission to blackmail, and in the long run the least expensive.

For a diplomat we know to have abhorred violence, Jefferson was
uncommonly diligent during his mission to France in investigating
the cost and size of a naval force sufficient to crush what Adams called
"these nests of Banditti." He proposed a fleet of 150 guns, half of it
in constant cruise, built, manned, and victualed for six months. To
this Adams' reply was the cold douche of a realist, though gently
applied. Had not Jefferson perhaps underestimated the strength of
the Algerians and thus the size of the fleet necessary to chastise them?
And although a vigorous, warlike policy instead of appeasement by
tribute must inspire all America, certainly not for years would Congress adopt one.

On this last point at least Adams was correct. In December 1790,
twenty-eight months after final ratification of a Constitution which
empowered the legislative "to provide and maintain a navy," the
recommendations of Thomas Jefferson (now Secretary of State) for
the creation of a Mediterranean squadron were read before Congress.
All they brought forth were additional appropriations for the ransom
of the Dey's captives (seven of whom had died meanwhile) and a
senatorial promise of a fleet when the country could afford it.

To criticize the members of those early sessions of Congress for
shortsightedness because they did not immediately acknowledge any
urgent need for a navy would be improper. For one thing, how could
it have been easy to stir up zeal for expensive enterprises of controversial value in the shadow of the towering national debt? The idea
of a naval force, foundering as a topic of the legislature, could and
did cut a lively wake through scattered private correspondence and
public pamphleteering. But for a decade after the struggle for independence, nothing especially seemed to warrant a navy, certainly not

the pirate threat. Indian unrest in the overland West had far greater impact upon the American consciousness than occasional depredations in a remote sea where profiteering shipmasters ventured at their own risk and which was, moreover, already policed by the Portuguese. For of all major European powers only Portugal was applying force to the pirate menace rather than bribery: since the summer of 1786 a Portuguese naval squadron had prevented the Algerians from breaking into the Atlantic and in addition extended protection to American merchantmen entering the Mediterranean. It is an indication of how little they cared about distant dangers that Americans could rely upon the Portuguese Navy untroubled by a sense of ignominy at sheltering behind a foreign shield.

We need not be puzzled, then, by the absence of any vehement drive for a fleet, even among a people who, George Washington had noted, possessed a "natural genius for naval affairs." Might not this very genius enable the country to conjure a fleet "almost in a moment," employing the "nursery of seamen" conveniently on hand in the merchant service and fisheries? This was not so farfetched. Few countries were as rich in maritime resources. Until the Revolution the sinews of Britain's sea strength were in large part American. Much of the timber, tar, pitch, rosin, and turpentine in her ships of war had been extracted from the seemingly infinite virgin timberland of the colonies. In 1775, one-third of the total tonnage on the British shipping register came from American shipyards. The colonies' own vessels numbered about 2,000 and their mariners were twenty times as numerous. The New England fisheries formed a bountiful source of bold and skillful man power for British warships. Indeed, few British institutions suffered more severely from the loss of America than the Royal Navy. "She was the fountain of our wealth," lamented the Earl of Chatham in 1777, "the nerve of our strength, the nursery and basis of our naval power."

America's own recognition of this unique naval potential was at first to consist of repeatedly sidestepping the means of ensuring that in future emergencies it could be effectively tapped. Each modest proposal from Henry Knox, whose duties as Secretary of War included attendance to naval questions, was scrutinized by politicians suspiciously alert for the slightest move toward a permanent fleet.

In the complex discussions over commerce and revenue which reflected congressional awakening to the responsibilities of independence, talk of a fleet became increasingly hard to avoid. And soon, although Henry Knox's naval messages to Congress continued to evoke only the barest response, he was no longer pouring his dutifully acquired estimates concerning personnel, equipment, sails, rigging, and ship construction into a vacuum of disinterest. Between 1791 and 1793 the tide of congressional feeling ran strong enough to float a revenue service of ten cutters under the banner of the Treasury Department.

The proponents were no organized bloc. Congressmen who held the belief that for the republic to survive, let alone prosper, in a troubled world would require the protection of a fleet were at first reluctant to express it. Public apathy and the strength of political opposition checked them. It is as if they awaited some dire token from abroad which would shock the people into realizing the need for a navy and galvanize their representatives into positive and unified advocacy of it. And at the close of 1793 the signal came, not as a result of the resumption of hostilities between England and France, but from an old trouble spot. On December 8, the schooner *Snow Queen* dropped anchor off New York with dispatches from the American Minister in Lisbon urging the government to sound an immediate alarm to all concerned in navigation. Portugal and Algiers had signed a treaty of peace, removing the long restraint on the Algerian corsairs and exposing American vessels bound for Europe to imminent hazard of seizure. Already, eight pirate ships of war had cleared the Straits of Gibraltar and were at large in the Atlantic. The envoy's warning, dated October 6, 1793, had taken sixty-three days to reach its destination. Long before its arrival the Algerians had celebrated their escape to the ocean with the capture of ten American merchant ships and their crews.

The *Snow Queen*'s news, followed by that of actual seizures, interrupted Congress in the middle of a slow-paced consideration of the Indian troubles at home and the failure of neutrality to receive its proper respect abroad. The tempo and direction of debate altered at once. Federalists in the House of Representatives pushed the passage of a resolution calling for the provision of a naval force, and a committee of nine men, all but one in favor of a fleet, was selected to decide on its strength, cost, and the ways and means to pay for it.

About this time (the exact date is unknown) two cabinet secretaries, Henry Knox and Alexander Hamilton, met with a group of Federalist senators and congressmen to plan a navy. Thanks to Hamilton, the proceedings of this private caucus went unrecorded except for five or six lines of estimates for a 44-gun frigate weighing 1,300 tons. Before Congressman William Loughton Smith of South Carolina, acting as secretary for the meeting, could write further, the Secretary of the Treasury took the pen from him, ostensibly to continue the minutes himself, and instead covered the sheet with flourishes and convolutions. This Hamiltonian sample of what a later generation would style "doodling," though almost hypnotic to gaze upon, provides no clue to the course of the discussion, but according to Smith it was this caucus that, while unattended by any member of the House select committee, led to the recommendation for the construction of six frigates.

The annals of House debates during this and subsequent sessions (no official record in detail was kept of Senate business) show the fleet's first legislative champion to have been William Loughton Smith. It would be pleasing enough to portray this genuine founder of the American Navy as an unsullied patriot who, like his fellow Federalists Hamilton and Knox, had fought for national independence, or at least supported the cause with inspired word. Instead Smith spent the revolutionary years as a law student in Europe, often hobnobbing with the aristocracy of England and Scotland, and his correspondence of the time indicates that the upheaval in his homeland left him unmoved. He returned to Charleston at the age of twenty-four, prospered as a lawyer serving powerful merchant interests, and in 1790 entered Congress, where he established prompt rapport with the northern Federalists and narrowly survived a scandal over questionable speculation in the South Carolina state debt. Favoring close trade ties with Britain, he was detested everywhere in his native South except in circles likely to profit from them. For his defense of John Jay's treaty with England, freeing northwestern outposts of British occupation for a price high in concession, he was hanged and burned in effigy, and among his papers is an anonymous but convincing threat of assassination by "15 republicans." To many who knew him well, he was a selfish, coldhearted, unscrupulous little Tory.

In the smoky, overheated chamber within the ill-ventilated brick building on Independence Square, this curiously dislikable South-erner expounded and analyzed, day upon day, session after session, making eloquent effort to show that not only did America's rising commerce need protection on the high seas but that she had in abundance the national resources to provide and maintain it. The roots of opposition to a federal navy were too firmly embedded in republican soil to be easily severed, however. Smith quite sensibly made no attempt to banish by polemic the familiar bugaboos—that sanction of a few ships would lead to a burdensome naval establish-ment, would plunge the country deeper into debt, and would pro-voke maritime wars. Nor did he scorn the Republicans' fiercest and most doctrinal obsession, that a navy would be the entering wedge of a new monarchy and a betrayal therefore of those who had bled to found a republic. He granted the possibility of risks, but still deemed himself "warranted in supporting it as a thing irresistibly and loudly called for."

The naval bill's chances of passage depended principally on its appeal to moderates among the opposition who, though steadfastly shunning grandiose dreams of America's destiny as a maritime power, might be induced to admit to present necessity. As a price for their approval, they demanded safeguards fore and aft: a preamble to the measure making plain that its purpose was limited to defense of commerce against Algerian piracy, and a ninth section providing for its suspension once the threat that had produced it was removed by negotiation. In final form the bill "To Provide A Naval Armament" sanctioned the construction of three frigates of 44 guns and three 36's, with a total establishment of 2,060 men. It passed by a vote of 50 to 39 and on March 27, 1794, received the President's signature— more than three months after the *Snow Queen* had arrived with its alarming dispatch from Lisbon. The agreement of Congress to a naval program did not remove it altogether from the rage and swirl of political contention. But henceforth its development could pro-ceed as well along the practical level of planning, design, and con-struction.

"The Navy was your child," George Washington is said by Mrs. Knox to have told her husband. John Adams, who privately regarded himself a fair candidate for that honor, was in his correspondence of later years to bestow it magnanimously upon Thomas Jefferson, while conceding that "Knox may have assisted in ushering [the Navy] into this world." To this day there exists a plurality of claims to U.S. Navy paternity, some which students have honestly put forward, others of dubious motive. We may regard Henry Knox's share in the event as no more than duty imposed by the office of Secretary of War, but one which he does seem to have discharged with something of the dedication of 1776, when, notwithstanding his hampering corpulence, he directed the hauling of the fifty-nine Ticonderoga cannon over a mountain wilderness in the dead of winter to rout the British from Boston. Often profane, chronically overweight (his wife almost equally so), Knox was a natural target for Republican ridicule, and he added to it by his vanity and pomposity. Known occasionally as the Philadelphia Nabob, he sported a gold-headed cane and kept a silken handkerchief over his left hand to conceal the stumps of two fingers destroyed in a youthful hunting accident.

The gun rates of the approved frigates had been based upon calculations of Algerian strength. It was now Knox's task to establish dimensions and costs to meet those rates. Since 1790 he had been soliciting estimates from seamen and shipbuilders and submitting them to Congress. We do not know which of the Secretary's several advisers exerted most influence on the final designs. The leading contender is Joshua Humphreys, and he has his loyal following of heirs and historians who advance him as a father of the Navy. A Quaker of Welsh descent, Humphreys had never been to sea or seen a ship of the line, but he was well read in marine architecture, had fitted out vessels for the old Continental fleet, and, owning a busy shipyard in the Southwark area of Philadelphia, was readily available to Knox for consultation. Knox hired him to prepare drafts and models of both frigate classes and on June 28, 1794, appointed him naval constructor, at an annual salary of $2,000, of the 44-gun ship to be built at Philadelphia. The other 44's were to be built at New York and Boston, the 36's at Norfolk, Baltimore, and Portsmouth, New Hampshire. There were professional objections to such decentralization of construction sites as awkward and expensive. But both President Washington and Knox, while agreeing with Captain Thomas Truxtun that to build south of Philadelphia might increase the costs by as much as 25 per cent, thought it politically prudent to "distribute the advantages."

America could not for years ahead produce more than a fraction of the number of ships possessed by any major European power. Joshua Humphreys therefore favored large, fast, and powerfully armed ships able to outmatch double-deckers in blowing weather when the lower gun ports could not be opened, and in calm or light winds to outsail them. In detail Humphreys' ideas encountered opposition, notably from Josiah Fox, who argued that such ships would be cumbersome and difficult to manage. A wealthy young Englishman who had served his apprenticeship in Plymouth Dockyard, Fox had relatives and friends in Philadelphia, and was visiting America to study timber when they persuaded him to stay on and help with the design of the new frigates. The professional relationship between Fox and Humphreys appears to have been cordial at first. Later, however, Humphreys, the elder of the two by twelve years, resented Fox's criticism and suspected him of trying to usurp his authority. Both men were assisted by Thomas Doughty, who, according to Fox, drew the building plans for the 36-gun ships. Many of Doughty's papers were accidentally burned by his family, and we know too little of his early years to grant him more than a subordinate role to those of Fox and Humphreys, but his subsequent long and distinguished career as designer for the American Navy is well attested.

The final designs, then, for the Navy's first frigates cannot be considered the sole work of any one man. They are best described as the creation of a trinity of shipbuilders—Humphreys, Fox, and Doughty —whose proud skills, jealous enthusiasms, and fiercely competitive imaginations guided the new Navy from War Department conference and drafting board to building stocks and eventual launch.

CHAPTER ⚓ TWO

Three Frigates

BY THE END OF 1794, shipyards had been leased or bought, naval constructors appointed, and purchasing agents hired. Six veterans of the Revolutionary War were made captains at a monthly salary of $75 and each assigned to superintend the building of a frigate. They were stubborn men whose opinions, for example, on spar dimensions, often conflicted with those of the constructors and one another. Problems of matériel had to be overcome. Nothing was available already fabricated. "The wood for the frames," Henry Knox reminded Congress, "is standing in the forest. The iron for the cannon lies in its natural bed, and the flax for sails and hemp for lines and rigging are perhaps in their seed."

The builders were hampered almost at once by a timber crisis. It had been decided that white oak, pitch pine, and locust would be employed, with knees and short timbers made from live oak and red cedar—valuable woods which, as the Secretary of War assured the House, "afford the United States the highest advantages in building ships, the durability of live oak being estimated at five times that of common white oak." The reliability of this estimate remains doubtful. At all events, the best specimens were believed to grow on the offshore islands of Georgia, but of fifty or more New England axmen sent down to aid John Morgan, the naval constructor from Norfolk, all but three found the climate unbearable and returned home. And when, after the molds had arrived from the north, a letter followed from Joshua Humphreys complaining of the delay, Morgan gave way

11

to anger and despair. "These molds frighten me," he wrote back to Humphreys, "they are so long. I cannot stand it, you say if I was there I should be mortified, if you was here you would curse live oak."

John Barry, captain of the vessel which Humphreys was impatient to begin, went down to inspect the situation for himself and reported that the wood might be ready by spring, an estimate soon revised to read "at least another year." The mishaps besetting the naval program when it had scarcely begun accumulated: some of the molds were destroyed by fire; a vessel sailing north from Georgia with a cargo of precious live oak was wrecked in a storm off Cape Hatteras; another bound for Baltimore was driven by gales from Chesapeake Bay clear to Martha's Vineyard. Thomas Truxtun, captain of the frigate building at Baltimore, had personally to scour the coasts of the Bay for suitable timber. Joshua Humphreys, needing large trees for the frigate at Philadelphia, penetrated the forest wilderness west of the Catskills. White-pine timbers for the construction at Boston, cut at Unity, Maine, were rolled and dragged to tidewater at Sheepscot River, whence they were towed by packet to the shipyard. Repeatedly, discouragement was fought by compromise and effort. But although Henry Knox had hoped that his frigates would be afloat in 1795, when he retired to private life in January of that year not one keel was yet on the blocks.

Succeeding Knox at the War Department, Timothy Pickering began by confessing total ignorance of shipbuilding, and he continued the policy of solicited advice and mutual exchange with which his predecessor had launched the program.

In December 1795, one month before he became Secretary of State (an office he had long coveted), Pickering proudly announced the laying of all six keels. William Loughton Smith, we may be sure, was not so much elated by the Secretary's message as dismayed that, in the twenty-one months since the adoption of the program for which he had so assiduously fought, this was as far as it had got. In any event, he was now apprehensive of a danger that it would advance no farther, for in the long-drawn-out negotiations with Algiers there were signs at last of a settlement. In vain Smith tried to head off the threat; the bill he hastily drafted to repeal Section 9 of the Naval Act was tabled. Four weeks later the President sent Congress a treaty of peace with Algiers, but, reluctant to halt abruptly all work on the ships, he threw responsibility for their fate into the laps of the legislators, and the political quarrel over the Navy broke out anew.

William Smith argued that to suspend all building would be degrading. Frigates were still needed to ensure Algerian adherence to the terms of the treaty, and moreover they would provide the country "with a kind of naval academy." James Madison of Virginia, after describing himself as one who set great value upon marine strength, proposed the completion of only those vessels whose construction was most advanced and postponement of a decision on the others. Fisher Ames of Massachusetts prophesied that a navy must promote the creation of an American nationality. And a newcomer to the House, an unprepossessing representative from Pennsylvania named Albert Gallatin, whose lifetime influence in the nation's affairs has yet to be adequately explored, observed that the best method of enhancing America's prestige was not to build ships but to pay off the national debt.

In the Senate, except to make an audacious demand on the Secretary of the Treasury for a detailed statement of government finances down to January 1, 1794, Gallatin had given no demonstration of his unique concern for the country's purse. Controversy over his eligibility for membership, on the issue of his alien birth, had kept him fretting on the defensive. But in the House he was fast becoming a Republican floor leader, prompt to pit his giant grasp of fiscal matters against Federalist thrusts to extravagance. Gallatin's reputation for social, domestic, and above all political frugality lends contemporary glimpses of his physical appearance a certain aptness. His soiled clothes a careless fit for his bony frame, nose and chin sharply pointed, his thin hair hanging straight and black, this genius of finance was a living caricature of parsimony. His speech suffered from a slow, embarrassed delivery in heavy Genevan accents, and the rigorous chopping movements of his right arm as he spoke seemed intended to drive each word firmly home.

His arguments that spring, 1796, combined with general dissatisfaction over the sluggishness of the shipbuilding program (notwithstanding an expenditure so far of close to half a million dollars), almost put an end to the fleet on its stocks. That his arguments failed can be explained by the surging popular demand for some show of strength against the affronts of not so much the Barbary pirates as the British and French, now at war. Even Gallatin recognized this new mood by modifying his earlier blanket opposition to all six frigates with a proposal that two be finished. It was defeated. The debate lasted intermittently until May and ended in a compromise bill authorizing completion of the 44's at Philadelphia and Boston, and the 36 at Baltimore.

For Gallatin this vote was merely the loss of an opening round, the first of many acts of attrition or direct assaults upon the national Treasury, whose defense in Congress and for thirteen years in the cabinet he claimed, one might almost think, by divine right. There was to be no more regular victim of his public thrift than the fleet he failed to strangle at birth. Yet Gallatin had married into a seafaring family. His father-in-law and two of his wife's uncles were veteran naval officers (one of them Samuel Nicholson, captain of the frigate under construction at Boston), and marriage also attached him to a number of younger relatives eager to be among the Navy's first midshipmen.

In the construction yards at Norfolk, New York, and Portsmouth tools were cast aside, workmen dismissed, and perishable material put up for sale. At Philadelphia, Baltimore, and Boston work was resumed with zest, as if to outstrip any further threats of suspension from the congressmen on both sides who were demanding to see something for the public money. What they would eventually see already bore impressive names. From a list prepared by Timothy Pickering, Joshua Humphreys, and the captains, President Washington had selected *United States, Constellation, Constitution.*

The bow and stern carvings of each vessel called for special craftsmanship. Patterns had already been solicited from William Rush, a prominent Philadelphia artist whose work, in addition to marine sculpture, included portrait busts, classical forms, and anatomical models for medical schools. In general, contemporaries speak admiringly of Rush's skill and realism. His "River God" head for the *Ganges* is said to have been so striking that when the merchantman put into Calcutta, Hindus swarmed out in boats to applaud and even worship. His Venuses, Junos, and Dianas, on the other hand, were criticized at home because, although properly clothed, they were shod in up-to-date high heels.

It was fashionable for popular patriotism to burst forth in flamboyant art, but Joshua Humphreys, a Quaker not fond of ostentation, must assuredly have winced when he read Rush's ideas for frigate decoration. Those for the *Constellation* provide an example. She should be represented (Rush wrote) "by an elegant female figure characteristic of indignant Nature, at the beginning of the American Revolution, determined on the formation of a new Creation. She should have a Flaming Torch in her right hand, setting fire to the Bursting World under her feet. The American Eagle in flight, soaring to Heaven to strike with Wisdom and Surprise the Wise Men of the East . . ." These, Rush concluded, were merely first thoughts; he hoped for better ones before the work began.

When that time came, the artist's dreams for the *Constellation* were modified only insofar as that Nature had lost her indignation and was now shown to be "in pleasing ecstasy," crested with fire, her waist encircled with the signs of the zodiac. A large central sphere, with emblematic figures of Navigation, Agriculture, and so forth extending to port and starboard quarterpieces, was to decorate the frigate's stern. Rush himself worked on the *Constellation*'s ornamentation, as he did on the Goddess of Liberty head for the *United States*, building at Philadelphia. His design for the bow of the *Constitution*, a full-length Hercules, one hand grasping a scroll and the other a club raised to strike, was executed by a Boston sculptor named John Skillen, whose instinctive comments when he saw what Rush wanted may have been worth hearing.

Early in 1797 James McHenry, the Irish-born Revolutionary War patriot who had succeeded Pickering to the War Department, received word from Joshua Humphreys' yard in Philadelphia that the hull of the *United States* was all planked and her principal decks laid and calked. By May everything appeared ready for launching. Held by rows of heavy timber stanchions braced firmly on the ground along both sides, the frigate's hull was visible many blocks away, rearing massively above the Old Swedish Mission and the roofs of Swanson Street. On May 9 the mood in Philadelphia was a blend of pride, festivity, and tense expectation. For John Barry, if all went well, tomorrow would be a day of honor as exalting as any he had known during his valiant command of the *Alliance* in the Revolutionary War. The fifty-two-year-old Philadelphian, born in County

Wexford, Ireland, was the senior captain of the new American Navy and his would be the first frigate launched.

The anxiety that had developed owing to abnormally low tides and persistently adverse winds vanished when May 10 dawned with a light breeze from the southeast and the tide showing promise of improvement. "At nine o'clock," begins Humphreys' report to the Secretary of War, "every preparation being made and only awaiting the tide at twelve, I gave orders to harden in the wedges to take a part of the burden of the ship off the whale shores." As if summoned by the thudding of the 110 carpenters' mallets, the crowds began to gather, some riding down from Chestnut Street in carriages, many on foot, more packed in boats along the Delaware. By early afternoon, 30,000 lined the wharves and grass banks, sentinels and constables moving protectively among them. Offshore, a hundred gaily decorated vessels rode at anchor, including the brig *Sophia* carrying the Secretaries of State, War, and Treasury but not the new President, John Adams, who had gone north to meet his Abigail coming down from Quincy.

Most of all this was Joshua Humphreys' hour, and we may picture him conferring and directing, confident yet concerned, an ungainly man by some accounts, with a large head, large eyes and nose, a barrel chest, and squat legs. There was a moment's consternation. "I gave orders to take the blocks from under the keel, but before they could be, the ship began to move." It is likely that her ways were too steep. Unaware that the descent was premature, spectators broke into cheers and the militia prepared to fire its salute. Humphreys issued quick orders for the spur shores to be knocked away, but the shuddering frame was still held, most precariously, by two hemp cables until Captain Barry, on board, shouted an order to cut them. Ax blades flashed, the cables parted, and the vessel gathered momentum. "This being the finishing part of the launch, the ship was left to herself only, to be conducted by her launching ways to her own element where she safely arrived, without straining or hogging more than one and a quarter inches, to my unspeakable satisfaction."

On the Patapsco River four months later the *Constellation* left her stocks. "A better launch I never saw," declared her captain, Thomas Truxtun. The only cavil was directed at her ornamentation, which, thought one critic, failed to express William Rush's original ideas.

The "dove of peace in the cap of liberty" could rather be likened to "a duck in a bag." Also, "Nature in pleasing ecstasy," as naked as modesty permitted, was usually represented as "having a row of breasts, wholly uncovered, to show her office of fostering all created beings." Clumsily costumed, the figure on the *Constellation* had only two.

The launch from Hartt's Shipyard, Boston, of the third frigate, *Constitution*, was set for September 20. Her descent to water proved embarrassingly piecemeal. In his anxiety to avoid the kind of precipitous launch that had imperiled the *United States*, the naval constructor, George Claghorn, had erred in the other direction and given the launch ways insufficient inclination. After two abortive attempts the launch was postponed until October 22.

On the eve of that date, despite an agreement to prohibit visitors in advance of the ceremony, Claghorn received on board a party of ladies and gentlemen whom Captain Samuel Nicholson had only just turned away. Nicholson, an elderly Republican in a nest of Bostonian Federalists, was considered by some of them to be "a rough, blustering tar." As if to prove it, he stormed on deck, collared Claghorn, and caned him in front of the visitors. Nicholson may have composed his temper in anticipation of hoisting the national flag over the new frigate the next day. If so, he was again frustrated, this time by a humble ship's calker who waited until the captain had gone to breakfast, then sent the *Constitution*'s colors, already bent to the halyards, fluttering up to the mizzen truck.

The gradual completion of the frigates for sea was overshadowed by continuous political strife. Unsuccessful in their bid to block all building of public warships, the antinaval forces mobilized to prevent the three that had escaped them and left their stocks from ever putting to sea. When William Loughton Smith introduced a batch of resolutions dealing with equipment, manning, and employment, Albert Gallatin and his colleagues systematically tore them to pieces. How could the frigates be manned without "recourse to the abominable practise of impressment?" How could additional moneys be spent without further undermining the already insecure national treasury? As for giving the Chief Executive discretionary power over use of the ships, as Smith proposed, would not this assuredly make the President complete master of the United States? And "if that were the case, the powers of this House were gone." Smith retorted that the President's hands ought not to be tied, and this sentiment, echoed so often down to our own day, was among his last utterances in Congress, for on June 6 he was appointed United States Minister to Portugal.

His place as foremost naval spokesman in the House was immediately filled by Robert Goodloe Harper, a Federalist whom Smith had himself plucked from the Piedmont back country of South Carolina. Like Smith, he was fiercely excoriated in much of that state, and such were his vanity and arrogance that he too offended both political parties. Most of his arguments for a navy can be found in his rebuttals to Albert Gallatin, whom he accused of measuring the country's rights, dignity, and honor "by counting-house standards."

It was suddenly a more dangerous time. French ire over John Jay's treaty of 1795 between the United States and Great Britain had ripened into active hostility. In 1796 Revolutionary France took to the sea. In the midsummer of 1797, Timothy Pickering (now Secretary of State) reported more than 300 American vessels seized by French privateers. Confident as never before of aroused popular support, the naval bloc in the House pressed passage, by a 78–25 final vote, of a new Act Providing for a Naval Armament, one which established salaries, uniforms, rules, and regulations, and empowered the President, should he wish, *"to cause the frigates United States, Constitution and Constellation to be manned and employed."*

John Adams was no war President: resisting objections from extremists within his party, he had just appointed a three-man bipartisan commission to sail for France and seek restoration of the close amity born in the desperate months between Saratoga and Yorktown. But he had always been of a mind for a standing navy, and even during that still vividly remembered struggle he had believed that American seamen "if let loose on the ocean, would greatly contribute to the relief of our wants and distress of the enemy." He had been a member of the small committee appointed by the Continental Congress to plan the interception of two British ammunition ships bound for Canada. Its first recommendation was that "a swift sailing vessel . . . be fitted with all possible dispatch for a cruise of three months." Three weeks later the small group was enlarged to seven men and officially labeled "a Naval Committee." It had suggested additional armed ships, and adopted a set of Rules for the Regulation of the Navy of the United Colonies which, governing discipline, rations, and pay, Adams had himself framed, basing them for the most part on British Navy law.

John Adams always regarded the proceedings of that time as the *true* origin and foundation of the Navy, and his share in them as historic and incontestable. His belief in a navy never faltered. Now, at the close of the Republic's second decade, with Federalists in firm control of both branches of Congress, and the French Directory replacing the Algerian Dey as the prime threat to America's right of passage on the seas, the nation had its Navy. It seems fitting that Adams should have been that Navy's first effective commander in chief.

By a twist of the fates Thomas Jefferson, actively unifying the opposition under his leadership, was now to be found among the opponents of sea power, an apparent change of heart which ceases to mystify when it is realized that Jefferson's lifelong notion of a navy was as a hastily cut switch with which to chastise barbaric primitives, never as a permanent and expensive sword to be brandished at civilized Europeans. But it was a European power that presently violated the United States flag, and when French outrage on the high seas was compounded by the cynical insult of attempted extortion which Talleyrand's agents X, Y, and Z flung at the American peace emissaries, a torrent of patriotic excitement flooded the country. It cast "bold Adams" to a new peak of popularity and all but buffeted the faithful friends of France out of political existence.

From all this the incipient Navy drew strength. Even Joshua Humphreys, once scornful of extravagant phraseology in the public sheets, raised toasts at a dinner in Philadelphia to "the infant Navy, may it even in its cradle strangle the serpents which would poison American glory." With ill-concealed derision the Republican newspaper *Aurora* reported on May 8, 1798, that "three hundred staunch Federalists drank no less than thirty-two staunch toasts." Two hundred and ninety-one cheers, "vulgarly called hurraws," burst forth, each accompanied by "the tossing of hats, caps and wigs in the air, merry-andrew jumps, and divers other irregularities and violent movements." One Federalist too harassed to share in the merriment was James McHenry, the Secretary of War, whose job it was to get that aggressive infant out of its cradle. He was under fire from two sides. Federalists blamed him for delays in completing the ships; Republicans attacked his naval expenditures as "pouring money into the sea." In vain he had urged the establishment of a separate department to deal with the multiplying naval problems; when, at last, the necessary resolution was brought before the House, a moment of discord in the affairs of high Federalists destroyed its chances for speedy passage.

The dispute had arisen over the proportion of naval to military strength needed to confront the French. Impelled by personal ambitions for military glory, Alexander Hamilton had grown cool toward naval expansion and favored rather a force of 50,000 armed men, 10,000 of them on horse, a notion which President Adams scorned as "proper only for Bedlam." If necessary, Hamilton had argued, additional ships could be borrowed from the British, who were only too anxious for joint action against the common foe. The British government did in fact offer to convoy American merchant ships, but refused to consider waiving the right to search them, even should an alliance be forged. When the British Minister traveled in late summer all the way to Quincy with his government's proposal, the President gently rebuffed him: "The people of this country are at present deliberating upon that question and it would perhaps not be wise to disturb their meditation."

The rift in Federalist thinking, what John Quincy Adams was to call "the first decisive symptom" of the party's disintegration, developed as Republican attacks on the naval program were sometimes crossing the bounds of political wisdom and violating patriotic sensibilities. Rather than make war, Albert Gallatin declared, he would even submit to French depredations in the hope that they would soon cease, a candid pronouncement that brought forth from all three semicircular rows of members' seats and the Speaker's chair opposite them exclamations of astonishment and anger. Ignoring charges of treason, Gallatin pressed on in his familiar labored tones, striving to extinguish with an outpouring of facts, figures, and dire prophesy each proposal to gird and mature the fledgling fleet. Nothing aroused his opposition more than the move to guarantee the growth of the Navy with the establishment of a cabinet office for its exclusive administration. The certainty that there could be no more

irreversible step toward a permanent force hardened Republican resistance generally, and the new disarray in Federalist ranks had the
effect of assisting it. Only after prolonged debate did McHenry get
his Navy Department, by the narrow margin of a 47–41 House vote.

It was another six weeks before the country's first Secretary of the
Navy could settle his personal affairs and take over from McHenry.
Conceivably, for Benjamin Stoddert it was a sizable task. Since the
Revolutionary War, in which he had fought as a major, been
wounded at Brandywine, and then served until peace as Secretary of
the Continental Board of War, he had virtually founded the commercial prosperity of Georgetown. By the time he was summoned to
Adams' cabinet at a salary of $3,000 per annum (raised to $4,500 the
next year), he had become an extensive property holder and president of the Bank of Columbia. He lacked maritime experience; was
broadly familiar with problems of administration, procurement, and
finance; and, like so many land speculators of his time, seems to have
lived on an abiding edge between the promise of yet greater affluence
and the threat of utter ruin. Devoted to his family, he once gave his
wife Rebecca $20 to buy a hobbyhorse for their children, but two
years later he wrote to Captain Barry, whose ship his young son had
joined as a midshipman, that the boy had been spoiled, was too
thoughtless to make a good sailor, and should not be singled out for
the captain's favors. Demanding loyalty from business associates, his
family, and soon his sea captains, Stoddert never stinted on giving his
own. Alone of John Adams' cabinet, it is the Secretary of the Navy
whose fidelity to the President remains historically sure.

He arrived in Philadelphia on June 12, 1798, to find that Mc-
Henry had left the city, apparently overcome by anxiety to jettison
his naval burdens. Without resentment, Stoddert quickly installed
himself, a chief clerk, four assistant clerks, and a messenger in two
offices at 139 Walnut Street. And when, at the close of his first busy
week, he confessed that he had scarcely had a moment to think, it was
not so much a complaint as an outburst of exhilaration.

Meanwhile the Navy continued to be a principal cause of congressional activity. Money was appropriated to resume completion of
the three frigates abandoned in the wake of the peace treaty with
Algiers. Two dozen small vessels of not more than 22 guns each were
to be built, bought, or hired. Retaliatory privateering against the

French received official sanction. And the marines were molded into a separate corps. With public feeling inflamed and a war party in Congress growing daily more impatient, accommodation with France seemed impossible. But Adams saw no necessity for total commitment by formal declaration of war. Instead he chose what he later termed *half-war* and on July 8 directed Stoddert to issue instructions authorizing his naval commanders, in home waters or on the high seas, "to subdue, seize and take any armed French vessel or vessels sailing under authority or pretense of authority from the French Republic."

Under the impetus of a half-war, then, the infant fleet was finally levered from its cradle. In those last unnerving weeks before handing it over, or rather abandoning it, to another's care, James McHenry had managed to advance preparations to ready the fleet for sea. Many of the problems were concerned with the purchase of equipment. Utensils, from quart tin mugs and tablespoons to bedpans and urinals. Stationery: inkstands, writing paper, batches of quills. Ship's pendants, drums and fifes, a dozen speaking trumpets, and 120 lanterns. The multifarious hardware of battle three frigates required: muskets, balls, and bayonets for marines. Three hundred boarding axes, 300 pikes, 550 cutlasses, 600 hand grenades. For the great guns: sponges and rammers, 670 barrels of powder, 1,600 chain or double shot, 10,000 round shot. And always the purchasing agents themselves needed to be watched in case dissatisfaction with their 2 per cent commission tempted them to unwarranted expenditure.

One ship of war, the *Ganges*, was already under sail. As the first vessel of the United States Navy to go to sea, this converted merchantman mounting 26 nine-pounders occupies a deserved niche in naval history. So does her captain, Richard Dale, a rough-mannered Revolutionary War officer who had fought briefly on the Tory side and been wounded, then shifted his allegiance and been wounded again while commanding the gun deck of the *Bonhomme Richard* in her battle with the *Serapis*. The maiden cruise of the *Ganges* as a ship of war was uneventful. The weather was so wretched that Dale would not have put out when he did had it not been reported that a 20-gun French ship was off the coast. The Frenchman eluded him and Dale thought he knew why: "Some *Dam Rascal* has been giveing him information of my giting out." The smaller armed merchantman *Delaware* commanded by Stephen Decatur, Sr., a Revolutionary War privateersman, has left a more notable mark by making the first capture. At sea no more than two days, she pursued and took the *Croyable* off the New Jersey shore and brought her in triumph up Delaware Bay while citizens lining the water's edge cheered and church bells were set pealing.

But it was the mighty frigates that Americans and in particular their government were anxious to see justify the heavy cost. McHenry had issued orders for recruiting able seamen at $17 a month and ordinary seamen at $10, a good deal less than salaries offered by shipping merchants, but comparing favorably with the $4 a month paid to Army privates. "Healthy, robust, and well-organized men" were required, the scorbutic and consumptive to be rejected. Judging by reports from Boston, however, delays in the manning of the *Constitution* were due not to scurvy and feeble lungs but the unpopularity of Captain Nicholson, whose "noise and vanity," wrote Stephen Higginson, the Federalist purchasing agent, "is disgusting to the sailors." His officers, according to Higginson's testimonials, were hardly better. The second lieutenant was "said to be intemperate and he looks it," and the surgeon "the opposite of what he ought to be in morals, politics and his profession. There is not a man in this town who would trust the life of a dog in his hands." Elsewhere the problem was yellow fever. Its recurrence in Philadelphia the previous autumn had transformed the seat of government into a ghost town. Her work crews reduced by epidemic and desertion, the *United States* fell into neglect. Seams in her decks and topsides split wide open; six of eight twelve-pounders being proved by Captain Barry burst the first day, and all but five the next.

Spring restored health and confidence. By summer, 1798, the frigate's officers had all been commissioned and Joshua Humphreys had calked her open seams. Recruiting was proceeding under the second lieutenant, John Mullowney, whose progress reports were good-humored but diffuse, misdated, or bearing no date at all. They finally caused Captain Barry to declare that "I am quite in the dark what you are doing." His exasperation is understandable. He was just then under pressure from James McHenry, whose haste to get the *United States* out suggested to Barry a lack of regard for her unprepared condition. It was with relief that he greeted the appointment of Benjamin Stoddert. Some have said that the captain was immediately retained as Stoddert's leading adviser, but the truth is that the Secretary canvassed aid from all "enlightened and patriotic men." He drew only on their maritime knowledge. No less essential to the running of a navy, especially one just founded, were drive and imagination, qualities not always manifest in the Secretary's sea captains but which he himself possessed in abundance.

Twin barriers to his objective of an efficient fleet ready for battle were political formality and the slowness of communication between his headquarters and the shipyards north and south. He pared to a minimum his consultations with cabinet and Congress, and reduced the volume of his correspondence by delegating wider powers of decision to his distant subordinates. Yet he never released his control of broad, general policy. Nor did he hesitate to intervene if the situation required. But on July 3, 1798, the report from the *United States* was that her people were quartered and the great guns ready for exercise by day and night. The last impediment to her departure was personally removed by the Secretary with a curt note to the Purveyor of Stores, from whom Captain Barry had been unable to draw two coils of rope and fifty pounds of butter. "The boat is waiting," wrote Stoddert. "Furnish these articles without the least delay." This done, the Secretary addressed himself to Barry: "The *United States* under your command, being equipped, manned and armed, you will proceed to sea with the first fair wind."

CHAPTER THREE

First Blood in a Half-War

> The floating castles of the United States have by this time made their appearance in the West Indies.
>
> —*Claypoole Advertiser,*
> September 12, 1798

IT IS NOT surprising that Americans, noted later in the year by an English observer as "absolutely mad" about their small fleet, would anticipate its early descent upon the Caribbean sea nests. For there lurked the privateers of France, and few but the most disgruntled Republicans doubted that there would be the United States Navy to hunt and destroy them. It was a faith as sturdy as the ships themselves, but one which in its simplicity failed to take into account the poverty of their number. Nor was allowance made for the temperament of the officers who commanded them. Popular excitement centered mainly upon the frigates. There was much to admire about them: masts rising in dignity to some 200 feet amid a soaring volume of canvas; the fast, sharp lines of their hulls; and the artistry of William Rush's figureheads, which, thought the architect Benjamin Latrobe, had about them such quality of motion they "seem rather to draw the ship after them than be impelled by the vessel." But in Benjamin Stoddert's view: "Heads are not useful, and I believe injure a ship. If we must preserve a useless ornament they ought not to be expensive."

The frigates were large for their gun rates: the 44's each measured

175 feet in length, about 43 feet in the beam, and displaced 1,576 tons. Respective dimensions for the 36's were 164 feet, 40 feet, and 1,278 tons. Longer and wider than British and French frigates of comparable rating, they had also an innovation of deck arrangement which substantially increased their firing power. The narrow gangways which customarily connected quarter and forecastle decks were so broadened as to create virtually a complete spar deck with an open waist amidships. On this level, quarterdeck and forecastle mounted at first twelve-pounders, soon to be replaced by the carronade, a short, quick-firing piece of large caliber invented in Scotland. The ship's principal battery of long guns occupied the main deck, more often thereafter called the gun deck. In general, historians of marine architecture have found little to criticize in the design of these first ships, which indeed influenced American frigate construction for almost the next five decades until the advent of steam.

The impressions one receives of their inner appearance range from spacious elegance to cramped, ill-lit squalor. Sealed from the rest of the vessel by removable bulkheads, roughly thirty feet of gun deck abaft the mizzenmast consists of the captain's ample quarters. As wide as the ship at this point stretches the great cabin, heated by a copper stove, well furnished with mahogany tables and eight or more Windsor chairs. On either side of the room two twenty-four-pounders squat in their carriages facing closed ports and flanked by wall racks lined with rammers, sponges, handspikes, and priming wires. From this commodious chamber the captain may retreat farther astern to a much smaller cabin with a row of six windows aft, curtained, and each of six panes. On either side of it is a yet smaller stateroom, each with access to water closet and bathtub in the quarter galleries. The lieutenants' quarters aft on the berth deck all but defy comparison. Their wardroom is a drab corridor forever denied natural light, and the row of doors on each hand opens to what so resemble prison cells they scarcely deserve to be called staterooms. These cheerless surroundings are shared by the lieutenants on equal footing with the marine officers, the sailing master, the purser, chaplain, and surgeon.

In the steerage forward of the wardroom live the midshipmen. A juvenile company of ambiguous status, their average age 16, patronized by officers and mocked by "the people," they strut the decks importantly, bantams in buff and blue. Among their variety of tasks they stand watch and assist at gun drill, inspect clothing and hammocks, supervise deck-cleaning details, and climb aloft in all weather to strain their treble voices with shouted orders from the yards to the topmen.

And *the people*, the three or four hundred of the common crew? Distributed by an endless subdivision of duties among stations from the clean swaying tops to the fetid depths of the orlop, they stand their watches in foul weather, fair wind, and calms, complainingly or in song, depending upon mood, health, and the elements. Theirs is a strange existence. In their closed and gloomy world between decks, gambling, thievery, and vice will breed and flourish. Yet fortitude, generosity, and humor are rarely absent, and a deep and disarmingly unsophisticated patriotism. They are allowed a daily ration of one and a half pounds of salt pork, beef, or salt fish, a pound of bread, a pound of rice, peas, or potatoes, with cheese, butter, and a half-pint of spirits, distributed in three awkwardly spaced meals which they consume as a rule seated cross-legged between the guns. They sleep in almost solid platoons of slung hammocks crowding the scarcely six feet of ill-ventilated space between gun deck and berth, and each man's hammock area is invested with sacred property rights. The situation had not changed forty-five years later when Herman Melville served briefly on the *United States*: "Every man is jealously watchful of the rights and privileges of his own proper hammock as settled by law and usage; your hammock is your Bastille and canvas jug; into which, or out of which, it is very hard to get; and where sleep is but a mockery and a name."

Late that summer, 1798, the *United States, Constitution*, and *Constellation* patrolled the Atlantic coast on what today would be called their shakedown cruise. At home, meanwhile, Congress had adjourned without a declaration of war against France, but that war nevertheless existed nobody realized better than Benjamin Stoddert. Strategic deployment of his few ships was now a duty of extreme importance. He was hampered in the successful discharge of it by the passage of communication through slow and insecure channels, but nothing much could be done about that. What soon pained him, however, was the wayward behavior of certain officers upon whose skill and initiative in distant waters he had ultimately to depend.

He had issued the first Navy Department orders for a mission of offense to Captain John Barry, directing him to the West Indies in search of privateers. But Barry seems to have been too bemused with pride in his new vessel to risk her in waters liable to hurricane. His letters those summer weeks are for the most part hymns to her smooth sailing and obedient steering, while Stoddert's correspondence of the same period betrays a mounting concern over his senior captain's lack of energy. On July 30 the Secretary, perhaps to reassure himself as much as John Adams, to whom the words are addressed, writes from Trenton, New Jersey (where his office functioned during a recurrence of yellow fever in Philadelphia), that "the hurricanes, I understand, are not so dangerous as they are generally believed." But it was at least partly due to the fear of them that Barry turned back, sailed up the Delaware, and, after one more paean in a letter to Joshua Humphreys extolling the *United States* beyond anything else afloat, showed himself at Trenton, to the consternation of Benjamin Stoddert, on September 21.

"I hope you will send him out again," wrote President Adams to the Secretary, and although in Stoddert's stern opinion men so easily deterred from their duty had no place in his Navy, he ordered him out to sea within a month. This time, 250 miles east of Hatteras, the *United States* ran into the weather Barry had most feared. Wind gusts split her foresail, a giant wave carried away part of William Rush's figurehead, and soon after, in a heavy sea, the ship sprang her bowsprit. The rigging slackened, loose shrouds endangered every mast, and each roll of the ship threatened to bring them down until James Barron, the third lieutenant, bracing himself against the sea which crashed across her decks, secured purchases, tautened the rigging, and restored stability to the ship. By midnight the gale had moderated, and Captain Barry wore his beloved, battered frigate for home.

With diminishing likelihood of French activity off the Atlantic coasts during the winter months, Stoddert decided to concentrate almost his entire force, about a score of frigates, brigs, sloops, and schooners, in the Caribbean for the protection of American sea trade. His plan was to station four squadrons there, two east of Puerto Rico, two in Cuban waters, under command of Barry and Thomas Truxtun, captains who could now call themselves *commodores*. Truxtun as Stoddert well knew, needed no persuasion to zeal; but the Secretary, still uneasy about Barry, delivered the latter on the eve of his sailing this eloquently broad hint: "A spirit of enterprise and adventure cannot be too much encouraged in your officers, nor can too many opportunities be afforded the enterprising to distinguish themselves. We have nothing to dread but inactivity." Off Martinique, however, the following February a lieutenant on the *United States* could only report "indifferent cruising," routine convoy duty, and the capture of a single 10-gun schooner privateer, the *Amour de la Patrie*. The *United States* then made for Guadeloupe, where Barry intended to negotiate a prisoner exchange, but short batteries fired on her as she entered Basse-Terre roads. Barry's guns replied. When the firing stopped, Étienne Desfourneaux, the French governor, sent word that no American captives were left on Guadeloupe; that he did not in any event recognize a state of war to exist; that as far as his island was concerned, American trade would always be welcome. And with these assurances Barry set course for home.

To the Secretary of the Navy, more impatient for news of American naval achievements than an amicable gesture of suspect sincerity, the commodore's unspectacular cruise was aggravating proof that no glory could be expected from officers who, once valiant, had grown old and fainthearted. The captain of the *Constitution*, next in seniority to Barry, was another problem. Little can be pieced together of Samuel Nicholson's early career. He took several prizes in the Revolutionary War, certainly, but the reason for his loss of command in 1782 and court-martial, which ended in acquittal, is not known. The political hue of his family background, more darkly Republican since Albert Gallatin established himself in it through marriage, was itself ample cause for Federalist distaste.

But his defects of character did not need the magnification of political prejudice to cast doubts upon his fitness for command. There was his well-known fondness for drink. And to maintain good order among the *Constitution*'s crew, he seems to have leaned too heavily upon the lash. Three Irishmen are flogged one day for "mutinous expression" and fighting with the master-at-arms. On the next a seaman is given a dozen lashes for striking his superior officer, and six others are made to "run the gauntlet"—are half stripped, seated each in turn in a tub, and hauled about the spar deck while the boatswain and members of the crew belabor them with knotted ropes. On the third day six more are flogged for fighting. A Robert Sharkey receives a dozen lashes for causing James Bates to plunge to his death from the main rigging, and a sailing master's mate is put in irons for inciting a mutiny. James Pity, a seaman on the *Constitution*, to whom we are indebted for these glimpses of unrest during her first important cruise, is himself arrested "without any reason," dismissed from the ship, and almost immediately reinstated by command from the Department.

Deaths on board the ships were common. Men fell from the tops, were swept overboard in storms, and, however regularly hammocks were scrubbed and spaces between decks fumigated with hot vinegar, succumbed to disease. The *Constitution* does indeed seem to have suffered more than her share of fatality under Nicholson's command; and to his avarice, as will be seen, a portion of it must be assigned.

But as on other vessels, the long days of monotony and hazard were relieved by lighthearted interludes. The mariner's legendary jollity has a strong base in truth; prolonged life at sea is even today surrounded by a rare loneliness which modern communications, while all but eliminating former perils, cannot entirely pierce. This loneliness was never more melancholy and oppressive than in the days of sail. So opportunities for traditional celebration were seized with a lively, childish pleasure. "Crossed the Tropic of Cancer," writes James Pity on January 12, 1799, "performed the usual ceremonies, viz., blacking, ducking and shaving which among 400 people produced a set of devils equal to any ever seen." And there is a philosophic briskness about his entry a month or so later: "Sold at the mainmast, the effects of several men deceased."

By then Samuel Nicholson's days as captain of the *Constitution* were numbered. They had been in fact since the fiasco of the previous September, when the frigate took the *Niger*, a 24-gun ship flying English colors which Nicholson, professedly misled by her papers and the French accents of some of her crew, assumed to be French. So diffuse and melodramatic was his report of the capture that Stoddert could make neither head nor tail of it, but inquiries quickly confirmed the vessel as British, thus trapping the administration in an embarrassing legal dispute with representatives of a nation whose feelings it earnestly desired to leave unruffled. Moreover, in his eagerness for condemnation of the *Niger* as his prize, Nicholson had brought her into Norfolk despite an epidemic of yellow fever there. His own son, a sixteen-year-old midshipman on the *Constitution*, became infected and died on board. The frigate's surgeon was stricken and died ashore.

Instead of being condemned as a legitimate American prize, the *Niger* had to be surrendered and $11,000 damages paid her owners. Worse still, Nicholson had exposed not only his crew to disease but the Atlantic seaboard, then under his protection, to French attack. Yet he was still idling in Hampton Roads on October 6 and, wrote Stoddert angrily on that date, "God knows how much longer." He hardly made amends when three months later he liberated a vessel from the French, found she was British, and returned her to her captors. Thereafter Stoddert was afraid to entrust him with command, but he hesitated to dismiss him for the *Niger* incident out of pity for his family, and he could find no one willing or able to persuade him to resign. The solution issued finally from his pronounced concern for Nicholson's immediate dependents. "As you have been a good deal absent from your family," he wrote, transferring him to the supervision of ship construction, "it is intended that you shall remain on shore."

The qualities which the Secretary had sought in vain in Barry and Nicholson were possessed in abundance by the third frigate captain at sea, Thomas Truxtun, and it was to him now that he and John Adams looked for such demonstration of sea power as would strengthen America's hand in the negotiations that the President, contrary to the wishes of some of his followers, planned to begin with the French. True, the commodore's ardor could sometimes be embarrassing and Adams appreciated the necessity of Stoddert's occasionally controlling it, but "I pray you," he wrote to him, "do so gently and with great delicacy. I would not have it dampened for all the world."

Truxtun became the first important architect of American naval tradition. In addition to the historic examples set the service by his victories in the West Indies, he brought to it new concepts of organization, navigation, and discipline, in some measure the product of his own reflection, or borrowed from the British and French. Following impressment at the age of sixteen aboard the 64-gun Royal Navy warship *Prudent,* he had returned to America markedly influenced by British laws and customs. At twenty he was master of his own merchant vessel, the *Charming Polly.* The Revolutionary War provided the first real opportunity to display his tactical skill as well as courage, and on a long cruise from the West Indies to the English Channel he captured a number of prizes. In 1783 he profited from the presence on his merchant ship *London Packet* of Benjamin Franklin, who sharpened if not awoke his scientific curiosity about the sea, and for much of the next decade he developed his knowledge of navigation while trading in the Indian Ocean and China Sea. In the summer of 1794 he produced a textbook on the subject entitled *Remarks, Instructions, and Examples Relating to the Latitude and Longitude* and, after digesting the work of probably the English tacticians Howe and Kempenfelt and certainly the French naval genius Mahé de la Bourdonnais, he wrote *Instructions, Signals and Explanations Offered for the United States Fleet* (the flyleaf of which, in a copy in possession of the U.S. Navy Department, contains in Truxtun's handwriting his only known essay into poetry: "The rights of America we will maintain/And then return to you, sweet girl, again").

The impression of Truxtun at sea as a tyrant, traceable to some apocryphal material in Admiral David Dixon Porter's biography of his father (a midshipman on the *Constellation*) and since repeated without question, is outweighed by contrary evidence. He could be harsh and was often fastidious. He abhorred drunkenness and was firm in matters relating to the cleanliness of the ship. Reprimanding a lieutenant for inattention to duty, he declared the man mistaken who expected a democratic system to prevail on board. He once stated that should his own son, a midshipman, misconduct himself, he would not only dismiss him from the Navy but disinherit him. (The young man died at sea in 1803. Truxtun disowned a second son years later, in circumstances unconnected with the Navy.) The *Constellation*'s marines disliked him for directing that they assist the crew in hauling at the capstan. He was especially severe with merchant captains under convoy who, despite his signaled instructions to stay together, allowed their vessels to become scattered, and he at least once threatened to fire into one unless the ship made more sail.

But it is difficult to view any of this as *tyranny*. Neither were his orders for running the ship unreasonable. Boatswain's mates were to keep her clean; carpenter's mates to stop all leaks and preserve the hull; her gunner and his mates must ensure that the guns were "in readiness at a moment's warning. A good lookout to be kept and in daylight a man at each masthead. The People as well as officers must repair to their stations whenever All Hands is called and they are not to leave their posts under any pretense. *We have an infant Navy to foster and it must be done."*

Good discipline, Truxtun thought, was better achieved by a particular deportment than by extreme severity. It became an officer to exercise restraint and show prudence in the use of his power. Men in inferior stations were to be treated as fellow creatures and cheerfully encouraged in the performance of their duty. For the punishment of most misdemeanors ways and means alternative to flogging ought to be devised. "Rigid discipline and good order are very different from tyranny—the one highly necessary and the other abominable." And Truxtun practiced what he preached. His preferred penalty even for the serious offense of sleeping on watch was the temporary stoppage of a rum allowance; and although some culprits might have regarded this as more a hardship than clemency, they could not but feel thankful that they had escaped the lash or worse.

Truxtum's tolerant administration passed its gravest test shortly after the *Constellation* put out, when symptoms of mutiny developed between her decks. He mustered the crew and read the Articles of War in the hope, "having the best disposition towards my People," that the misled would perceive the error of their course and the mischief-makers be shunned like serpents. Loyalty triumphed, and the agitator was exposed as John Watson, an old and bloody hand at the game; late a topman on the British ship of war *Hermione*, he had conspired in the murders of her insanely brutal captain and most of the other officers. Truxtun sent him ashore under guard into the custody of the British consul at Norfolk. (Watson was ultimately hanged.) Throughout this tense and dangerous time Truxtun had avoided use of the lash. One wonders how Captain Nicholson would have handled the affair.

Truxtun was above average height, his eyes were blue, and his hair was brown. His best portrait shows a tolerably mild countenance, appropriate to what we have seen of his character. And we may confidently imagine him in his buff, blue, and gold on the *Constellation*'s quarterdeck as she bears south, not so much tyrant as vigilant, inquiring, hopefully omniscient parent. Thus he might have appeared at noon on February 9, 1799, in the Leeward Islands when, his masthead lookout sighting a strange vessel standing fifteen miles to westward, he ordered all hands to make sail and bear down on her. Noting the event on a slip of paper for later entry in the *Constellation*'s log, he added: "I take her for a ship of war."

As a result of a correspondence in the summer of 1798 between the Adams administration and the British Minister to the United States, a complex system of private signals existed to reduce the risk of British and American ships firing upon one another. Devised by Vice-Admiral George Vandeput, commanding a British squadron off the American coast, it involved combinations of colors at the maintop and foretop differing daily, a form of password (names of cities were employed: London, Plymouth, Boston, etc.) when the vessels were within mutual hailing distance, and nightly arrangements at the mastheads of lights and false fires. Truxtun threw out the private signal of the day for a British ship, and the stranger replied by hoisting an American ensign. He then tried the private signal for an American ship of war, and when this time there was no response he ordered: *Beat all hands to quarters.* By midafternoon there was no doubt. Standing to the northwest, the other ship replaced her false flag with the French tricolor and fired a cannon to windward.

She was the *Insurgente*, a 36-gun vessel under command of Captain Barreaut, and though her compliment of 409 was larger than that of the *Constellation* she was somewhat smaller in size. After the chase had continued for two and a half hours, the sky darkened suddenly and a squall bore down on both ships. "We now housed the lee guns and ran out those on the weather side," wrote John Hoxe, a carpenter on the *Constellation*. "Just at that moment the squall struck us, and as we had all our sail set, such a cracking and snapping I never heard before. Our studding-sail boom snapped, the studding-sails flying in the air, and our ship going before it like a racehorse." The wind injured the Frenchman far more. His main-topmast collapsed and tumbled over the side while the topgallant sails were being taken in. This disaster Barreaut blamed for his subsequent misfortunes; also, according to his official report of the action, he had no idea that the ship of a nation so befriended by his own would attack him.

In rough sea the *Constellation* came up on the Frenchman's lee quarter. Barreaut hailed several times, but was not answered. Instead the American ship made preparations to fire. Barreaut, by his own account, was in something of a dilemma because of superior orders not to fire on an American. But "I found myself in no position to avoid an engagement." The loss of his main-topmast, however, swung the advantage to his attacker. "I was obliged to receive a full broadside from a frigate of 24 and 12-pounders deliberately aimed at pistol shot." He tried to carry the *Constellation* by boarding, and might have succeeded, such was his superior man power, but the *Insurgente* responded sluggishly. The *Constellation*, all sails set, ran on ahead and crossed the Frenchman's bows. Maneuvering with difficulty in the heavy weather, the *Insurgente* fired three broadsides.

The projectiles flew high into the *Constellation*'s rigging. An eighteen-pound ball struck the fore-topmast and left it swaying for a fall. From his station in the foretop, Midshipman David Porter hailed below for instructions, but his young voice foundered in the roar of cannon and the bellow of the wind. On his own initiative he climbed aloft, cut the slings, and lowered the yard, relieving the mast of the topsail's dragging weight. Most of the few American casualties were in the tops. Shot lacerated the legs of a man in the foretop, another in the maintop lost a foot, and the leg was torn off a third in the mizzentop. "The wind of a cannon ball" broke another's back.

The value of the gunnery drill enforced by Truxtun on the long voyage out was now vividly demonstrated. Aiming low, his gunners fired double-shotted broadsides, the very first of which wrecked the Frenchman's quarterdeck. Both vessels were rated 36 guns, but the *Constellation*'s armament was the more powerful, her broadsides some fifty pounds heavier. There were other telling factors: she was less hurt than her opponent by the squall, and her officers and crew had become under Truxtun's shrewd direction a loyal and aggressive company, as quick to expunge any suspicion of cravenness in its own ranks as it was ardent for battle with the foe of its flag. If Captain Barreaut's protestations of surprise are to be believed, no such will to victory excited the crew of his ship. And now her lame condition allowed a broad application of the American's tactical skills. The French ship, as Truxtun afterward acknowledged, fought back manfully, but she was raked from every quarter as the *Constellation* almost encircled her. Her rigging hung in tatters and many of her crew lay dead. Corpses were found in the tops eighteen hours after the guns had rested.

Barreaut's surrender was transacted on both sides by all the gestures of chivalry, but the Frenchman could not refrain from sorrowfully warning the man who had bested him that the consequence of his action must be war. Truxtun was undismayed. He had never been at ease with the indecisive nature of the conflict with France. As he wrote Stoddert the day after the battle: "I detest things being done by halves." His first lieutenant, John Rodgers, went aboard the stricken *Insurgente* and described as the most gratifying sight in his experience "seventy French pirates wallowing in their gore." Impelled by that same callousness, which is after all a counterpart of pride and bravado, the *Constellation*'s third lieutenant, Andrew Sterrett, had accounted for the only American fatality of the action: at its height a seaman named Neal Harvey had fled his post and Sterrett, drawing his sword, had run him through. We cannot be sure that Truxtun knew or approved of his lieutenant's deed at the moment of execution. Sterrett was one of the three officers afterward commended by him for their zeal and swift obedience to orders. Sterrett in any event had no apologies, for, as he told his brother, "We would put a man to death for looking pale on this ship."

This first major victory of the American Navy produced some interesting results. Governor Desfourneaux declared his island of Guadeloupe to be at war with the United States. The British, whose own performance against the French in West Indian waters had been unremarkable, unanimously applauded Truxtun, and the ship brokers of Lloyd's Coffee House in London sent him a silver urn. Meanwhile, in the commodore's own country, the reaction was not of unqualified pride but fierce controversy. The savagery of Sterrett's letter, which appeared in the public prints, was widely deplored, and even sympathy for Captain Barreaut was aroused by published reminders that his vessel had always respected the American flag. But the battle's most important significance was probably political, a widening of the division between John Adams, still working for a diplomatic adjustment with France, and those of his party who scorned such efforts. For they could now declare with their leader Timothy Pickering, the cabinet's leading "hawk" where France was concerned, that the only safe and honorable negotiation was that begun so resoundingly by Commodore Truxtun.

After putting into St. Kitts to unload her French prisoners and undergo repairs, the *Constellation* sailed home. Half her crew, whose time of service had expired, were paid off and a rendezvous opened in Hampton Roads to recruit for another year's cruise. As an inducement to old hands Truxtun promised each a beaver hat, black silk handkerchief, two months' advance pay, and two weeks' liberty ashore. Most of the men re-enlisted and in twenty days the *Constellation* was again ready for sea, her crew presumably inspired by the lively words of their redoubtable commodore: "On the ocean is our field to reap fresh laurels; let the capstan then be well-manned, trip cheerfully our anchor, spread the sails, give three cheers, and away to hunt up our enemies."

There had in the meantime occurred two incidents, neither to the Navy's credit, which were to assume added significance long after John Adams' half-war had ended. The affair of the *Baltimore* is immediately notable both as an illustration of Federalist anxiety to avoid friction with the British and in its revelation of the ruthless aspect of Benjamin Stoddert's nature which he managed to conceal except when personal or political exigency thrust it into view. The Secretary's circular to his captains accompanying copies of the Act of Congress which authorized them to seize French ships had contained a warning against the molestation of any flying another flag. "I wish to particularly impress on your mind, that should you even see an American vessel captured by the armed ship of any nation at war with whom we are at peace, you can not lawfully interfere to prevent the capture, for it is to be presumed that the courts of such nation will render justice." Or as Commodore Truxtun succinctly observed: "Our government wishes to be on good terms with Great Britain and we must not counteract what it desires."

Six weeks later, Captain Isaac Phillips, to whom Truxtun's words had been addressed, was convoying thirty sail from Charleston, South Carolina, to Havana when his vessel, the 20-gun merchantman

Baltimore, was intercepted off the Morro by a British squadron composed of two frigates and three ships of the line. Phillips signaled his convoy to make all sail into Havana and bore up for the English flagship *Carnatick* in order, he subsequently explained, to divert her attention from the scattering merchant fleet. Invited on board, he was informed by the commanding officer of the squadron, Admiral Loring, that any of the *Baltimore*'s crew not carrying American protection papers would be taken out of her. When he returned to the *Baltimore*, Phillips found a British lieutenant aboard her, muster roll in hand, her crew assembled on deck before him. The captain suffered fifty-five men, almost one-third of his compliment, to be taken off, and then he hauled down his flag, but this formal act of surrender was ignored. Admiral Loring returned all but four of the men and sailed away.

When news of the incident was received, only Benjamin Stoddert of the predominantly Anglophile Adams cabinet showed any strong reaction. No doubt he feared its effects upon the ambitious program he had just sent to a Congress still hotly divided on the subject of naval expansion; and as domestic figurehead of the fleet, he might well have felt as personally affronted as had been his captain. Yet granting either possibility, it is hard to perceive just what good dwelt in the attitude he proceeded to take, and we can only conjecture the true motives behind his merciless treatment of Isaac Phillips. He rejected the captain's attempts to justify admittedly pliant conduct as the result of impressions given him by letters from the Secretary and Commodore Truxtun directing him to (in his words) "keep on good terms with the British by every act of conciliation." For the *Baltimore*'s first lieutenant, Josias Speake (Stoddert's distant cousin), who had yielded the muster roll in Phillips' absence, the Secretary had not a word of censure, but instead he placed him in temporary command of the *Baltimore* while holding her captain alone accountable for "tame submission to a British lieutenant." Every ship in Phillips' convoy had reached Havana safely, including three briefly detained by a British ship, yet the Secretary charged that Phillips had assisted "in throwing these vessels into British hands." The circumstances being "too degrading" for Phillips to retain his commission, "I am commanded by the President to inform you that your services are no longer required."

After an unsuccessful protest against condemnation without trial, Phillips belatedly disclosed that a captain's commission had never been received by him, that therefore he should never have been burdened with the responsibilities of the rank. The "lost" commission, dated July 3, 1798, was supposed to have been issued by the Navy Department six days later. The incident off the Morro occurred in November of the same year. It was now January 1799, and on the ninth of that month a duplicate commission, bearing the original date, was sent to Phillips. And the very next day he was dismissed from the Navy. The Secretary, under no obligation to defend his actions to Commodore Truxtun, nevertheless outlined for him his reasons for Phillips' dismissal, and no doubt to allay possible uneasiness he added that, although the President possessed the power to dismiss an officer without trial, it was not one to be lightly employed. Recounting the affair in his *History of the Navy of the United States*, James Fenimore Cooper, ever alert to real or fancied naval injustices, went further: "It is at all times a dangerous and in scarcely any instance a necessary practice."[1]

A circular issued by Stoddert to all ship captains two weeks before he dismissed Isaac Phillips appeared to leave no doubt of the gravity with which he viewed the captain's offense. Since it was to take on more dramatic relevance in later years, its salient paragraph may be noted here: "It is the positive command of the President that on no pretense whatever you permit the public vessel under your command to be detained or searched, nor any of the officers or men to be taken from her, by the ships of any foreign nation, so long as you are in a capacity to repel. When overpowered by a superior force, you are to strike your flag and thus yield your men—but never your men, without your vessel."

Lieutenant William Bainbridge had surrendered both. His vessel was the captured French privateer *Croyable*, refitted as a 14-gun

---

[1] In 1820, seven years after Stoddert's death, Phillips revived the case in a plea for reinstatement and quoted from recent private letters of John Adams denying any recollection of directing or consenting to the dismissal. "Indeed," the former President had just written, "I suspect he [Phillips] never was dismissed, and that he is now a captain in the Navy as much as he ever was[!]." Belittling this testimony as the failing memory of an old man, and chiding Phillips for bitterly asserting that he was sacrificed to screen Benjamin Stoddert and his cousin, the Navy Secretary rejected the petition.

schooner and renamed *Retaliation*, and on November 20, 1798, she had come under the guns of the *Insurgente*. Bainbridge, who had taken her for British despite her failure to answer his private signals, realized his mistake too late. That a show of resistance by his little vessel against the Frenchman would bring swift disaster officers more audacious than William Bainbridge would have acknowledged. Without firing a shot he struck his flag and was taken to Guadeloupe a prisoner. The *Insurgente*, having forever fettered his reputation with the drab distinction of being the first officer of the national Navy to surrender his ship, sailed on toward her own appointed destiny with Commodore Truxtun and the *Constellation*.

It was not yet the custom of the Navy Department to order courts of inquiry into the loss during battle of armed vessels. Had one been held to investigate the surrender of the *Retaliation*, it would probably have acquitted Bainbridge of all blame. And his conduct while in captivity, his refusal to demean himself before Governor Desfourneaux, and his concern for the well-being of his incarcerated crew earned him the sympathetic approval of his government. But no official praise or exculpation could remove the unique burden now left upon his pride. Much more will be heard of William Bainbridge. Sorry luck, professional misjudgment, the manipulation of rivals, are repeatedly to confound him, and each succeeding humiliation, stirring anew his chronic apprehensions of odium, will distort his personality even as he rises in the Navy to a position of eminence.

CHAPTER FOUR

Stoddert and Truxtun

THE PROPOSALS which Benjamin Stoddert sent to Congress in December 1798 have been called the high-water mark of Federalist navy policy. Their stated purpose was to command the friendship of the powerful and the respect of the unprincipled. He asked approval for the construction of a dozen 74-gun ships of the line, as many frigates, twenty or thirty smaller vessels, and the extensive shore facilities which a fleet of this size would require. His case was strengthened by statistics showing the country's investment in armed ships to be already reaping profit, for instance, in the substantial reduction of insurance rates on merchant cargoes to and from Russia, Britain, and Italy. But the opposition of a party suspicious of high-seas fleets, indifferent to foreign trade, and wedded instead to an ideal of domestic agrarian development could not be overcome by statistics of this sort. Albert Gallatin, now its leading spokesman in Congress, drew yet again on the inexhaustible supply of his own brand to forewarn of the economic catastrophe awaiting the nation should she squander her Treasury on Federalist pretensions. And when he had succeeded in forcing a revision of the proposals, he continued to attack them because they now were inadequate. The truth was, he concluded, not now or at any time in a future of unknown duration would America be in a position to afford a fleet strong enough to confront any European foe.

Not for the first time, rebuttals to his remarks contained stinging aspersions upon his loyalty. "As often as it suits his purposes,"

Robert Harper said of him, "he blazons forth the vast naval power of England, places before our eyes her six hundred ships of war and then, with a most anti-patriotic triumph, asks us what our six 74s and ten or fifteen frigates can do against this mighty colossus. I grant that we shall not be able to contend with this force, nor do I wish it. I am not for dominion but defense. To protect our commerce we can and ought to aspire. The difference between dominion and defense constitutes the difference between that gentleman's arguments and truth." When the debate ended in February 1799, the naval bloc had won approval of six 74's, six frigates, and two repair docks.

Sixteen years were to pass before the first 74 left the stocks, and not until the 1830's were dry docks in service. Shipbuilding facilities, however, were permanently established almost at once, six sites having been bought by Stoddert at Norfolk, Washington, Philadelphia, New York (Brooklyn), Boston, and Portsmouth, New Hampshire. On these were founded the great Atlantic coast navy yards that for more than a century and a half, from sail to nuclear power, played a special role in America's naval history. The Brooklyn Navy Yard closed down in June 1966, with the Portsmouth Navy Yard scheduled for extinction in 1974. The Washington Navy Yard functioned for about a hundred years mainly as a naval weapons plant, but today, though its naval facilities share space with a number of government agencies unconnected with the sea, it still exists at least in name. The remaining yards continue in full operation, especially the giant naval complex at Norfolk.

In contrast to the future immensity of those installations whose creation he secured, Stoddert's fleet seems impossibly small to have waged even a quasi war. And of little help was the fact that its officers were, many of them, men of incredible perversity. With some, Stoddert could afford to be brusque, as he was with William Bainbridge, who, still fearful of official disfavor notwithstanding the promotion given him after his surrender, had complained of being overlooked for another. Thomas Truxtun, on the other hand, so valuable to the Navy, required treatment of the utmost delicacy. A number of Stoddert's successors in the Navy Department were in some degree to encounter the same problem; of such towering obstinacy and fragile pride were America's naval officers under sail that among a Secretary's prime requisites, if he aspired to any success at all, was high proficiency in the art of controlling the intractable. But Stoddert was the first to learn this, and he did not take easily to the consumption of time and patience which the process involved.

It was the contrariness of two senior officers, one of them Truxtun, that wrecked the Secretary's dream in 1799 of showing the American flag off the shores of France. His plan, taking advantage of the lull in Caribbean operations during the hurricane season, called for the *United States* and *Constitution* to strike the French coast south of Brest, cruise ten or twelve days in the Bay of Biscay, and be back in the West Indies in time for the all-important winter campaign. Even if no prizes were taken, "our officers and men will learn that they are not always to be nursed at home, our very fine ships will be seen in Europe, the French will be impressed to a little more caution in their depredations on our commerce." It was a project full of exciting possibilities and enjoyed John Adams' warm endorsement. Unfortunately, most of that summer the ships idled in port and Stoddert's efforts were preoccupied with a wrangle made all the harder to adjust by the intervention of the President himself.

The trouble began when Silas Talbot, commanding one of the frigates left unfinished by the settlement with Algiers, was reappointed captain *with no loss of seniority* when construction was resumed under the impetus of the crisis with France. The suspension of Talbot's pay and subsistence, John Adams was to argue, no more deprived him of his seniority than "shaking off the apples is cutting down the tree." But Commodore Truxtun's pride, puffed by adulation following his victory over the *Insurgente*, could not now endure a subordinate status to that of Talbot, whom he had always regarded as a landsman impossible to transform into a sailor, and he violently protested. To Adams this was only a manifestation of Truxtun's vanity and ambition, traits which, however, the Secretary of the Navy forthwith appeased by deciding the seniority in his favor. Talbot, who had as a soldier been wounded seventeen times in the Revolutionary War, considered himself as a mariner the equal of any Truxtun, and notwithstanding that it delayed departure of the *Constitution*, whose command he had been given, he refused the new commission.

Talbot's action was as dismaying a shock to John Adams as to Stoddert. "The *Constitution* occupies my thoughts by day and dreams by night," the President confessed. He wrote imploringly to Talbot and expressed willingness even to board the frigate daily for personal discussion with him except that to do so might arouse a sensation. Adams appears to have courted indignity by the lengths he was prepared to go in mollifying Talbot. It was not so much a case of the President's loving Truxtun less but cherishing Talbot more. Rather, he feared resentment in Boston political and commercial circles should Talbot, a popular son of New England, appear to be victimized. Truxtun came from New Jersey, a locality which did not weigh so heavily upon the President's political consciousness.

He furnished Stoddert with an extraordinarily detailed account of Silas Talbot's patriotic services, continued to prevail upon the latter, and eventually got him to sea. But it was now August, the season too advanced to permit a European diversion, and so, Stoddert wrote gloomily, "I give it up."

Now it was Truxtun's turn to resign his commission, and after delivering an emotional farewell address to his officers he quit the *Constellation*. Before the end of the year Stoddert got him back again by returning his commission with a guarantee against the possibility of Talbot's ever asserting control over him. Thus did the Navy survive its first crisis of jealousy. There would be many, many others, of more profound bitterness and with sometimes tragic consequences. Foreboding as well as immediate chagrin may have inspired the words Stoddert wrote that year to a cabinet colleague: "This avarice of rank in the infancy of our service is the Devil."

On Christmas Eve the *Constellation* once again stood for sea. It had been found that the frigates were overloaded with armament, thereby increasing their tendency to hog, or arch upward along the keel. For her present cruise the *Constellation*'s main battery was reduced by exchanging the twenty-four-pound long guns for twenty-eight eighteen-pounders, with twenty-four-pound carronades on her quarterdeck. On February 1, 1800, eight days short of the anniversary of his engagement with the *Insurgente*, Truxtun sighted the frigate *Vengeance* off St. Kitts and gave chase. On that earlier occasion, contrary to exaggerated claims (Truxtun's among them) of the *Insurgente*'s fire power, she had been definitely the weaker ship. Now the situation was reversed: the *Vengeance*, with fifty-two guns, was far superior. The weight of her broadside has been estimated at

516 pounds, while that of the *Constellation* was now, with her modified armament, 372 pounds.

Captain Pitot of the *Vengeance*, like Captain Barreaut before him,
was not seeking a fight. Bound from Guadeloupe to France, his vessel
carried thirty-six American prisoners, considerable specie, and some
eighty French Army officers and civilian officials. But it was the
captain's present misfortune to be pursued by one to whom forfeiture
of a battle on which the heart was set was no more palatable than
defeat itself. Commodore Truxtun intensified the chase. "Every inch
of canvas was set that could be of any service," John Hoxe tells us.
"We got within hail of him, hoisted our ensign, had the candles in
the battle lanterns all lighted and the large trumpet in the lee gangway ready to speak him and demand his surrender." In the hope of
disabling his pursuer, Pitot commenced firing with his stern chasers
and quarter guns, and when the *Constellation* maintained her approach he ordered the *Vengeance* into the wind and a broadside
discharged. On the *Constellation* Truxtun sensed this would be no
easy fight. At his side always during action stood the sailing master
and two midshipmen for messengers. Now he hastened one, Henry
Vandyke, to the gun divisions below with orders to take good aim
into the enemy's hull, to load and fire without confusion and as fast
as possible.

The French gunners, as was their practice, directed their main fire
at the *Constellation*'s rigging and spars. Her headsails were soon carried away, her mainmast shrouds badly cut up. Night fell and under
a pale moon broadsides flashed and thundered from the leaping guns
of the two ships. At 10 o'clock the *Constellation* was creeping ever
closer and raking the Frenchman with musketry and cannon from
gun deck, quarterdeck, forecastle, and waist. Now the ships were
almost board to board, with the *Constellation*'s forty-three-foot-long
flying jib boom fouling the French ship's mizzen shrouds, and Captain Pitot calling bravely upon his crew to repel. But it was not
Truxtun's intention to board, and as the Frenchmen swarmed to
their quarterdeck a torrent of grape shot and musket balls fell upon
them.

Despite her frightful casualties, as the *Vengeance* bore away she
was still hurling broadsides. A ball struck John Hoxe, who was stationed near the *Constellation*'s pumps, tore open his side, and almost

severed his arm. He crawled forward along the berth deck to the sick bay, where he waited for attention among the other mutilated. When his turn came, "I was taken up, laid on a table, my wounds washed clean, my arm amputated and thrown overboard." During the battle Surgeon Isaac Henry performed six amputations. Busy with knife, needle, and sponge, aided by the surgeon's mate and his young assistant, called the loblolly boy, he could remove shattered limbs and stitch wounds, but mitigate no agony. In the ill-ventilated shambles of the sick bay, he waged his own private, ghastly struggle, one he could never hope fully to win, for and against the unappeasable wounded.

Three times the *Vengeance* hauled down her colors, but desperate tokens of surrender were obscured by darkness, spray, and battle smoke. The *Constellation* continued her fire. A cannon ball swept Captain Pitot's speaking trumpet away and struck off a lieutenant's arm. Shot sundered the vessel's shrouds and the mainmast crashed to the bow. Fouling some of the other rigging in its descent, it brought down the fore-topmast and mizzen-topmast as well, with eight unfortunate topmen. A crippled hulk, the *Vengeance* reeled away into the night, fifty dead and 110 wounded on her decks, her hull pierced above and below the water line. The generals and citizen passengers, mindful of the *égalité* of the new France, helped the crew plug leaks and bail the five feet of water which flooded her hold.

It was after midnight when the *Constellation*'s guns rested. She was in scarcely better shape than the now vanished *Vengeance*. Some of her sails were missing and the badly torn shrouds had left the mainmast, 150 feet tall and almost three feet thick, dangerously unsupported. Truxtun ordered all hands to rig temporary stays, but the strong wind and buffeting seas gave them no chance. Though the ship rolled heavily, Midshipman James Jarvis, "an amiable young gentleman" commanding the maintop, refused to descend or permit his topmen to leave their station, and he with all save one perished when the mainmast toppled at last into the sea. This brought the *Constellation*'s fatalities to fourteen and, of twenty-five badly wounded, eleven more would die.

His disappointment at an inconclusive end to the fight tempered by a conviction that such was her damage the *Vengeance* must surely sink, Commodore Truxtun buried his dead at sea and ran the *Con-*

stellation down to Jamaica for repairs. "You can have no idea of the figure we cut," wrote one of his lieutenants. "There is not a spar or fathom of rigging abaft the fore-mast. Our hull is very much battered." Two months later Truxtun heard to his surprise that the *Vengeance* had stayed afloat. She limped into Curaçao "in a most distressed condition," wrote an eyewitness, "without a mast standing except the lower fore and mizzen-masts and not an original rope except the fore and bobstay that was not knitted or spliced."

News of the punishment inflicted upon the *Vengeance* by an American vessel of smaller fire power reached Paris as peace talks began and was an important and perhaps decisive factor affecting their outcome. It must already have been apparent to the French, certainly to Bonaparte, who had just gained sole power upon the fall of the Directory, that the alienation of America was a foolish error. The French Navy had been drawn into an unanticipated quarrel when its qualities and resources were at an ebb. Much of the old naval nobility had perished under the guillotine. Many of its present officers were former privateersmen and merchant mariners with no experience of command. In morale as well as matériel it had not recovered from the annihilation of Admiral Brueys' fleet on August 1, 1798. And even as those twenty-one frigates and ships of the line foundered or surrendered in Abukir Bay under Admiral Nelson's guns, there was emerging from the other side of the Atlantic this new Navy, small but threatening, cast into virtual alliance with France's foe at a most critical stage in her naval fortunes by the rashness of France herself.

Sensibly, Bonaparte reduced his naval commitment in the Caribbean, and the "half-war" entered a phase of pursuits and scattered conflicts between American naval ships and French privateers, with an incidental campaign against a local form of corsair, called picaroons, who sailed out to plunder in huge barges. A few episodes are noteworthy because they involved young men marked for renown. On New Year's Day, 1800, the 12-gun American schooner *Experiment*, Lieutenant William Maley, lay becalmed in the Bight of Léogane off Haiti with her convoy of four merchantmen when twelve barges appeared, manned by roughly 600 picaroons armed with muskets, sabers, boarding pikes, and four-pound cannon and swivels in the bow. They were identified as followers of Benoît Joseph André

Rigaud, a mulatto dissident waging guerrilla war on land and piracy afloat against the cautiously pro-American administration of Toussaint L'Ouverture, the former slave who now ruled Haiti. Lieutenant Maley, using his sweeps, maneuvered the *Experiment* into the center of his little merchant fleet, prepared the great guns, and placed a strong body of musketry on forecastle and quarterdeck. The picaroon barge fleet deployed into three squadrons and converged upon the schooner "with shrieks and menaces."

Maley's gunners destroyed two barges almost immediately, whereupon the rest turned their attention to the merchantmen. Two tried to take the brig *Mary*. A ball from the *Experiment* which flew neatly between the *Mary*'s masts sank one, but the other succeeded in boarding. The *Mary*'s crew, however, had fled or jumped overboard. After killing the only man remaining on deck (the *Mary*'s master, already wounded by a musket ball), the picaroons abandoned her. All the barges now withdrew and Maley's oarsmen were unable to overtake them.

Stories were soon circulating that Maley had been of a mind to surrender when the picaroons drew near and was inspired to resist by his first lieutenant, David Porter. This cannot be proved: no official inquiry was held and five months after the attack Maley, charged with drunkenness and looting French captives, including women and children, was forced out of the Navy. We hear no more of him. And it is to be expected, if not entirely applauded, that Porter's biographers trace their hero's valor from the picaroon incident, according him full credit for preventing wholesale capture and massacre.

Isaac Hull made his bold debut as Captain Talbot's first lieutenant on the *Constitution*, the ship with which his name would be even more illustriously linked twelve years hence. Early that year, 1800, Talbot had sighted a handsome French letter of marque at anchor in Puerto Plata, on the Spanish side of Santo Domingo, under protection of the fort's three heavy cannon. She proved to be a former British packet, the *Sandwich*, and was awaiting only a cargo of coffee before beginning the run to France. Talbot was no immature hothead and the risks of raiding in a neutral port must have been perfectly clear to him. One is led to suspect that he was overanxious to justify by some achievement the President's rare support of him in the seniority dispute, if he could not conspicuously show himself (since French men of war were now so scarce in the West Indies) Thomas Truxtun's equal. Under his command so far the *Constitution* had fought no battles and seized but one or two insignificant prizes. He decided to capture the *Sandwich* or destroy her in port.

He could not run the *Constitution* in because of harbor shoals, so he manned a sloop, the *Sally*, with ninety seamen and marines under Lieutenant Hull and on May 12 sent them in under bright noon sun. The raiders concealed themselves below decks, reminding Daniel Carmick, who was in charge of the marine contingent, of the wooden horse of Troy. Captain Carmick and his marines left the *Sally* some distance out, waded ashore in neck-deep water, and spiked the cannon before the garrison commander realized what was afoot. The *Sally* meanwhile had run alongside the *Sandwich* and Lieutenant Hull, sword in hand, led his men aboard her "like devils." They suffered no loss, and although the packet was stripped when taken, her shrouds coiled and stowed below, by sunset Hull had her cleared, rigged, and ready for service. "No enterprise of like moment was ever better carried out," Talbot claimed proudly, and himself described it as "a daring act." It was of course also an illegal one. The *Sandwich* had finally to be surrendered, and damages for the violation of Spanish neutrality were met at least in part by the forfeiture of prize money due the *Constitution*'s crew from a more legitimate routine seizure.

The contribution, if it amounts to that, made by John Rodgers in the conflict with France was a characteristic start to an oddly mixed career of fame and frustration. He had left the *Constellation* to command the 20-gun sloop *Maryland* with orders to protect shipping along the northern coastline of South America. But from July to December 1799 he fell in with no France ships and all he took was an American vessel found trading with the enemy under Swedish colors. John Shaw, on the other hand, in command of the swift little *Enterprise*, a 12-gun schooner, achieved excellent results during the same period. At the end of the year Shaw summed up: "I have in my last cruise made 300 French prisoners, killed and wounded 61 men, taken 42 pieces of artillery and 180 stand of musketry, which is really more than I could have contemplated."

As the year 1800 began, Benjamin Stoddert controlled a navy of almost fifty vessels and 6,000 men. His correspondence makes clear that, warmly abetted by President Adams, he had little compunction about hurrying them to sea even at some risk. "Neither want of men or marines must detain the *Boston*'s sailing," he had written to Captain George Little in the fall of 1799. "The British often go out understaffed." There was a brief concern when, weeks after the *Boston*'s departure, no word had come from Captain Little. "One of the bravest men in one of the finest ships in the world," wrote John Adams apprehensively, "I am afraid has been driven out to sea without a proper compliment of seamen. Yet we did right. . . ."

Little, as it happened, was quite safe in waters northeast of Guadeloupe and soon to be heard from. On October 12, in a two hours' battle which left both ships shattered, the *Boston* had captured a small French frigate, *Le Berceau*. Anyway, Benjamin Stoddert refused to allow the disturbing possibilities behind Captain Little's silence to deter him from bullying yet another ship to sea, notwithstanding her unfinished carpentry. He ordered this one to weigh anchor immediately, assuring her captain that the Department would take full responsibility. It is possible to detect in some of Stoddert's hastening directives the quality of imperative persuasion present in so many minutes and memoranda of Winston Churchill. A fascinating similarity of mode is in fact suggested by comparison of a letter from the British First Lord of the Admiralty in November 1914 to the commander in chief at Devonport with one issued by the American Secretary of the Navy 115 years earlier almost to the day. Churchill is ordering out, on the following Wednesday, two battlecruisers urgently needed in the South Atlantic to hunt Admiral von Spee's squadron. Stoddert is rushing the brand-new sloop of war *Patapsco* out of Baltimore by the next Sunday. Both missives, in words that seem almost to echo each other, propose that, if necessary, shore technicians should sail with the ships, finish their tasks at sea, and return home (in Churchill's words) "as opportunity may offer." In both cases the tactic succeeded: work was completed, probably at a cost of some overtime, and all three ships left promptly.

There is nothing wanton in Stoddert's apparent disregard of hazard to his ships and men. Without a mariner's appreciation of safety factors at sea, he could hardly have displayed a mariner's caution. And he was by no means wrong in attributing many of the delays to laziness or inefficiency in the shipyards. At all events, if there was peril in haste, it just had to be courted. Confident that he himself was perfectly willing to take political risks for the good of the service, he did not think it asking too much that his captains accept the risks, in whatever form, of their calling. On July 15, 1800, he ordered the *Insurgente* to sea "whether prepared or not." Following her capture, the French frigate had been brought into Hampton Roads and from thence to Baltimore for thorough repairs under the nominal supervision of Captain Alexander Murray. Some discussion arose over the fitness of her spars: Murray thought they should be renewed and Commodore Truxtun overruled him, although, Murray wrote, "by his own account he says they may serve for a short cruise only." There is no evidence that the spars were renewed. Now French privateers were suddenly infesting America's home waters, and the *Insurgente* was the only ship of strength conveniently available to pit against them. "If she is only half-manned or half-fitted she must sail." Brutal words indeed, but Stoddert was not afraid to let them go into the record. And sail she did that summer with 300 men under command of Captain Patrick Fletcher. She was last spoken off Cape Henry on August 10, shortly before a hurricane swept up the Atlantic. She was never heard from again.

Her loss is usually ascribed to the storm. Certainly weather tested the structure of the frigates and the mettle of those who manned them more cruelly than did any Frenchman's cannon. Nothing illustrates this better than the ordeal of the *Essex* and the *Congress*. Conceiving that French privateers might attempt to intercept the return of richly laden American merchantmen from the Dutch East Indies, Stoddert had ordered the two frigates halfway around the world to escort them home. No American ships of war had ventured so far to the eastward. The *Essex*, a 32-gun ship built at Salem by popular subscription, sailed on January 9, 1800, with a favoring wind. Edward Preble, her New England captain, has been described as tall and stalwart, and a clergyman who observed him and a celebrated Indian chieftain simultaneously on the streets of Boston thought them both the noblest human specimens he had ever seen. This must have been before Preble's imprisonment during the Revolutionary War on board the English hulk *New Jersey*, for his health had declined thereafter. But he was known to possess a sturdy voice, heard often ashore in patriotic song and the recital of naval odes, and on the quarterdeck during the fits of temper for which he was notorious. His quicksilver temperament concealed a painful shyness; this thirty-eight-year-old mariner, agitated on the eve of his long voyage by a desperate passion for a Portland widow, beseeched her favors indirectly through anguished letters to her mother. Then he set out, and was soon demonstrating qualities of seamanship, command, and calculated boldness which were to distinguish Preble's short but influential naval career.

Five days out, the *Essex* was struck by a heavy gale, which caused her to spring her mainmast between decks, and carried her main shrouds and all the topmast stays into the sea. As darkness fell and the wind blew harder, Preble ordered the topgallant yard and masts lowered, took in the mainsail, and set up the weather shrouds. Far into the night the crew labored. They succeeded in easing the strain upon the mainmast, but at dawn the weather had not moderated. Preble aroused his carpenters before 6 o'clock to prepare "fishes"— strengthening pieces—with which to brace the mast, and in this fashion, under the captain's indefatigable direction, the *Essex* rode out the storm and proceeded on her ordered course. The *Congress* was in less sure hands. In the opinion of many contemporaries, Captain James Sever was too inflexible a disciplinarian and too inefficient a seaman. Almost the only good words one can find of him are those of a midshipman, Charles Morris, who thought him "austere and distant but cool and self-possessed in trying situations." Sever, most probably, experienced few situations more trying than when the winter storm assailing the *Essex* overtook his vessel three days out of Newport. Like the *Essex* she sprang her mainmast, eight feet above the spar deck, and Sever ordered the main yard lowered and main-topmast removed to save it. Nathaniel Bosworth, the fourth lieutenant, climbed aloft followed by five men. "Poor Bosworth," a fellow officer wrote afterward, "the word to cut away the topmast was no sooner passed than he was up shrouds." And he was no sooner aloft when the mainmast collapsed, flinging him to his death in heavy seas and carrying with it the mizzen-topmast and mizzen-masthead. Several men were injured; Midshipman Morris, entangled in the main-topgallant brace, was swept as high as the mizzentop and then let fall to the deck, breaking an arm. Now Sever concentrated on securing his foremast and bowsprit: both had sprung. But the wind refused to slacken. Wallowing helplessly in a trough, the *Congress* rolled away her fore-topmast while her crew were struggling to lash the heel of the jib boom in an effort to at least save the bowsprit.

A dismasted wreck, the *Congress* crept into Hampton Roads, Sever seeking consolation in a presumption that the *Essex*, an inferior ship, must be in even worse plight. It is not hard to imagine his feelings when he heard that she had withstood the tempest and was steadfastly approaching the coast of South Africa.

She anchored in Table Bay on March 11. Captain Preble delivered the private signals to the admiral of the British squadron, dined with him, and heard his officers admire the American frigate's beauty. Two months later Preble was off Batavia, and in August on his way home with fourteen ships under convoy carrying coffee, sugar, pepper, and tea. Autumnal gales repeatedly scattered the vessels and Preble had also to contend with a mutiny in mid-ocean, but he quickly put it down, struggled to reassemble his dispersed merchantmen, and on November 28, 1800, shepherded eleven of them into New York Harbor. This was two months after the Treaty of Morfontaine had ended the quasi war with the French.

To political historians, this strange conflict provides a dramatic illustration of presidential resistance to party pressures. But its greatest significance can be perceived as naval rather than political. Until then, the maritime nations of Europe had not taken seriously America's pretensions to statehood, much less considered her a likely equal or rival. But beyond mere possession of a public fleet (in the European tradition itself an acceptable token of national sovereignty), Truxtun's resounding triumphs in the Caribbean and Preble's appearance east of Table Bay convinced the Old World that the former colonies of the New were an imminent naval power to be reckoned with.

The exploits of the captains and commodores which won this first guarded respect from Europeans were only possible through less glamorous accomplishments in organization, administration, and strategic deployment. By these we may fairly measure Benjamin Stoddert. Few men more foresighted and dedicated could have been found for the job. It is true that in his dealings with officers his alternating characteristics of tolerance and ruthlessness were at times misapplied. He is vulnerable in his handling of the *Baltimore* affair, and was unwise to the point of folly in the magnitude of the authority with which he invested Thomas Truxtun. If there is nothing in the commodore's career to justify the brand of the tyrant, he had in the spring of 1800 become dangerously conceited, and encouraging him to act "as if you had command of the whole Navy" was a reckless invitation to trouble. Yet those were Stoddert's words directing him to investigate a case of unrest aboard the *Congress*, and in what had begun to resemble joint control of the Navy by Stoddert and Truxtun it was soon impossible to tell who was senior partner. The limit was struck when Truxton ordered the *Constellation*, now under command of Captain Murray, to sail for St. Kitts without Department orders. Murray obeyed, but took good care to inform the Secretary just before putting out. Stoddert, who wanted the *Constellation* on the Santo Domingo station, 500 miles from St. Kitts, was furious, all the more, we can presume, because Truxtun's prestige and value, and the Navy's (or Stoddert's) reliance upon him, precluded the court-martial that his astonishing arrogance invited. Stoddert had to content himself with some of the angriest words he had penned on Department stationery: "In sending off Murray without instructions from the President you assumed the direction in a case belonging to the Executive exclusively, and God knows what inconveniences may result from it."

But however arguable these aspects of Stoddert's administration, it is certain that uppermost in his thoughts most of the time was the good of the service he had nursed into existence. And when in the spring of 1801 America's political leadership passed from the divided Federalists to a party united under Jefferson and Gallatin and sworn to eliminate war expenditures, his final task was to establish safeguards for its future. In size it now amounted to at least fifty ships, thirteen of them frigates; the number of men had increased to 8,000; the officers' list now showed 28 captains, 7 master-commandants, 110 lieutenants, and 354 midshipmen. Stoddert decided that the best guarantee for preserving at least a nucleus of a fleet was a set of proposals so modest no Republican could patriotically oppose it. He recommended the retention of thirteen vessels, six in active service, seven in a prepared state "in ordinary," with a corresponding reduction in man power. For what it was worth, he outlined to Congress his general philosophy on the subject: "When the United States owns twelve ships of 74 guns and double the number of strong frigates, and it is known they possess the means of increasing with facility their naval strength, we may then avoid those wars in which we have no interest, and without submitting to be plundered." These observations made no particular impression, and a bill to reduce the Navy was passed on March 3. Then, having devoted three years to the creation of the service, and having brought about its partial liquidation in a calculated attempt to save it from total extinction, Benjamin Stoddert returned to private life.

It was a ruinous one. Never again did he come anywhere near the business prosperity he had enjoyed before his appointment as the nation's first Secretary of the Navy. He accumulated many debts, some of which Truxtun helped him settle by persuading friends to buy property lots from him, but he never fully recovered and when he died on December 17, 1813, at the age of sixty-two he was still heavily in debt.

As for Truxtun, although he was one of the captains retained by the Jefferson administration, his career lasted scarcely a year longer and dribbled to an inauspicious end. He had been assigned to command a squadron in the Mediterranean, where, thanks to the existence of her Navy (albeit depleted), America was able to counter with force a brigandage it had once appeased. Eagerly the commodore had set out for Norfolk, where he was to board the frigate *Chesapeake*. But if his enthusiasm was not dampened in Washington (where an apparently indifferent Jefferson, with whom he dined, asked him if he was headed north or south), it was thoroughly quenched at Norfolk by the vessel's unprepared state and shortage of men. Most galling of all, although Truxtun had expected that a captain would be appointed to run the flagship on which he sailed as commodore, none was sent. Angrily, he refused the command, only to have the new administration interpret his act as resignation from the Navy. The commodore, not yet fifty, retreated in a fury to his stately home on the New Jersey shore. Here he sulked for many idle years, convinced that he was a victim of Thomas Jefferson's vengeance for having trounced the French. He wrote many rambling and acrimonious letters to the Navy Department, meanwhile confiding his grievances to Aaron Burr, who consequently tried to recruit the embittered commodore for treason. But this was Burr's mistake. Much as Truxtun detested Jefferson's government, disloyalty to it would have betrayed that service from which, no matter what the new occupants of the Navy Department thought, he could not bring himself to accept separation, a service which in his own valorous and supremely egotistical fashion, he had helped launch and undoubtedly loved.

CHAPTER FIVE

The Mediterranean Squadron

As if surrendering the *Retaliation* to the *Insurgente* in the Caribbean in 1798 was not bad enough, further mortification awaited William Bainbridge in the Mediterranean. During America's preoccupation with France, her annual tribute to Algiers had fallen into three years' arrears. When payment was resumed, the John Adams administration decided that some accompanying show of naval strength might impress both the Dey and her coastal neighbors, and with this aim he sent the gifts, which included chinaware and Irish linen, aboard the 32-gun converted merchantman *George Washington*. By her very name this vessel has attached to the episode a sour irony. She sailed from the Delaware on August 8, 1800, in Bainbridge's command and anchored forty days later off the mole at Algiers. The abject nature of the mission, though less discreditable to the captain than to the diplomats and politicians responsible for the treaty, had already inflamed the wound dealt his pride by the capitulation off Guadeloupe. Now the Dey applied the salt: he wished to press the *George Washington* into his service for conveying emissaries and a good-will cargo to the Sultan of the Ottoman Empire.

The fourth son of a respected Princeton physician, William Bainbridge had been privately educated by his maternal grandfather, under whose influence he acquired a predilection for knowledge and cultural self-improvement. As a young merchant mariner he proved uncompromisingly forceful. His quick instincts and powerful build had helped to suppress at least two mutinies, and while commanding the armed merchantman *Hope* at the age of nineteen he had not hesitated to defy and even fire upon British ships exercising their controversial right of search.

In the Navy his personality underwent a change, the result perhaps of new self-discipline and a burgeoning humanitarianism. At moments of crisis he showed an increasing disposition to assess odds. It was an unfortunate time to develop the habit. Manifest boldness was becoming an essential to naval eminence; caution ran the risk of contempt. The character of Bainbridge gave evidence of being a mixture of the two. As events were in later years to prove, he had not altogether ceased to be a determined and dangerous foe. But in his early naval service at least, that period when, in the glibness of some historians, he was simply "a child of misfortune," it was as much miscalculation and uncertainty as bad luck that precipitated disaster and left him prey to the only thing that he mortally feared: the censure of his countrymen.

Richard O'Brien, the American consul at Algiers, joined Bainbridge in arguing with the Dey and his ministers for three or four weeks; but since the French and British had on occasion favored him by transporting his goods, he professed to see no reason why the Americans should not fall into the same line of self-interest and appeasement. While the potentate resorted to alternating tactics of tantrum, cajolery, and threat, Bainbridge anxiously prophesied in letters home that continued refusal would only provoke him into renouncing the treaty with America and unleashing his corsairs once more against her commerce. On the other hand, to serve as the Dey's agent would invite grave possibilities. What if the *George Washington* were attacked by a ship of a European power at war with Barbary? Should Bainbridge fight to defend the Dey's goods and passengers? Would not America be charged in any case with a breach of neutrality?

Even if nothing of that kind happened, ferrying high-ranking infidels to a strange domain where by all accounts the plague raged and the United States was quite unknown would subject Bainbridge to "the worst of purgatories." Yet what choice had he but to submit? Thus he wrote in letters of chagrin and excuse. He thought the Navy Department's orders to awe foreigners with a disciplined and military showing were hardly compatible with the purpose of his voyage to Algiers in the first place, and they could be properly executed by not one but ten or twelve American frigates. "I hope I may never again be sent to Algiers with tribute," he wrote fervidly, "unless I am authorized to deliver it from the mouth of a cannon."

At 2 P.M. on October 9, again the flag of a vessel commanded by William Bainbridge was lowered, and the crimson colors of Algiers hoisted at the main. Some of the Americans who, in the words of the ship's log, had been "big with the expectation of returning to the land of liberty" openly wept. Ten days later the *George Washington* set course for Constantinople with an exotic passenger list made up of the Algerian ambassador to Turkey, his personal suite of a hundred, and as many male and female slaves. She might have been a fabled treasure ship, for the Dey's propitiatory cargo was valued at more than half a million dollars. She was a Noah's Ark bearing lions, tigers, antelope, parrots, horses, cattle, sheep, and ostriches. And without claim to glory she deserves a niche in history, for, once beyond range of the Algerian batteries, Bainbridge rehoisted his country's colors and they were borne past the twin forts commanding the Dardanelles and across the Sea of Marmara to be flown for the first time at the mouth of the Golden Horn.

The significance of the event as a herald of American interest in this area was not lost on Constantinople's foreign diplomats, and they remarked as well on the *George Washington*'s cleanliness and the good behavior of her crew. In the Sultan's circle it was observed with delight that the United States flag, like Turkey's, featured celestial details. A sorry situation had its positive side after all, and when Bainbridge by word and deportment established a basis for future good relations between the two countries so vastly separated and totally dissimilar, he was, to his credit, making the very best of it.

He returned to Algiers with a firman from the Grand Admiral of the Turkish Fleet guaranteeing the Sultan's special protection throughout the Islamic world. A mere flourish of it before the Dey not only cut short an attempted resumption of impositions but reduced him, Bainbridge said, to "a mild, humble and even crouching dependent." The firman was also key to the rescue of fifty-six French civilians of Algiers whom the Dey had imprisoned when, out of further servility to the Sultan—an ally of England's in the struggle against Bonaparte—he declared war on France. Bainbridge's act of humanity was all the greater, for he did not yet know that American hostilities with France were at an end.

Early in 1801 the *George Washington* sailed home. Although the new administration had fretted over the reports that she had been dragooned for the convenience of a heathen despot, Jefferson greeted Captain Bainbridge sympathetically enough and termed his conduct "judicious" under trying circumstances. But the first American warship to span the Mediterranean from Gibraltar to the Orient had completed the voyage as a pirate's lackey, a fact that was not altered by the official acceptance of Bainbridge's and Consul O'Brien's explanation that knuckling to the Dey had preserved the peace. And it would take more than the President's charity to rid William Bainbridge of suspicions that a politely concealed disillusionment with him had now crept into existence.

A month after his arrival home, developments in the Mediterranean virtually assured Bainbridge's return to that sea and an opportunity to brighten a so far murky service record. Envious of the flow of tribute to Algiers, Yusuf Karamanli, Bashaw of Tripoli, began rattling his sabers for an increase in his own blackmail income from America. The Bey of Tunis joined the avaricious chorus, but did little more. The dynamic personality of William Eaton, the American consul, held him in check. A hundred Eatons, however, would have had difficulty curbing Karamanli's greed and jealousy. To gain the Tripolitan throne he had slain his eldest brother before their mother's eyes, exiled a second brother to Tunis, and probably poisoned his father. Angered by the American silence in response to his demands for tribute commensurate with that furnished his major rival in the Ottoman satrap system, he sent a squad of men to the terrace of the United States consulate, where they hacked down the flagpole, a Barbary signal of war.

The challenge did not catch President Jefferson off guard; neither was it entirely unwelcome. That the settlement of disputes between civilized parties or nations ought not to be sought in armed force was one of his most preciously held tenets. It accounts for his political leadership of men fundamentally opposed to a permanent navy, and many expected when he came to power that the minimal fleet bequeathed by the previous administration would founder completely under his. But Jefferson's philosophy did not always rule out the use of force. When the declared aim was to supplant a corrupt nobility with popular democracy, he could pardon even the bloody industry of the guillotine. And to destroy piracy rather than finance it in payment for doubtful immunity had always seemed to him sanctioned by morality *and* thrift. In short, force should be avoided between nations of comparable maturity but was justified against aristocrats and barbarians. This double standard explains Jefferson's paradoxical role in naval history. He had urged the creation of a navy and was to begin his Presidency by accelerating its growth. Yet on general principle he abominated it.

He was not sure he understood it either. The Navy Department, by his own admission, was the branch of government that most baffled him. His first three selections for successor to Benjamin Stoddert declined the position, and when it seemed that he might have to advertise publicly for a volunteer, Samuel Smith, an influential Maryland senator, pushed his brother Robert into the office. The new Secretary was a courteous, somewhat vain, and gossipy man who owned the biggest maritime law practice in Baltimore and had been mildly active in state politics, hardly the best equipment for the most taxing, disdained, and understaffed of all the cabinet departments prior to 1812. Assuredly Smith would have withstood the pressure of his brother and even the persuasions of the President had he had foreknowledge of the work and perplexity the job involved. His principal responsibility was the repair, construction, and most useful deployment of the small fleet. The six navy yards under his supervision were beset by staff intrigue and labor unrest. He had to decide on the most economical disbursement of usually insufficient funds which passed through the hands of sometimes dishonest purchasing agents. And always he had to contend with self-willed sea officers.

It was a big enough drain on Smith's capabilities trying to deflect Albert Gallatin's economy blade when it swooped upon the recommendations for naval improvement and expansion which he conscientiously laid before the cabinet. The Secretary of the Treasury, as Smith must have known, considered him to be an extravagant dolt. Moreover, Smith could not count on his brother to support ideas that might just annoy the President; in any case Samuel Smith's sphere of influence did not extend far beyond the Senate. In the

House of Representatives, which had the final word on expenditures, Robert Smith's proposals ran into a Ways and Means Committee dominated by Gallatin's cousin by marriage and political intimate, Joseph Hopper Nicholson. To make matters more difficult, Nicholson was chairman of a committee appointed in December 1801 to investigate the expenditures of the Federalist administrations. (In this capacity he asked the former Secretary of the Navy by what authority he purchased six navy yards. Benjamin Stoddert could not recall the precise legislative occasion. But, he reminded Nicholson, authority for the construction of the 74's would have been sufficient, for one could no more build ships of the line without shipyards than without keels.)

Smith's management of naval affairs was repeatedly governed by the influence Gallatin and Nicholson could exert upon the Chief Executive. Gallatin's economic philosophy so dovetailed Jefferson's brand of pacifism that he became the cabinet oracle to whom the President most often turned. And Joseph Nicholson had placed Jefferson squarely in his debt by a dramatic display of loyalty at a critical moment. During the balloting on the electoral tie in February 1801, he had left a sickbed, crossed through snow to the drafty Capitol, and for seventeen successive days, in spite of a raging fever, cast his Maryland vote for Jefferson.

Nicholson's republicanism established him firmly in the ranks of opposition to a national Navy. And his status and power enabled him to intercede when necessary on behalf of the several Nicholsons who were members of it. He had been expressly charged by his uncle, Captain Samuel Nicholson, to "use your influence with the Navy Department to benefit me, my children, and our connections in the naval service." Samuel Nicholson was himself a beneficiary when his nephew, writing an earnest letter to Thomas Jefferson three weeks after his inauguration as President, secured his uncle's retention in the reduced Navy and obtained for him command of the new Navy Yard at Charlestown, Massachusetts.

In general, naval policy during Jefferson's first term was shaped by the exigencies of the Mediterranean situation. As so often since with elected visionaries, foreign developments obliged Jefferson to tack about as soon as he grasped the nation's helm. It was an adjustment of conviction which had the approval of Albert Gallatin, who, although he regarded the Navy as a "profligate excrescence," was sufficiently a realist to acknowledge practical necessity. His plans for the liquidation of the Navy were quietly set aside, though not abandoned. The cabinet, as yet unaware that the Bashaw of Tripoli had declared war, but already compelled by "proofs of hostile purposes" to take steps for the protection of Mediterranean commerce, voted unanimously on May 15 to send out three frigates and a sloop under Commodore Richard Dale.

That officer's first orders limited him to reconnaissance, convoy duty, and demonstrations of strength; only if war had been declared by the time of his arrival was he free to sink, burn, or otherwise disable the enemy's shipping. Clashes with vessels of nations with whom America was at peace were to be avoided. "We do not mean that you are to submit to unequivocal insults," wrote Robert Smith and, paraphrasing Stoddert's instructions to the fleet's captains after the British search of the *Baltimore,* he continued, "and particularly you are not to suffer your ships to be entered, or your men examined or taken out, but to resist such attempts to your uttermost, yielding only to superior force, and surrendering, if overcome, your vessel and men, but never your men without your vessel."

The first American battle squadron to cross the Atlantic consisted of the schooner *Enterprise* and frigates *Philadelphia, Essex,* and *President,* the latter flying the commodore's broad pendant. They sailed past Cádiz, where the sight of six British ships of the line blockading the port afforded a reminder of the Napoleonic power struggle convulsing Europe, and on July 1, 1801, entered Gibraltar Harbor.

Two Tripolitan ships were anchored there: a 28-gun schooner and a 14-gun brig, commanded by Murad Reis, the Grand Admiral of the Tripolitan Navy, less exaltedly identified as a Clydebank renegade, born Peter Lisle. Little more can be told of this Scotsman than that his ascent from captive deckhand to the Bashaw's naval chieftain was the probable result of the value placed upon his seamanship, his adoption of the Moslem faith and tongue, and his marriage to the Bashaw's daughter. Hailing him, Dale politely inquired if their countries were at war, to which Murad Reis lied that they were not. But from subsequent reports on shore, Dale presumed otherwise and before continuing his eastward cruise he detailed Captain Samuel Barron of the *Philadelphia* to remain behind and intercept the

Tripolitans when they came out. The American consul at Gibraltar stationed himself on the Rock meanwhile, ready to dispatch a boat and alert Barron should the corsairs show signs of leaving. Thus blockaded at the start were two of the Bashaw's best ships with his son-in-law, the admiral, and some 400 seamen. Their capture, wrote William Eaton from Tunis, would end the war immediately, for without them Karamanli was helpless.

Dale carried on to Tripoli, where, communicating through Nicholas Nissen, the Danish consul, he invited the Bashaw's terms for restoration of peace. He declined to enter actual negotiations, however, despite indications that the Tripolitan ruler, in some anxiety about his vessels at Gibraltar, was willing to talk. Instead Dale dispatched the *Enterprise*, Lieutenant Andrew Sterrett, north to Malta for water; directed Captain Bainbridge, who now commanded the *Essex*, to convoy American trade; and he himself set up a single-vessel blockade before Tripoli with his flagship *President*.

At 9 A.M. on August 1 the 12-gun *Enterprise*, approaching Malta under British colors, fell in with a polacre, a three-masted Mediterranean merchantman, armed with fourteen guns and named the *Tripoli*. Sterrett hailed for the purpose of her cruise. The *Tripoli*'s commander replied that he was hunting Americans but had so far found none. Sterrett immediately hauled down the false colors and ran up the American flag, letting him know he need seek no farther. The ships closed to pistol range, throwing broadsides and small-arms fire at each other. James Leander Cathcart, ex-consul at Tripoli and an old Mediterranean hand, had once written that after a single broadside and attempted intimidation by shouting the Bashaw's seamen would try to board, but "if you beat them off once they seldom risk a second encounter." Instead of conforming to Cathcart's brief on Barbary assault tactics, the crew of the *Tripoli*, armed with pistols, knives, and blunderbusses, tried three times to board, and then resorted to a ruse the ex-consul had not mentioned—feigned surrender and a surprise attack when the Americans, guns at rest, were closing to take possession. But treachery only inspired Sterrett's crew to equal cunning and deadlier gunnery. Certainly the lieutenant who had run a man through for cowardice on the *Constellation* felt no such necessity aboard the *Enterprise* that morning. At the end of three hours not an American was hurt, but half of the ninety or so aboard the polacre, including her surgeon, lay dead or wounded. Surrender this time was no pretense. The commander appeared at the gangway, flung his flag into the sea, and then prostrated himself. Sterrett dismantled the polacre except for a sail and a spar and sent her struggling back to Tripoli, where defeat so early in hostilities was not to be taken lightly: the Bashaw ordered the commander seated backward on an ass, paraded in disgrace through the streets, and given 500 bastinadoes.

When the triumphant *Enterprise* reappeared off Tripoli, she took over the *President's* blockade, and Dale returned to Gibraltar, where the *Philadelphia* maintained her vigil outside the harbor. The Tripolitan ships were still there. But as Dale soon learned, they were stripped and unmanned: their crews had stolen across the Straits to Tetuán in small boats at night and were by now on their long overland journey home. Admiral Murad Reis took the sea route: he reached Malta in a British ship, made his way thence to the North African shore, and landed in furtive safety thirty miles east of Tripoli.

The failure to capture Murad Reis established the lackluster pattern of Dale's whole campaign. Sterrett's victory—which earned his crew an extra month's pay each and himself the congressional promise (still unfulfilled four years later) of a commemorative sword— remained its single achievement. At home disappointment grew, much of it traceable to want of understanding. No administration, least of all Jefferson's, could have properly appreciated the real difficulties of Dale's far-off command: the worsening weather as the year waned, the problems of liaison and supply inevitable to so few ships operating from foreign and not always friendly ports, the evaporating zeal and proficiency of men whose periods of enlistment were expiring. Naturally, the cause of trouble most magnified by those incapable of comprehending any other was the dilatoriness of the commodore. Dale, "a man of singular simplicity and moderation," Fenimore Cooper calls him, was summoned home after only five months on the Mediterranean station and allowed to resign.

Partly to blame for the indifferent results of that first campaign was an early self-handicap of Jefferson himself as President: his restricted view of the constitutional powers of the office, and in consequence a reluctance to adopt, without congressional sanction, any warlike measures beyond those manifestly related to home defense. Fortunately, his resolve to resist piracy, instead of subsidizing it, remained strong and he was soon making what were, for him, daring representations to the legislature. He found he had only to ask. In February 1802 Congress gave him full discretion in the employment of the Navy for *offense*. Too late to help Dale but promising great benefit to his successor, this new political initiative increased the limit of a seaman's service from one year to two and almost doubled the strength of the Mediterranean fleet.

Its command was now offered to Thomas Truxtun, who (as we have seen) refused it and resigned because a flag captain did not come with it. Little time or care was wasted looking for somebody else. Indeed, the next appointment would be difficult to reconcile with Jefferson's earnest desire to chastise the pirates if one did not bear in mind his limited grasp of the qualifications essential to naval command. No record exists to show that Richard Valentine Morris possessed any that were outstanding, and his name is missing from the original list of officers retained by Jefferson's administration. The appointment is sometimes hinted at as purely political. (And so it might have been; Morris' brother, a Federalist congressman, had abstained from the House vote on the electoral tie in 1801 and freed the Vermont delegation to cast its ballot for Thomas Jefferson.) Richard Morris accepted command of the squadron, and almost immediately his wife asked permission to accompany him overseas. Robert Smith gallantly assented. In due course she followed the commodore on board the frigate *Chesapeake*, taking their son and a colored servant with her.

In the prolix volumes of captains' correspondence, Secretary's letters to vessels of war, private diaries, and ships' logs which comprise the sea-stained record of the Barbary War, Richard Morris' fifteen months in the Mediterranean have the tragicomic impact of a harlequinade on a battlefield. His blockade was no more effective than Dale's. Bashaw Karamanli's xebecs and galleys came and went as they pleased, usually keeping close to shore, where the large American ships could not safely intercept them. Yet hazards were sometimes forgotten in the heat of pursuit. Captain Alexander Murray chased eight enemy gunboats into twelve-fathom water and was almost running the *Constellation* on Tripolitan sands when 6,000 native cavalry, by Murray's estimate, galloped down to the beach. After an exchange of shots between the frigate and the horsemen, Murray withdrew.

The captain's boldness here is worth remarking, for he was of the old naval breed distinguished more for seamanship than dash. Half deaf, the result of an accidental discharge of a cannon in the Revolutionary War, Murray may also have had vision trouble, for he later permitted a Tripolitan cruiser carrying pirate loot and captive Americans to approach the *Constellation* and, after mutual salutes, to proceed without hindrance. It was this kind of thing that provoked William Eaton to sneer that the government "might as well send out Quaker meeting houses to float about the sea as frigates with Murrays in command."

The acidulous consul at Tunis ought to have directed some of his shafts at Daniel McNeil, about whose eccentricities the general silence suggests that they beggared comment. Commanding the 28-gun frigate *Boston*, McNeil roamed the Mediterranean at will, failed to communicate with the rest of the squadron, maintained indifferent contact with the Department and none at all with his commodore, and was so absent-minded he could sometimes forget men he had sent ashore on duty and sail away leaving them there. He offset the lack of three officers thus abandoned at Toulon by departing with three French dinner guests who were finally landed on the African shore and obliged to return to France in a fishing boat. McNeil's known irresponsibilities overshadow his probable accomplishments. At least he prevented four Tunisian merchantmen from running wheat, oil, and barley into Tripoli, but this also annoyed the Bey of Tunis and threw fresh problems on Consul Eaton's desk. McNeil was soon brought home and dismissed from the Navy.

Commodore Morris lost little if any sleep over the erratic conduct of the *Boston*'s captain, and he may have been as heedless, if not ignorant, of the rumors circulating among the ships, relayed to the consulates and echoing back to the Navy Department, that he was spending so much time in the safe comfort of European ports he had lost sight of the object of his mission. The dependable Eaton had a gibe ready—next the government might try confronting Tripoli with "a company of comedians and a seraglio." Sarcasm arose in the steerage too. Aboard the *Chesapeake* it was whispered that command of the squadron had passed into the delicate hands of the commodore's lady, who, wrote a midshipman, "is not beautiful, or even handsome, but looks very well in a veil."

While it has done little for his reputation, the evidence shows that Morris was not permanently idle. On January 30, 1803, he sent the squadron to Tripoli with the intention of frightening the Bashaw to terms. But a gale sprang up, nearly dismasted the *Chesapeake*, and blew for two weeks. When Morris next put out, it was for Tunis, where a quarrel between William Eaton and the Bey threatened to start another war. After conferences with the Tunisians which Morris thought had gone tolerably well, he and Captain John Rodgers were placed under surprise arrest and a ransom of $34,000 was demanded for their release. This was the amount allegedly owed the Bey by Eaton, who had borrowed it to finance an overland march on Tripoli to install Hamet Karamanli, the Bashaw's exiled brother, as rightful ruler. A flurry of arguments and name-calling in the Bey's palace abruptly ended Eaton's consular career, and upon some financial aid from the French and Danish envoys, the naval officers were freed.

In April Commodore Morris transferred his flag to the frigate *New York* and again made for Tripoli with the hope of intimidating the Bashaw. But on the tenth, just as the drum began beating for grog, powder exploded in the *New York*'s cockpit close by the magazine and started a fire. Ignoring the commodore's order to lower boats, his crew, fearing fresh explosions, fled to the ship's extremities—fore, aft, and aloft. A confused quartermaster told to signal *"fire on board"* ran up *"mutiny on board"* instead, which brought the *John Adams* and *Enterprise* ranging under the flagship's stern, crews at battle stations and guns run out. Isaac Chauncey, the *New York*'s first lieutenant, assembled some of the more frightened men and reminded them that they might as well be blown through three decks as one. His logic reassured them. They followed him and Lieutenant David Porter below, where for ten minutes they fought the flames with sodden blankets and buckets of water. The *New York* was saved, but of nineteen men terribly burned fourteen died, including two midshipmen, the surgeon's mate, the commodore's secretary and a loblolly boy.

The record of Commodore Morris' campaign is not entirely a catalogue of misadventure. On a sunlit morning in June lieutenants Porter and James Lawrence led fifty men in a spirited amphibious attempt to destroy a dozen grain feluccas high and dry on a crescent beach thirty-five miles west of Tripoli. Under a covering bombardment from the *New York*, *John Adams*, and *Enterprise*, the Americans came ashore in nine boats, two laden with combustibles, and were met by musket fire from a breastwork thrown up of sails, yards, boulders, and grain sacks. Tripolitan cavalry pranced to and fro farther inland, kept at a distance by the ships' cannonade. The raiders sped with their combustibles to the foot of the breastwork, where the feluccas lay side by side, set them alight, and in good order swung left and right to allow their supporting fire a clear target.

But the defenders came swarming from behind the shelter, discharging muskets and waving swords. Some scooped sand and pebbles and flung it in the Americans' faces. Others beat at the flames devouring their precious craft and cargo. They managed to save half the boats, then joined their comrades, slashing and shooting at the raiders as they fell back to the surf. The Americans counted fifteen casualties afterward, an unknown number of them fatal. The toll among the Tripolitans was far heavier. " 'Twas good sport, I must confess," wrote a midshipman who had participated, and Lieutenant Porter, despite wounds in both thighs, was all for going back to finish off the feluccas, but the commodore ruled against it. Impulsiveness was a driving trait in David Porter's nature. Only recently, just before coming out, he had brawled with a Baltimore tavern keeper while on a hunt for deserters and stabbed the man to death. The civil authorities at first indicted Porter for murder, but evidence supplied by his victim's widow pointed to self-defense on the lieutenant's part and the charges against him were dropped.

Peace negotiations opened by Commodore Morris the following week quickly collapsed, and the *New York* at once pressed all sail for Malta, where the commodore's pregnant wife awaited him. During his absence the *John Adams* and *Enterprise* had trapped a polacre in a narrow inlet east of Tripoli and pounded the outgunned vessel for forty-five minutes until her crew fled overboard and she blew up. Captain Rodgers of the *John Adams* presumed her to be the largest cruiser in Murad Reis's fleet, and he described the explosion as one of the grandest spectacles he had ever seen. If John Rodgers was making a singular achievement out of this single conquest, well he might, for in the many years ahead of him he was to be repeatedly balked in his reach for battle honors.

The *New York* meanwhile anchored in Malta Harbor, where next day the Royal Navy frigate *Amphion* appeared with Admiral Lord Nelson in command. Nelson and the *Amphion* cleared Malta within three days. Morris was still there after nearly a month and by then had gathered his entire squadron about him. The American block-ade of Tripoli, such as it had been, was lifted, and, apparently as-sured that it had taught the Tripolitans a lesson, Morris sailed next for Naples. Storms and treacherous currents almost wrecked his ships in the Straits of Messina, but they managed to swing northward for Leghorn, and finally pointed their bowsprits to the west again. On September 9 off Málaga the Americans caught an impressive glimpse of British naval power when a fleet of six sail of the line—one of them H.M.S. *Victory*, with Nelson now aboard her—and two frigates rode by. Following an undetailed exchange of greetings with the British admiral, the American commodore put into Málaga, where three days later a letter from the Secretary of the Navy relieved him of his command.

Robert Smith believed that Morris had "not done that which ought to have been done," and when the commodore got home a court of inquiry composed of three officers junior to him charged him with indolence and incompetence. Whatever political fortune once blessed him had disappeared. "What is the next step?" Jefferson asked his Navy Secretary. "I am not military jurist enough to say. But if it be a court-martial, pray let it be done without delay." Morris was spared this, however, and was merely informed that the President considered his services no longer in the public interest. On September 12 the third American squadron reached Gibraltar, com-manded by Edward Preble, his broad pendant secured to the mast-head of the frigate *Constitution*.

CHAPTER SIX

The Ordeal of William Bainbridge

> How glorious it would have been to have perished with
> the ship. National honor and pride demanded the sacrifice.
> —American Minister in Leghorn, 1804,
> on the loss of the *Philadelphia*

AT FIRST no love was lost between Commodore Preble and his officers. They bridled at his sharp tongue and were disgusted by his
storms of anger. For his part Preble, aged forty-two, resented their
youth—none was over thirty—and sourly belittled them as "a parcel
of children." Time they might have better spent in professional self-
training had been frittered away in dalliance, particularly under
Morris, and their lives gambled and sometimes lost in senseless dueling. Preble's stern discipline corrected much of this, but not without
harsh feelings on both sides. He was a sick man, enfeebled by tuberculosis, and had probably resigned himself to a scant married life
with the Portland lady he had so anxiously wooed and finally won.
These things he kept to himself. He never strove for intimacy with
his officers or sought their sympathy. And in the end he won their
devotion.

He ran his ship well, and although his Rules and Regulations for
the *Constitution* did not markedly differ from those drawn up by the
captains of other vessels, it can be safely said that no one enforced
them more thoroughly. The time by the glass would be attended to
with precise regularity, the bell at the call of the quartermaster from

the lee gangway struck promptly every half-hour and rang every four hours. The lookouts would be tensely alert night and day, the pumps sounded every two hours, and the ship pumped out scrupulously "whenever there are three inches more water in the well than the ship sucks at." The commodore would be notified immediately on the sighting of a strange sail. There would be no cuffing or cursing on the quarterdeck and no Sunday duty "except such as washing or wetting the ship and trimming the sails." No one on Preble's ship would have dawdled beyond the hour allotted for each meal, and heaven help the cook if he failed to draw his salt meats every sundown and keep them well washed and soaked in the steep tubs. The rum would be served twice a day at noon and 4 P.M., and those who wished could wash it down at the scuttlebutt of water kept filled and lashed near the mainmast. Blasphemy, profanity, "all species of obscenity and immorality" would summon forth Preble's terrible wrath. The officers would make sure to familiarize themselves with the people and thus address men by their own names when ordering them aloft or elsewhere. At home in port women would be allowed on board, an indulgence, however, granted only the deserving; the master-at-arms would keep a "Women's List" detailing their names, marital status, duration on board, and general conduct.

Tobacco smoking other than in the established place under the forecastle was forbidden. So was the wearing of best clothes at work, and for swabbing decks the people must be barefoot, trousers tucked up. The log of the *Constitution* shows Preble to have been as ready to flog for misdemeanor as was ever Samuel Nicholson, his predecessor on the frigate in the late war with France. But there was this important difference. Preble's brilliant seamanship, deliberate boldness, and perhaps above all the close sympathy which—notwithstanding his irascibility—he would always extend those with just grievance made the people esteem no less than fear him. Thus a confidence was bred among the crew of the *Constitution* under his command.

Preble's first test was awaiting him when he arrived at Gibraltar. William Bainbridge had surprised a Moorish gunboat in the act of plundering an American brig. This was strange since Morocco was the least aggressive of the Barbary States and an earlier dispute with her had been easily settled by an American gift of a hundred gun

The *Philadelphia* under construction. Financed by Philadelphia merchants, the frigate was launched in the spring of 1800. Drawn and engraved by W. Birch and Son. *Courtesy of the Franklin D. Roosevelt Library*

Benjamin Stoddert, first Secretary of the Navy: June 1798–March 1801. Original painting by E. F. Andrews in the Navy Department. *United States Navy*

Thomas Truxtun wearing his Order of Cincinnati. From a painting by Bass Otis in the Long Island Historical Society. *United States Navy*

Edward Preble. From a painting by Rembrandt Peale. *United States Navy*

carriages. The *Philadelphia*, Bainbridge's new command, towed the gunboat into Gibraltar, where Preble interrogated the captain and discovered that the Governor of Tangiers had issued orders for Moorish vessels to capture those not only of American but of Sweden, Denmark, Holland, Russia, and Prussia. Not the type to deal with provincial subordinates, Preble decided at once to make a direct protest to the Emperor of Morocco. After ordering the *Philadelphia* out again, with the schooner *Vixen*, to convoy merchantmen as far as Tripoli and then begin blockading it, Preble took the rest of his squadron into Tangiers. Before going ashore, he left his officers with instructions that, should he be prevented from returning, they were to "attack the castle, the city and the troops, regardless of my personal safety." But the sight of the *Constitution, New York, John Adams*, and *Nautilus* was enough. The Emperor disavowed the action of the Governor of Tangiers, cashiered the captain of the gunboat Bainbridge had taken, pressed gifts of livestock upon Commodore Preble, and swore eternal affection for the United States. Then he swept his entourage to the shore for a review of Preble's fleet. The Imperial Guard stood to attention in colorful ranks nearly three miles long. The *Constitution*'s guns thundered twenty-one times, the fort batteries replied, and the Imperial Moroccan Band blew a traditional march of friendship.

The incident helped stir Preble's optimism. Orders from the Department recalling the frigates *New York* and *John Adams* sharply reduced the weight of his Mediterranean force, but the need for light cruisers to operate in coastal waters had induced Congress to approve construction of more brigs and schooners. The *Syren, Nautilus*, and *Vixen* had recently come out. In Preble's opinion this type of craft, with his two frigates *Constitution* and *Philadelphia* in strong offshore support, were, if boldly and strategically employed, all that would be needed to defeat Tripoli. In this spirit he promised his government that peace could be expected by the following spring, and a week later again wrote the Navy Department, reporting the arrival of the brig *Argus*, Lieutenant Stephen Decatur: "The order she is in does great credit to her commander." Preble's pride in his officers, soon to be mutual, had begun to show itself. "There shall not be an idle vessel in my squadron," he wrote. His confidence remained buoyant as the *Constitution* cruised eastward through the

Mediterranean. On the morning of November 24 it was shattered, with all his hopes and plans, when he spoke the British frigate *Amazon* and heard her news. He had lost to the enemy his only other frigate, the beautiful *Philadelphia*, with her captain, all twenty-two officers of the quarterdeck, and her people.

William Bainbridge had committed the first of two serious errors when he detached the schooner *Vixen* and left the *Philadelphia* on her own. It was a decision that ran counter to Preble's wishes without quite amounting to disobedience of his will. Preble thought ships should never patrol the Tripolitan coast singly. If one became grounded or otherwise disabled, another ought to be on hand for her succor and protection. Moreover, the lighter draft of the *Vixen*—a fast, new schooner weighing 170 tons and mounting fourteen six-pounders—made her far better suited than the *Philadelphia* for blockade. Preble's memos and missives of September 18 and 19, 1803, were hurriedly written but they leave no doubt of his intentions. On the first date he signaled Bainbridge and Lieutenant John Smith of the *Vixen* to join him aboard the flagship, where he ordered the captain to use the *Vixen* while cruising eastward as he saw fit, sending her "well in shore to look into the bays and snug places along the coast." The vessels were to pause for provision at Malta no longer than a day before continuing to Tripoli, where Bainbridge was to "maintain as effectual a blockade as can be done with the force you have with you." In a sardonic tone Preble wrote to the Navy Department that some time having passed since an American squadron was seen off Tripoli, and not wishing the Bashaw to feel neglected, he had dispatched the *Philadelphia* and *Vixen* to pay him a visit. "I had not time to give Lieutenant Smith such full orders as I wished," added the commodore, "therefore I directed him to sail in company with Captain Bainbridge and follow his directions." And in his memorandum book next day Preble noted: "Sent the *Philadelphia* and *Vixen* to blockade Tripoli."

The vessels stationed themselves before the port on October 7. Twelve days later an Austrian brig came out and from her Bainbridge learned that two Tripolitan cruisers were at sea. He ordered Lieutenant Smith off immediately to search for them in the vicinity of Cape Bon, the Tunisian promontory which forms with Sicily a strategic bottleneck between east and west Mediterranean. Bainbridge's conviction that this was the most useful area to intercept the pirates has some justification. It may be argued, however, whether the likelihood of encountering an enemy cruiser, based on questionable intelligence, warranted a surrender of vigilance before Tripoli. In any event, leaving the *Philadelphia* unescorted proved folly enough.

Perhaps Bainbridge did not give the matter sufficient thought, for he was in a very dissatisfied mood. Blockade duty was dull. In a letter to Preble dated October 22, two days after the *Vixen*'s departure (and rather surprisingly containing no explanation for the division of his little force), he complains that he has been "on this solitary station" a fortnight without sighting anything of the foe except behind his shore fortifications. The advancing gale season would curtail operations beyond November 20, but, he ended somewhat doggedly, although the weather was even now dangerous, "fervent zeal in the cause of my country, and desirous of giving you satisfaction in my conduct, will induce me to persevere to the last." The weather was indeed bad. A violent storm flung the *Philadelphia* eighteen miles east of her position. She was attempting to regain it when at 9 A.M. on October 31 she sighted a sail to windward making for port. The vessel was already quite close to shore, but Bainbridge ordered immediate pursuit. And that was his second fatal step.

All that we know in any detail of subsequent events that day comes from widely disparate accounts: the captain's, succinctly confirmed by his lieutenants, and the caustic tale made public in 1808 by William Ray, marine private. Historians who freely utilize Ray's version of later woes seem not to trust his story of the mishap which produced them. Yet it may be an error to disregard Ray altogether as a legitimate alternative to the testimony of Bainbridge and those who shared his responsibility. Ray was no undereducated misfit paying off shipboard grudges but a reasonably bright Connecticut clerk who had entered the Navy at a mature thirty-two in order to get out of debt. It is true he did not take easily to life between decks and he confessed himself repelled by the practice of young midshipmen "to command, to insult, to strike in the face men old enough to be their grandfathers." A number of deserters from the British Navy who were members of the *Philadelphia*'s crew complained of treatment harsher than any they had known in their old service and were, Ray tells us, close to mutiny. This state of affairs, he would have us believe, was caused by David Porter, the first lieutenant. His appraisal of Porter as a petulant bully might be colored by the knowledge—it was in general currency—of the lieutenant's having slain a tavern keeper. For the most part Ray deals kindly with the officers, including Captain Bainbridge, whose principal fault the marine divined as an unfortunate tendency to rely on his subordinates in moments of crisis.

Shoal and sunken rock slowed the *Philadelphia*'s passage. It took her two hours to bring the Tripolitan vessel within gunshot, and even before she opened fire with her bow guns it was apparent that the chase was carrying her into unsafe shallows. Granting Bainbridge's anxiety for a triumphant feat of arms, he was not the sort to pursue a diminishing promise of success amid rapidly increasing hazards, and, according to Ray, men on the quarterdeck observed that he was beginning to show signs of doubt. They also overheard Lieutenant Porter remark that the vessel was in no danger; that he was well acquainted with these waters, having reconnoitered them in a small boat prior to his raid on the grain feluccas.

The xebec lured the frigate to a line of reef running parallel to the coast, uncharted at this time but certainly familiar to local mariners. Both vessels rounded the eastern end of the reef, entered the inner channel, and sailed southwest toward the harbor. After thirty minutes of fruitless firing, Bainbridge called off the chase; the frigate was only four miles east of the city and would shortly come within range of enemy batteries. But to Bainbridge's consternation, although the *Philadelphia* now made for open sea, the water was becoming *shallower. Eight fathoms*, the sounding party called and then *seven*. At *half-six* Bainbridge ordered the helm put hard down and the yards braced sharp up, but the *Philadelphia* plowed on at eight knots. The commodore had sent his first lieutenant aloft for a view of the city. He was no more than halfway up the mizzen shrouds when the masts quivered, almost throwing him to the deck. The frigate shuddered— and became utterly motionless, her bow lifted six feet higher in the water.

She had veered for sea too soon, struck the reef barrier, and now lay undamaged on a shelf of sand and rock with fourteen feet of water under her fore-chains and seventeen feet astern. Her normal draft was eighteen and a half feet forward and twenty and a half aft. Bainbridge's immediate reaction was to crowd all sail in an effort to force the frigate over the reef, but this only worsened her plight, for her bow held all the faster. To complete matters, a rising swell pushed her even harder on the reef and simultaneously listed her to port.

The xebec meanwhile had taken word of the frigate into harbor. Now nine gunboats could be seen putting out. The atmosphere aboard the *Philadelphia* grew more desperate. Bainbridge ordered the foremast cut down, bow guns cast loose and tipped into the sea. Still she would not move. That no effort was made to warp her free Bainbridge explained long afterward as due principally to a lack of boats strong enough to carry an anchor. The frigate was in fact equipped with a barge, a launch, a pinnace, and a jolly boat. In William Ray's account, Boatswain George Hodger put forward the suggestion of casting a stern anchor and the officers rejected it. The most likely explanation why kedging was not tried may be found in Bainbridge's additional excuse, corroborated by his officers, that enemy gunboats dominated the sea area where the operation would have to be conducted.

The Tripolitans did open fire, but to avoid damaging their anticipated prize they aimed their shots into her rigging. When Bainbridge endeavored to reply, some of the ship's stern had to be cut away so that his guns could be brought to bear from her sloping deck. But then their discharges ignited the ship's timber. After extinguishing a blaze, Bainbridge called his officers together for "a deliberate consideration of our situation." One of the gunboats had placed itself on the *Philadelphia*'s starboard, in no danger from her guns since they pointed at the sky. But still no strong attack came. The enemy fire remained desultory and no move was made to board. The final officers' council was held · about four hours after the grounding. It produced, in Bainbridge's subsequent words, "the unanimous opinion that it was impossible to get the ship off, and that all further resistance would be but unnecessarily exposing men in a situation where neither perseverance nor fortitude would be of any benefit to our country or ourselves. Therefore it was unanimously agreed that the only thing left for us to do was to surrender to the enemy."

Considering David Porter's known boldness in speech as well as deed, that he would meekly consent to submission is difficult to credit, unless for once silence was forced on him by an acute sense of some responsibility for the calamity.

Preparations were made for scuttling. The captain tore the pages of his coded signal book and a midshipman burned the pieces or threw them overboard. The ship's gunner flooded the powder magazine. The carpenter and two mates pierced the vessel's bottom with chisels and augers. If Ray is to be believed, on this occasion the patriotism of the people was in worthier display than that of the officers. They were astonished by the command to lower the colors and the man at the halyards refused to do so until a midshipman threatened to run him through. There took place "a general mourning of the crew," and in this at least the captain joined. Throughout the afternoon, in Porter's subsequent testimony, he had shown coolness and deliberation, but now, as for the third time he lowered his flag in bloodless capitulation, Bainbridge wept.

Though the Tripolitans had ceased firing, they appeared in no hurry, and after what must have been an acutely embarrassing wait Bainbridge sent his first lieutenant in the barge to tell the nearest foe that the Americans really meant it—the *Philadelphia* had struck. It was after sunset when gunboats swarmed around her and the Tripolitans climbed aboard, to manhandle her officers and strip them of valuables and outer garments. A flash of the younger Bainbridge showed when he beat off one pirate who tried to tear from his throat the locket containing a miniature of his wife. Then Murad Reis arrived. He foiled the scuttling at once by ordering every hole firmly plugged. An assortment of native craft bore the *Philadelphia*'s complement of 307 officers and men, including 41 marines, across the rough waves and at 10 P.M. landed them, miserable and soaked with spray, at the foot of Bashaw Yusuf Karamanli's castle.

In the old American consular building where the officers were confined, Bainbridge's agony began. It did not stem from the cruelty of his captors but was self-inflicted. Writing to his wife from his prison cell, he laid bare the terrors of censure which now tormented him. He even regretted that a merciful Providence had not beheaded him with a Tripolitan ball while his ship wallowed on the reef. It was true his officers had absolved him from blame, but this was only, he feared, out of loyal sympathy. He controlled himself sufficiently for reports to Commodore Preble, ruefully conceding his mistake in having sent away the *Vixen*, but asserting that when the *Philadelphia* grounded he had done all that could be expected of him. "Some fanatics may say that blowing up the ship would have been the proper course. I never presumed to think I had the liberty of putting to death 306 souls because they were placed under my command." Not for long could his despair be hidden even in letters to Preble.

He had, he wrote, tried hard to avoid accidents, but "misfortune has attended my naval life. Guadeloupe and Algiers have witnessed part of it but Tripoli strikes the death blow to my future prospects."

The words were no sooner penned than, forty hours after his surrender, fate applied the ultimate mortification. A powerful wind coming out of the northwest piled the seas along Tripoli's coast and raised the *Philadelphia* off the reef. Murad Reis's seamen salvaged her guns, shot, and anchors, replaced them on board, and towed her under the Bashaw's colors into the harbor.

Preble wrote back to Bainbridge in a charitable tone, assuring him of constant friendship, and professionally approving the efforts made to save the frigate. But this was partly inspired by Christian concern for captives of Islam and must actually have required great restraint on Preble's part, for he was beyond dispute horrified by the disaster and nonplused by Bainbridge's failure to disable the vessel totally before the colors were struck. On the propriety of the surrender, Preble had nothing to say to the captain, but to the Secretary of the Navy he wrote, "Would to God that the officers and crew had one and all determined to prefer death to slavery."

The shift in the balance of Mediterranean naval power presaged new diplomatic difficulties. Tobias Lear, lately installed as United States consul in Algiers but possessing a Jeffersonian mandate for the settlement of affairs with all the Barbary States, saw his mission doomed. The first words to reach him were that the *Philadelphia* had run aground while chasing a corsair and had fought off gunboat attacks for almost two days. Clearly apprehensive of the damage to American prestige should the latest incoming reports of a bloodless surrender prove correct, Lear added that he "conceived" the *Philadelphia* had been carried by boarding only after suffering heavy casualties.

Bainbridge sent him the dismal truth in a letter which all but reproached the Tripolitans for unfair tactics. Would that a boarding had been tried instead of a plan that risked them nothing—"Our situation was like a man tied to a stake attacked by another with arms." This is a hasty analogy, for of course no serious attack had been made. As Bainbridge's letter goes on to say, casualties would have resulted if the Tripolitans had fired into the *Philadelphia*'s hull. What the captain did not dwell on was the fact that their plan had been, discernibly, to take the handsome prize undamaged. They elected to wait, perhaps for reinforcements, certainly for darkness, before making an attempt, notwithstanding the possiblity of a wind change in the meantime floating the ship free. The *Philadelphia*'s officers might have drawn hopes of holding out from that same possibility. But of the swell that did in fact float her free within two days, Bainbridge protested, "We were not gods to foresee the wind."

The frigate, though helpless, had not been under serious attack. Her officers, instead of voting to keep their colors flying and await whichever came first, a heaven-sent wind change or Tripolitan boarders, had chosen instant surrender. These were the unfortunate facts, and the renegade Murad Reis made the most of them, scoffing at the captain before the embarrassed American crew.

That the captive officers were never physically maltreated was as much due to the regular intervention of the Danish consul, Nicholas Nissen, as to the Bashaw's awareness that dead men fetch no ransom. The *Philadelphia*'s people, quartered separately from the officers, were less precious property and therefore less comfortably off. Their prison was a three-story warehouse ordinarily used for smoking hides, and already crowded by 600 slaves of different nationalities. The Americans were shackled, the unskilled put to labor on the harbor ramparts, and the carpenters, sailmakers, and blacksmiths were compelled into the maintenance of the Bashaw's fleet. When Bainbridge heard about this practice, he complained that it gave the enemy a "great advantage." But it would be better, he felt, if the order to stop it came from Commodore Preble rather than himself. His contacts with the men were confined to their occasional petitions for prison improvements. When they asked for a money allowance to supplement their daily diet of two black loaves and oil with fruit purchased from the market place, he responded with promises and inspiration: while awaiting the results of his efforts to better their condition, they were to "conduct yourselves as becoming American seamen and soldiers. Keep your spirits up and hope for better days." A good half of the *Philadelphia*'s crew were in fact English-born, causing Bainbridge to suggest in a letter to Preble that Admiral Lord Nelson might be persuaded to enforce a demand for their freedom. Representation was made to the British, but their consular authorities showed no interest and Nelson was understood to say that the captives deserved hanging—whether because they had broken allegiance to their motherland or lost their ship is not known.

Twice the *Philadelphia*'s officers tried to escape by digging tunnels, but the roof caved in each time. Other attempts came to naught. Bainbridge approved but did not join them, preferring to stay behind with those who, like himself, could not swim.

The one ruse to achieve success was the captain's essay into clandestine correspondence. Using as ink lemon juice diluted with water, he wrote secret messages to Preble and the American diplomats describing the Bashaw's defense system and offering suggestions for attack. The "invisible" paragraphs were appended to the regular letters which Bainbridge was allowed to send through Nissen in Tripoli and the Danish consul at Malta. The writing was supposed to become legible when the paper was scorched—over a hot fire, the consul at Tunis told Tobias Lear, but Bainbridge advised that while this was suitable for thin paper, the extractions on the thicker variety, which facilitated writing on both sides, were best made "by the blaze of a candle following the line." Preble, who entered the spirit of the thing, ended one of his letters to Bainbridge: "I would have you attend to the *juice* of this letter and hope you will find it *sweet to the palate.*"

By this method Bainbridge early in December conveyed his idea for destroying the *Philadelphia* by fire. The frigate rode at anchor in the shadow of the Bashaw's castle. Bainbridge maintained that it was impossible to remove her from the place "and thus restore this beautiful vessel to our Navy" (a conclusion later disputed), but she could be boarded and burned by a party concealed in small craft. He wrote again on February 16, 1804: "She lays about three-quarters of a mile from the shore. Let the boats be well prepared with combustibles. . . ."

This message was unnecessary. The very night after he had laboriously scratched it in his invisible ink and sent it off, he was aroused by a tumult within the city. According to Surgeon Jonathan Cowdery, who had earlier that day been administering to the Bashaw's ailing young daughter, there was much screaming and cannon fire. "Opening the window which faced the harbor, we saw the *Philadelphia* in flames."

CHAPTER SEVEN

Decatur Leaps to Glory

> This evening, My Dear Mother, I sail for Tripoli for the
> purpose of burning the frigate *Philadelphia*.
> —A midshipman on the *Constitution*,
> February 1804

THE MOST POPULAR version of Stephen Decatur's entrance at the age
of nineteen into the United States Navy ascribes it to instincts for the
sea inherited from his father and so irresistible that he procured a
midshipman's warrant without the knowledge or consent of either
parent. A less romantic explanation charges him with having struck
"a woman of doubtful integrity" who consequently died and Decatur
was brought to trial. Two attorneys, friends of the family, obtained
his acquittal, but he was advised to enlist on board the *United States*,
then preparing to sail. So runs the story. In any event the young
Decatur is known to have been headstrong and willful.

He was born on January 5, 1779, in a log cabin at Sinepuxent on
the Atlantic shore of Maryland, whence his parents had fled during
the British occupation of Philadelphia. Scots, Irish, and French
blood ran in his veins. His father was a competent seaman, a privateer in the Revolutionary War and a favored captain during the
Federalist administration. The boy studied at the Protestant Episco-
pal Academy in Philadelphia and attended the University of Pennsylvania for less than a year. At seventeen he took employment as
clerk with Gurney and Smith, a merchant shipping firm in which his

father had a business interest and which was the purchasing agent for the building of the *United States*. Decatur is believed to have handled the procurement of her keel pieces and stood upon her deck with Captain John Barry when she was launched.

He was certainly on board when she first sailed out. His fellow midshipmen included two close friends: Charles Stewart, with a career stretching ahead of him into the age of steam and ironclads, and Richard Somers, whose life was soon to end spectacularly. But the relationship aboard the *United States* on which developing tragedy focused was that between Decatur and Lieutenant James Barron. It was later said that Decatur confessed himself grateful for Barron's guidance and loved him as his own father. We need hardly doubt that he was a frequent target for the arrows of nautical and moral counsel which came from Barron's inexhaustible quiver: the inevitable hazard of every naval aspirant who entered his sphere. We can be equally sure that Decatur witnessed an illustration of the older man's proficiency when almost singlehandedly Barron saved the ship in the storm off Cape Hatteras during the fall of 1798.

Dueling was already established among naval officers as the most fashionable method of settling quarrels; two-thirds as many were to die from this cause as in all America's sea fights between 1798 and the Civil War. The victims were usually midshipmen or junior lieutenants. On the rare occasion of a duel between high-ranking officers, complex motives and profoundly aggrieved sensibilities were involved. But to the unthinking and largely unfeeling young, dueling was an excuse for bravado, a game in which courage was affirmed and insult avenged. Into it the Navy's juveniles plunged with zest and they fell by the score. Stephen Decatur, as principal or second, participated in several duels or near duels. Such was its terminal nature that the pastime can scarcely be called habit-forming, otherwise he may be said to have been an addict. Yet he was not bloodthirsty. An excellent marksman who never shot to kill, he could place the pistol ball wherever he wished—as on the occasion of his first duel, when his adversary, the mate of an Indiaman he accused of stealing seamen recruited for the *United States,* fell wounded in the hip.

Pretexts for duels were difficult to avoid. Decatur unintentionally provided one when he chanced to call his friend Somers a fool. His apology was readily accepted, but six other midshipmen showed what they thought of Somers' courage by refusing to drink wine with him. From Somers' standpoint this left him no alternative: he challenged all six to duels. Decatur sprang to his side as second. Somers' first opponent wounded him in his right arm and the next one shot him in the thigh. He declined Decatur's offer to replace him for the remaining bouts, but allowed him to support his weakened arm while he continued in a painful sitting position. In the third exchange of shots he wounded his opponent, whereupon the affair—somewhat incredible even for its day—ended in unanimous accord that Midshipman Somers' honor indeed bore no stain.

Two years later a duel on Malta nearly finished Decatur's career. In a theater lobby Midshipman Joseph Bainbridge (William's younger brother) had overheard the Governor's private secretary, Mr. Cochrane, insult the American character, and had immediately challenged him. Since Bainbridge was inexperienced with a pistol and Cochrane reputed to be an expert, Decatur, quick to act as the midshipman's friend, insisted on four paces instead of the customary ten. "This, sir, looks like murder," Cochrane's second protested, and so it proved, for Cochrane fell mortally wounded. The Governor of Malta issued an order for the arrest of the American pair, but Commodore Morris hastily shipped them home. To Decatur, escape from trial in a foreign port was no compensation for so inglorious a retreat from the Mediterranean, and according to James Barron, his confidant in those days, he threatened to quit the Navy. "By advice and arguments," Barron would later remind him, "I saved you from resigning the service of your country in a pet." Decatur was to deny this. Barron was also to recall that a letter of recommendation he had written, and Decatur delivered, to the Secretary of the Navy was instrumental in getting the lieutenant his first command. The letter, of which no trace can now be found, was never denied by Decatur, but he sharply rejected Barron's assumption of credit for his advancement. These claims and refutations flew back and forth years later, after shame and glory had been liberally apportioned. All that can be stated with verity of Decatur's first command is that the Secretary of the Navy appointed him to the brig *Argus* in the fall of 1803, entrusted him with $30,000 in gold and silver for Commodore Preble's expenses, and sent him back to the Mediterranean.

The moment he heard of the *Philadelphia*'s capture, Preble determined upon her destruction. Bainbridge's secret messages suggested the method. Lieutenant Decatur, yielding command of the *Argus* to Lieutenant Isaac Hull, his senior, took the smaller *Enterprise* and two days before Christmas captured a 64-ton Barbary slave ketch called the *Mastico*. Thus Preble was supplied with a lateen-rigged vessel able to approach the Tripoli shore without stirring suspicion. Off Syracuse, where his little squadron was based, he summoned his officers to the *Constitution*'s great cabin, and the zeal shown by the young man who commanded the *Enterprise* appealed to him instantly. Decatur was even now of striking appearance—darkly complexioned, swarthy almost, his nose slightly aquiline, his eyes piercing and almost black. The upward tilt of his head conveyed the hint of nobility (or, to many later, of arrogance), and his carriage could be stately or he could be as "active as a panther." Robert Spence, a midshipman who had known him on the *United States*, thought him "calculated to rivet the eye" and went on: "I had often pictured to myself the form and look of a hero such as my favorite Homer had delineated. Here I saw it embodied." Preble had already recognized in him excellent qualities of command, and he quickly chose him to lead the expedition. As would become typical of the loyalty Decatur invariably attracted from his people, the crew of the *Enterprise* begged as one man to go with him.

In the midst of Preble's preparations he was notified that the Bashaw had reduced his conditions for peace negotiations—now all he wanted was a schooner, the repatriation of Tripolitan prisoners, and $120,000 ransom for the *Philadelphia*'s crew. "If it were not for our unfortunate countrymen," Preble remarked, "I should be sorry to have peace with the Bashaw until we could make him beg for it." He rejected the new terms. In another development Hamet Karamanli, the exiled contender for the Tripolitan throne, made his first contact with Preble in a request for arms and money to implement William Eaton's old idea of a land campaign against his brother. Preble added his endorsement to the plan and transmitted it to Washington for the government's consideration. Then he turned again to the business of the *Philadelphia*. By the first week in February everything was ready.

Two vessels set forth on the mission, one of them the ketch *Mastico*, now renamed *Intrepid*. She was no more than sixty feet long, with a beam of twelve feet, and rarely in her slaving days could she have been so loaded. The lieutenants James Lawrence and Joseph Bainbridge were cooped up in the tiny cabin with a surgeon's mate and Salvador Catalano, a Sicilian pilot familiar with the approaches to Tripoli. Seventy midshipmen, seamen, and marines crowded the rest of the craft. Occasionally Decatur was on board, but much of the time before the actual boarding he spent in the relative comfort of the brig *Syren*, commanded by Lieutenant Charles Stewart, whose assignment was to supply reinforcements immediately before the seizure of the *Philadelphia* and afterward cover the *Intrepid*'s withdrawal. At dusk on February 7 the vessels were a few miles outside the harbor when a gale swept upon them and the rough seas prompted Catalano to warn against continuing. Decatur, refusing to accept the Sicilian's instinctive opinion as decisive, ordered him to row a small boat with muffled oars and make a closer inspection of the seas at the harbor entrance. He sent Midshipman Charles Morris along, too, because Catalano's word, Morris later recalled, was sure to be doubted "as the offspring of apprehension." After wind and waves almost battered the little boat to fragments, they managed to get back to the ketch with a report that Morris, confronted by impatient and skeptical faces, gave only with reluctance: under present conditions entry into habor would be hazardous, retreat impossible.

The weather grew worse and to the discomforts of the cramped men on the *Intrepid* was added hunger: their salt beef had putrefied, forcing them to subsist on hardtack and water. The storm raged more than a week and although by the sixteenth it was dying, the seas still ran high. However, the break in the weather might not last. Further delay could ruin already depleted chances for success. Decatur's order for the *Intrepid* to proceed without awaiting the *Syren*'s extra men was justified by the circumstances—more so, as it turned out, since the *Syren* had lost an anchor in the storm and was hardly in the best position right then to play her part. In any case it was the kind of decision Decatur relished making, and we need not doubt Morris' recollection that as the *Intrepid*, flying British colors and towing her small boat, crept into Tripoli Harbor through the dying light of the day, he turned to him with the remark: *"The fewer the number, the greater the glory."*

The ports of the captured frigate glowed mournfully in the dusk.

She looked bare, stunted, and skeletal. She still lacked a foremast, her main and mizzen topmasts were housed, and her lower yards were on her gunwales. She was moored within range of some 115 of the Bashaw's cannon and four cable lengths from four of his war vessels. The *Intrepid* steadily closed, Decatur and perhaps half a dozen others upright on her deck, disguised in loose Maltese dress, the rest of the party stretched or huddled in the shadows. Charles Morris wondered if he would face death in a manner of which his friends at home would approve. He was also calculating how best "to secure a prominent position when boarding." No pistols were to be used; as Lieutenant Decatur had reminded them, the *Philadelphia* was to be taken quietly, with naked steel.

At about 10 P.M. lookouts on the frigate sighted the ketch and hailed. From the *Intrepid*'s helm Catalano replied that his vessel was a trader, had lost an anchor in the gale, and wished to make fast to the frigate and ride out the night alongside her. At the same time the *Intrepid*'s small boat put out with a line. Still unsuspecting, the Tripolitans inquired about the brig they had observed in the outer harbor. This would be the *Syren*. Catalano, cued by an alert Decatur, answered that the vessel was a former British man-of-war, bought at Malta and coming in to join the Bashaw's fleet. During this conversation, the *Intrepid*'s line was made fast to the frigate's fore-chains and the concealed Americans began hauling in closer to her port side. Ten yards separated the two vessels when the "lost" anchor was spotted and a cry went up from the Tripolitans— "*Americanos!*"

One of the lookouts slid down a fore-chain and cut the line, but momentum carried the ketch alongside and again it was secured. Leaping to the chain plate before he had even given the order to board, Decatur for an instant lost his grip and Midshipman Morris, who had jumped at the same time, was the first of the raiders to set foot on the *Philadelphia*'s deck. Decatur alighted a moment later and, unaware that he had been preceded, he mistook Morris for a Tripolitan. His sword was raised to strike him when, says Morris, "I accidentally turned and stayed his uplifted arm by the watchword [*Philadelphia*] and mutual recognition."

The rest of the party now came clambering over the rail and squirming through the gun ports. Not more than twenty Tripolitans put up any fight and those who were not driven overboard were quickly subdued. Catalano now suggested taking the frigate out, the wind and current being favorable and the *Syren* in a position to give covering fire. Decatur must have been powerfully tempted. But he was under contrary orders of the commodore, based on Captain Bainbridge's opinion that a recapture of the ship he had surrendered was out of the question "owing to the difficulty of the channel." So the combustibles were hauled up and distributed, to the *Philadelphia*'s storeroom, her gun room, cockpit, and berth deck. Morris' task was to set the cockpit burning. Passing below, he again ran into Decatur and was again obliged to identify himself to avoid the lieutenant's hasty sword. Two other parties were dispersing themselves according to plan, Lieutenant Lawrence's to fire the berth deck and forward storeroom, Lieutenant Bainbridge's to attend to the wardroom and steerage. Decatur and sixteen men, meanwhile, guarded the upper deck. For some reason Morris' combustibles were delayed, and by the time he had started a blaze in the cockpit sections of the ship over his head were fiercely burning. He had to fight through barriers of smoke and sparks in his flight from the cockpit and up the forward hatches to rejoin the others, who were now going over the side. Lieutenant Decatur, if not first to board the *Philadelphia* certainly the last to leave her, sprang into the *Intrepid*'s shrouds as she swung away.

Flames raced across the frigate's deck timbers, burst out of her gun ports. Now the harbor batteries were in action, but the ketch *Intrepid* stood in greater peril from proximity to the *Philadelphia*. The wind had slackened and she dropped astern, a sail fouling the *Philadelphia*'s blazing quarter gallery, sparks and glowing debris fluttering down on the tarpaulin covering her ammunition. Swords hacked the ketch free; pikes and sweeps pushed her safely away from the fiery rain. Shot came hurtling from the shore and a ball struck the ketch, piercing her topgallant sail, but this was the sum of her damage and only one American was wounded. Morris tells us that the men, pulling vigorously on their long oars, seemed less alive to danger than awed by the sad splendor of the once proud ship now dying, tar bubbling down her sides, flame spiraling up the length of her two remaining masts. Some of her cannon discharged. Around midnight her charred cables parted, she drifted ashore, and there blew up.

When the returning *Intrepid* and *Syren* hove in sight of the squadron waiting at Syracuse, cheers broke out to welcome them. Decatur, reporting triumph to the commodore, was generous with praise: "Every support that could be given I received from my officers." He spoke too of the "important services" of Salvador Catalano. His warmest words were reserved for the men. In the increasingly crowded competition for glory, no one was to play the game more ruthlessly than Stephen Decatur; but while often infuriating his rivals of equal rank, he never lost the fondness and admiration of the *people*. At times he seems to have enjoyed a livelier affinity with seamen than with captains and lieutenants. Now he paid tribute to the "coolness and intrepidity of the brave fellows I had the honor to command."

Charles Morris, many years later, had some afterthoughts on the exploit. He recalled discounting any applause for the accident of being first on the *Philadelphia*'s deck and pointing out that whatever praise he deserved was "for my faithful report against an attempt to enter harbor when we first arrived." Had he allowed fear of derision to influence him into making any other, disaster most probably would have resulted. But Morris, who would one day be appraised as the ablest sea officer of his time, was then a mere midshipman and there is no evidence that any particular acclaim tended in his direction at all. In any case, prudence, which has its share in the successful execution of most bold enterprises, is rarely given its proper due. Thus it was the audacity of destroying the *Philadelphia* under the enemy's guns that contemporaries lauded and posterity has celebrated; and Stephen Decatur became the American Navy's most romantic embodiment of audacity.

Preble, describing him to the Secretary as "an officer of too much value to be neglected," requested his instant promotion; the reward would benefit the whole service as an incentive. But when Robert Smith sent out a captain's commission for "the Hero," it had a different effect. Many officers, especially seven lieutenants ahead of Decatur in seniority, were incensed and Andrew Sterrett, protesting that his capture of the fully manned *Tripoli* two years before had been at least as meritorious as the destruction of a captive frigate defended by a handful, resigned from the service. It was a reaction foreseen by Charles Goldsborough, chief clerk of the Navy Department, who had frankly proposed in a letter to Preble that Decatur be urged to decline the promotion—a noble act which would not only silence the resentment of his colleagues but would immortalize him. Commodore Preble is unlikely to have passed the idea along. Certainly the promotion was not refused. As for immortality, Decatur had already achieved it.

CHAPTER EIGHT

Assault and Appeasement

Two DOZEN VESSELS moored in line of battle guarded the entrance to Tripoli: a brig, two 8-gun schooners, two galleys, and nineteen gunboats. Each of the latter mounted a heavy cannon in the bow, two brass howitzers on the quarter, and carried thirty or forty men. To ships of the *Constitution*'s draft, their position among the rocks and shoal was virtually unassailable. In addition, the Bashaw's castle and forts overlooking the harbor contained 115 heavy cannon and were manned by perhaps 25,000 men. In general, the odds confronting the Americans were formidable.

But Preble had determined to "beat the Bashaw into a better humor" and in the weeks following Decatur's exploit he made active preparations for a direct thrust at the harbor defense fleet. From King Ferdinand of the Two Sicilies he borrowed six gunboats, a couple of bomb ketches, eight long brass cannon, and ninety-six Neapolitan sailors—altogether a loan short of expectations considering that Ferdinand was himself supposed to be fighting the Bashaw. Preble had the eight cannon installed on the *Constitution*'s spar deck. The gunboats, flat-bottomed barges each mounting a single twenty-five-pounder, were designed for coastal defense. In deep water they became almost unmanageable either by oar or under sail, and had to be towed to Tripoli. Gales in which they all but foundered delayed operations until August 3, 1804, a clear day with a warm easterly breeze. In the morning fourteen of the Bashaw's gunboats, as if to warn off the assembled American squadron, ventured beyond

the reef and stationed themselves in two sections. The stronger—
nine vessels—lay to the eastward, and when at 2 P.M. Preble signaled
the attack to begin and six of his gunboats cast off under sweeps,
they steered in that direction.

They proceeded in two divisions commanded by Stephen Decatur
and his stanch friend Richard Somers. Shore batteries opened on
them at once, and were as promptly engaged by guns of the *Constitution, Syren, Argus, Nautilus, Vixen, Enterprise,* and a Maltese brig
originally destined for the Bashaw but intercepted by Preble and
rechristened *Scourge.* Round shot struck the *Constitution's* mainmast and a quarter-deck gun but failed to put the frigate out of
action. The two Sicilian bomb ketches were also busy, hurling projectiles from their thirteen-inch brass sea mortars. But half the gunboats miscarried. Somers' vessel, moving sluggishly in a contrary
wind, had slipped far behind. The gunboat commanded by Lieutenant Joshua Blake stood off firing grape and round shot without
effect, a circumstance he blamed on misunderstood signals but which
inevitably threw doubts upon his courage. A Tripolitan ball carried
Lieutenant Joseph Bainbridge's lateen yard over the side, and the
remaining gunboats, pitching dangerously in a swell churned by falling shot, bore down on the waiting enemy.

For more than a century, events and personalities connected with
the early Navy have been too often recalled in a spirit of juvenile
romanticism. Yet this may be easy to forgive. No amount of sober
detachment brought to the examination of archival records can resist
the impression at times of a series of idealized adventure prints
sprung to life. The battle of the gunboats off Tripoli was one such
episode. Lieutenant Decatur, cutlass drawn, leaps into the bow of an
enemy gunboat, on his heels Midshipmen Jonathan Thorn and
Thomas Macdonough, behind them fifteen sailors whooping like
Red Indians and brandishing dirks, swords, pistols, boarding pikes,
and axes. Never have the Tripolitans known such savage zeal. The
swords are swept from their grasp; their torsos and throats are
stabbed or pierced; limbs and heads are cleaved. Back go the survivors down the length of the boat, along both sides of the gangway,
to jump overboard or die fighting in the stern. (Nothing emphasized
the ferocity of the attackers better than the casualty figures: thirty-
one pirates out of thirty-six killed or wounded, three Americans

wounded.) Finally an exhilarated Decatur hauls down the Tripolitan colors and takes the blood-drenched prize in tow. Meanwhile Lieutenant Trippe's party wages a perilous struggle. They are in the act of boarding when their gunboat becomes detached, leaving Trippe and ten men stranded in the enemy vessel and fighting on, unassisted, outnumbered three to one.

No great future glory was in store for John Trippe, but his personal daring before Tripoli was the equal of anybody's. He singled out the Moslem commander and tried to fell him with a boarding pike, but was himself beaten to his knees by saber blows. Bleeding from eight wounds in the head and two in the chest, he nevertheless managed to ram the pike upward in the Tripolitan's groin. By this time Trippe's vessel had made fast again, and, reinforced, the boarders quickly gained the upper hand. But in the confusion no one remembered to lower the enemy's colors until a broadside from the *Vixen* brought the mast and lateen yard tumbling down on the victors' heads.

Lieutenant James Decatur, Stephen's younger brother, commanded the third American gunboat. The Tripolitan he came alongside feigned an early surrender, but the moment Decatur stepped on board a musket ball struck him in the head. When the news reached Stephen, he left his prize in Midshipman Thorn's charge and set forth with Macdonough and eight men in search of the treacherous enemy commander. We cannot be positive that he was the huge Tripolitan whom Decatur finally encountered, but vengeance of a kind was bloodily wrought. They fought knee-deep among the inert and writhing victims of the Americans' preliminary grape and musketry fire. Decatur slashed at the other's pike with a cutlass and, when its blade broke off and whirled away, he fastened his arms about the giant's waist and wrestled him to the deck. Gaining the upper hand, the Tripolitan alternately tried throttling and stabbing Decatur until the American managed to free his pistol and fire it into his foe's broad back. "I found that hand-to-hand is not child's play," Decatur wrote to a friend later, " 'tis kill or be killed. The first boat, they were thirty-six to twenty; we carried it without much fuss. The second was twenty-four to ten; they also went to leeward. Some of the Turks died like men but much the greater died like women." Decatur's wounds healed; his lasting souvenir of the battle of the gunboats was a small, well-bound volume of excerpts from the Koran which he took from one of his victims.

The immediate fruits of the action—three enemy boats captured, their crews practically annihilated—were not to Preble's satisfaction. But we can now perceive enduring and significant results. It was upon this savage clash in Tripoli Harbor that the ideal of personal courage in the American Navy was founded. Gunnery duels, ship against ship, give ample scope for valor, but boarding and close combat on the enemy's deck with a foe believed—if he was not always to prove—merciless and powerful demanded a special kind of fearlessness. The establishment of a naval tradition then, one which subsequent wars would both test and enhance, was the prime achievement of August 3, 1804.

James Decatur died at sunset the day after on board the *Constitution*, and the brother whom he had trailed in many a youthful escapade along the Schuylkill was at his side. Next afternoon the lieutenant's remains were sewed in heavily shotted canvas and, after a eulogy spoken by Commodore Preble, were committed to the Mediterranean. There is no need to doubt the words Stephen is said to have uttered during the all-night vigil beside his brother's body. "I would rather see him thus than living with any cloud on his conduct."

On August 7 Preble had just launched another assault, directed now at the Bashaw's shore batteries, when the *John Adams* arrived with news that four more frigates were on the way. Since only two captains junior to Preble had been available, this meant two must outrank him. To the senior, Commodore Samuel Barron, he was to surrender his command. It has been suggested that had Preble been less of a favorite with New England Federalists, Jefferson might somehow have contrived to retain his valuable services. However, this is to overlook the fact that while Preble's excellent seamanship was well known, the full evidence of his qualities had yet to reach Washington when plans were drawn up to send a stronger squadron. That decision was in fact a reaction to the first news of the loss of the *Philadelphia*. Thus the administration could not have been aware of any special reason to favor Preble by circumventing the proper procedure. It nevertheless anticipated his disappointment, and Robert Smith tried to mollify him with assurances of the President's esteem.

But, as the commodore wrote that night in his journal, "how much my feelings are lacerated by the supercedure at the moment of victory cannot be described."

His dismay was understandable, his assumption of victory premature. Only six of the enemy shore cannon were silenced that day. Many shells failed to explode—all but one, wrote Bainbridge—and this lame demonstration cost Preble a gunboat with most of its crew of twenty-eight, destroyed by a Tripolitan red-hot shot. Midshipman Robert Spence, blown into the air by the explosion, alighted conveniently near the forward gun he had been manning and to the intense cheers of fellow survivors swimming around him he resumed firing until the gun and the wreckage to which it was attached sank beneath him. (In neither this nor subsequent attacks was the *John Adams* of any use to Preble, for she had left her gun carriages in Hampton Roads to allow more space for provisions. They were brought out later.)

Whatever their effect in material loss to the Bashaw, the American assaults and the threat of more induced further reductions in the price he demanded for peace. Still it failed to meet Preble's terms. The imminence of a transfer of command might have posed a handicap to the commodore's planning, but days passed with no sign of his successor and early on August 24 the squadron again stood in for Tripoli. Cannon balls flew at the castle and forts. The commodore, a slight figure on the *Constitution*'s quarterdeck, ordered her moved closer inshore and from this position her divisions hurled 300 round shot, grape, and canister. Meanwhile eight gunboats under Captain Decatur engaged thirteen enemy galleys, sank one, and scattered the remainder. Preble withdrew to nine miles, repaired the damage to his vessels, and less than a week later struck again. The pattern of assault was much as before: led by Decatur and Somers, the gunboats penetrated the reefs to attack their Tripolitan counterparts while the bomb ketches ran in under barrage from mole, castle, and forts to fire directly into the town. The *Constitution*, herself daringly close and within range of seventy enemy guns, pounded the shore with eleven broadsides. Terror spread through Tripoli; many inhabitants, including foreign consuls, fled. A party which the Bashaw had assembled on his terrace to witness the dispatch of the American fleet by his gunners quickly broke up. But no amount of the misery imposed

Bombardment of Tripoli, August 3, 1804. The towering *Constitution* is flanked by gunboats and mortarboats. At rear can be seen the Bashaw's lateen-rigged vessels. Artist: Michel F. Corné. *United States Navy*

Burning of the *Philadelphia* in Tripoli harbor, February 16, 1804. From a contemporary painting by G. Brookings, in the collection of the Naval Historical Foundation. *United States Navy*

William Bainbridge, c. 1813. From a painting by Gilbert Stuart. *United States Navy*

Stephen Decatur, c. 1815. Artist: John W. Jarvis. *U.S. National Archives*

James Barron. Engraved by J. W. Steel from a portrait by Neagle. *United States Navy*

on his people affected him. As Nicholas Nissen testified, the Tripolitan ruler cared little for their safety. Nissen stayed on in the town, a reliable source of aid and solace to the American captives, particularly to Bainbridge, for whom he felt genuine sympathy. After one of Preble's attacks, the diplomat wrote, "Poor Captain B. was nearly killed. A 24-pounder passed his head within a few inches while he was in bed and covered him with mortar." The projectile, by another account a thirty-six-pound ball, knocked down a wall on the captain's bed and left him lame for months.

Until then Bainbridge's incarceration had been at least tolerable. He read and wrote all that he could. Through assiduous study and the cultivation of select correspondents, he was to aspire to an erudition somewhat more elevated than that attained by most mariners of his day. Flashes of historical vision occasionally relieved the torment of self-rebuke and the dread of obloquy which haunted the interminable hours of his imprisonment. "Ere long," he wrote in conventional ink to one of the Mediterranean diplomats, "great revolutions must take place in Europe and in this part of the world. America's rising glory will make her friendship courted." Of immediate contingencies, however, Bainbridge felt less confident. Bombardment had at first appealed to him as the means most likely to expedite his release, but he quickly lost faith in it and now wrote, "I wish to God our country would send troops to take this place." He prayed desperately for his deliverance. Moored in the harbor under Tripolitan colors, the frigate he had surrendered had been a gaunt symbol of shame. That it was, as he had proposed, destroyed by fire gave him a hollow satisfaction while the opportunity for positive expiation remained denied him. "Cursed fate," he lamented bitterly, "which deprives me of sharing the danger and the glory."

Yet frustration and confinement had not hardened the captain's nature into callousness and he would have been shocked by the careless barbarity which bloodletting produced in the attitude of Preble's youthful veterans. "They seem to talk of butchery and cutting up a Turk," observed a new arrival to the Mediterranean, "with as much indifference as one is accustomed to carve a turkey or chicken." The writer, a purser aboard the *John Adams*, also sensed an anxiety to force terms on Tripoli before Samuel Barron's squadron arrived to take the credit. Certainly Preble chafed to see the white flag hoisted

above the Bashaw's castle, and that late summer of 1804 he sanctioned a venture even more of a gamble than the burning of the
Philadelphia.

We can be sure in fact that it was largely inspired by a compulsion
to surpass Decatur's exploit. Richard Somers' accomplishments
before Tripoli had so far been eclipsed by his principal rival in
audacity. Now with the season for active operations drawing to a
close he intended, with the commodore's blessing, to destroy not one
but the host of the enemy's ships by sailing an infernal cargo into
their midst.

Once again the ketch *Intrepid* was employed. A hundred barrels of
powder were stacked on board and a fuse was set connecting them to
combustibles in a room aft. A hundred thirteen-inch and fifty nine-
inch shells were piled on the deck above. The crew would have
fifteen minutes to pull away in rowboats while the fuse burned. Midshipman Henry Wadsworth was appointed as Somers' second in command and the volunteer party swelled to thirteen when another midshipman stole aboard at the last minute. A final offer by Lieutenant
Somers that any who wished might still honorably withdraw was
greeted with three cheers and a clamor for the privilege of applying
the match. At about 9 P.M. on September 3 the *Argus*, the *Vixen*,
and the *Nautilus* accompanied the *Intrepid* toward Tripoli Harbor
as far as the shoals. Before bidding farewell to Decatur and Charles
Stewart, his most intimate friends, Somers took the ring from his
finger, broke it into three fragments, gave them each one, and kept
the other. Three enemy gunboats were sighted within the mole, near
the western entrance through which the ketch would pass, but
Somers' only comment upon this was that lately the foe had become
shy; they would undoubtedly be first to flee.

"All took their leave in the most cheerful manner with a shake of
the hands," Charles Ridgley, then a midshipman, was to recall, "and
one another, as they passed over the side to take their post in the
ketch, might be heard, in their own peculiar manner, to cry out 'I
say, Sam Jones, I leave you my blue jacket and duck trousers, stowed
in my bag' and 'Bill Curtis, you may have the tarpaulin hat, the
Guernsey frock, and them petticoat trousers I got in Malta—and
mind, boys, when you get home, give a good account of us.' " In
Ridgley's retrospective opinion, every man knew he was doomed.

Through his night glass the midshipman watched the fire ketch recede into the darkness. A very short time elapsed. At 9:47 the silence and blackness were awesomely sundered as the *Intrepid* exploded.

Accidental detonation? An unlucky hit from a gunboat or shore battery? In all likelihood one or the other, for the *Intrepid* could not possibly have gained the harbor mole in those brief minutes. Yet officially at least, Preble fixed upon the third alternative—relished by romantics ever since—that the *Intrepid* did reach the mole; that she was intercepted and boarded; that "the gallant Somers and heroes of his party, determined at once to preferring death to slavery, put a match to the train leading directly to the magazine." They chose suicide before surrender, Preble asserted, so that "their country should never pay ransom for them, nor the enemy receive a supply of powder through their means." It is as if the commodore clothed unprovable supposition in the authority of categorical report because the temptation of contrast with the *Philadelphia*'s bloodless capitulation was impossible to resist. The contrast may not have been absent from William Bainbridge's thoughts either as, under Tripolitan guard, he examined six American bodies washed up on shore after the explosion, so mutilated he could not even distinguish officer from seaman.

Edward Preble's zeal and energies had been nothing less than dynamic, if the word can be applied to one whose health was in steady decline, and his encouragement of bold enterprises had established daring as a permanent ideal of his country's naval service. Like Truxtun before him, Preble was a builder of tradition. But his seven weeks in front of Tripoli must be accounted a failure—although had he been allowed more time, the result would probably have been different. In any event, he had not forced the Bashaw to terms, and the new American command of Samuel Barron off Tripoli was to show, in spite of augmented fleet strength, a tendency to accommodate the Bashaw rather than come to grips with him. The new policy reduced the status of the strengthened naval squadron from the tactical assault weapon Preble had envisaged to little more than an intimidating factor at the bargaining table.

A week after the *Intrepid* disaster—Preble's last gamble—two sails hove in sight: the *President*, Commodore Samuel Barron, and the

Constellation, Captain Hugh Campbell. Preble yielded command and, after settling his accounts at Malta, Syracuse, Messina, and Palermo, departed for home early in December on board the *John Adams.* With him went a written declaration of regret at his going and affection for his character, its fifty-three signatures headed by Captain Decatur's and including those of many who had once detested him.

The fleet campaigns against Tripoli had neither eliminated piracy nor liberated the Bashaw's captives. William Eaton, sensing his government's disillusionment, fed it with extravagant accounts of naval stupidity and talked Jefferson into the approval of his pet scheme for the exploitation of Hamet Karamanli as a rallying point of insurgency against the *de facto* regime in Tripoli. The ex-consul returned to the Mediterranean aboard the *President,* the nature of his mission hopefully concealed beneath the title he bore of Naval Agent to Several Barbary States. But Eaton, an adventurer of wild notions and rumored intemperance, had not been given carte blanche: the Navy had full authority over the enterprise. And had there existed any kind of intelligence system, a couple of facts brought to light would have promptly aborted the plan. But only after Eaton had landed in Egypt, searched for the exile with a company of marines, and found him hiding in a Mameluke village did it transpire that popular support for his cause was imaginary, diminishing whatever hopes were nurtured in the young Tripolitan for asserting his royal legitimacy.

Yet Eaton's ardor persisted. Encouraging Hamet into taking his princely place at the head of the column, he named himself general and spent the $20,000 advanced him by Commodore Barron in the recruitment of contentious nomads and European soldiers of fortune. On foot, horse, and camel the motley army set out westward from Alexandria, while offshore the *Argus,* Master-Commandant Isaac Hull, sailed along a parallel cruise, maintaining some sort of liaison. One is tempted to pursue in greater detail the 500-mile desert march of this force led by Eaton and his protégé, the reluctant pretender. But it was not an exclusively naval undertaking —although to the "General's" everlasting ire, it was scuttled on the imminence of success by naval policy under diplomatic direction.

Tobias Lear might reasonably be called the prototype of an

American phenomenon in overseas diplomacy identified in our day as a State Department troubleshooter. To the adjustment of difficulties accompanying the growth of American interests in the Caribbean and the Mediterranean, this Harvard graduate, George Washington's friend and private secretary, applied his skills of guile and negotiation. Instinctively preferring a bartered peace to continued blockade or renewed bombardment, he was particularly scornful of the kind of venture Eaton had plunged into. At the close of 1804, through the offices of the Spanish consul, he had visited Tripoli and thought he detected a willingness to negotiate. To institute peace talks required naval concurrence, something even Lear could never have cajoled out of Preble, but with Samuel Barron in command of the squadron the pathway to peaceful settlement became clearer. Barron had fought bravely enough in the Revolutionary War as commander of the Virginia state navy, but now his health was at least as poor as his predecessor's and he had none of Preble's aggressive spirit. Neither did Lear anticipate any objection from the government. The President's faith in total naval victory over the pirates had been shaken, and in light of the reports of Hamet's indifference and the refusal of the Arab populace to flock to his banner, who now could take "General" Eaton's expedition seriously?

Certainly the failure of force by land and sea appeared to prove the wisdom of Jefferson's deepest prejudices against it as an effective remedy. His cabinet henchman Albert Gallatin increasingly begrudged every dollar spent in the maintenance of American arms in the Mediterranean whether under sail or across desert sands. Other factors encouraged Lear. Captain Bainbridge had now abandoned the hopes for an overland rescue which had replaced his earlier advocacy of bombardment, and was writing letters to Lear full of fearful hints that any more attacks from whatever quarter would tempt the Bashaw to slaughter his captives. The reality of this threat became controversial. There were naval officers off Tripoli—Captain John Rodgers for one—who thought it exaggerated, although Surgeon Cowdery's prison journal records the Bashaw's vow, should the Americans bring his brother against him, to burn all the *Philadelphia*'s officers and men except Cowdery, who had saved his sick child's life. No further help could be expected from the King of the Sicilies; Captain James Barron, sent by the commodore to the Court of Naples for twice as many gunboats and bomb ketches as Preble had borrowed (and with an offer of double pay to the Sicilians who manned them), returned to his brother empty-handed.

But nothing better favored Lear's chances of fresh diplomatic laurels than the liver disease which had stricken Samuel Barron. Prostrate ashore in Malta, the commodore clung to life and his command as if to defy the physicians who despaired of the former and the officer next in seniority, Captain Rodgers, who coveted the latter. But he was helpless to resist, even had he been so inclined, the calculated persuasiveness of Tobias Lear, and in the third week of May 1805 he agreed to peace talks with Tripoli and then turned over control of the squadron to Rodgers.

With the co-ordinated fire of the *Argus*, *Nautilus*, and *Hornet*, Eaton had just captured Derna at a cost of only fourteen casualties, and was strenuously reorganizing for the resumption of his long march, when on June 11 the news arrived that wrecked his desert dream. Within two weeks Lear had secured a treaty of peace which freed the captives of both sides and ended payments of tribute. It also enriched the Bashaw with $60,000 to compensate for the comparatively few Tripolitans he would be getting back in the prisoner exchange—though Thomas Jefferson's very purpose in strengthening the naval force under Barron had been to end contemplation of *any* monetary payment. The Bashaw gave guarantees against future molestation of American commerce and promised the release of Hamet's wife and children, whom he had held in hostage. Hamet actually was obliged to wait more than two years for a family reunion, the result of a "secret" declaration to the Bashaw signed by Lear without consulting his government and not made fully public until long after the diplomat's apparently motiveless suicide in 1816.

The treaty aroused much criticism among the naval officers eager for a summer offensive, yet none was voiced by the new commodore —in utterance certainly the most bellicose of them all. Only recently Rodgers had announced that before paying a cent for ransom he would write his name in blood on Tripoli's walls. He had fretted for an opportunity of compelling "this monster"—the Bashaw—to reason. Now he was left without "a hope of receiving a button for my services, much less a medal." But ferocity of manner—and, one gathers from his portraits, of countenance—was a characteristic that Rodgers rarely managed to justify with action. In this case he was hampered by a debt of friendship. In the spring of 1802, as master of a Baltimore merchant schooner, he had become involved in General LeClerc's brutal campaign to crush the mulatto insurgency on Santo Domingo and reassert French rule. He assisted Tobias Lear's efforts to protect American lives and property, and when LeClerc had him jailed for allegedly spreading anti-French propaganda it was Lear who engineered his release. Now Rodgers could also feel grateful to the diplomat for having prised command of the squadron from Samuel Barron's death grip. The new commodore's diatribes against the Bashaw abruptly ceased and he said nothing to embarrass Lear's latest diplomatic coup.

Its most felicitous consequence was the liberation of the *Philadelphia*'s company. An entry in Lear's diary provides both a glimpse of the men's pathetic rapture and the sense of discipline which not even nineteen months' captivity had drained from their captain. "The intoxication of liberty and liquor had deranged the faculties as well as the dress of many of the sailors and Captain B. wishes them all on board quite clean and in order." The court of inquiry Bainbridge desired to investigate the loss of his ship was speedily arranged and conducted on board the *President* off Syracuse. Captain James Barron sat as president, Stephen Decatur and Hugh Campbell served, and William Eaton suppressed his rage against Lear and all connected with the treaty long enough to act as judge advocate.

Bainbridge's concise testimony that every rational effort had been made to get the frigate off the reef was endorsed by his lieutenants. As for the surrender, "The usage of nations appears that when there is no probability of successful defense and all means of escape have been tried, the flag may be struck without injuring the captain's honor—these tacit but admitted regulations are forwarded on principles of humanity, and a nice and delicate attention to national and individual honor." No time was wasted questioning this supposition. Captain James Barron, almost as if he foresaw the day when despair would wring from him a similar plea before a tribunal including the officer now facing his peers, issued approvingly the court's decided opinion "that Captain William Bainbridge acted with fortitude and good conduct in the loss of his ship and no degree of censure should attach itself to him."

The idleness of peace fostered ugly quarrels. Officers passing on routine duty from ship to ship became couriers of calumny. The bitterest feud was the top-level wrangle dominated by the sullen Commodore John Rodgers. Inheriting the squadron command too late for a war in which to flaunt it, Rodgers brooded and blustered about the *Constitution*'s great cabin and quarterdeck like a thundercloud seeking a lightning rod on which to discharge its swollen fury. Tobias Lear remained insulated. The Barrons took the shock, Samuel, whose responsibility for the negotiations with Tripoli ought to "forever damn his reputation," and James, the Judas brother who had used every cunning to keep the command in Samuel's sick hands while deceiving Rodgers into thinking that he was persuading his brother to step down. Thus Rodgers raved. But neither Barron was in a position to do much about it, Samuel for obvious reasons, while James was preparing to take him home on board the *President*, an overloaded frigate carrying Captain Bainbridge and most of the *Philadelphia*'s crew besides her own.

James Barron sent Rodgers a curt note, putting off an accounting for his insults until "a proper place and time." According to Captain Bainbridge, who conveyed the message, Rodgers retorted with a boast of readiness to meet either Barron at any time, and should he not hear from James in America, "I shall impute it to a want in him of what no gentleman wearing a uniform should be deficient." This was as much a typical affirmation of his own masculinity as a crude slight on Barron's courage. The exigencies of "manliness" so pervaded John Rodgers' mind that he sometimes lost sleep worrying whether he had the previous day properly obeyed them.

Yet if a hardy life at sea gave evidence of manhood, Rodgers had no cause for concern. At an early age he had left his birthplace, a farm near Havre de Grace, Maryland, for an apprenticeship aboard a Baltimore merchantman which plied between French and West Indian ports. Not yet eighteen, he was first mate of the *Jane* and two years later her master. But though he brought experienced seamanship into the Navy with him, he was among those dismissed under the naval reduction program of 1801. In less than a year, following his affray with General LeClerc in Santo Domingo, reinstatement with no loss of rank was offered to him and, forgetting the angry oath he had sworn to perish before he ever donned uniform again, he accepted. Thereafter, direct combat, though often within reach, constantly eluded him. Never in war or private feud did he quite succeed in coming to grips with his adversary.

Near the close of summer, 1805, the prospects of combat which had faded with the end of the Tripolitan War brightened when the Bey of Tunis demanded restoration of a blockade runner taken by the Americans off Tripoli. George Davies, who had succeeded William Eaton as consul, parried the Bey's claims as long as he could, then relayed them to the *Constitution* with a postcript reminder that any response ought to be written in Italian or French. That was enough for Commodore Rodgers. In a fever to "discuss the subject by the language of our cannon," he wrote the Bey a lengthy note in English which contained an ultimatum expiring after thirty-six hours and would have required about as long to translate. But this meant war, protested the consul, who obviously failed to perceive with what relish this likelihood was anticipated. Alas for Rodgers' hopes, the very sight off Tunis of the power at his command—the *Constitution, Constellation, Essex, John Adams*, brigs, schooners, sloops, and gunboats, eighteen ships in all—was all it required to preserve the peace. The Bey proclaimed a desire for friendship with America and appointed an ambassador to present his case personally before the government in Washington. George Davies, who felt himself somehow by-passed, expressed an inclination to resign. Rodgers, after consulting with Tobias Lear, promptly replaced Davies as consul with the *Constitution*'s physician.

The Tunisian Ambassador sailed for America on the *Congress* as the honored guest of her captain, Stephen Decatur. In the dissension between John Rodgers and the Barrons, Decatur had taken no part. Much of the time he had spent enjoying the fruits of his Mediterranean fame. Lord Nelson was reported to have called the burning of the *Philadelphia* the boldest act of the age, and the Governor of Malta, Sir Alexander Ball, reflecting the sentiment of the admiral he had fought under at the Battle of the Nile, hosted Decatur with lavish cordiality.

The first extensive fleet activity by Americans outside the Western Hemisphere thus came to an end in 1805. The deeds of valor performed off Barbary would pass into naval folklore. More immediately, the campaigns had provided lessons in tactics, supply, and organization which would have to be assimilated before the Navy matured as an effective and cohesive fighting service. There was a long way still to go, and, quite apart from political fluctuations at home, few things impeded the Navy's growth more than the spreading rash of personal envies and conflicts. Stubborn and fanatic illy proud, many officers appeared simply incapable of subordina ing private jealousies to the general good of the service or even, de: pite a fiercely boasted patriotism, to that of their country.

Now the commodores and captains were going home. Decatun, on the *Congress*, entertaining his exotic passenger and basking ir the confident expectation of a hero's welcome in Hampton Roads. James Barron, professionally attentive to the *President*'s overload (she was weighed to the water line with more than 500 souls) and generally unhappy over the state of the Navy and his future in it—already "the Navy has almost ruined me." Samuel, his brother, lingering on without promise of full recovery. And on the same ship, William Bainbridge, relishing his physical liberty while captive to fears of scorn for which there seemed no ransom.

John Rodgers simmered off Syracuse. Although ordered to send home all ships except the *Constitution* and the sloop *Hornet*, provided peace in the Mediterranean remained unbroken, he was not yet ready to turn his back on the slightest chance of leading them in battle. But with the onset of winter, discontent plagued every vessel, none more than the commodore's flagship. Disease-ridden and mutinous, the men of the *Constitution* developed a weary hatred of the white walls of Barbary, of the monotonous blue of the Mediterranean, and of the massif dominating its western gateway through which it seemed they were doomed never to sail. Some were flogged through the fleet for sedition; the lash fell on others guilty of "boxing about the grog tub."

Meanwhile, Barbary offered Rodgers no further opportunity for action and when, late in the spring of 1806, another call came to bring the ships home, he prepared at once for departure. But it was not just the unconditional tone of Robert Smith's latest order which made the commodore lose no time. The sloop that brought it out hummed with a report that his character was under attack at home, and Rodgers did not doubt that the slanderer was James Barron. Removing his pendant to the *Essex* and pausing only to collect male and female Barbary broadtail sheep for President Jefferson, he set course for home, swearing, if it cost him his life, to defend "that such as no man shall ever defame with impunity."

He took most of the squadron with him and left the *Constitution* in Captain Hugh Campbell's command. Another winter came and went with no summons home and no prospect of relief. Campbell wrote the Department an alarming letter. The situation on board had become critical following the death of the *Constitution*'s physician. There was no one to treat the sick "except a loblolly boy who has acquired some skill and judgement in drawing of teeth and applying the lancet to a well-filled vein." In the spring, 1807, Campbell received word that a relief frigate was at last about to come out. He passed the welcome news to his crew and with the *Hornet* and schooner *Enterprise* in company the *Constitution* sailed on June 12, calling at Leghorn, where marble was taken on board for the proposed monument to George Washington, before continuing westward for Gibraltar. There she met the schooner *Wasp*, just arrived from America with shattering news. The *Constitution*'s relief had certainly begun her voyage, but had failed to get five leagues beyond the capes of Virginia.

CHAPTER NINE

The *Chesapeake* Delayed

> You are to have command of the *Chesapeake* and to proceed
> with her to the Mediterranean. The *Wasp* is also fitting
> out for the same service, to relieve the frigate *Constitution*
> and the schooner *Enterprise*.
>
> —Secretary of the Navy to
> Captain James Barron,
> January 17, 1807

WASHINGTON in the first few years of the nineteenth century was a
scattered village of shacks, lodginghouses, and one or two buildings
of yet unrealized splendor. Choked by dust or drowning in mud, the
new capital was assailed by Republican and Federalist alike as a $15
million investment that only proved no community could thrive
there. Members of Congress sickened at an alarming rate and the
most professional medical services were centered at the Navy Yard
under the direction of the young naval surgeon John Bullus. A one-
and-a-half-mile track through forest and swamp connected the President's sandstone mansion with the single completed wing of the
Capitol Building. To the northwest stood the so-called Six Buildings,
housing the cabinet offices. Amid these uninspiring surroundings
great decisions were made which had their impact upon naval development.

As the Barbary threat diminished, fiscal economy became more
intensely the keynote of the administration's policies, and the Navy
was the first branch of service to suffer. This was in spite of the fact

that Spain seemed about to follow the example set by British, French, and Barbary pirates in preying on American shipping. On September 16, 1805, Robert Smith, whose personal fortunes were involved in maritime commerce, had advised the President that congressional approval should be sought for building more gunboats, putting all frigates in a state of preparedness, completing the six 74's for which the principal materials had been procured, and building six more. To safeguard American sea trade against not merely the present Spanish threat but future contingency, "we ought to prepare the means of offensive as well as defensive war." But the following December, in his opening speech to the new session of Congress, all that Jefferson did was ask for more gunboats and leave the fate of the already authorized 74's "to the further will of the legislature." Of additional 74's he had nothing to say.

His words reflected not only the shift in naval emphasis from overseas expedition to domestic port and harbor defense but an obsession with gunboats as the most suitable means of effecting it. The idea was nourished and may have been inspired by letters from Thomas Paine in Paris which glowingly described Napoleon's plans for the construction of a vast fleet of small, cheap craft (some fitted with bow ramps in the fashion of Second World War assault boats) with which to invade England. Contrary to some accounts, Jefferson's gunboat policy was not universally scoffed at by professional men. But its few naval supporters—with the exception of Edward Preble, whose favorable opinion was founded on gunboat performance before Tripoli —were, not surprisingly, officers characteristically lacking in offensive zeal.

Gunboat design differed according to the creative whims of the sea captains and constructors appointed to oversee building, and to the accessibility of materials. In general, however, the craft were about seventy feet long and eighteen feet in the beam, and variously rigged as fore-and-aft ketch, or lateen, or dandy rigged, and armed with two long eighteen-, twenty-four-, or thirty-two pounders on pivots. Since recoil from broadside discharges almost capsized them, the trend in their design altered to boats with limited traverse fire ahead and astern. A gunboat under Stephen Decatur's direction did capsize and sank in six fathoms. Describing the event in a letter to Bainbridge, he could not resist wondering, "What would be the real national loss if all the gunboats were sunk in 100 fathoms of water." Difficulties in maneuverability also faced the gunboat designers. But the technical inadequacies of any naval program pursued under Jefferson's two administrations were apt to be lost on him. Even during the Tripolitan War, only a fraction of funds appropriated for the Navy had gone into improvement of shipyards, and the establishment which was probably in the poorest condition was that closest to the seat of government. It was on the Potomac's eastern branch (now the Anacostia River), where depths seldom exceeded eighteen feet, with the result that frigates could enter only on the highest tides. Congress had rejected proposals for a dry dock designed by Benjamin Latrobe, and while naval stores decayed along the Washington waterfront several fine vessels, the *Chesapeake* among them, rotted in the Potomac mud. Of the eleven frigates in the United States Navy, only the *Constitution*, according to an estimate reached by Commodore Preble in 1805, was in good repair.

Jefferson, of course, had enough on his mind. Destiny had given him control of his country's affairs and opportunities as they were rushing into collision with the long-accepted global interests of old Europe. But historic command failed to exhilarate him. The almost simultaneous challenges of Napoleonic decrees and British orders in council, not to mention the western scheming of his former Vice President, Aaron Burr, only intensified his yearning for the leisure of retirement in which to contemplate advances in science and exploration.

Yet however limited his vision of tactical realities in naval and political spheres, he was still capable of sweeping pronouncements. On May 4, 1806, he wrote to James Monroe in London that "we begin to broach the idea that we consider the whole Gulf Stream as of our waters, in which hostilities and cruising are to be frowned on for the present and prohibited as soon as either consent or force will permit us. We shall never permit another privateer to cruise within it and shall forbid our harbors to national cruisers." These were brave words coming from a President who did not think it especially alarming or even anomalous that, while the growth of America's commercial shipping approached a million tons, only a single American warship should cruise abroad to protect it; who could base a national defense posture upon coastal batteries and fifty small gunboats; who in his second term as Chief Executive appeared perfectly willing to preside over the atrophy of the high-seas fleet.

Robert Smith, meanwhile, was doing his utmost to keep the Navy alive. Notwithstanding a Republican majority in Congress, he had received occasional support from sympathetic legislators. However, on January 27, 1806, foes of the Navy pushed through a resolution requiring him to state in detail estimates of repair and man-power costs for all his war vessels, to report on their condition, and to list "those such as it may be in the national interest to dispose of instead of repair." Smith replied that five frigates, four brigs, and two schooners were fit for service. Six frigates needed repair—the cost impossible to assess. Icily the Secretary added: "I know of no vessel belonging to the Navy which I consider it would be 'the interest of the United States to dispose of rather than repair.' "

The House debated on February 28. George Clinton thought the only issue to be one of national defense, whether of batteries, gunboats, or an increase in fleet strength. But assuredly, declared the New York representative, "something must be done." Nathaniel Macon, leading the Republican gunboat bloc, suggested what this ought to be, after first warning his listeners that his proposal might surprise them: Should war ever come, why not lend America's Navy to another nation which happened also to be at war with the same foe? ". . . for I think such nation would manage it more to our advantage than ourselves." The anti-Navy faction also raised the old fearful cry of tyranny, upon which Orchard Cook of Massachusetts threw mild scorn. "Generals have overthrown the liberties of nations," he observed, "but I have certainly never read of an admiral that made himself a despot." On March 25 the House voted to spend $150,000 on the protection of ports and harbors and $250,000 to construct fifty additional gunboats. A proposal to complete the six 74's went down in defeat.

One month later Congress approved a limited extension of the so-called Mediterranean fund to protect American commerce against piracy, thus enabling Smith to alert Captain James Barron for departure in the *Chesapeake*. But simultaneously came a congressional proposal to fix the total number of able seamen, ordinary seamen, and boys in the Navy at 925. Already that figure had been exceeded. Should the bill pass, the *Chesapeake* would have to wait until the arrival of the vessels Commodore Rodgers had been ordered the previous October to send home, which were nowhere yet in sight. Hastily Smith scribbled a note informing the President. But no help came from that quarter and the bill became law one week later. Ten months were to elapse before Congress raised the man-power figure by 500.

Reluctantly Robert Smith canceled plans for the *Chesapeake's* early departure and issued the positive order that brought home from the Mediterranean all the capital vessels of war but one—the *Constitution*. And, with what must surely have been relief, the Secretary turned to issues of personnel welfare. Here he had somewhat better luck. He succeeded in providing a modest pension scheme for officers, and for the people he replaced the traditional issue of rum with whisky. It was, he thought, a more wholesome and economical drink. "In time the sailors will become perfectly reconciled to it." The annual consumption of rum by the Navy was about 45,000 gallons. Smith suggested 20,000 gallons of whisky for the ensuing year, "but it must be pure rye whiskey of third and second proof." Whether or not the seamen became reconciled to it, ship's whisky thereafter was often alluded to as "pure Bob Smith."

At the end of the year Burr's continued movements impelled the administration to raise a naval force in support of the militia guarding the lower Mississippi. By January 1807 it amounted to 126 marines, two mortar ketches, and four gunboats under the direction of Master Commandant John Shaw. At the same time, with Rodgers' return from the Mediterranean, prospects had brightened for the dispatch of the *Chesapeake* to the relief of the *Constitution* and her long-suffering crew. James Barron was ordered to lose no time completing the gunboat construction he supervised at Hampton Roads. This meant his uninterrupted presence at the site. "You will not move from that place," Robert Smith wrote to him, "without special orders from me."

The Secretary's stern prohibition supports the belief that he was determined to prevent a duel between Barron and John Rodgers. That affair now appeared to those who had followed its course from the Mediterranean to its ebb and flow between Hampton Roads, Washington, and Havre de Grace as less dispute than pursuit, the hounding of an apparently spiritless Barron by a choleric commodore bent on dueling with him. Now pleading sickness in Hampton Roads, now hurriedly terminating a visit to Washington when Rodgers was descending upon the capital to meet him, Barron was soon the target for rumors that "he will not stand fire."

The final decision for the *Chesapeake* to sail required Barron's presence in Washington to supervise her fitting out. Again it became necessary for the Secretary to keep his feuding officers apart. This time he restricted Rodgers' movements, confining him to the gunboats building at Havre de Grace. At the same time Smith made clear to the commodore's friend, Captain Thomas Tingey, that a settlement of the quarrel had better be arranged quickly. As commandant of the Washington Navy Yard and constantly under Department pressure, Tingey was in no position to argue. He composed conciliatory statements for each party to sign, though he quite failed to cool off privately the smoldering Rodgers with reflections on how he would have felt "if by your hand a widow and orphan children had been left to mourn."

The episode affords a good example of the special peace-keeping talents demanded of a Secretary of the Navy in the days of sail. It also sheds some light on the character of an officer who seems hardly to have been cut out for naval service in the first place. James Barron entered it without ambitions of glory. Male members of this family of mariners who originated in the port of Bristol, England, were expected to sail out as early in life as possible and master the ways of the sea. Barron fulfilled these expectations thoroughly. As boys, he and his brother Samuel had fought in the little Virginia state fleet commanded by their father during the Revolutionary War. He was now a proficient seaman. But in the new Navy boldness and dash were as essential to distinction as proficiency, and these he lacked. One can sense the suggestion of a miscast role in the few impressions of his likeness that have survived. Neither the truculent glare nor the haughty self-confidence that leaps to the gaze from so many portraits of his naval contemporaries is present here. In face and physique Barron is heavily rotund, a grave smile plays about his mouth, and above the plump nose his eyes narrow, the result, one naturally assumes of his known defective sight, but also, given his nature, as fairly attributable to a frown of chronic apprehension.

He is at thirty-nine a bulky composite of benevolence and bemused concern, something of a meddler, tactlessly free with moral, professional, and generally unsolicited counsel. He is good-natured, well-meaning, and doomed to misadventure, an ill-fated Pickwick on the quarterdeck.

The same week that the Secretary of the Navy assigned James Barron to command of the *Chesapeake,* an application for active service reached him in the familiar hand of Master-Commandant Charles Gordon, who had been inactive for a year and was now "heartily tired of an idle life." Smith attached him to the *Chesapeake,* but in terms which the young officer promptly demanded be clarified to leave no question of his status on board. Obediently, the Secretary reworded his order: Barron, with a command embracing more than one vessel, would carry the courtesy title of commodore. The captain of the frigate would be Charles Gordon.

The significance of this dispensation of rank, with its bearing upon areas of responsibility, was to gather importance. But at the time it seemed no more than a prudent adjustment to suit Gordon's vanity. Few young officers enjoyed more favorable connections in the President's circle. His uncles included three stanch Jeffersonian Republicans with Revolutionary War backgrounds. Joseph Hopper Nicholson, former leader of the House Ways and Means Committee and now a Maryland circuit court judge, was a cousin. Three female cousins had married prominent Republican jurists or politicians. And he was firmly linked to the cabinet itself by Hannah Nicholson's union with Albert Gallatin, Secretary of the Treasury.

Yet Gordon was burdened with a legacy of shame. Following the collapse of the Scottish Jacobite Rebellion in 1746, his father, taken by the English, was saved from the noose only through the intercession of an aristocratic cousin in London. He fled to the American colonies and married into the prestigious republican clan of Nicholsons, on the eastern shore of Chesapeake Bay, but when the Revolution started he abandoned them to aid actively his old foes, the English. Arrested and charged with treason by the Continental Congress, he was again saved from hanging through cousinly intercession —the Nicholsons, acting on behalf of his distraught wife. As before, exile was the price of salvation. He returned to Scotland, leaving his eight children in the Nicholsons' custody.

Charles Gordon's guardians no doubt encouraged him to seek all means of erasing the stain on the family bequeathed by his father, and very likely the younger Nicholsons in the Navy taunted him into doing so. But the foppish and self-indulgent Gordon was aged twenty before he followed uncles and cousins into the service. Promotion, however, came quickly, and when necessary he sought the influence of his powerful relatives ashore, Judge Nicholson and Albert Gallatin. Intercession blessed the son as it had his disreputable father.

James Barron's opinion, based on earlier contact with Gordon in the Mediterranean, was that he loved pleasure too much for the business of running a ship. On learning that he was to be his flag captain, the commodore requested that he himself be relieved of the command. The risk of thus being made accessible to John Rodgers evidently operated less upon him than the prospect of a lengthy cruise with an undependable executive officer. But Robert Smith refused him. And Barron's anxiety worsened when his lieutenants were named, for to a man they were known cronies of John Rodgers, particularly William Henry Allen, "a most vindictive rascal," in Barron's view, who would come aboard poisoned against him by "all the prejudices his friend Rodgers could inculcate."

All this was bad enough. In addition Barron was dissatisfied with the gunpowder supplied him and with Robert Smith's suggestion that if he found it inferior, other powder might be bought cheaply at Malta. Another problem was the *Chesapeake*'s crew. Procurement of fully trained American seamen had become a recruiting officer's nightmare. The salary of $12 a month fixed by government economists was hardly an allurement for experienced men who could get $26 a month from merchants. Expectedly, Barron's people would be a motley crowd, a few with skill and simple patriotism, the majority riffraff, tavern dregs of Norfolk, Baltimore, and Philadelphia, physically poor, strangers to discipline, and among them, no doubt, deserters from foreign flags. Their refinement into trained and loyal men would be Charles Gordon's responsibility, not his. But could he be certain, knowing Gordon, that it would be conscientiously discharged?

All in all, the prospect of sailing out with an indolent captain, lieutenants of questionable trust, and a shiftless crew, not to mention defective gunpowder, could hardly have stimulated the brightest optimist, far less Commodore James Barron. Trouble seemed bound to follow the *Chesapeake* like an albatross. And events already in motion involving diplomats, the American government, and deserters from the British Navy predestined that the albatross would surely overtake her.

CHAPTER TEN

The Admiral's Directive

> More than half the seamen in the United States Navy are
> foreigners, many of them British and Irish. They are the
> best seamen we have.
>
> —Lieutenant William Henry Allen,
> March 1807

IN AUGUST 1806 a hurricane had swept out of the South Atlantic,
interrupted the pursuit of a French squadron by a British, and scattered the ships of both to the northwest. Two of the French sought
shelter in American waters: the *Patriot*, her topmasts gone and several guns thrown overboard, struggled up Chesapeake Bay to Annapolis while the dismasted frigate *Cybelle* managed to make safe
harbor in Norfolk. Within a short time the news reached the Honorable George Cranfield Berkeley, Vice-Admiral of the White, commander in chief of His Majesty's ships on the North American
station. And there subsequently appeared off the Virginia capes a
sizable British naval force to prevent the French, once they were
able, from regaining the Atlantic.

The blockade lasted all winter. British officers became regular and
not unwelcome visitors to Norfolk and Hampton seeking fresh water,
supplies, and relaxation of one form or another. To their people,
however, the continued proximity to a neutral shore offered tempt-
ing opportunities for desertion.

On a squally evening in March five men and a midshipman put

out in a jolly boat from the sloop *Halifax* off Hampton Roads to weigh her kedge anchor. The men attacked the midshipman, rowed off into the gathering dusk and rain, and touched land at Sewell's Point, creeping ashore in the darkness. One of the deserters, a sail-maker with "Jenkin Ratford" tattooed on his left arm, showed up at the United States Navy rendezvous in Norfolk, where Lieutenant Arthur Sinclair was briskly and with little discrimination recruiting for the *Chesapeake*. The sailmaker enlisted as John Wilson, was issued a note of American citizenship, and marched next day along Main Street with some thirty more, the first draft of the frigate's crew. On hearing that Ratford had been seen "patrolling the streets in triumph," Captain Lord James Townshend of the *Halifax* put ashore to demand his surrender. Lieutenant Sinclair denied recruiting anybody of the name, but Townshend soon sighted the runaway parading confidently beneath the American flag. He ordered him back to the *Halifax*. Ratford's reply was a rude gesture and a shout: "I will be damned if I go back! I am safe in the land of liberty!"

The captain took his complaints before John Hamilton, British consul in Norfolk, to whom they were all too familiar. Only recently he had tried unsuccessfully to recover four men who had deserted from the frigate *Melampus*. That these were now also among the *Chesapeake*'s crew Sinclair did not trouble to deny, but he did say that only the local magistracy could decide their release. After Townshend had left him, Hamilton applied to the Mayor of Norfolk for the surrender of both the *Melampus* and *Halifax* deserters, but the Mayor was advised by the young and gifted attorney Littleton Waller Tazewell to do nothing: the ships in question were *armed public vessels*, ineligible for benefit under the Act of 1805, which authorized city magistrates to arrest and hand over deserters from foreign *merchant vessels*. Tazewell was confident of his ground, having himself introduced the act while a member of the Virginia legislature.

Hamilton transmitted a full report of the situation to David Montague Erskine, the British Minister in Washington, whose endeavors to maintain cordiality between his country and the United States were none the less sincere for the inspiration he drew from his Philadelphia wife and the popularity both enjoyed in the new capital's incipient but vibrant society. He was, though, a naïve, often confused young man who, it was said, owed his position to the importance of his father, the Lord Chancellor of England. It is likely that impressments and desertions nettled Erskine as much as they did his subordinate in Norfolk. But he did not feel it incumbent upon him to inquire in detail into every "trifling" case and considered none of them inimical to United States–British relations. On receipt of Hamilton's letter, which had been forwarded with copies of the consul's correspondence with the Mayor of Norfolk, he formally applied to the Secretary of State for restoration of the deserters and was prepared to take no further interest in the matter.

Mr. Madison turned it over to the Secretary of the Navy, who on April 6 ordered James Barron at the Washington Navy Yard to investigate. Robert Smith added a belated warning against signing on deserters from British ships—his original recruiting instructions had cautioned only against enlisting the scorbutic and unskilled. Lieutenant Sinclair's recruits having just come up by ketch from the south, Barron was able to examine them without delay on the *Chesapeake*'s spar deck. His findings were quickly in the Secretary's hands. The *Melampus* deserters were positively native Americans: one the son of a Maryland tobacco planter and mulatto mother, the second also a Marylander, the third a Negro from Massachusetts. (The fourth had dropped out of sight and was never accounted for.) Affidavits were produced by their earlier employers. All three men had been impressed from an American merchant ship in the Bay of Biscay.

Most significantly, as things developed, Barron's report dealt only with the *Melampus* case—Smith's order had contained no reference to deserters from the *Halifax* or any other ship, for David Erskine, writing to Madison, had claimed only the *Melampus* men. Informed by Madison that, being definitely American, the men could not be surrendered, Erskine notified Admiral Berkeley, stationed at Halifax, Nova Scotia, and, as was his custom in such annoyances, added no comment.

Commodore Barron meanwhile had left Washington, his task at the Navy Yard completed. He would board the ship when she came down to Hampton Roads. Regarding the *Melampus* case, at least, his mind was at ease; his government had assured him (or so he later testified) that the British Minister was quite satisfied with the result of his investigation. But if the diplomats had forgotten John Wilson —Jenkin Ratford—he was still very much on the Royal Navy's mind.

His impudent defection, above all, the public insult to Lord Townshend, had infuriated British officers from Hampton Roads to Halifax. Discipline and the necessity of redressing the humiliation of a
nobleman and captain demanded the sailmaker's due punishment,
which would, moreover, serve as a sober deterrent at a time when
desertions from His Majesty's service were increasing at an alarming
rate. The recovery of Jenkin Ratford from the Americans, therefore,
became an imperative. To this end, Berkeley had believed, the
British envoys ashore were active. The admiral and his captains to
the south were unaware that Ratford's surrender had not even been
asked in Washington. As spring advanced into summer, their anger
mounted at what seemed stubborn refusal to give him up. Estimates
of the number of British seamen in American service grew more and
more inflammatory: Captain Lord Townshend alleged that over
thirty-five were on board the *Chesapeake*; Captain John Douglas,
commanding the squadron in Hampton Roads, reported that the
majority of her people were British. To the Lords of the Admiralty,
Berkeley complained that there were "above ten thousand British
seamen in United States employ."

By such figures he hoped to convince his government that the time
for mere words had passed. His own patience expired. Waiting no
longer for further word from London, he issued a general order on
June 1 which would subsequently be variously described as plain,
peremptory, and studiously ambiguous. It asserted that British seamen had deserted his Majesty's ships *Bellisle*, *Bellona*, *Triumph*,
Chichester, *Halifax*, and *Zenobia*, and joined the *Chesapeake*. All
captains were directed, should they meet her at sea and outside
American territorial waters, "to shew to the captain of her, this
order, and to require to search his ship for deserters from the above
mentioned ships, and to proceed and search for the same."

The absence of the *Melampus* from Berkeley's list indicates that he
had accepted the American opinion concerning her deserters—which
Erskine had conveyed to him—or at least considered it insufficiently
resolved in British favor for his purposes. In any event, he lost no
righteous ground for action by a casual disregard of the *Melampus*
now. There were other aggrieved captains besides hers, notably Lord
Townshend, and his ship *Halifax* was on the list. The admiral's order
was dispatched southward, in the custody of Salisbury Pryce Humphreys, captain of the 56-gun warship *Leopard*.

CHAPTER ⚓ ELEVEN

The *Leopard*'s Prey

Commences with clear weather. Wind from the Southd. and
Eastd. People on various ship's duty. At half-past ten A.M.
Commodore Barron came on board. Hoisted the Broad
Pendant.

—Log of the *Chesapeake*,
Hampton Roads, June 6, 1807

WHILE MOST NORMAL MEN found the American capital all but unin-
habitable, Captain Thomas Tingey loved "our rural city" and had
helped pioneer its principal community amusement, the Dancing
Assembly. He presided over balls often held on the Navy Yard property and usually enlivened each function with patriotic songs, performed in harmony with his wife. The disposition of this English-
born officer, who had left the Royal Navy to command an American
armed merchantman in the conflict with France, was so merry that
British diplomats found it easy to forgive him for abandoning the
service of the King.

But during the early months of 1807 Tingey's social activities were
hampered by his wife's poor health and the management of his friend
John Rodgers' turbulent affairs. On top of it all, he was required to
outfit the *Chesapeake* at what he complained to be short notice. In
this task trouble beset him at every turn. The frigate was in sorry
shape, her officers were meddlesome, and the blacksmiths hired to
work on her, objecting to salary reductions and Yard regulations
prohibiting drinking on the premises, kept threatening a strike.

Furthermore, the Secretary of the Navy had grown quite unreasonable. When Tingey requested eight good journeymen imported from Philadelphia, Smith demanded to know why their need had not been perceived earlier. Ample warning had been given of the decision to send the frigate out. "You will inform me in detail," Tingey read with the incredulity of one who is rarely rebuked, "the causes of this great delay." They were exposing themselves to distress and ridicule, for "our means of keeping up a Navy must look feeble and contemptible indeed if such a long time is needed to fit a frigate for sea." Tingey's hurt reply blamed wintry weather and the tedious alterations forced upon him by the fussiness of Commodore Barron, Captain Gordon, and their lieutenants. The commandant proceeded with the *Chesapeake*'s victualing. He was under Department orders to procure, for twelve months' cruising: 60 barrels of flour, 63,875 loaves of bread, 1,500 pounds of butter, 3,900 pounds of cheese, 163 bushels of beans or peas, 650 gallons of molasses, 225 barrels of beef, 225 barrels of pork, 650 gallons of vinegar, and 4,563 gallons of spirit. And at long last, to Tingey's overwhelming relief, the *Chesapeake* was towed beyond his domain.

Her passage down the Potomac was studded with mishap. She had been hauled scarcely two miles along the Eastern Branch when she grounded on Greenleaf Point and Captain Gordon had to order all hands to heave her clear. The following Sunday morning, off Alexandria, her fore-topgallant yard came unhitched and the thirty-six-foot spar crashed to the forecastle, killing a seaman and a boy. Eleven days after leaving the Navy Yard, the frigate only lay abreast of Mount Vernon; and when Gordon prepared to fire a salute in memory of the late President, he found half his sponges and cartridges too small for the guns. "Had we been engaged in an active war," he wrote in a fury to Robert Smith, "I should suspect the officers of the Yard with having a design on my character." And that day a seaman fell overboard and drowned. Strong headwinds slowed the vessel as she entered Chesapeake Bay. Desertions multiplied. In the last week of May, nine men made off with the cutter. A jolly boat put out in search of them and the crew of that mutinied as well and disappeared.

Twenty-six days after leaving Captain Tingey's care, the *Chesapeake* dropped anchor in Hampton Roads. All she needed now were some final equipment, the commodore's arrival, and fair winds. Barron boarded her the next morning, but stayed less than three hours. He inspected the upper deck and officers' quarters, accompanied by Captain Gordon, but did not visit the magazine or do more than glance over the eighteen-pound guns, only twelve of which were mounted. The ship had left Washington with her armament incomplete, a precaution against grounding on the Potomac shoals. However, even as Barron picked his way across her lumbered deck, sixteen guns with their shot, just come down by ketch, were being hoisted on board.

As if to balance his instinctive doubts, Barron decided to accord the officers every measure of fairness. Before leaving the ship he expressed satisfaction with her condition and at home that evening was inspired by feelings "of particular pleasure" to report to the Secretary on the "extreme cleanliness and order" he had found on board. "Captain Gordon speaks in high terms of his lieutenants. The state of the ship proves the justice of his encomiums." On June 10 he made a second visit to her and found arrangements afoot for "a ball," which Gordon later recalled as nothing more than a small party for a few friends. Barron and his lady were invited, but did not attend. The commodore was not even aware of a second party held by the lieutenants the following Saturday, for he was still ashore, where he received a note from Gordon blaming further delay on local piety: the watering boat would not come out on Sunday; "the religion of Hampton will not even allow the pumps to be worked."

Two hundred barrels of bread, with twelve thirty-two-pound carronades for the quarterdeck armament, completed the *Chesapeake*'s loading, but no sooner had Barron been notified and bade his farewells when the wind shifted northeast and blew a gale. Gordon let him know on June 19 that since the ship was windbound he was not expected; the only concern now appeared to be two pillows ordered from a Georgetown upholsterer and not yet come aboard. But the ship was unmoored "and ready for weighing the first fair wind. All station bills are completed. The guns are all charged and if possible we have an exercise this evening." It was noon on Sunday, June 21, when Commodore Barron boarded the ship for departure.

At 7 A.M. next day, her sails spread to the pressure of a west-southwest breeze and her tall masts stirring against the brightening sky, the *Chesapeake* stood for the Atlantic. Barron's sailing orders contained a reminder of the offshore presence of British ships. "Our interest as well as good faith," Secretary Smith had written, "requires that we should cautiously avoid whatever may have a tendency to bring us into collision with any other power." Barron carried another letter, written in the neat if cramped hand of Thomas Jefferson, asking him to arrange the safe transport home from Malta of a pipe of good Madeira and wishing him a pleasant voyage.

At 9 o'clock the *Chesapeake* sailed past Lynnhaven Bay, where the British squadron lay at anchor. Two vessels, the *Melampus* and *Bellona*, began immediately signaling to each other and to a third standing out in the Roads three miles north of Cape Henry Light. The third ship hoisted anchor and backed south, preceding the *Chesapeake* into the Atlantic, to vanish behind the glistening dunes of the Cape. She was the *Leopard*.

On the *Chesapeake* Barron observed these movements through his glass, read nothing disquieting in them, and, of course, could not interpret the signals. He was in any case preoccupied with activity aboard his own ship. In contrast to the sunlit calm of the sea she glided over, her decks were plateaus of disorder.

She carried a crew of 339 men and boys with a marine contingent of 52. The young wife of the Marine captain, John Hall, was also aboard. So were Doctor John Bullus, his wife Charlotte, their three children, maidservant, and Negro boy. Bullus, a good friend of Jefferson and occasionally the President's physician, had served aboard the *United States* during the half-war with France. His post now was to be navy agent in the Mediterranean. Baggage and furniture belonging to the Halls and Bulluses were piled high on the *Chesapeake*'s gun deck along with empty water casks, the armorer's forge and bellows, cases of claret, and dozens of sick men in hammocks. More sick were quartered on the spar deck in the sun by order of Surgeon Hunt. There were some sixty men on the sick list. Finally, herded below decks were a dozen or more Sicilian musicians with their instruments and families. Recruited in the Mediterranean as a band for the Marine Corps, they had been declared unwanted and were being sent home.

The events of that afternoon off the Virginia coast may be reconstructed with some assurance. The breeze had slackened and the

Chesapeake, having cleared Cape Henry around 2 o'clock, tacked inshore to await the boat taking back the pilot. In the commodore's spacious and curtained cabin aft, Captain Gordon, Captain Hall, and the Bulluses joined him for the first dinner of the cruise. Hetty Hall, a bride of less than six months, felt unwell and remained in her cabin. Through the open ports Barron and his guests could see the *Leopard*, now a mile or two to the south; she too had tacked inshore. After dinner the *Chesapeake* stood off again to the eastward and was three leagues east of Cape Henry when the *Leopard* wore and stood down for her. By 3:30 the English ship had rounded up on the *Chesapeake*'s windward quarter and advanced to within sixty yards.

Across the water came her captain's polite hail that he had dispatches for the American. Barron, near the starboard gangway, replied through his speaking trumpet: "We will heave to and you can send your boat." A British lieutenant named Meade came on board and was shown to the commodore's cabin, where he displayed Admiral Berkeley's search order and handed Barron a note from the *Leopard*'s captain which expressed the hope that an adjustment would be reached without disturbance between their two countries. After reading the documents, Barron passed them to Doctor Bullus, whose presence he had requested during the Englishman's visit.

The absence of the *Melampus* from the admiral's order did not surprise Barron; her desertions had been the only subject of complaint by the British and the omission must mean, he felt, that, confronted by proof of their American nationality, even a British admiral realized the impropriety of seeking their return. These men, the only "deserters" he knew of a fact to be aboard the *Chesapeake*, Barron felt at liberty to discuss, and he did so even to the extent of recounting Mr. Erskine's "satisfaction." And Doctor Bullus (here Barron gestured at him) was privy to the affair. To all this Lieutenant Meade made little comment, beyond indicating that he had no idea who Mr. Erskine was. Following a brief consultation with Bullus, the commodore drafted his answer, denying knowledge of any deserters from ships mentioned in Berkeley's list and refusing to allow anybody other than the *Chesapeake*'s officers to muster her crew for a search. Meade, who had been on board more than half an hour, left with Barron's reply, and he also took back with him the copy of Berkeley's order.

Motivated by "an ardent desire to prevent bloodshed," Captain Humphreys of the *Leopard* decided against forcing an immediate search. He resumed hailing. The *Leopard* lay only half a cable's length from the *Chesapeake* and Barron could see that the tompions were out of her guns. He turned to Captain Gordon. "I do not know what they intend," he said. "But you had better clear our gun deck." And to Humphreys' persistant hailing he repeatedly answered: "I do not hear what you say, sir."

Humphreys' next words, heard on the *Chesapeake* or not, were ominous. *"Captain Barron, you must be aware of the necessity I am under of complying with orders."* Barron's response, bellowed through the speaking trumpet and fading over the calm water, was as before: he could not hear. During the uncertain pause which followed, he directed Gordon to hurry the men to quarters *secretly*, without benefit of drumbeat and taking care not to show themselves through the ports. "If we are seen going to quarters," Barron explained, "they will charge us with making the first hostile show." Gordon relayed these instructions to the first lieutenant, Benjamin Smith, and descended to his cabin for sidearms. John Bullus herded Charlotte and the children below into the fetid security of the cockpit. Captain Hall, after ordering his sergeant to have the marines draw and load their muskets, went to fetch his sword and found his wife in a state of upset. He bade her get dressed, and carried her to the cockpit.

Commodore Barron, near the gangway, peering out at the *Leopard* as if to fathom her captain's intentions from the activity on her decks, was startled by a burst of drumming from his own. He swung around imploring for silence. Captain Gordon struck the hapless drummer with the hilt of his sword and the bold tattoo abruptly ceased. Many of those animated by it wavered. But the lieutenants were quickly at their stations. William Montgomery Crane aroused his good friend Allen from the wardroom, collected his sidearms, and raced to the first-division forward battery. It was cluttered by the armorer's forge, the anvil, the carpenter's workbench, a pile of boards, a heavy grindstone, and several casks. He had them cleared, ordered the guns cast loose, and sent boys to the magazine for matches and powder horns. Midshipman Charles Norton hailed down the wardroom hatch to hurry them up, but the shout echoed back that not a powder horn was ready. Lieutenant Allen meanwhile cleaned his second division amidships of three pork barrels (one of them full), the grog tub, and a range of cable. In addition, over and abreast of his guns hung nine sick men in hammocks, their utensils stacked against the carriages. Allen ordered the men carried below to the cockpit and their belongings were thrown down the main hatch after them. John Orde Creighton, the junior lieutenant, recovered from a momentary hesitation at the foot of the after-hatch ladder caused by the arrested drum flourish, and hastened to his third-division after battery. He found it encumbered by a table, some chairs, a large canvas screen, and an oaken sideboard. "By God," he exclaimed, putting his shoulder to the sideboard, "we will have our division cleared, at any rate." He was energetically assisted by Midshipman Jesse Duncan Elliott. Barefooted seamen rushed fore and aft to their stations. At each gun division young midshipmen called off the quarter bills in hushed treble tones. The divisions were soon free from obstruction and properly manned, but this was of little avail without equal headway below. Captain Gordon had come upon the ship's gunner, William Hook, loitering on the quarterdeck. He angrily ordered him to his station in the magazine where the gunner's mate waited at the locked door. But Hook had not yet reached it with the key when he heard, as did everybody aboard the *Chesapeake*, the thunder of the *Leopard*'s opening fire.

The ball flew athwart the frigate's bow and was followed seconds later by another which whistled over her stern. Commodore Barron gave a cry of dismay, Gordon exclaimed that there was now no time to lose, and, before either man could utter another sound, twenty-five of the *Leopard*'s guns from a distance of less than seventy yards hurled a broadside of solid shot and canister. The *Chesapeake*'s stout timbers shook, her tall masts quivered, and shrapnel shredded her canvas. Shouts rang from the men about the guns, and below decks the sick groaned in their hammocks. From his magazine, Gunner Hook issued seven powder horns, all that were filled of the fifty-four aboard, and with the gunner's mate began topping the rest. Elsewhere a current of fear immobilized many of the *Chesapeake*'s crew. Some were heard to declare that the ship was not prepared to fight.

She was still unprepared when the British guns discharged a second broadside which cut her main skysail in two and lacerated her foresail with grape. Lieutenant Sidney Smith, whom Gordon had hurried below to investigate the delay at the magazine, was blocked at the magazine door by a crowd of midshipmen and boys, shrill young voices clamoring for horns, loggerheads, and matches. Captain Gordon had left the quarterdeck when Smith returned, but the commodore was much in evidence, apparently agitated, pacing to and fro, and hailing the gun deck for action. The divisions were no longer obstructed and the guns had been loaded before the *Chesapeake* sailed out, but none could be primed without powder or discharged except by lighted match or heated iron loggerhead. Again the *Leopard*'s cannon roared and still the American's were mute. Bombardment at close range without the means to fire back was something none of the *Chesapeake*'s people had signed on for, but only a few fled their posts. Enraged frustration was their principal reaction, and as the rumbling echoes of each broadside died, there could be heard above the sob and gasp of wounded, loud protests against "having to stand like sheep and be shot at."

Through the acrid British gunsmoke rolling over the *Chesapeake*, Commodore Barron limped aft. He had been standing at the gangway, the most exposed part of the ship, and the *Leopard*'s opening fire had left seven wounds in his right leg and thigh. When Sailing Master Samuel Brook offered to bind them, Barron said, "It is of no consequence." They were not words of bravado. Perhaps the commodore was oblivious to bodily pain just then, his senses numbed by what his mind conceived as the perfidy of his officers. Disloyalty and dereliction—in such terms was he to recall the failure of Allen, Crane, and Creighton to fire their guns, and the ineptness of the lieutenants stationed on the quarterdeck. Even allowing for a recollection distorted by bitterness, there seems no doubt that the *Leopard*'s unanswered broadsides instantly scattered Barron's fair intentions toward his officers.

There is certainly less indication that they infuriated him against his actual attackers. It was not, of course, Barron's nature to strike warlike attitudes. Moreover, the only practical demonstration of a determination to fight was through the cannon's mouth. Since the *Chesapeake*'s guns were unquestionably silent, of what use, it could be asked, was a display of defiance on the quarterdeck when futility commanded the gun deck? Nevertheless, if Commodore Barron appeared instinctively to blame his own officers rather than square off against the British, some of them no less instinctively construed his behavior as confirmation of the whispers they had heard ashore and afloat casting doubts upon his courage.

The commodore mounted a signal locker to see better, and Sailing Master Brook bound his wounds with a handkerchief. "Is it possible," Barron asked, "that we cannot get one gun to fire?" Supporting himself against a starboard quarterdeck gun, he looked across at the *Leopard*, her outlines blurred by gunsmoke, and he lifted his speaking trumpet to hail. His voice was indistinct, but Captain Hall, who had just returned to the quarterdeck, where his marines stood with muskets at the ready, thought his words ended: ". . . we will send our boat on board of you." This Barron subsequently explained as a *ruse de guerre*, intended to beguile Captain Humphreys "until I was in a situation to repel him."

When he turned to his own vessel again, the commodore wore an expression of profound distress. "Look at those braces and that rigging," he called. "Will no one lend a hand to secure them?" The two Lieutenants Smith were within sound of his voice, but neither officer, Barron said later, had the use of his reason from the moment the *Leopard* started firing. No one answered. Hall's marines stared doggedly before them. From mizzenmast to forecastle, the *Chesapeake*'s spar deck was littered with tangled cable, torn shrouds, and splintered portions of the shattered foretop and skysail mast. Groups of seamen huddled among the debris, some of them weeping from the pain of unsalved wounds—Surgeon Hunt was below, himself wounded. The first cutter hung askew, pierced by shot. Through the open hatches rose the vain clamor from the gun deck. A stench of blood mingled on the warm air with the reek of gunsmoke. Near the mizzenmast, Commodore Barron stood as erect as his wounds would permit, surveyed the length of his hurt and impotent ship, and cried aloud: *"For God's sake, gentlemen, will nobody do his duty?"*

If answer was made, none heard it as the guns of the *Leopard* spoke again and a storm of shot raked the American frigate. Still her guns stayed silent. So did the marines' muskets; Captain Hall would not permit them to fire unless Commodore Barron signaled him to. Had they done so, Hall was to say, it would have been to good effect: the *Leopard's* marine commander presented a particularly conspicuous target. Barron's acknowledgment of Captain Hall's report that the *Chesapeake*'s marines were ready for action had been merely an absent "very well," and when the same announcement was made to Captain Gordon, Hall got no response at all.

Gordon returned to the quarterdeck. He had been below urging Gunner Hook to hurry up. Barron beseeched him to try to get a gun working himself, whereupon the captain descended to the gun deck and asked Lieutenant John Orde Creighton why his third-division guns were not firing. "Sir," replied Creighton, "we have nothing to fire them with." One man dispatched by Midshipman Elliott to the magazine for matches or loggerheads had dutifully crawled back to his station, body agape with wounds and the loggerhead he still stubbornly clutched grown cold. Gordon turned to Lieutenant Allen, but the second division was a shambles: two men had each lost an arm, another's leg was torn off, and a fourth, struck full in the chest by a ball, had died at Allen's feet. Blood ran down the gun barrels and streamed between deck timbers. The lieutenant's blue tunic was dappled crimson.

On the quarterdeck, meanwhile, Barron pleaded with Captain Hall to go down and "ask them for God's sake to fire one gun for the honor of the flag. I mean to strike." It was just then that Captain Gordon caught a boy rushing up from the magazine with two full powder horns. He snatched them from him, doubled along the gun deck, and flung them across the hatch to Allen, who immediately primed three guns himself. But when the lieutenant tried to fire one, the sole loggerhead he had obtained was not hot enough. Throwing it aside, he ran along the gun deck to the galley and plucked a burning coal from the stove, some thought with his bare fingers. In the smoke and confusion, witnesses received varying impressions of how that red-hot nub traveled from galley stove to gun, but Allen's prompt inspiration secured the only pride of the sorry afternoon. The eighteen-pounder fired, leaping in recoil the length of its breechings, and although a slow swirl of smoke blurred the *Leopard*'s outlines, some of the *Chesapeake*'s crew cheered as if they clearly saw the ball strike her hull—as in fact it did, penetrating to the wardroom.

At once Commodore Barron's voice rang down the hatchway. "Stop firing, stop firing. We have struck!" The men around the guns heard someone above and aft echo harshly: *"God damn you, haul down the colors!"* Preparing to fire a second time, Lieutenant Allen paused. Again Barron hailed the gun deck. "How many guns have been fired?"

"One, sir," Allen called back.

"You have fired two, you have fired two."

"No, sir, but one."

The *Leopard*'s guns put a stop to this exchange. The sixth or seventh broadside—few Americans were keeping count—crashed into the *Chesapeake,* although her flag had already struck the taffrail. Hasty orders were bellowed to the maintop, where the commodore's broad pendant still flew. Down it fluttered and the *Leopard*'s guns finally rested. The attack had lasted almost half an hour. Fourteen shot had pounded the *Chesapeake*'s hull; her main and mizzen masts were irreparably damaged; all her sails were torn by grape and round shot. Fatalities were few: three men lay dead below decks, but of the score wounded many were frightfully mutilated and at least one more would die.

Commodore Barron braced himself against the fife rail and dictated a note: *"Sir, I consider the frigate Chesapeake your prize, and am ready to deliver her to an officer authorized to receive her."* He ordered Lieutenant Benjamin Smith to take it in a boat to the *Leopard,* but even this last mortifying rite of surrender was denied the dignity of competent performance. As the gig containing the lieutenant was being lowered, a seaman got his hand jammed in the block. He was about to free it by severing the tackle when Smith shouted at him, *"If you cut this boat's fall I will cut your throat."* Neither measure became necessary and the gig was lowered.

A light breeze raised the smoke until it veiled the afternoon sun and hung like shreds of mourning above the capitulation.

Distressed and exhausted, Barron retired to his cabin. When Lieutenant Smith returned, he was followed by the *Leopard*'s boat bringing her purser, a master's mate, and two lieutenants, one of whom requested Captain Gordon to muster the *Chesapeake*'s crew. He was referred to the commodore, who thereupon ordered the muster roll handed over and all hands assembled on deck. They shuffled into line for British inspection, a sight so distasteful to Gordon that he withdrew to his cabin and did not emerge until summoned to Barron's quarters. He found Lieutenant Creighton, who had come to ask the commodore if he might secure his guns.

"I have nothing more to do with this ship," Barron told him. "She is surrendered."

Gordon entered. "I regret we had not gone to quarters," he said, pounding the commodore's table with his hand, "and returned the *Leopard*'s fire."

Barron endeavored to restrain him. "You may have to speak of it elsewhere." He added: "I am the victim, no one else."

The other lieutenants were sent for, the servant ordered outside, and the doors shut. Barron asked for comment on the situation and Gordon spoke first: although continued bloodshed had been avoided, "a few broadsides would have been more to our credit." Lieutenant Crane said bluntly, "It had been better if the *Chesapeake* were blown from under us than be thus dishonored." As for William Henry Allen, he had difficulty concealing his disgust. He had seen the men of his division fall at their guns, had felt their warm blood upon him. Their agony might have been avenged, the honor of the ship and her company certainly sustained, had not her colors been struck, had not the commodore broken off an engagement which, though belatedly entered, could have been bravely continued. As the savagery of Allen's private observations makes clear, no forewarning from even his mentor John Rodgers could possibly have prepared him for what was, in his proud view, an unforgivable act of cowardice. In the commodore's cabin the lieutenant came near to cursing Barron, and his self-restraint was less out of respect for superior rank than from a conviction that the commodore's own conscience would justly scourge him. "While he possesses the power of recollection," wrote Allen, "no curses can add to his tortures." Even so, the lieutenant did not mince words. To Barron's face he declared, "We have disgraced ourselves." This was enough. Before anyone else could venture an opinion, the commodore dismissed them.

When Gordon returned to the quarterdeck, four men alleged by the *Leopard*'s officers to be British deserters were standing apart from the others. Three were the *Melampus* men. Only the fourth came from a vessel on Admiral Berkeley's list. It had taken a thorough search of the *Chesapeake* to find Jenkin Ratford, but he was quickly identified by the English officers, for he had once served some years on their ship. They found him in the *Chesapeake*'s coal hole, where he had hid throughout the attack.

After all four had been taken off, Barron received his last message from Captain Humphreys. The Englishman had "nothing more to desire." He deplored "that any lives should have been lost in the execution of a service which might have been adjusted more amicably" and by implication he rejected Barron's offer of the *Chesapeake* as a prize of war. The *Leopard* made sail and stood to the north. On the *Chesapeake* the people spliced and patched, or pumped the three feet of water she had taken in her holds. Boys scattered sand over the bloodied timbers. Warm dusk enveloped the bruised frigate and her splintered decks were silent. But within the wardroom, five lieutenants seated in the glow of a battle lantern discussed the unprecedented step which outraged pride and an almost pathological concept of honor demanded they should take. As for what course their ship must now pursue, her condition allowed no argument. She tacked about and in the morning, as fine weather changed to rain squalls, matching her wretchedness with its own, she crept back into Hampton Roads, her sails tattered and patched, her colors missing, to drop anchor at half-past meridian.

Doctor John Bullus and Captain Gordon left for Washington in the frigate's pilot boat with the commodore's report. But Gordon also carried an important communication from the lieutenants. Allen's fingers, if they had indeed held a searing coal, had healed sufficiently for him to compose and sign a petition to which his colleagues and Sailing Master Brook added their signatures. While certifying to a sense of shame, it proclaimed that their desire had been to resist the *Leopard*. And it became their "imperious duty" to request an order for the arrest of Commodore Barron on two charges which they pledged themselves to prove true: that on the probability of an engagement he had neglected to clear his ship for action; that he had failed to do "his utmost to take or destroy a vessel which we conceive it his duty to have done." Less than a week after this astonishing missive reached Robert Smith, it was reproduced in the pro-administration newspaper *National Intelligencer*. Not so Barron's version of the encounter. Three months were to pass before the communications between himself and Captain Humphreys appeared in American newspapers—and then borrowed from British sources.

The commodore's official and private views seem at first glance in utter conflict. To the Secretary he speaks of "our unprepared and unsuspicious state" when the *Leopard* opened fire, but drops no hint of dissatisfaction with the conduct of his officers. When Gordon returned to Norfolk and demanded to know whether Barron was responsible for local rumors charging him with delinquency, the commodore wrote back, "I have done you all the justice in my power. I attach no blame to you." But in this same letter he excoriated the lieutenants as "the greatest cowards that ever stood on a ship's deck." Writing at about the same time to John Bullus, who had remained in Washington, he renewed his attack on them and tilted at Gordon too for lingering on the quarterdeck when he should have been below quelling the "panic." None of his officers had paid heed to his orders. Only when commanded to strike did they move with alacrity; and they found voice only when it was seen, after the lowering of the ensign, that the pendant still flew. Then "all those heretofore dumb fellows bawled out to the topmen to haul it down." Elsewhere in the letter he asserted that never in his life had he sailed in a ship so unprepared for defense as the *Chesapeake*.

Since Barron did not make these things known in his official report, we may be forgiven for assuming that they are of little value as testimony but, rather, were irrationalities issuing from mental anguish. Yet valid explanations can be made for his failure to file countercharges against his officers. He might already have suspected, as events would prove, that against the word of certain favored personnel his own would carry little weight. Since he was basically a kind man, it is not improbable either that his official silence was a result of the same misguided paternal sense of fair play which had produced that letter to the Secretary, one he now profoundly regretted, complimenting his subordinates upon the *Chesapeake*'s condition. And surely Barron's magnanimity toward them *immediately* after the incident in Hampton Roads was leavened with the hope that they would reciprocate, would forgo personal animosities and close ranks with him, as loyally as the officers of the surrendered *Philadelphia* had done when Captain Bainbridge faced official inquiry and the threat of censure. Instead the commodore found his charity rewarded only by the propagation of slurs upon his name and a well-publicized demand for his arrest.

Upon receipt of the news from the south, Robert Smith issued three brief letters. One ordered Captain Stephen Decatur to take instant command of the *Chesapeake* and restore her to seaworthiness. Another relieved James Barron of his command and informed him of Decatur's succession. "You will deliver to him all the letters you have received from this Department since you had command of the *Chesapeake,* and will remain at Hampton until you shall hear from me." Charles Gordon, however, was permitted to continue on board as captain. As for the lieutenants' petition, the Secretary applauded it and gave assurance of proper action.

At noon on July 1, Stephen Decatur boarded the *Chesapeake* and in the commodore's cabin took possession of all ships' documents and Department orders. This business completed, Commodore Barron came up the hatchway to the quarterdeck. Against a pleasant sky the broad pendant flew once more above the frigate, but no longer to signify his command. The officers were lined on deck to witness his departure. In an agony of mind and spirit, he limped past dry and scornful eyes and just before reaching the gangway he stumbled, appearing as if about to faint. Then he steadied himself before descending the ladder to the cutter waiting alongside. And at 4 P.M. Commodore Barron quit the frigate *Chesapeake.*

CHAPTER TWELVE

Zest for War

I hope you mind the published accounts of this affair as
little as I do. We must make allowances for the heated
state of the populace in a country where every tie, both
civil and religious, is treated so lightly.
                                    —Admiral Berkeley to
                              Captain Humphreys, July 4, 1807

BY AND LARGE, the nation of some six million Americans reacted to
the attack on the *Chesapeake* as to a cruel surprise blow. Not even
the sinking of the *Lusitania* in 1915 touched off such a patriotic
storm, and one must advance another quarter-century to the raid on
Pearl Harbor to find a close comparison. What Admiral Berkeley's
compatriots, caught in the popular tempest ashore, may have
thought of his haughty complacence in the safety of Halifax can best
be imagined. Both John Hamilton in Norfolk and David Erskine in
Washington could see their assiduously developed social reputations
foundering overnight. Hamilton's position was the least enviable.
Norfolk's anger knew no bounds from the moment the first passengers on the drays and phaetons jolting along the rutted thorough-
fares brought word of the outrage in the Roads. Excited speculation
filled mansions, coffeehouses, and stores, while in streets near the
wharves ship's chandlers, blacksmiths, joiners, and sailmakers
downed tools and made for tavern meetings or set out in rowboats to
question the crew of every incoming vessel.

"All doubt was relieved [reported the Norfolk *Gazette and Public*

Ledger] by a spectacle which was calculated, and did not fail, to arouse the indignation of every American present, and we trust that it will *never* subside until ample satisfaction has been made—eleven of our wounded fellow citizens arrived in a boat despatched from the *Chesapeake* . . . three of the crew were killed . . . the independence of our country has been attacked, and in defending it our fellow citizens have been killed. Submission to the demands made on Commodore Barron could not have been made, without relinquishing our right as an independent nation. Every national ship is considered as a part of the nation's territory; as well might the government of Great Britain instruct her officers to land in our country and assume the right of punishing those who may have offended her laws, as to enter our ships of war for the same purpose." A citizens' committee of protest quickly convened at the Town Hall and voted for the suspension of all contact with British warships. The prohibition applied equally to the supply of provisions and the services of pilots. The British almost certainly had no idea of the combustible mood of coastal citizens until their schooner *Hope* sailed up the Elizabeth River to land a lieutenant with dispatches for John Hamilton. A crowd would have lynched him but for the intervention of the local militia.

Meanwhile, Stephen Decatur's arrival on board the *Chesapeake* had transformed the atmosphere in her wardroom from shameful gloom to a gusto for battle. Henceforward her crew were regularly beat to quarters and the great guns exercised daily. To twenty shipwrights under Josiah Fox fell the task of stitching and bolting the frigate back into seaworthy condition, but the repair of her reputation was held to be the prime duty of Commodore Barron's successor. No one acquainted with him doubted for a moment that he relished it. Three weeks after he took command, two boatloads of Virginian militiamen passing the ship were cheered by men in her shrouds but given no gun salute. The French frigate *Cybelle*, on the other hand, had just paid them the signal honor of hoisting her national flag five times. Why, it was asked, could not an American ship salute them in proper fashion? Answer was given that according to naval tradition a vessel without honor can confer none on others. "We heard the explanation with a sigh," wrote a militia officer, "but immediately exclaimed 'if Barron has disgraced you, Decatur will retrieve your honor.' "

From reports Decatur now began sending to Washington, that opportunity was imminent. British movements were "extremely suspicious"; they had brought to, by firing, every vessel passing the capes and had sent "many insolent and menacing messages to Norfolk" threatening, if the people did not supply them with wanted articles, to capture the *Chesapeake* and cut out the *Cybelle.* All these reports were based on hearsay, and as if in refutation the British turned refreshingly benign. Captain Douglas, warning of his power to obstruct the entire trade of Chesapeake Bay, had at first demanded that the Norfolk citizens' committee resolution be annulled. But when Littleton Tazewell, the eminent Norfolk attorney, brought him the Mayor's reply, appropriately dated July 4, defying the British to do their worst, Douglas blandly disclaimed the slightest notion of aggression. And Tazewell, conveying the captain's peaceful assurances back to the Mayor, paid tribute to the gentlemanly behavior he encountered while on board H.M.S. *Bellona.* All of which left Stephen Decatur unimpressed. So Captain Douglas meant no hostility? His actions following Tazewell's visit belied his words. "He has lightened his ship and fired many shots at an Eastern Shore man," Decatur alleged. But should any of his ships enter the Elizabeth River, "I think I am not over sanguine when I say I believe they will not all go down again." The *Chesapeake* could now meet the British without fear, and he would stake his reputation in her "alongside any of their proudest ships of equal force. If put to the test, the event would prove me not a vain boaster."

The chances of such a trial developing rested upon what course the President decided to take. He was staying on in Washington that summer to manipulate by mail the prosecution of Aaron Burr in Richmond. But on receipt of a firsthand account of the *Leopard*'s attack from Bullus and Charles Gordon, he recalled his cabinet, which, like Congress, had deserted the capital for "the sickly season." Around his long council table, amid the maps, charts, and window-boxed flowers he so carefully tended, the five members heard him propose a proclamation banishing all British ships from American waters. Communication with any that refused to leave would be forbidden. Exchanges between the two governments would not be affected, but their conveyance to and from British vessels would be managed by American port customs authorities. The cabinet approved without hesitation.

Privately Thomas Jefferson had little faith in his proclamation. Madison—whose first draft of it had been too warlike for the President's tastes—explained to a port collector that it meant British ships would henceforth be treated as enemies. But the President was under no illusion that they would obey it. Moreover, as an index of the administration's earnestness, it was hardly guaranteed to satisfy an aroused nation. Popular feeling ran high. Even in Washington, an unlikely place in midsummer for emotion to thrive, the July 4 celebrations were more fervidly patriotic than any Jefferson could recall. The mood everywhere was an intoxicating blend of pride, dauntlessness, and a confident zest for war. As the *National Intelligencer* boasted: "What We Did In The Weakness of Infancy, It Will Be Strange If We Cannot Repeat In The Vigor Of Manhood."

Against all this fever Jefferson's instincts rebelled. But though he told John Randolph that he had "ceased to believe anybody belonging to any kind of vessel" because he was overwhelmed by "reports and fables," he felt obliged to act upon the missives from Captain Decatur portraying British commanders as "having their foot on the threshold of war." With, therefore, no choice but to prepare for it, he mustered all state militias, placed coastal areas on an emergency footing, and contemplated a winter march into Canada.

His Secretary of the Treasury favored an immediate recall of Congress, reasoning that, so notorious was Washington's summer unhealthiness, no step was better calculated to impress the British with what gravity the American government viewed the offenses of the Royal Navy. In the meantime, to lessen the risk of further incidents, Gallatin would have pilot boats cruise off Virginia to warn incoming American vessels against entering Hampton Roads. He seems also to have wondered whether, if Captain Decatur would only offer them water, the British ships would not all go away.

But as that summer of 1807 advanced, the British ships ventured no further hostility. The national mood steadied. The country's defenses were manned as best as could be imagined under an administration sworn to peaceful neutrality. The Virginia coast was fortified, 3,000 armed men patrolled the shores of Chesapeake Bay, and from Hampton Roads, the area most exposed to threat, official reports told of nine eighteen-pound guns mounted at Fort Norfolk and the combat-readiness of the militia. The Secretary of the Navy had dispatched his fastest schooner to the Mediterranean for the recall of Captain Hugh Campbell and the lone *Constitution*. The vigilant and indefatigable Decatur had restored the *Chesapeake* to fighting trim and stood ready to attack with all his abundant energies should the British come up the Elizabeth. The schooner *Revenge* was bound for England with dispatches, in the custody of Doctor Bullus, demanding not only indemnity in the *Chesapeake* affair but an end to the prolonged and aggravating practice of impressment.

Everything to be expected of the government had been set in motion, including the quest for culpability. The anger of press and public had in general been directed at the British, with only an occasional deflection of aim toward the ship with the stained flag and those who stood in the shadow of her dishonor. But any day now the court of inquiry called by Robert Smith would begin to investigate the surrender that Commodore Barron had made, in the words of the Secretary's order, "without that defense being shown which might have been expected from the known valor of Americans."

Jefferson thought of the *Chesapeake* incident as "an interlude during the suspension of the Burr trial." He could do nothing more about it now. Politically the next move was up to the British. It was unnecessary to recall Congress just yet and summer ailments had afflicted Madison and Gallatin. To have detained the cabinet in Washington any longer would have been inhuman as well as needless, so Jefferson dismissed it. He ordered his horse saddled and on August 1 rode off in relief to Monticello.

The British maintained their new show of restraint. David Erskine, in New York when news of the *Leopard*'s attack reached him, had hastened to Washington and publicly denied that his government had authorized it. He wrote an urgent letter beseeching John Hamilton in Norfolk to curb the Royal Navy's officers. But Captain Douglas had by then sailed in the *Bellona* for Halifax and taken the captives from the *Chesapeake* with him. His successor in command, Captain Sir Thomas Masterman Hardy, removed a second provocation from the Virginia coast by ordering Captain Humphreys and the *Leopard* to Bermuda. Then Hardy retired his squadron to an innocuous position beyond the capes, a manifestation of prudence promptly acknowledged in a relaxation of tension ashore. Groups of militia were disbanded and the men sent home.

Grateful for the moderation shown by Captain Hardy in the south, David Erskine made no secret of his displeasure with the admiral to the north. Rejecting Berkeley's attempts to justify the *Leopard*'s action as dictated by an American "refusal" to surrender deserters, the minister emphasized that, proper though it was to resist any attack upon the British flag, "in this instance the aggression has been on our part." Nor could Erskine share the admiral's optimism that his superiors in London would condone the order of June 1. And he proved right. Locked in one titanic struggle beyond the Channel, the British were not impatient to provoke another on a new front across the ocean. Far from approving George Berkeley's conduct, the Lords of the Admiralty delivered a sharp rebuke and called him home, a decision Berkeley resentfully deduced as the product of political expediency. Before leaving Halifax, he performed certain noteworthy functions. One was the issue of a proclamation offering the king's pardon to all deserters, provided they returned to their ships immediately. Its preamble was a patriotic blandishment: "As the hearts of all true British seamen are like their native oak, honest, tough and unchangeable, they can never be induced to countenance hostility against Old England. . . ." But the fate of Jenkin Ratford in Halifax Harbor the same week was enough to daunt the most oaken-hearted penitent from rushing back with outstretched arms to embrace the Royal Ensign.

Described as a thirty-four-year-old Londoner, he was charged before a court-martial with desertion, mutiny, and contempt. His declaration that on no account would he have ever fought against his country was ignored. Even Captain Lord Townshend's charitable testimony that before his desertion the accused had not been a bad sort was of no avail. On August 31, 1807, Ratford was hanged from the yardarm of the sloop *Halifax*. His final words were to correct the record. With who knows what last spark of pride he informed his executioners that he had not been born in London, but was a Yorkshireman.

Admiral Berkeley's most agreeable task during his closing weeks on the North American station would have been that of attending the marriage of his daughter to Sir Thomas Masterman Hardy, who had sailed up from Virginia for the event. And when Hardy returned in the *Triumph* at the end of the year, the Norfolk *Ledger* reassured its readers that as "the captain carries his new married lady with him, it does not appear that he expects to have much fighting to do." Moreover, the reason for the British squadron's appearance in American waters in the first place no longer existed. During Hardy's felicitous absence in the north, the repaired French ships *Cybelle* and *Patriot* had hoisted anchor and (after being blockaded sixteen months) made all sail for the Atlantic. In the manner of their departure the *Ledger* perceived a lesson for Americans on the impolicy of depending upon any force other than their own. The government had come to regard the French vessels as part of the Chesapeake Bay defense system. Now they were gone "without leave or notice, having taken what we used to call French leave. We wish Monsieur a good passage to France." The only brief hindrance to it came from Captain Decatur, who took from the *Patriot* a French-born seaman charged with deserting the United States Navy to rejoin the service of his motherland.

Meanwhile the official inquiry into the *Chesapeake*'s surrender had taken place in October. Robert Smith had at first summoned Edward Preble to preside over it. The commodore acknowledged Smith's letter with the typical assertion that he had "enough blood in my veins to boil with indignation at the recent insult," but he died six weeks later and Smith appointed Alexander Murray, one of Charles Gordon's several patronly cousins, who had additional cause for bias against Barron: the latter was known to have criticized Murray's methods of reconditioning the *Insurgente* and to have predicted her fate. Barron was aware of Murray's feelings. And Murray was merely the first of several whom he would regard as depressing choices to pass judgment upon him. Perhaps his selection contributed to Barron's renewed spell of ill-health. At any rate, pleas of indisposition forced one adjournment after another until Littleton Tazewell, hired by the government as Judge Advocate, lost his patience and protested to the Secretary of the Navy. "Events not improbable," he wrote, "may at any moment suddenly deprive the United States of all testimony." Tazewell meant the possibility of war. He lost one important witness that same week when Lieutenant Benjamin Smith died on board the *Chesapeake* of bilious fever.

Barron attended only the first week's hearings and was represented thereafter by Robert Barraud Taylor, a Norfolk attorney whose professional brilliance was outshone locally only by that of Littleton Tazewell. From Captain John Hall of the marines and three midshipmen Taylor extracted testimony that during the *Leopard*'s broadsides Barron had been "calm . . . collected," "firm . . . showed no agitation . . . acted bravely." But a formidable array of officers paraded by Tazewell thought otherwise. According to Captain Gordon, it had never been Barron's intention to do other than "fire a few guns and surrender the ship." "He surrendered out of fear," testified Lieutenant Crane. To Lieutenants Allen and Sidney Smith the commodore had shown "want of courage," and although Lieutenant Creighton confessed himself unable to "blast his character by a positive charge of cowardice," he thought that Barron had certainly been confused and irresolute. Even Sailing Master Brook was "doubtful of his courage." This near unanimity of censure seems not to have registered upon Barron's counsel. "I deem it unnecessary," he said, "to offer any defense of Commodore Barron. The court is capable of judging correctly without any comment from me."

Robert Taylor might have held a different view had he seen the letter which Murray, with or without the knowledge of Captains Isaac Hull and Isaac Chauncey, the other officers on the court, dispatched to Washington when it finally adjourned. Ostensibly to save Robert Smith the trouble of plodding through the "prolix and elaborate" record, he had solicitously summarized it, adding only "some appropriate observations." The accused (Murray's term for Barron) knew that deserters were aboard his ship, that threats had been made to search for them, and from his failure to take proper measures "the inference is strong that he did not mean to defend her." America's state of peace was no excuse. "A ship of war so nobly equipped as the *Chesapeake* then was should never be taken off her guard. Behold the reverse, after an attack of a few minutes he struck his colors without consulting a single officer, thereby disgracing the flag of the United States." The detailed record, which reached Smith early in November, contained twenty-eight accusatory opinions, none of which cast the merest hint of culpability upon Captain Gordon or indeed mentioned his name. The final article carried a reference to "those whose duty it was to remedy the deficiencies of the ship," suggesting for the first and only time a possible plurality of candidates for blame. But as if to remove any flicker of doubt where blame truly belonged, Littleton Tazewell sent the Secretary a further court opinion, emphasizing that the cause of the frigate's surrender was the failure of Commodore Barron to prepare his ship against an attack which he was given abundant reason to expect.

An exchange now occurred between the Secretary of the Navy and Littleton Tazewell which leaves one with the odd impression that for a fleeting instant Albert Gallatin voluntarily released his grip on government expenditures. Robert Smith asked Tazewell to repeat the office of Judge Advocate at the court-martial made mandatory by the results of the court of inquiry and invited his estimate of a fee for services rendered so far. In reply Tazewell suggested $500, acknowledging it to be a large amount and explaining that his temporary abandonment of the court of civil law had exposed him to financial loss. The attorney need not have been reticent. Within two weeks he received a draft from the United States Treasury for $600 and the promise of "further suitable compensation" for service on the court-martial. (The practice of employing civilians as judge advocates on naval courts continued until after the Civil War. In March 1865 legislation was passed limiting their fee to $200, but not until June 1880 did Congress authorize the President to appoint within the Department the office of Judge Advocate of the Navy, carrying with it the rank of captain.)

The imminence of a court-martial caused widespread excitement. The national commotion stirred up by the attack on the *Chesapeake* had subsided, but, in the taverns of Norfolk at least, argument over the conduct of her officers ran sufficiently hot to generate insults and challenges. Two *Chesapeake* midshipmen named Crump and Broom fought a duel which left Crump wounded in the thigh; and even as Secretary Smith issued a worried order to Captain Decatur urging the prohibition of further dueling by his officers, Charles Gordon met two Norfolk citizens, both, in Decatur's opinion, beneath his notice. But Gordon had already noticed them and on the field he consented to a curious arrangement that allowed a principal's second to shoot if the opponent fired too soon. This resulted in such a genuine confusion of aims that a second duel was fought for clarification. It left Gordon and his two opponents each slightly wounded.

Meanwhile Congress had reassembled in October and plunged into a discussion of national defense. When this spent itself in a conflict of opinion, not much of an active Navy survived but Thomas Jefferson's gunboats. Except for a few Federalists, no one wanted to vote money on what John Randolph called a fleet "degraded and disgraced." Robert Smith showed no inclination to fight for his frigates, and after a full cabinet meeting it was decided to confine them to port in wartime, where they would serve "as receptacles for enlisting seamen to fill the gunboats occasionally."

The period of political inaction due to the lack of news from Europe promised to end as ships which had sailed from that continent only a month before came home, their voyages shortened by prevailing easterly winds. On December 12, the *Revenge* brought back Doctor Bullus with dispatches reporting Bonaparte's determination to enforce the Berlin Decrees sealing continental ports to British shipping. December 13 the *Augustus* reached Norfolk with James Monroe aboard, his diplomatic career in Europe at an end. And on the following day the *Brutus* sailed into New York, bringing London papers which outlined Britain's plans to prevent neutral commerce with her enemy, France. All in all, the tidings from Europe were disheartening, but they gave Jefferson the opportunity to test as never before his cherished theories of peaceful coercion. With Madison's assistance he drafted a message to Congress warning of "the increasing danger with which our merchandise, our vessels, and our seamen are threatened on the high seas and elsewhere from the belligerent powers of Europe," and he recommended an end to all trade with them. Three days before Christmas—four after Congress had authorized the construction of 188 additional gunboats, making altogether 257—the Embargo Act became law.

None of this made much impression upon Commodore James Barron, who, when he contemplated President Jefferson at all, did so with deep resentment. His brusque removal from command, even before an official inquiry had been held, had left him with the conviction that whatever the tribulations ahead he could not count on the Jefferson administration for succor.

In the Navy, Barron's name had become an object of scorn. The attitude taken by the national press was somewhat less painful, although here and there Benjamin Stoddert's stern injunction against permitting seamen to be taken out of American warships was recalled—to the commodore's discredit. In general, Republican newspapers expressed sympathy for Barron as a prey to British aggression. Federalist sheets depicted him as a victim of Jefferson's folly. Just once did Barron find it necessary to protest, in a letter to the Norfolk *Ledger*, against "publications calculated to injure my character." He spent the last month of 1807 quietly at the home his father had titled "Little England"—not the most fortunate choice of names that season —and, comforted by his attorney Robert Taylor, endeavored to brace himself for the court-martial.

CHAPTER THIRTEEN

A Commodore on Trial

> Every commander or other officer who shall, upon signal for
> battle or other probability of engagement, neglect to clear
> his ship for action, or shall not use his utmost exertions to
> bring his ship into battle, or shall fail to encourage in his
> own person the inferior officers and men to fight courageously,
> such officer shall suffer death or such other punishment
> as a court-martial shall adjudge.
>
> —Article Four, Rules for the
> Better Government of the
> United States Navy, 1801

THE WEEK BEFORE CHRISTMAS, 1807, Robert Smith had ordered
Commodore John Rodgers to Norfolk with instructions to arrest
Barron, Captain Gordon, Captain Hall, and Gunner William Hook.
Barron was charged with negligent performance of duty, neglect on
the probability of an engagement to clear his ship for action, failure
to encourage his officers and men to fight bravely, and failure to do
his utmost to take or destroy the *Leopard*.

No senior officer of the United States Navy had faced accusations
of so serious a nature, and those of the commodore's peers who read
the court of inquiry opinions were quick to reach a verdict of guilty.
At least one of them arrived at a suitable penalty. Since quitting the
Navy, Thomas Truxtun had assumed the posture of an elder naval
statesman full of advice and acerbity. His perspectives may have been
warped by gout and unwanted leisure. But he would not have lacked

support for certain remarks which he addressed to Captain Isaac Chauncey recalling the case of Admiral Byng—"as brave a man and as loyal as ever was Howe, Jarvis, Duncan, Rodney and Nelson," and even so "it was the policy of England at that moment that he should be disgraced and die a premature death." Truxtun suggested that naval discipline might be enhanced and America's sovereignty better respected abroad if a similar example was made of Commodore Barron. He asked Chauncey to consider these sentiments as a seasonable gift from an old friend, having written them on Christmas Day.

Commodore Rodgers left the gunboats whose construction he supervised at New York and hastened south. The court over which he had been appointed to preside would be judging a man who had excited his contempt and venom. If the passage of ten months had allowed these feelings to ebb, nothing had occurred in that time, certainly not Barron's surrender of the *Chesapeake*, to supplant them with any more charitable. There is no evidence that Rodgers sought release from the appointment on grounds of prejudice, but we know that Stephen Decatur did.

However strong an affinity had developed between James Barron and Decatur during the early cruises of the *United States*, its dissolution may be traced to an incident which had taken place on a Norfolk street in January 1806. After escorting the Tunisian Ambassador to Washington, the hero of Tripoli had gone to visit his parents in Philadelphia and also to break off a romantic attachment which Barron for one had understood nothing could sever. But Decatur had fallen in love with Susan, the attractive, accomplished, and controversial daughter of Luke Marbury Wheeler, the seventy-third Mayor of Norfolk. Three years the captain's senior, Susan was not inexperienced in amorous affairs and her romantic involvements—the latest with Napoleon Bonaparte's brother Jérôme—were meat for town gossips. Spice was added by the mistiness of her origins. Her father's unsteady business activities are first recorded in the Elk Ridge region of Maryland, and there Susan was born, but of her mother nothing is known except for fragmentary evidence that she was of lowly station and possibly mulatto. When Decatur reappeared in Norfolk bent on marrying Susan (he did so less than two months later), James Barron in his presence scolded a third party who had jocularly attributed Decatur's swift return to the attraction of a new belle. The exact words which passed during this street encounter are unknown, but Barron's were a typically fatuous intrusion or at least were resented as such, for "from that day Decatur was an altered man to me." It never occurred to James Barron that his paternal solicitude, if it amounted to that, had become less of a necessity than a nuisance the moment Decatur gained national renown, or that in any event it ought to have stopped short of the twenty-six-year-old officer's romantic affairs.

And then Rodgers had come home. Barron's embarrassing performance, the undignified evasions, the inconclusive settlement of the feud, operated further upon Decatur's feelings, and his "opinion of him as a soldier was not favorable," a judgment ruthlessly confirmed when the *Chesapeake* struck her colors. Then Decatur "formed and expressed an opinion that Commodore Barron had not done his duty." He had attended the court of inquiry as a spectator; heard all the evidence; examined the findings and thought them lenient. He ended his letter to the Secretary: "It is probable that I am prejudiced against Commodore Barron. Nothing should occasion me so much regret as to be compelled to serve on the court-martial that tries him." Robert Smith replied that he had no doubt Decatur would do justice to the accused and to the country—and he turned down his request. Decatur thereupon sent copies of the correspondence to James Barron.

Decatur's attempt to disqualify himself, and his furnishing Barron with documentary grounds for protesting his seat on the court, have been cited by his biographers as an example of his magnanimity. This may be. Yet it is hard to see how he could have honorably remained silent, particularly since his prejudice was, by his own admission, no secret. (It is still harder to pardon the omission in at least one biography of the words *"and expressed"* from an otherwise verbatim text of this significant passage of Decatur's letter.) As for the copies sent to Barron, here again Decatur's aversion was already a matter of knowledge—during a final strained meeting between the two just before the *Chesapeake* sailed, he had not troubled to conceal it.

Barron was all for acting upon the written evidence of prejudice now in his possession, and furthermore for objecting to the presidency of John Rodgers on similar grounds. But Robert Taylor saw things differently. The participation of men *known* to be hostile would serve to emphasize Barron's final vindication, an outcome which Taylor professed not to doubt; what court on earth could in this case reach anything but a favorable verdict? Barron was unable to share his counsel's confidence, but he yielded to his advice and forgave it long afterward as coming from a man "too honorable for such work as was then going on."

For a number of reasons the *Chesapeake* trials occupy a unique position in American naval history. Historians have suggested without furnishing evidence that they proceeded from a Jeffersonian thirst for scapegoats, or that their purpose was to palliate wounded national feelings. The court-martial of James Barron, however, achieves its true notability less from unsupported speculation than from certain attestable features which are far more intriguing. For one thing, it was the only occasion in American naval history on which a commanding officer was formally charged with failure to prepare against expected attack. The court of inquiry ordered by the Navy Department to investigate the Pearl Harbor disaster of 1941 produced not dissimilar accusations against an admiral, but he escaped court-martial. Then there is the irony of Barron's alleged offense having occurred while the two nations involved were in a state of peace with each other and wished to remain so. From a legal standpoint, the *Chesapeake* tribunal was said to have "first set the example to the service of rigid adherence to principles, forms, and precepts"; yet as a model of dispassionate justice it is short on luster, for it is marked by prejudice and duplicity. And as have few other court-martials, it cast its own long shadow of bitterness and tragedy.

A small throng of spectators, some of them Barron's friends and relatives, attended the trial in the *Chesapeake*'s great cabin. The officers of the court settled themselves around the table in stiff solemnity, their gold lace and blue cloth lending some slight color to the January pallor filtering through the ports. Not counting Rodgers, ten officers would judge the commodore: Captains William Bainbridge, Hugh Campbell, Stephen Decatur, and John Shaw; Master-Commandants John Smith and David Porter; Lieutenants Joseph Tarbell, Jacob Jones, James Lawrence, and Charles Ludlow. At one end of the table was Littleton Tazewell, with Commodore John Rodgers, heavy-browed and portentous, at the other. Off to Tazewell's right stood a smaller table with two chairs for the accused and his counsel. On the left, a single chair awaited the first witness. At the desk used by Commodore Barron during his brief command sat a clerk to record the proceedings of his trial. The discharge of a gun from the frigate's quarterdeck signaled the formal opening of court and the recital of charges.

Littleton Tazewell, aged thirty-three and already firmly established in law and state politics, was said to be in discourse "mathematical, quick as lightning, sportive and cool." He also evidenced so unemotional a manner as to embarrass friends, who thought him callous toward even his own family. He courted the society of naval officers with the special warmth often shown by intellectual giants for men of dash, and was on particularly close terms with Stephen Decatur.

Tazewell followed the recital of charges with a reading of the court of inquiry report, a procedure Robert Taylor, Barron's counsel, did not then protest although its propriety was eventually to be questioned. Taylor had earned Norfolk's gratitude during the summer crisis by his command of a cavalry troop in the area's defense system. In the popular view Commodore Barron was a less defensible cause, and by shouldering the burden of it (perhaps because he was a cousin) Taylor exposed to some risk a political future already jeopardized by his avowed federalism. But it cannot be said that he gambled with it recklessly as James Barron's advocate.

It was Littleton Tazewell's purpose to extract evidence showing that an attack on the *Chesapeake* should have been and was expected. William Montgomery Crane, the first witness, described the signs of "hostile determination" he had seen: "After we got under weigh the *Leopard* did the same because of a signal made by the *Bellona*. She hauled around the cape, so as to get the weather gauge of us, as the wind then stood." When the wind became light and baffling, as if about to shift, the *Leopard* stood off from land in order to take advantage of it. The wind did change, and the *Leopard* shortened sail. "I noticed she had her lower deck ports triced up. About three P.M. she bore down on us." These circumstances alone (Crane said) would have led him to prepare his ship for action had he been in command. When Master-Commandant Porter asked him how he knew that the *Bellona*'s signal had prompted the *Leopard*'s departure, he replied that he learned the fact afterward. "But I would have inferred it. No other ship in the squadron paid attention to the signal but the *Leopard*." After the lieutenant had testified that Barron did not consult him on the decision to surrender, Captain Decatur inquired if he considered it a commander's duty to do so. Crane replied that in certain cases it was and that this was one of them. When Robert Taylor asked under what circumstances a commander was exempted from so doing, the lieutenant gave a ready answer: "After he has made a gallant defense."

Taylor ignored the slight upon his client and suggested that Crane's interpretation of the British movements might be exaggerated. After all, had not there been a British squadron lying in Chesapeake Bay long before that day?

"There is no doubt of this," Littleton Tazewell interposed. "It is a matter of some notoriety, you may save yourself the trouble of proving it."

Robert Taylor inquired whether it was not usual for a two-decker in warm weather to have her lower ports triced up.

"I never saw it before," Crane answered. "It might be possibly so in a calm, but at this time there was so much sea that her lower ports were dripping before she came alongside of us."

Crane admitted that his division was badly cluttered when the *Chesapeake* passed the Virginia capes, but denied that it was his duty to clear it until ordered.

"What is the force of the *Leopard*?"

"A two-decker, rated as a fifty gun ship, with 24-pounders on her lower deck."

"And the *Chesapeake*?"

"She carried forty guns. Twenty-eight 18-pounders and twelve 32-pound carronades."

"Do you believe the *Chesapeake*, with the best disciplined crew, had any reasonable hope of taking the *Leopard*?"

"No, but she might have fought her a long time."

Lieutenant Crane voiced the opinion that the drummer should not have been forbidden to beat the men to quarters. And when Taylor asked at once if the drum would not have been heard on board the *Leopard*, all the disdain for cautiousness then growing fashionable among young naval officers seemed concentrated in his curt reply: "Certainly it would."

On January 7—the fourth day of the trial—Lieutenant William Henry Allen replaced Crane in the witness chair. Throughout the months following the attack, Allen's sense of shame had lost none of its fanatic intensity. He conceived of himself on trial, with an exoneration of Barron the verdict of his guilt, and he had written to his father: *"If I am acquitted honorably, you may see me again. If not, never."* Now, in words which echoed Crane's, he recounted the maneuvers which induced him to expect trouble from the *Leopard*. Tazewell asked if it was usual for a ship that meant no harm to round to windward of another when she wished to speak. Allen said no. "They generally pass to leeward."

"Could not the *Leopard* have easily passed to leeward of the *Chesapeake* and then spoke her?"

"Certainly she could."

At once David Porter inquired if the witness would consider every windward movement of a vessel as indicating hostile intent. Allen admitted he would not. Porter also drew his supposal that it might be proper for a commander to get his crew to quarters secretly—but only (he added) if the ship were surprised at night. He was asked about the message brought on board by the British lieutenant and of the commodore's impressions of it. "From Commodore Barron himself," Allen replied, "I understood afterwards that the purport of the communication was to demand certain men from us and if they were not delivered, to take them by force." On this point the other officers gave substantially the same answer. None of them had *read* Admiral Berkeley's order, but Commodore Barron, following the attack, had conveyed an impression of it as a threat of force.

Of all the officers on the court, indeed in the entire Navy, none more than William Bainbridge knew the mortification of surrender. The specter of public censure had not been completely exorcised from his mind by the court of inquiry which, under the direction of the officer now accused, had acquitted him of blame for losing the *Philadelphia*. Now he asked the third witness, Lieutenant John Orde Creighton, if the *Chesapeake*'s casualties and damage had warranted surrender. It was an interesting question, coming from the captain who had yielded his frigate intact to an enemy.

Creighton answered: "No, sir."

Littleton Tazewell then asked if any part of Barron's conduct in getting the crew to quarters had been unbecoming the character of an American officer. Before the lieutenant could reply, Taylor objected. The cabin emptied while the court deliberated, and afterward the spectators re-entered, with cheeks whipped a fresh crimson by the wind off the Roads, to hear Tazewell declare that no reason existed for sustaining the defense counsel's objection. "The same question has already been asked of other witnesses," he reminded the court, "and has not been objected to." This was so. It had been asked of Crane and Allen, and both had answered. If the question was improper now, it was so on those occasions, yet Taylor had not protested. It was repeated. *Was Barron's conduct unbecoming the character of an American officer?* Creighton answered *yes.*

Lieutenant Sidney Smith was the first witness to be asked if he or any other officer had reported to Barron their belief that the movements of the *Leopard* meant she intended to attack. Smith replied that he had not. He refused to answer for the others and was interrogated no further on this point. Instead the questioner—Porter—inquired if any aspect of Barron's conduct had indicated a lack of determination to defend the *Chesapeake.* In his affirmative answer Smith cited "the manner of going secretly to quarters, his not subdividing the marines, and not having the gun deck cleared during the full forty minutes that the British officer was aboard." The lieutenant was asked by Tazewell if anything in Barron's behavior appeared to be caused by fear. Smith answered: "The commodore appeared much agitated. When he called for his officers the first time, and I went up and offered my services, he appeared to hesitate, as if not knowing what order to give."

Taylor took over the questioning. "Other than this agitation you speak of, was there anything else from which you could infer a want of courage in Commodore Barron?"

"There was not."

"And you believe this agitation produced from fear?"

"I thought it was."

"How did he exhibit this agitation?" Taylor pressed. "In what did it consist?"

Such persistence may have nettled the lieutenant. "I have stated my impression. I can add nothing more."

But the attorney had one last question. "Were you ever in an engagement before?"

"Never."

Captain John Hall was called. His answers to Taylor were unhesitating. Was Barron agitated? No. Were his orders firm and distinct? Perfectly. Did he fail to encourage his subordinates to fight bravely? "No, sir," answered Hall. "Everything which he did, I thought, was calculated to encourage them."

"Did you see Lieutenant Sidney Smith during the attack?"

"I did."

"Where was he, generally?"

"He was on the larboard side of the mizzen mast."

"How was he occupied?"

"He was standing up with his sword in hand, tolerably close to the mast."

The picture of contrasting attitudes conveyed by Hall's testimony —the commodore's steadfast calm while his present derogator had sheltered behind the mizzenmast from the *Leopard*'s fire—was not likely to influence the court seriously. For against the word of a lieutenant of the Navy, it was that of a man himself under accusation and who was, moreover, a marine.

On January 8 Littleton Tazewell addressed the following to James Madison, Secretary of State: "James Barron having represented that your testimony will be material to his defence, you are hereby summoned to give your attendance at the court-martial forthwith, in order to your being examined as a witness." The idea was to prove Barron's word that he had been informed by his government that the British Minister was satisfied on the question of deserters. But the commodore could have had little hope that the summons would be obeyed. Both Madison and Robert Smith had already displayed curious reticence on this aspect of the affair, even after David Erskine made public that he had been far from satisfied. If Erskine's denial was true, it meant either that Barron had misunderstood his government or had been misled by it. This is also to assume that Barron was telling the truth. No written evidence existed to support his claim of government reassurance that the case of the deserters demanded by the British had been cleared up to everybody's satisfaction. At any rate, a statement from Madison or Smith would have helped, but the likelihood of one became suddenly even more remote. Tazewell's summons reached Mr. Madison only a few hours after the British ship *Statira* entered the Potomac bringing George Henry Rose, envoy extraordinary from the British government, to discuss American demands relating to the attack on the *Chesapeake*.

Madison, as things turned out, had less to do with Rose than Robert Smith. That Federalists strove hard to capture the visitor's confidence surprised nobody, but even those treading the shallows of conspiracy against the administration failed to achieve the close liaison with him rapidly established by Jefferson's Secretary of the Navy. Smith was in fact acting on the President's authority. Perceiving that Rose would "open himself more frankly" to Robert Smith than to Madison, he privately appointed him "the medium of obtaining an understanding." Madison, who was feeling unwell, raised no objection to being shunted aside for a week or so. As Jefferson later recalled in a discussion of the incident, "the harmony among us was so perfect that whatever instrument appeared most likely to effect the object was always used without jealousy." Jefferson himself played little part in the talks. Having resolved not to seek a third term, he was counting the days to Monticello and, moreover, was suffering from a jaw infection and a recurrence of his migraine.

Instead of the redress which the American government wished, George Rose had brought demands of his own, and was under orders to refrain from any serious negotiations unless they were first met. The demands were, notably, the withdrawal of the President's July 1807 proclamation, and an official "disavowal" of any of its officers found "sheltering deserters." Rose was correct in sizing up Robert Smith as at least one American cabinet minister anxious for conciliation at any price. The Secretary's private distaste for Jefferson's Embargo and his anxiety for a rapport with Britain equaled that of any Federalist, and had his mandate to negotiate continued, there is no telling what concessions might have been made to the British visitor. But at the end of the week James Madison moved back into the talks and informed George Rose that no disavowal of American officers would be made unless His Majesty's government first disavowed Admiral Berkeley. Madison refused to budge from this position and on February 16 Rose, declaring the talks a failure, packed his bags for home.

More than anything else on Madison's mind those wintry days was the struggle within the Republican party to nominate a successor for the Presidency. He knew himself to be Jefferson's personal choice, but a movement in Virginia supporting James Monroe for the office was gathering momentum. At the core of the Monroe faction stood Littleton Tazewell, and it might be speculated with what amusement if not cold planning the enigmatic Norfolk attorney savored the idea of the Secretary of State in the witness chair at Barron's trial. But Madison's response to the summons read, "My memory does not apprise me of any circumstance which could be of importance to the trial." The hearing continued, with Charles Gordon called to the witness chair.

Did the captain report to the commodore (Robert Taylor asked) about the *Leopard*'s movements, or those of any other British ships on the passage through Hampton Roads to the sea? "I did not." answered Gordon, and corrected himself immediately. "Yes, I did. At nine A.M. the *Bellona* and *Melampus* were conversing with their signals and the *Leopard* was getting under weigh. I reported these things to Commodore Barron in his cabin. Afterwards I made no report since he was on deck himself." At dinner, he recalled, Barron glanced through one of the ports at the distant *Leopard* and remarked "to no particular person" that "her movements appeared suspicious but that she could have nothing to do with us." He admitted that after the British lieutenant had left, Commodore Barron told him to clear the gun deck, but "I do not think this can be called a decisive order. Rather a request."

"Did Commodore Barron fail to encourage his officers and men to fight courageously?"

"He did not encourage them in my presence."

Soon came the question he must have known Taylor would ask him. *Did he discover any deficiencies in the gunner's department?*

"I must decline to answer, and claim the privilege which the court has granted me." Littleton Tazewell had properly reminded him that in view of his own forthcoming trial he was at liberty to avoid self-incrimination. And when Robert Taylor asked that the witness be compelled to answer, the Judge Advocate refused.

Taylor altered tack. "Did you fire a salute when passing Mount Vernon?"

"Yes, sir."

"Did you encounter difficulty?"

"I decline to answer."

"After descending Chesapeake Bay did you report to Commodore Barron that your ship was ready for sea?" Again Gordon would not answer, neither did he when Taylor produced the letter he had written Barron June 19, 1807, describing the readiness of the vessel and her armament. But it bore his signature. Taylor finally got him to acknowledge it. He passed it to the Judge Advocate, who read it to the court. But when he tried to draw Gordon into a discussion of its contents, the captain once more declined to answer.

Later he alleged that even before the *Chesapeake* left the Washington Navy Yard, Barron appeared to share his own conviction that the deserters sought by the British would be demanded at sea. But it was the commodore's words over dinner when the frigate had put out that riveted his attention on the imminence of trouble. Had anyone present (asked Taylor) commented on Barron's remark? Gordon did not recall. But did not these apprehensions induce him after dinner to order the gun deck cleared?

"There was no need of such an order."

"Did you go to the gun deck and examine its state?"

"No. I considered it my duty to be on the quarterdeck."

"Did your suspicions induce you to ask the gunner about the state of his magazine?"

Gordon refused to answer.

At Taylor's request, Captain John Hall took the witness chair. "Did you dine with Commodore Barron on the day of the attack?"

"I did."

"Did you hear him express any suspicion as to the movements of the *Leopard* during dinner?"

"I did not."

"Did you hear any person at the table express suspicion of her movements?"

"I heard none."

Hall was dismissed. Again it was his word against that of a naval officer. But there was another dinner guest to be heard from. Doctor Bullus could, moreover, support the defense on an additional point, for it was Barron's understanding that he had received the same impression as himself, and from the same government source, that Erskine had accepted the American statement regarding the deserters. John Bullus was popular with all the officers, and there can be no doubt that Barron anticipated a decisive measure of help from his testimony. Robert Taylor urged the Judge Advocate to request Bullus' early attendance. Tazewell also asked the Secretary of the Navy to send Fitz Henry Babbitt, a *Chesapeake* midshipman reported to have aired views in tavern and on ship's deck marking him as a potentially useful prosecution witness. "I would issue summonses," Tazewell wrote, "but I do not know their whereabouts." While the court awaited the missing witnesses, he introduced written exhibits, including Robert Smith's letter of caution to Barron, which, as a reflection of the administration's pacific policies, might have helped in some measure to vindicate the commodore's hesitation under the *Leopard's* guns. But the document which had the greatest effect was his report to the Secretary of the Navy dated June 23, 1807. Since Lieutenant Meade had taken Admiral Berkeley's order back to his ship, Barron had been obliged to rely on his memory for its substance. The purport of it (he had written) was that "each and every vessel of the British squadron should take, by force if they could not be obtained by other means, any British deserters found on board the *Chesapeake*."

Barron's memory had ill-served him: Berkeley's order (a copy of which Captain Douglas had since sent Barron on his request) nowhere mentioned force, and neither is the implication of it crystal clear. Yet if this was indeed the construction Barron had placed upon the admiral's words, was not his failure to seize the opportunity offered by the presence of the British officer on board his ship and prepare her for action cast in a justly reprehensible light?

Even as the court was in session, the narrow avoidance of another crisis over deserters disclosed emphatically just how heavy a proportion of the *Chesapeake's* crew consisted of Englishmen. Captain Bromley of the *Statira*, awaiting George Rose in Hampton Roads, had protested the forcible detention of seven who wished to avail themselves of the royal pardon and return to British service. Under instructions from the Department to discharge all foreigners, Stephen Decatur ordered a general muster of the crew. According to two Englishmen among them, he called only those who wished to join the *Statira* to step forward and at once "the whole fell back as though fired on by musketry." Decatur, in fact, discharged 175, the majority of them British, but denied Bromley the benefit of their services by transporting them up Chesapeake Bay in a gunboat and putting them ashore at Baltimore.

Meanwhile the weather in Hampton Roads worsened. Ice encrusted the *Chesapeake*'s masts and rigging, and while being rowed back to the ship at 3 A.M. after attending a ball ashore "graced by sixty ladies," Lieutenant Allen thought it one of the coldest nights he could remember. The weather drove the court to adjourn from the *Chesapeake* to a lodginghouse in Norfolk, but little business was done there. It was assumed that the witnesses from the north were unable to travel owing to snow and ice. Not until January 29 did the trial resume on board the *Chesapeake*, and almost immediately Commodore Rodgers received a letter from the Secretary of the Navy. Doctor Bullus had returned from his mission to England, where he had delivered the government's demand for indemnity, to find his family in financial difficulties. Under the circumstances it had been decided to grant "his earnest entreaties" and excuse him from attending the trial. At the same time, Smith indicated that if his presence was essential, the doctor would go. As for Fitz Henry Babbitt, he was on his way down in a gunboat.

It had already been emphasized to the Secretary that the defense needed Bullus' testimony, but Smith's letter, though vaguely contradictory, carried a clear implication that Barron would be imposing additional hardship upon Bullus and his family if he caused him to make the journey. Robert Taylor took the hint and gave up. Bullus did submit a brief and guarded deposition, of little value. Anonymous reports reached Barron now that John Bullus was "sometimes his friend, at others, his enemy." The commodore was probably inclined to believe them. Certainly he had lost, or been robbed of, his key witness.

Fitz Henry Babbitt's value to the other side is hard to assess. A seventeen-year-old midshipman and jaunty chatterbox, Babbitt testified that Barron had ordered the men on the weather guns to keep their heads down or be cut to pieces.

"What were the men doing?" Robert Taylor asked.

"Standing upon the guns, looking over the hammocks."

"Did Commodore Barron intend his voice to be heard?"

"I suppose so—he spoke pretty loud."

The ill-fated *Chesapeake* as she might have looked to the *Leopard* on June 22, 1807. *Courtesy of the Portsmouth Naval Shipyard Museum*

The *Chesapeake* and the *Shannon* off Boston, June 1, 1813. The English have boarded and are taking possession. Painted and engraved by William Elmes. *United States Navy*

John Rodgers. From a painting by John W. Jarvis in the U.S. Naval Academy, Annapolis. *United States Navy*

Isaac Hull, c. 1815. Artist: John W. Jarvis. *Courtesy of the New York Arts Commission*

James Lawrence in master-commandant's insignia. From a painting by Alonzo Chappel. *United States Navy*

"Are you certain that the expression was 'we shall all be cut to pieces'? Was it 'you will all be cut to pieces'?"

Babbitt was unshaken. "It was 'we shall all be cut to pieces.' "

His admission that the men were in any event unnecessarily exposed ended the testimony which he had descended the Potomac River and Chesapeake Bay in a gunboat to deliver. Next, Lieutenant Arthur Sinclair admitted that the forty men he recruited in Norfolk included a person said to be a deserter from the *Halifax*.

"Before the *Chesapeake* sailed, did you inform Commodore Barron that you had recruited such a man?"

"I did not."

"Have you any reason to believe that previous to June 22, Commodore Barron knew this man to be aboard his ship?"

"I have not."

Taylor had finished, but Littleton Tazewell detained the lieutenant to ask if he was not aware that his recruits also included three men who had deserted from the *Melampus*. The question wrenched from Barron his only outburst of the trial. "These I knew to be aboard," he cried before Sinclair could answer, "and that they were said to be deserters."

Robert Taylor called Charles Nuttrell, pilot, who spoke of the weather on June 22, 1807. "Did it blow heavy, was there a high sea?"

"No, sir."

"Was there such a breeze as to make a two-decker shut her lower ports?"

"I do not know about a two-decker. There was a fresh breeze, but the sea was smooth. The wind had not been blowing long enough to raise any sea."

"Was the breeze such as to bring the lower ports of a line of battle ship under water?"

"Apparently not, for the *Leopard*'s ports were not under."

Taylor, having drawn this sharp contradiction of Lieutenant Crane's testimony at the outset of the hearing, inquired if there had been any sign of fear or cowardice in Commodore Barron's words or manner during the attack. "I did not discover any," replied Nuttrell. He added candidly, "I was too bad scared myself to observe him particularly."

Taylor created a mild sensation next morning by declaring his wish to examine the Judge Advocate. But Tazewell raised no objection, and if he felt puzzled or concerned he was not the man to show it. After Commodore Rodgers administered the oath, he took his seat in the witness chair while the spectators forgot their chilled and cramped discomfort before the rare sight of Norfolk's two most brilliant attorneys in confrontation. Taylor, by directing Littleton Tazewell to read aloud testimony taken at the court of inquiry and before the present court, implicitly accused Charles Gordon of having perjured himself. The captain's original sworn position was that, previous to the *Chesapeake*'s departure, neither he nor Commodore Barron had expected a demand for deserters at sea. Before the court-martial, however, he had testified that he had expected, and Barron had appeared to expect, that such a demand would be made, a substantially different response, in harmony with the objectives of the present prosecution. Here indeed was the first serious indication of a connivance already rumored as having been at work to Barron's disadvantage during the three months' delay between the two tribunals. The very least result of Taylor's tactic was to cast doubts upon the reliability of Charles Gordon's memory. And the court seemed to leave it at that. No officer showed any inclination to probe further. Neither did Robert Taylor, who evidently considered his duty to his client faithfully done by having brought the matter up.

Barron was not called upon to testify, and the trial approached its end. His closing plea, read for him by Robert Taylor, ran to 18,000 words and was obviously, if only from the florid rhetoric which occasionally obscured its substance, the handiwork of the attorney. Barron did take personal exception to certain flatteries—the "intelligent and impartial tribunal," the "justice and honor of my judges"—but Taylor nevertheless left them in. The speech was largely a matter of denial. Denial of responsibility rightly Gordon's—here Taylor quoted from Naval Regulations, which ruled that *"A captain or a master commandant, whether sailing alone or in a squadron, shall at all times have his ship ready for immediate action. He must muster his crew at least once a week in port or at sea, and is frequently to exercise them in the use of the great guns and small arms. He is responsible for the whole conduct and good government of the ship."*

There was denial of Barron's alleged remark at dinner. Denial that he had read in the Berkeley order a threat of force: what he had described in his report to the Secretary was not his original impression of that document but a distorted recollection induced by the *Leopard*'s attack and formed under extreme bodily and mental anguish. And finally, denial that any proper course had been left him but to surrender the *Chesapeake*.

Why had Captain Gordon testified falsely? Because "the web of his destiny is interwoven with mine; my condemnation is the pledge of his acquittal; if it be not proved that the catastrophe resulted from my misconduct, the charge will revert to him from whose neglect of discipline and arrangement the surrender flowed. His examination has unalterably fixed the connection between us. To the prosecution his innermost soul is cheerfully unfolded. To me he is as cold as death, and silent as the tomb." Now the commodore's fate was in the hands of his judges. "Life, honor, the heritage which ten years of service enables me to bestow on posterity hang on your decision."

To arrive at it the court went into private session at the lodging-house ashore. After somebody (Porter?) had unsuccessfully raised a motion regretting that the court of inquiry opinions were annexed to the statement of charges, the officers proceeded to find Barron guilty on one of them. The first could not be sustained in the teeth of Naval Regulations: responsibility in detail for the state of a ship was not the commodore's while a master-commandant acted as captain. The third charge—failure to encourage his men to fight—was insufficiently supported by only two of ten specifications and in effect freed him from the suggestion of cowardice. As to the fourth, certainly the *Leopard*'s broadsides had not been boldly met and the damage suffered by the *Chesapeake* did not justify striking the flag; but since she was in no condition to repel, surrender became necessary.

In its deliberations on the second charge the court disagreed that the *Leopard*'s putting to sea or her triced-up ports (in warm weather and on a smooth sea) were of themselves indications of hostile determination. But Commodore Barron "did receive from the commanding officer of the *Leopard* a communication which clearly intimated that if certain men were not delivered up he would proceed to use force." (By "communication" the court of course meant Admiral Berkeley's order. Not even Littleton Tazewell could have persuaded anybody to read a threat in Captain Humphreys' covering note, an innocently worded missive which the court at no time brought into evidence.) That Barron understood it to mean force was manifest in his own written word and the testimony of those to whom he had spoken on the subject, and yet he had neglected to clear his ship for action. Thus were Barron's denials brushed aside; thus was the commodore damned by his hapless report to Robert Smith and remarks he had made to his officers.

Yet as their testimony reveals, with none of them had Barron discussed the admiral's order *before* the *Leopard* opened fire. In narrow fact, the report to Secretary Smith and evidence from the officers alike on this point could only reflect Barron's recollection of an impression received two or three hours earlier. That his memory deceived him in so short a time (even under the trauma of the *Leopard*'s attack) may not be wholly convincing. But in any event the court had taken the view that nobody could have escaped the admiral's meaning. And the only American able to testify with authority, one way or the other, on Barron's impression of the British document *at the moment he read it* was the absent witness for the defense, Doctor John Bullus.

On the following Monday morning, the officers of the court adjourned to the *Chesapeake*'s cabin, where Littleton Tazewell read through the formal litany of diminishing penalties, beginning: *Shall Commodore Barron suffer death . . . ?* To each, the court voted no, until he reached: *Shall Commodore Barron be suspended from all commands . . . ?* And then the court voted yes: *without pay or official emoluments of any kind, for the term of five years.*

CHAPTER FOURTEEN

Clemency for a Captain

> There was an influence in the cabinet of that day which protected Captain Gordon.
>
> —Commodore James Barron

GORDON'S TRIAL opened and closed within one week. At the outset he was permitted to have read for him by Littleton Tazewell an unexpectedly frank confession. It was true that while in sole command of the *Chesapeake* from May 1 until June 6, 1807, he had not once exercised his guns, true that his crew were called to quarters only three times, and true that he did not minutely examine the gun fittings or order a regular report from his gunner on the state of the ship's armament. Conscience alone drove him to take this step (he declared), for he employed no defense counsel but relied on the "intelligent fairness" of his judges. The statement revealed nothing of the towering wrath he had felt for Thomas Tingey's Navy Yard when his guns failed him off Mount Vernon, and the subsequent testimony of the lieutenants approached a panegyric to his vigilance at the Yard and his professional competence during the descent of the Potomac.

A jarring note was introduced by Midshipman Jesse Elliott. After the encounter with the *Leopard* (he testified) the third-division guns at least were found defectively mounted, and he had ordered their carriages sawn down to make them fit. But the midshipman was quickly put in his place. Stephen Decatur thought the fault he had described a minor one, and the remedy he had adopted clumsy and unwarranted. By next questioning the *Chesapeake*'s carpenter, Decatur established that sawing had been unnecessary; Elliott could have secured the guns by simply knocking down the clamps with a maul.

Commodore Barron was called to the witness chair. The result of his trial had yet to be made known to him, but there was a lassitude about his responses suggesting that he had resigned himself to an adverse verdict. Questioned, one suspects not unkindly, by David Porter, he aroused himself to accuse Gordon of having deceived him with reports of the *Chesapeake*'s fitness for sea, but he suffered the captain's cross-examination with what reads like apathy.

"On your first visit to the ship in Hampton Roads, did you not express to me your entire approbation of her?"

"All but the armament. Of that I could not speak."

"Did I not state to you in Hampton, at your home, the deficiencies I had discovered coming down the Potomac?"

"I presume you did. I do not recollect the particulars."

Barron's June 6 letter to the Secretary of the Navy, lauding Captain Gordon and his lieutenants, found its way into the case—certainly at no instigation of the commodore's. Now he heard the words he had written in a spirit of naïve magnanimity made public to Gordon's advantage and his detriment. "Is it customary in the American Navy," Gordon then asked, "to exercise the men on the guns while coming down the Potomac, with all your guns not yet aboard and your crew not complete?"

"I do not believe it is."

"Was I to blame for the lumbered state of the ship?"

"No. The government had authorized a number of passengers in the ship. Their luggage could not be moved without offending them."

"Do you know that a ship in a perfect state of discipline cannot be got to quarters without confusion, if surprised by any enemy?"

Gordon's question seemed to stir Barron. "It certainly had that effect aboard this ship."

Littleton Tazewell read the captain's defense speech for him. Compared with Robert Taylor's embroidered oratory, it was a model of simplicity and frankness, opening with an admonition to his audience not to expect "ornaments of art or beauties of style," and quickly getting down to substances. If his were not a candid nature, he, Gordon, might be tempted to argue that his authority aboard the *Chesapeake* had been superseded the moment Commodore Barron hoisted his broad pendant. Instead, he would grant that it *was* his duty to exercise the guns after they were all aboard. But his men were either sick or too busy; an exercise would have further delayed the ship's departure. "When we were at war with Tripoli," he went on, "I was a junior officer, but I well know that the guns of the *New York* were never exercised until we got far into the Atlantic." He reminded the court that the *New York*'s captain was then James Barron. He denied all knowledge of badly mounted guns—"I might as well be made responsible for not succeeding with a torpedo in blowing up the *Leopard*"—and that he had reported the ship ready for sea to Barron. In sum, Gordon declared, "The stain on the *Chesapeake*'s flag proceeded not from any errors of mine. Although my whole conduct from the first of May had been scrutinized with an eye so accurate as to distinguish between two musket balls differing from each other about one pennyweight only, yet no charge is brought against me based upon the disastrous events of that memorable day. If the guns were not securely fitted in their carriages, they certainly did not jump out that day. If the sponges and wads were not of the proper sizes, neither sponge nor wad was that day used. If the powder horns were not all filled, those filled were not used that day. If the matches were not primed, no effort was made to light them that day. If the marines were not supplied with enough cartridges, they were supplied with more than were that day consumed. If I have been guilty of omissions, they were mere neglects of duty, from which no evil consequence has been felt. But when you reflect on the evidence, I feel confident that you will not say I have omitted anything which I ought to have done."

His confidence was generously rewarded. The court accepted his reasons for not exercising the guns and held him blameless for misleading Barron about the preparedness of the ship. (Barron must have misunderstood; therefore the error was his.) Although his failure to call for written gunnery reports established some guilt, he was entitled to the utmost leniency. The court sentenced him to be privately reprimanded by the Secretary of the Navy, adding that, since his offense was "a very slight one" had an even lighter penalty been available it would have been imposed.

John Hall's trial was brief. He had, he declared, reported his marines' lack of cartridges to Gordon, but conceded the captain might have been too busy to notice. Hall closed his remarks with the hope that, although he had no objection to his present judges, it would not become the rule for a marine to be tried before an exclusively naval tribunal. Without comment on this, the court sentenced him to a reprimand. Less than a day was wasted on Gunner Hook. He stammered badly, an affliction which Master-Commandant Porter alluded to in a good-natured try for mitigation when Lieutenant Allen testified that Hook had told him seventeen powder horns were filled before the *Chesepeake* sailed. "As Mr. Hook stammers," Porter said, "is it not possible that instead of seventeen he may have said seven?" "He does stammer a good deal," replied the lieutenant, "but I did not mistake him." William Hook had seen seven years' service as a gunner and was one of Decatur's boarding party that burned the *Philadelphia*. The court on board the *Chesapeake* found him guilty of willful neglect, weighed "the fatal consequences which in a great degree resulted from it," and dismissed him from the Navy.

Gordon was allowed to remain as acting captain of the *Chesapeake* —the Secretary wished to avoid embarrassing him with anything which might be considered "degradation"—but Captain Hall, at his own request, was relieved of his post.

The Secretary of the Navy had good cause for satisfaction. Culpability had been legally apportioned and confined south of the Potomac. Nothing could be laid at the Department's door. Even the reputation of the Washington Navy Yard and its dancing commandant had survived. Judgment had been meted and, with the issue of another $600 draft to Littleton Tazewell, services rewarded. From the standpoint of naval discipline and good order, Robert Smith could consider the case of the *Chesapeake* closed. Politically, he was far from through with it.

In a most tragic manner it was to alter the destinies of certain officers. In part at least, the trouble arose from a disturbing riddle: Was Charles Gordon protected by high influence? Had secret manipulation from Washington preserved a captain's reputation by the sacrifice of a commodore's? The record of the trial stirs doubts right from the opening prosecution tactic of bolstering the charges against Barron with court of inquiry opinions clearly founded on *ex parte* evidence. Under Tazewell's direction the court not only refused to accept Barron's denials that he had expected an attack but made evident in its summation that he was the *sole* officer on board who had good reason to expect one. Nothing prior to Barron's receipt of Admiral Berkeley's order, not even the *Leopard*'s maneuvers, was (in the court's opinion) of a significance to warrant anticipation of trouble. This ran counter to the attested viewpoints of the lieutenants, but it had the result of bringing Barron's guilt into sharper focus. Nothing except the communication ordering a search of the *Chesapeake* and "clearly intimating" a threat of force (the court held) could have justified immediate active steps for defense; and no naval officer but Barron, the evidence indicated, had read or even known of it before the attack. The court had every right to determine Barron's culpability on the sole issue of his response or lack of it to the Berkeley document, and even to impose a heavy-handed sentence. But one does not need to criticize either the judgment or the penalty in Barron's case to question whether Charles Gordon was so much less reprehensible that the court would scout his proven guilt, deliberately seek the softest punishment it could find for him, and announce that it had done so as if in public apology for having accused him in the first place.

By dismissing the first charge against Barron, the court had committed itself to the view that responsibility for the *Chesapeake*'s "state and condition" was rightly Captain Gordon's. Then how could it so easily have condoned his neglect to have her ready for instant engagement, *at all times*, while condemning Barron for failure to clear her for action in less than an hour? The reason given was that "no evil" resulted from Gordon's omissions. But had his vessel been ready for prompt retaliation, as Naval Regulations required, even that short space of time would not have been needed to get her guns firing.

And what are we to make of the reluctance to investigate the fact that a portion of Gordon's testimony before the court of inquiry was strikingly recast to suit the prosecution strategy at Barron's trial? Or of the captain's ostensibly unprofessional pleas which won him such extraordinary clemency? In content and style they were not unworthy of the man who had read them for him. Coincidence? Or corroboration of Gordon's own boast afterward that the Judge Advocate had a hand in composing his defense?

It is not hard to imagine a network of protection about Charles Gordon, with Joseph Hopper Nicholson and particularly Albert Gallatin in position at the seat of government while Littleton Tazewell handled things at Norfolk. It smacks suspiciously of gratitude for favors received that Gordon tried later, on his own initiative, to drum up support for Tazewell's appointment as Secretary of the Navy. One is also tempted to connect the oddity of Tazewell's court fees that, authorized by the captain's ordinarily thrifty kinsman in Thomas Jefferson's cabinet, were larger than the attorney had asked for, equal in sum to that of a naval captain's annual salary. To recall finally that Littleton Tazewell's closest friends sometimes found cause to lament the flexibility of his ethics is only to deepen the shadow of doubt that hangs above the entire record of the *Chesapeake* trials from the selection of court officers to the issue of a couple of United States Treasury drafts.

Gordon remained acting captain of the *Chesapeake*, cruising along the Atlantic coast, until early 1809, when he received command of the brig *Syren*, carrying dispatches to France. The close of that year found him once more in American waters. He was visiting his relatives in the Annapolis area when he read the caustic "Reflections" on the *Chesapeake* affair appearing in Alexander Contee Hanson's *Federal Republican*. It may have appeared to Gordon that the *Chesapeake*'s honor was once more under attack, by one who was politically if not in blood an Englishman. He challenged Hanson to a duel, which took place near Washington on January 10, 1810. The young Federalist was a deadly shot: His pistol ball struck Gordon in the stomach. The captain was borne to the home of the Secretary of the Treasury, where Hannah Gallatin nursed him from the brink of death, though he was never to recover fully. Early in 1811 he was sent back to the *Chesapeake*—an unwanted assignment, but since a new administration had replaced Robert Smith's at the Department, his favored position was far less secure. The frigate was at Boston in ordinary, her inglorious function now to serve as a receiving ship for enlisted seamen. To John Bullus (navy agent at New York since his escape from the necessity of testifying at Barron's trial), Gordon described his woes. He was forced by his still suppurating wound to live onshore surrounded by "the greatest set of rascally English-blooded Federalists I ever saw," his abhorrent duty the command of a degraded vessel, "that unfortunate, unhappy ship on board of which all my wretchedness and misery commenced."

James Barron meanwhile struggled with the viscissitudes of suspension without pay. As master of a merchant brig he earned a brief livelihood in the West Indies, but his chances of profitable employment were limited by his age, the disgrace which shadowed him, and the severe blight on trade resulting from the Embargo Act. Adding to the family misfortunes, Barron's brother Samuel died, only a few hours after the new Secretary had named him commandant of the Norfolk Navy Yard. Then Barron's wife fell chronically sick. "God only knows what I am to witness in a world of torment," he wrote. But Madison's repeal of the Embargo improved commercial prospects, and in 1811 Barron's brother-in-law, a Norfolk merchant, gave him command of the *Portia*, a 170-ton vessel carrying merchandise between Lisbon and Copenhagen. His salary was to be $40 a month, supplemented by a 2½ per cent commission on the profits he made for his employer. He took up quarters on the *Portia* and sailed out of Hampton Roads for Europe on April 5, 1812.

CHAPTER FIFTEEN

To Whip an Englishman

> Our Navy is so lilliputian that Hercules after a hasty dinner
> would sink it by setting his foot on it; I had like to say that
> Gulliver might bury it in the deep by making water on it.
>
> —John Adams to his grandson, June 15, 1812

THERE IS AN ELEMENT of unreality about the refusal of James Madison's administration and the Eleventh Congress, while contemplating war against the greatest naval power, to bring the American Navy up to a confident fighting strength. True, the pitiful gunboat program so earnestly promoted by his predecessor (even in anonymous contributions to the *National Intelligencer*) had been abandoned and all the completed craft, except those stationed on the Mississippi, decommissioned. The orders were issued from Paul Hamilton, former South Carolinian governor and planter, who had succeeded Robert Smith in the Navy Department. But although Madison approved the scuttling of the "Jeffs," as disrespectful wits had called the gunboats, he took no action on the Secretary's suggestion that fast, well-armed frigates be built in their place.

For a time the President's avoidance of war measures was not inappropriate. What he called the "rusty and corrosive affair" of the *Chesapeake* had been to all appearances healed as a result of private talks and exchanged notes between David Erskine and Robert Smith, whom the President had been virtually blackmailed by a congressional clique into naming his Secretary of State. Erskine pledged his government to concessions that included withdrawal of the Orders in Council, a disavowal of Admiral Berkeley's conduct, payment of indemnities, and restoration of men taken from the *Chesapeake*. Smith offered in return American resumption of trade with Britain and continuance of restrictions against France. Madison promised that American ports would once more be open to British commerce. For once, both American political parties were united in satisfaction. But when George Canning, the British Foreign Secretary, received his copy of the agreement, he immediately repudiated it as an impertinence and with, for that day, bewildering speed David Erskine was recalled to England. Canning next sent out Francis Jackson, a notorious boor whose uncouth manner and heavy-handed courtship of extreme Federalists soon drove Madison early in 1810 to request his recall as well. From this point nothing occurred to alter America's course toward an armed conflict with Britain. And still precious little was done to repair the country's obvious inadequacy for one. This is what mystifies.

The anomaly is reflected by Navy Department orders. The captains must be ready and determined "at every hazard" to restore the honor of the service and "revive the drooping Spirits of the nation." This was demanded of them even though they were forbidden to patrol more than a marine league seaward. The government dared not risk losing any of its handful of sloops and frigates—yet the captains must not disappoint the country. There was indeed more to it than just the necessity of gratifying popular expectations, for should they fail "every man, woman and child in our country will be active in consigning our names to disgrace, and even the very vessels of our little navy to the worms." However overwrought, these words addressed by Commodore John Rodgers to his officers expressed a genuine fear prevalent in the Navy up to the very eve of war—a fear not merely of its arrested development but of its outright dissolution. The Navy existed by a thread which domestic foes, given half a chance by a timid administration, would gladly sever.

That same year the establishment had also to contend with heresy. When the naval hierarchy looked to the future at all, it saw progress almost solely in terms of larger ships, faster lines, and greater gunnery, advances in these categories to be made beneath the canopy of irreplaceable sail. Thus Robert Fulton's ideas were instinctively derided by several prominent captains and commodores, showing that professional conservatism which has, in one form or another, impeded developments in every technology from steam to space rocketry.

Fulton, the indefatigable visionary, had encountered ridicule in Europe and returned home to more. On August 17, 1807, he had launched upon the Hudson a craft 133 feet long and 18 feet deep installed with a 20-foot boiler housed in brick and an open 24-horse-power British-built Boulton and Watt steam engine, the whole contraption sandwiched between two giant paddle wheels. And even though the *Clermont* made the passage from New York to Albany in thirty-two hours without accident, perhaps it was as well for Fulton that the *Chesapeake-Leopard* crisis and the Burr treason trial dominated newspaper space. Additional publicity might only have embarrassed him with louder sarcasm than he in fact received. In any case, the revolutionary possibilities demonstrated by the steamboat's successful cruise appear to have been quite lost on naval officers.

Fulton's torpedo trials in 1810 were to make no deeper impression. Commodore Rodgers, from the start, had either mocked his theories as the hallucinations of an unbalanced mind or—had not the inventor long resided in England?—suspected them as cunning distractions to lower America's guard. Now Rodgers would have the chance of exposing their absurdity. Congress, attracted to anything which could envisage the abolition of the warship, voted $5,000 to finance public experiments. They were held in the East River with the 300-ton brig *Argus*, Master-Commandant James Lawrence, acting as theoretical target ship. Using clockwork torpedoes, Fulton had already blown up brigs in New York Harbor, off the Normandy coast, and outside Deal, England. In his latest demonstration he intended to row the weapon (charged with about seventy pounds of gunpowder) out to the brig, cast it adrift, and let the current carry it against her hull. Rodgers represented the Navy on the predominantly civilian commission to review the trials and, since Fulton described his method of attack in advance, was enabled to plan in detail the *Argus'* defense. He directed Lawrence to encircle the vessel with his own frigate *President*'s splinter net and a cordon of spars, and to suspend grapnels and pieces of kentledge from yards and booms. Thus the display, required by Congress to prove "the practical use of the torpedo, or submarine explosion," emphasized instead the methods that ingenious naval men might devise to neutralize it. Fulton had to admit the impossibility of getting the torpedo anywhere within effective range of the target ship, and in consequence the commission decided that his invention was too imperfectly developed for consideration as a defensive weapon. We have come to accept the surprise factor as of primary importance in successful torpedo attack, but it was the would-be attacker who on this occasion confessed himself "taken unawares." Still, Fulton was, by his own admission, "always big with some project" and he lost no time in disclosing his next, a torpedo blockship with cannonproof sides and musket-ballproof deck, maneuvered by a hand-driven screw propeller. Foreseeably, John Rodgers ridiculed this as well. All in all, the Navy's senior officers derived nothing from Fulton's demonstrations except confirmation that none of them, now or ever, deserved serious attention. And no one speculated upon the fact, although it could hardly have escaped them, that the elaborate arrangements which the commodore had found necessary to repel the torpedo attack had just as effectively immobilized the ship.

Fulton had provided the fleet with an interlude of trivia and amusement. The main thing now was to sustain that zeal for vengeance which the Secretary of the Navy sought to inculcate in his officers, one of whom, he felt, had badly let him down. "I had fondly cherished the hope that our officers only needed an opportunity to vindicate the wounded honor of our flag—in this I have been disappointed." Hamilton addressed these pained words to John Trippe, the scarred and handsome commander of No. 6 Gunboat before Tripoli. On June 26, Trippe, while in command of the *Vixen* off the Bahama Bank, refused a second opportunity for bloodshed and glory by withholding the vessel's fire—though he had cleared her for action—after the British brig *Moselle* had carried away her boom with two shots. Trippe accepted the British plea of mistaken identity and then put into Havana, having conducted himself prudently in the opinion of Captain David Porter, while another old comrade, Stephen Decatur, thought his "moderation" had lost him "a glorious opportunity to cancel the blot under which our flag suffers." This was the view Hamilton preferred, too, and he summoned Trippe home to face inquiry. But the lieutenant was spared unkind words and possible disgrace. Before the Secretary's letter could reach him in Havana, he succumbed to a sudden fever. "Poor Trippe," wrote Hamilton on learning the news, "died at a most unseasonable moment."

Injury wrought upon a mere brig would not have appeased the thirst for vengeance as consummately as a blow struck at a predatory frigate, and none craved that honor more than John Rodgers. His chance appeared early in May 1811 when the British frigate *Guerrière* was reported interfering with American shipping off Sandy Hook. Orders were rushed immediately to Rodgers, off Annapolis in command of the *President,* and on the 10th he sailed out, to a Godspeed from the Richmond *Enquirer*—"May the wounds of the *Chesapeake* and *Vixen* now be washed away." No sooner did the *President*'s topsails vanish below the eastern horizon than an intensity of anticipation along the Atlantic seaboard produced a flurry of rumored engagements, one of them illuminated by an imaginative watcher on the shore with 200 gun flashes. There was an encounter, but one rather less vivid.

On May 16, fifty miles east of Cape Henry, the *President*'s lookouts sighted an unknown ship. It was late afternoon, and though Rodgers pressed on all sail, dusk had fallen before he came within hailing range. But all hands on his frigate were eager to believe they had overhauled the *Guerrière*. Official accounts of what then took place conflict, the American version carrying the greater weight in testimony. Between 8 and 9 P.M., without revealing the identity of his own vessel, Rodgers hailed for the other's "and before I had time to take the trumpet from my mouth, was answered by a 32-pound shot and canister," which damaged the *President*'s mainmast and severed a boy's arm. The American gun divisions, in a tense state of preparedness, thundered back with broadsides. The stranger's weaker fire quickly flickered out, and next morning Rodgers reported with mortification that he had been compelled to fight and disable a 22-gun British sloop, the *Little Belt*. She suffered thirty-two casualties, some fatal.

The subsequent inquiry into Rodgers' conduct was held for no other reason than to silence Federalist papers gloating over a British court opinion that the *President* had fired the first shot without provocation. Its outcome was no surprise. Stephen Decatur arrived in New York Harbor to be appointed president of the court, sent Rodgers a breezy letter inviting his choice of time and place for it, and added, "May you live a thousand years." Then he closed with a blissful postscript: "I do not know what I have written above. I am in such haste to see my little wife." And in this beatific mood he presided over an inquiry which, after hearing fifty witnesses swear that the *Little Belt* had fired first, found Rodgers' conduct to have been not merely blameless but altogether praiseworthy. But Decatur was not an unqualified admirer of John Rodgers, and one feels that there were times when he regarded the senior commodore with an amused irreverence. On this occasion certainly, he cannot have thought that the near annihilation of twenty-two guns by forty-four entitled him to lavish praise. Nor does he appear to have taken seriously the Secretary's latest dramatic inference of events. It had now become, Hamilton explained, the turn of the British to lust after vengeance, and John Rodgers would assuredly be the target—a conclusion Rodgers himself proudly endorsed. It was therefore "important" that Decatur end his patrol off Virginia and stay with Rodgers until further notice. To dash forth and escort an overrated commodore must have struck Decatur as gratuitous—certainly it opposed his instincts to seek and fight singly—and furthermore placed his claim to the title of commodore in some jeopardy. And in any case, since Decatur anticipated the day when opportunity would favor him to "whip an Englishman" (the popular expression for what had become a mandatory naval ambition), he wanted no presence or circumstances to blur the result. It had to be something quite distinct from the series of ambiguous encounters which had destroyed Barron's reputation, tarnished Trippe's, and not altogether elevated that of John Rodgers.

Decatur informed the Secretary that British ships including the *Guerrière* were in his vicinity. Rodgers would have to wait until he satisfied himself that they were up to no mischief. In the main, though, his letter was a request for an official guarantee of his commodore's title, "a subject of some delicacy to me." He sailed for New York in the *United States* on June 9. She did not fall in with the *Guerrière*, but two other British warships, the *Eurydice* and *Atlanta*, stood down for her off the Virginia coast. Their captains explained that they bore dispatches for the American government. When they stood off again, a cannonball from one of Decatur's long twenty-four's flew after them, discharged, the commodore reported, "by accident."

Meanwhile Augustus Foster, a British envoy more competent than Erskine, more civilized than Francis Jackson, had secured a settlement of the *Chesapeake* affair under terms virtually identical with those Canning had repudiated in 1809. He negotiated with a new Secretary of State. President Madison, no longer able to tolerate Robert Smith on his team, had charged him with disloyalty and replaced him with James Monroe.

Most importantly, the *Chesapeake* settlement reflected the beginning of a moderation in British attitude which America's discriminatory trade legislation had forced upon her. Britain's warehouses were becoming clogged with unsold goods, her factories had closed down, and the ranks of her discontented unemployed lengthened. Moreover, the situation was seriously affecting the supply lines to Wellington's forces on the Iberian Peninsula. Pressure from British manufacturers and members of Parliament to revoke the anti-American Orders in Council began to build. Spencer Perceval, the Prime Minister, clung mulishly to them and when on May 11, 1812, a madman's bullet killed him in the lobby of Commons, an ensuing period of political anarchy further postponed the now inevitable steps toward an adjustment with America. It was an especially unfortunate delay, for by then the winds of change were sweeping America too, born of a fierce nationalism centered west of the Appalachians and soon shaking the Twelfth Congress with storm velocities.

The traditional distaste which Republicans professed for war had always tended to evaporate when the prospective foe was Britain. It had become almost a party duty to criticize conciliatory moves whether toward or from her—thus her contribution to the *Chesapeake* settlement was likened to "restoring a hair after fracturing the skull." But invariably it was a case of all hostility short of war. The brink might be approached but never crossed. Republican foreign policy was rooted in safety and submission. But now came violent reaction. With startling suddenness after their triumphs at the polls in 1810, a new Republican breed dominated Congress, a company of vigorous and hot-tempered frontiersmen who rejoiced in the nickname "War Hawks," who preached force against Britain, rekindled the tired spirits of surviving party elders, and who by the power of their personality as much as actual political strength attained such popular influence that the President himself, facing re-election, ignored them at his risk.

After all that has been written of James Madison and the War of 1812, it remains impossible to gauge accurately the determination of his efforts to avoid it. But it would no doubt be far less obscure to us had he become aware in time of the change of heart in London. Instead, echoes of British perfidy were now reaching him from the western wilderness, where, according to reliable intelligence, the Shawnees responsible for the massacre of sixty-one American soldiers on November 6, 1811, had been armed with British weapons. While those grave communiqués from General William Harrison's bivouac on the Tippecanoe were being exploited for all they were worth by the war bloc in Washington, the administration itself released documents that had fallen into Monroe's hands implicating the Canadian government in a three-year-old plan to foment New England disaffection. These disclosures further coincided with publication of a five-part series in the *National Intelligencer* sermonizing against the evils of impressment. French diplomatic chicanery was scarcely necessary to worsen relations between Britain and her former colony, yet this too was afoot as Bonaparte, swinging his legions about for the attack on Russia, sought to reduce Britain's pressure on his rear by embroiling her elsewhere.

If war with England, why not with France? The question was heard often enough, particularly when a French naval squadron, eluding a British blockade, burned or sank several American ships in the Baltic. "The Devil himself," wrote the Republican Nathaniel Macon, "could not tell which government, England or France, is the most wicked." But England, by her possession of Canada and her manipulation of Indian savagery, constituted the immediate obstacle to frontier expansion. It was to destroy England in Canada that the War Hawks successfully advocated vast increases in militia strength. At the same time, blind to the importance of maritime security because obsessed by frontier fears and ambitions, they joined the surviving Republican diehards in antinaval alignment. The political hazard of proposing naval increases right now would have been obvious to Madison even had he not been himself imbued with a Republican's traditional distrust of large public fleets. All he asked when Congress met late in 1811 was such provision as the existing naval force might require and the creation of a reserve stockpile of materials. His Secretary of the Navy went to the other extreme with a request for twelve 74-gun ships of the line and twenty frigates, including the ten already in being—five of which needed repair. More attuned to the congressional mood, the House Naval Committee confined its proposals to construction of ten new frigates, but even this moderate program came under violent attack. Langdon Cheves, the committee chairman, a militant South Carolinian who possessed classically oratorical gifts, led the fight to save it. He attacked as absurd the idea of a land assault against Canada without a corresponding power of challenge on the seas, deplored the present sorry state of the Navy, and proclaimed the all-important question now to be "whether we will suffer it to go down entirely." His arguments to keep it afloat filled a marathon speech that lasted two days. The Republicans answered with an anticlimactic rehash of shopworn scares—"press gangs would disturb the peace, your seaports would become the constant theatres of riot and debauchery," and so on—before the debate moved into an examination of whether England stood in her present peril from possession of a navy or whether her existence depended upon it.

The debate's chief sensation was produced on January 22 by Henry Clay, Speaker of the House and acknowledged leader of the frontiersmen, who shocked his colleagues with a plea in support of the Cheves bill. Seated in the Speaker's chair on the rostrum beneath the great stone eagle, he spoke as earnestly as he had ever addressed a Kentucky court during his youthful career in criminal law. Yet his eloquence had little more impact on landlocked imaginations than to bring forth inanities. John Rhea, an old-guard Tennessee Republican, professed himself puzzled by the suggestion that warships were as necessary to the protection of western interior interests as to those of the seaboard, and wondered how this could possibly be "except they meant to use them against the Indians." On January 27 the bill to increase the Navy was defeated by three votes. Less than three months later the *National Intelligencer*, virtually a government publication, ran a headline: "Declare War Now. What Are We Waiting For?"

Captains and their connections were anticipating it in a variety of ways. Minerva Rodgers sent her husband extra-warm shirts to safeguard him against rheumatism on the expected long cruises. Stephen Decatur teamed his father-in-law Luke Wheeler with the lawyer Littleton Tazewell to act as his prize agents. Charles Gordon, the blood still seeping from his duel wound, wanly assured his friend Bullus that "I shall be sending in a fine English prize this summer." William Bainbridge in far-off Russia ceased his efforts to market indigo, secured travel papers from the U.S. Minister in St. Petersburg (Leningrad), and set out on a hazardous journey across the Finnish wastes. The Russians had supplied him with a horse-drawn carriage, driver, and footman. At Abo the party found the Gulf of Bothnia partly ice-covered and the ferry inoperative. The carriage was dismantled and taken across section by section in hired boats which had sometimes to be dragged bodily over vast ice floes. They reached shore at Stockholm, struck out across Sweden, and were within sight of the spires of Gothenburg when their carriage skidded off a cliff and plunged thirty feet, killing the driver and horses, and injuring the servant. Bruised and fatigued, Bainbridge carried the man into the city. He boarded the first vessel bound for America and finally reached Boston exhausted, plagued with a cough, and richer by seven or eight thousand dollars.

On June 1, 1812, President Madison called Congress into session to hear him recount the grievances against Britain. The Orders in Council, long a principal aggravation, were now at the foot of the list. Madison had instead selected as the foremost irritation something which the British, no matter how conciliatory they might grow, were far less likely to surrender—the exercise of impressment. Many Americans had in fact become resigned to the practice as a chronic weakness of incorrigible Albion and were not disposed to go to war over it. There were indeed some, not all Federalists, able to perceive it for what it essentially was, a manifestation less of arrogance than desperation, a symptom of Britain's need while fighting for her life to sustain her naval strength against a man-power leakage to the west of about 2,500 seamen a year. But it was still possible to fan the embers of resentment over wanton seizure from American merchant ships (often in American territorial waters) into a white-hot patriotic rage. That British naval officers had been ordered to exercise more caution and avoid taking out bona fide American citizens was not yet known. Neither were Americans aware how rapidly the preservation of peace with them was becoming a salient objective of Britain's foreign policy.

On June 23 the British government repealed the Orders in Council—the London *Times* wondering editorially why they had ever been sanctioned. The signals flying over Westminster this early summer of 1812 were unmistakable. They heralded the beginning of a long-overdue realization that America ought not any more to be trifled with. Though the process would demand of England some political modification and a certain swallowing of national pride, her precarious economy and the enervating struggle with Bonaparte were, after three inflexible decades, forcing her into a more respectful regard for the people she no longer governed.

But it was coming about tragically late. Five days before Britain scrapped the Orders in Council, America declared war upon her. The decision has been variously ascribed to Madison's political weakness, to self-righteous principle, to a diehard prejudice against British Toryism, to an overhasty assumption of Bonaparte's invincibility. And Madison may well have felt himself bound under the Constitution, whose genesis he had so devotedly assisted, to comply with the majority wishes of Congress, which were in this instance almost fanatically martial. The range of possible motives is wide and all may have been involved. But it is very hard to find excuse or even explanation for the attitude toward sea power of the many congressmen who clamored loudest for hostilities. The resolution to fight Britain passed in the House of Representatives by a 79–49 vote. Of those seventy-nine advocates of war, fifty-three had, no more than five months earlier, cast their ballots against the Navy.

Comparisons of its size with that of the British conjures at once a vision of David challenging Goliath. In ten years the only increase in its number of vessels (except for gunboats) had been two sloops, two brigs, and four schooners. The total force did not exceed seventeen deep-water craft, of which only five frigates were seaworthy. Britain had almost 700 warships at sea, over one-third of them ships of the line and frigates. However, most of these were blockading the European coast from the Baltic to the Mediterranean or on convoy duty along the sea lanes to the Peninsula. If they had not been so engaged, it is still doubtful whether the Lords of the Admiralty would have transferred large squadrons in a hurry to the North American station. Their lordships' estimate of the United States as a naval threat amounted to little beyond her capacity for seducing valuable seamen from British service. One could not expect any impressions left by the exploits of Truxtun, Preble, and Decatur to have survived a period during which, the British knew, Americans had allowed their Navy to rot. Economic realities might be forcing Britain's industrialists and politicians to take a new, serious look at the United States of America, but her admirals continued to regard that country with amusement and contempt, partly inspired by the reports in the *Times* of American congressmen arguing interminably "whether six or two frigates shall be built to cope with the Navy of England."

Thus the British were self-induced to maintain on the North American station a naval force short of adequate for the double duty of guarding convoys and reconnoitering the Atlantic coastline. John Rodgers, reliably informed that it consisted of the 64-gun ship of the line *Africa*, seven frigates, seven sloops, seven brigs, and two or three schooners, felt confident that a surprise blow at them before their captains could know of the war declaration would equalize the balance. Rodgers was no lightheaded optimist bedazzled by prospects of glory. The enemy enjoyed excellent port and dock facilities at Halifax, Bermuda, and in the West Indies (in contrast to America's impoverished navy yards), but the vast sea area between their bases stretched the patrolling fleet dangerously thin and it would be months before reinforcements could arrive. Thus the odds were attractive that American ships cruising in company might fall upon one or two isolated enemies and eliminate them. Even the *Africa*, a thirty-one-year-old veteran, would have been no match for two of the American 44's. But Rodgers waited in vain for appropriate orders. A government which had neglected its Navy could hardly be looked to for ready-made naval war policy.

The Department correspondence of those last months of peace is pervaded with indecision and uncertainty, occasionally relieved by Hamilton's flamboyance. Early in April a communication from Wilmington had informed the Secretary that the English frigates *Guerrière* and *Belvidera* were molesting merchantmen off the Delaware capes. He sent Rodgers out to drive them off, exclaiming "Commodore, our eyes are upon you." Nothing came of this, however, although the cruise ranged from New York to Hatteras and back, and afterward Rodgers was again confined to New York Harbor. As late as May 21 the Secretary, baffled by the problem of how best to employ without risk "our little navy" for the annoyance of British trade, was soliciting proposals from his two most active commodores. Decatur, in a reply brimming with self-assurance, recommended that the ships cruise separately and remain out as long as possible, unfettered by departmental orders, their operations subject only to "the enterprise of their officers." Consequently, Decatur thought, the enemy would be forced to end his patrol of the seaboard and concentrate his ships for safety. Rodgers had similar ends in view, but proposed quite different means. Except for a few small vessels sent to cruise in British and West Indian waters, he would keep the ships in company close to home—and, it was superfluous to add, under his command—as a combined weapon. Hamilton was, in other words, presented with a choice of policies which can be summarized as lone-wolf errant versus wolf-pack leashed. But time was too short for thoughtful study of either.

With war imminent Hamilton focused concern on the small frigate *Essex*, hove down at the Brooklyn Navy Yard with a defective foremast, a badly fouled hull, and a captain, David Porter, who, to the Secretary's annoyance, had selected this moment to demand a drum and fife, music being "indispensably necessary in getting the crew speedily to quarters." On June 13 Hamilton urged Commodore Rodgers to have the *Essex* ready for immediate service. He added, "For God's sake get ready and let us strike a good blow." He had already ordered Commodore Decatur, at Norfolk, to form his *United States*, *Congress*, and *Argus* at once as part of Rodgers' force. On June 30 Decatur reported his ships off Sandy Hook and blamed adverse winds for the delay. Coming up he had fallen in with the British sloop *Tartarus* and a schooner, and had he known war was declared, "the harbor of New York would have been graced by their appearances as prizes." These vessels had been in Paul Hamilton's thoughts on June 18, the Thursday on which war was declared, when he sent John Rodgers the first battle instructions. They were neither resolute nor explicit. For the present Rodgers must "remain in such a position as to enable you to most conveniently receive further extensive and more particular orders which will be conveyed to you through New York." But since one or more enemy cruisers were believed to be near Sandy Hook, "you are at your discretion free to strike at them, returning immediately after into port." On the following Sunday, Hamilton, still searching for a suitable naval strategy, received his first practical guidance from a somewhat unexpected quarter. Albert Gallatin was less intent upon the harassment of British commerce than the safe homecoming of America's. Trade which he valued at from one to one and a half million dollars weekly would be flowing into domestic ports. To the Secretary of the Treasury's incisive mind it was obvious that the protection of these ships and the coastal traders constituted the nation's most urgent responsibility. "I think that orders to that effect," Gallatin told the President on June 22, "ought to have been sent yesterday and that, at all events, not one day longer ought to be lost." Next morning a courier raced out of Washington for New York with revised instructions. Now the naval force had again to be divided, Rodgers' squadron patrolling north of the Virginia capes while Decatur's ships plied southward from Sandy Hook, their zones overlapping at the busy approaches to New York, the Delaware, and the Chesapeake. "May the God of battles be with you," the Secretary concluded typically. But when this latest order reached New York after its three-day journey, the commodore and his fleet had already sailed.

Rodgers had received Hamilton's first timid war directive on Sunday morning—Gallatin was then urging on the President in Washington the measure which would supersede it. The commodore reacted at once to those words which granted him discretion. He had been privately informed that a hundred or more Jamaican merchantmen, weakly escorted, stood "about southeast of us on the edge of the Gulf" bound for England. He did not overlook the possibility of taking local enemy cruisers by surprise, but his principal thought now was to intercept and destroy the convoy. Probably his next senior officer encouraged him in his decision. Beyond question, Stephen Decatur was restive in his subordinate role and cannot have been too happy with the necessity of having to sail in company. But a lengthy cruise at least was now possible, and the great wealth of the Jamaican fleet gave promise of its being a highly profitable one. The two commodores signed an agreement to share equally all prize money earned by either one. Then the squadron stood for the Atlantic.

There was, then, no clarion call to arms, no swift dispersal of ships to battle stations. The declaration of war had been accompanied by no sign of a dramatic change in the ruling party's firmly fixed idea of a Navy limited to coastal defense. There were no prospects of an imminent shipbuilding boom—the industry had not yet recovered from the results of Jefferson's Embargo. A powerful British naval response to the announcement of hostilities, once the news reached London, might follow at any one of several points, but the Department had no plans drawn for contingencies. Naval supplies and munitions were lacking, crews were hard to recruit, and there existed no reserve of trained seamen. So small was the Navy that its distribution can be quickly stated. Captain John Shaw kept watch along the Gulf coast with the brigs *Syren* and *Viper* and a dozen or so gunboats. The *Constitution*, Captain Isaac Hull, was recruiting at Annapolis and on standing orders to join Commodore Rodgers. The repair of the *Essex* continued at Brooklyn, and William Bainbridge supervised the refit of the forlorn "receiving ship" *Chesapeake* at Boston. The frigate *Adams* was being leisurely cut down to a flush-deck corvette, and the *New York, John Adams,* and *Boston,* frigates proudly built from citizens' contributions, were rotting at Washington and Norfolk. Also at Washington, the *Constellation* approached completion after seven years' intermittent overhaul. The brigs *Nautilus* and *Enterprise* were at sea or ready to sail. A lone brig, the *Oneida,* represented American naval strength on the Great Lakes. And Rodgers' squadron—the *President, United States, Congress,* the sloop *Hornet,* and the brig *Argus*—had entered the Atlantic. Thus the United States Navy groped into the war with perhaps sixteen seaworthy ships mounting little more than 400 guns, manned by some 5,000 greenhorns and seafarers, their senior officers not altogether the heroic automata that two generations of juvenile romanticism has made them to appear but a company of proud and seasoned mariners with fiercely individual traits, whose patriotic incentives were sometimes hard to distinguish from glittering dreams of prize money.

CHAPTER SIXTEEN

Ocean Duels

AT 3:30 A.M. on June 23, 1812, Commodore Rodgers learned from a brig out of Bermuda that the Jamaican convoy had roughly a 300-mile start on him. Four hours later, however, he altered course to investigate a strange sail sighted to northeast. He was not abandoning the convoy: once the stranger was identified and settled with, the commodore planned to crowd all sail after the convoy, notwithstanding Hamilton's orders to return to port after action. At 1:30 in the afternoon Captain Richard Byron of the 32-gun frigate *Belvidera* sighted the approaching Americans and, entertaining no doubt of their hostile intentions, made all sail to escape. For two hours the chase continued over a smooth sea. But for their different flags, pursuer and pursued looked pretty much alike; American frigates of this period were painted in British fashion, black with a bright yellow streak along the gun ports. The wind freshened from the south and the American flagship, already far ahead of her consorts, gained rapidly until, shortly after 4 o'clock, she entered gunshot. Now Rodgers, so often thwarted, could scent triumph. Now the odds were more evenly matched than when he had stumbled on the *Little Belt*. Now he might once and for all remove that persistently invoked *Chesapeake* stain, to the country's—and Paul Hamilton's—unqualified satisfaction. When, at a range of half a mile, the *President* began the action with her starboard bow guns, the commodore himself fired one of them.

Every shot struck home. Captain Byron ceased speculating on the motives behind an apparently unprovoked attack and ordered the

Belvidera's stern chasers to reply. But the concussion that almost immediately shook the *President* was not the result of British fire. A starboard bow chaser on the American ship had burst, killing or wounding sixteen men, half wrecking the forecastle, and hurling Rodgers to the deck with a broken leg. Limping painfully but in firm control, he shouted for broadsides, hoping to crush the *Belvidera* with a full weight of shot. It did not matter that each necessary yaw to fire port and starboard batteries would cost him valuable distance. He preferred this mode of attack to laying his superior force alongside under the enemy fire. Historians have criticized him for this. But it should be remembered that the commodore, for all his intimidating personal presence, was not one to gamble boldly even when favored by the odds.

Before the margin grew too wide for effective fire, each vessel managed to damage the other's rigging extensively. The *Belvidera* lost two men killed and twenty-two were wounded. Most of the *President*'s total of twenty-two casualties resulted from the defective gun. Now the *Belvidera* increased speed by casting away her two anchors and the *President*, yawing futilely and hampered by torn shrouds, fell farther astern. A new threat to Byron developed when the *Congress*, Captain John Smith, came up. But over the *Belvidera*'s side went her barge, yawl, and jolly boat, while her crew pumped out fourteen tons of water. The *Congress* fell astern then, and the English frigate disappeared northward for Halifax in the gathering dusk.

After a day spent on the flagship's repairs, Rodgers resumed his stalking of the Jamaica fleet. On June 29 he fell in with a schooner bound for New York and learned the convoy's position as of two days ago. Calculating that it might yet be overtaken before entering home waters, he urged the *President* on at all possible speed. His leg mended but slowly. He had himself carried to the forecastle daily; he would not undress even for sleeping. And in the first week of July scraps of orange peel and coconut shells drifted by on the waves, tantalizing signs that the merchantmen might not be very far off now, perhaps just below the eastern horizon. The debris cast in the convoy's wake was all John Rodgers was to see of it. His ships plunged into dense and widespread fog, and when they emerged at the close of another week they were within one day's sail of the Cornish coast.

Now the commodore might have garnered a spectacular compensa-

tion. Bold forages among the abundant shipping clustered around
the British Isles could have seriously harassed the enemy's trade and
confronted the British Admiralty with a critical dilemma. To form
the squadron necessary for driving the Americans away would have
meant depleting the already overburdened force blockading Bonaparte's coast. Rather than do this England might very well have
sought an end to the war with the United States on the latter's terms.
It was in any event worth a try; and while the enterprise would
require daring, it could hardly be dismissed as unprecedented. John
Paul Jones had set a vivid example in 1778, and even earlier Lambert Wickes had spread havoc in England's home waters with a force
no stronger than a sloop and two cutters. Rodgers' own "favorite
lieutenant," William Henry Allen, was to demonstrate its feasibility
audaciously in this war. Certainly the gleaming prospects must have
occurred to the commodore. Yet they do not seem to have inspired
him, all the evidence suggesting that weariness and frustration
burdened his mind. Stephen Decatur's desire to strike daring blows
before recrossing the Atlantic can safely be assumed. But he was not
the senior commodore. And on July 13 Rodgers ordered his
squadron to wheel away from the mouth of the English Channel and
set course for the southward.

At home meanwhile his whereabouts had become a source of mysti-
fication and, after the *Belvidera*'s narrow escape to Halifax, British
interest in them was just as strong. On July 5 the *Belvidera* sailed
again, this time in company with the *Aeolus*, 32; the *Shannon*, 38;
and the *Africa*. Four days later, off Nantucket, they were joined by
the *Guerrière*. Word of the British force quickly reached New York
and Washington, where no one doubted that its purpose was to intercept Rodgers. He must therefore be apprised. But the American government was no better informed of his position than was the
enemy. On July 14 the *Nautilus* under William Montgomery Crane
put to sea from New York with the Department's letter of warning.
Instead of finding Rodgers the sloop fell in with the English squadron, and after a six-hour chase, during which Crane cast all his lee
guns over the side, he was forced to surrender with 106 officers and
men. The British vessels continued southward, and before the day
was much older sighted yet another American ship under orders to
join the missing commodore.

Isaac Hull had put out only a few hours after the *Constitution* had received her last batch of a hundred recruits—most of them strangers to a vessel of war. The Secretary had advised him not to engage even the inferior *Belvidera* without sufficient confidence in his men and now, in the late afternoon of July 17 off the New Jersey coast, Hull and his untried crew could make out not one but four strange sail ahead, close inshore, and a fifth farther out to sea. Hull waited for darkness and then, taking advantage of a southeast breeze, he bore down on the isolated vessel—the *Guerrière*—and made the private signals. They went unanswered and he maintained course. Silently, in the deepening summer night, the two vessels closed. At 3:00 A.M. they were only half a mile apart and the *Guerrière* too was busily making signals, unnoticed not only by Hull but the four other ships to leeward. Tension and uncertainty gripped every vessel. It was possible, as Hull hoped, that all five unidentified ships might turn out to be Commodore Rodgers'. Captain Richard Dacres of the *Guerrière* faced the same possibility regarding four of them—and he already knew his immediate shadower to be American. The closest of the four ships to leeward was in fact the *Belvidera*, whose captain had misunderstood or failed to see the *Guerrière*'s signals and had decided that she as well as the *Constitution* must be American. About 4 o'clock this strange, nocturnal comedy, possible only in an age without reliable night communication systems, was abandoned by Dacres, who fired two guns and a rocket to announce an enemy in view, then made all sail before the wind. Spreading daylight ended the confusion of identities. The *Constitution* saw herself to be alone among enemies, of which the closest to her, the *Belvidera*, lay just four miles off her lee quarter.

Hull ordered the *Constitution* tacked to the south. He had few illusions about his chances for escape. But registering cool optimism and professional ingenuity, he inspired his raw crew to extraordinary effort. At his orders they sawed away part of the taffrail, mounted a twenty-four-pounder hauled from the gun deck and an eighteen-pounder from the forecastle, and ran two more twenty-four-pounders out of the cabin ports. Thus the frigate showed a formidable quartet of stern chasers. Still she must make a run for it and only superior speed could save her. Hull ordered all sail set. The men obeyed with zeal if not professional smoothness. But their trial had only begun. Shortly after 5 P.M. the fragile breeze died completely.

Isaac Hull might have been more suited to a merchant's exchange than the quarterdeck. He was short, thickset, and friendly, and whenever possible showed a penchant for business enterprise which more than once landed him in trouble. He ran away from home to become a cabin boy and was thereafter, at least when ashore, the ward of his uncle William, an Army officer of high repute. In the records of the conflicts with France and Tripoli, he left a worthy mark. In December 1811, Joel Barlow, who had crossed to France in Hull's ship to take up duties as Ambassador, wrote that he could not overpraise the captain's merits. Hull was to need all the character references he could get. It was during that European mission that he reportedly used the *Constitution* as a passenger ferry between Portsmouth and France, charging 25 guineas per head. It was also subsequently alleged that he returned home with quantities of French merchandise aboard the frigate which he sold profitably ashore. These stories almost certainly came to Paul Hamilton's attention. According to at least one naval officer, charges were being prepared against Isaac Hull when the war intervened. At any rate, Hull could feel assured of the loyalty of his crew. Unlike so many contemporaries, he was not given to endless bravado—but he does seem to have enjoyed, as did Decatur, easier relations with the people than with his fellow officers. Nothing more dramatically illustrates the rapport between Hull and his lubberly crew than the contest of seamanship, perseverance, and labor which now began as the *Constitution* and six British ships—with a seventh, the *Africa*, hull up on the horizon—found themselves trapped together in a sultry calm.

The lone American frigate and the enemy sail might have been model vessels glued to a sheet of glass but for their decks astir with perspiring seamen and anxious officers. No one needed to puzzle himself with problems of battle maneuver. Friend and foe, the captains could apply their minds to a single purpose. That of the Englishman was to overhaul the American. Hull's determination was simply to escape. Shortly after 5 A.M. the preliminary moves were taken. Hull set his boats out to tow. The British did likewise. After two hours of hard rowing, Hull was outstripping his pursuers. The captain of the British flagship *Shannon*, Philip Broke, summoned all the squadron's boats to her, and drawn by their combined man power, with her sails all furled, she steadily gained on the American.

This, in the words of Charles Morris, Hull's first lieutenant, "seemed to divine our fate." But the *Constitution*'s sounding lead showed only twenty-six fathoms and, "with our minds excited to the utmost," Morris now recalled how kedging had once propelled the *President*, his old ship, to speeds of almost three miles an hour. Hull promptly ordered rigging and cable spliced into a line some 5,000 feet long and secured to the capstan. A kedge anchor bent to the other end was taken under oars as far forward as the line would stretch and dropped to the bottom. While men straining at the capstan bars warped the ship ahead, a second line and kedge were speedily prepared. In merciless heat, the *Constitution*, like a cherished and carefully aided cripple, worked slowly over the first anchor and as this was hauled up the second, at the forward limit of its line, was dropped and the brutal labor resumed.

The British quickly realized what the Americans were up to, and in short order Captain Byron of the *Belvidera* was applying the same tactics. Eagerly the *Belvidera*'s gunners opened fire and Hull replied. All the shots fell short. How close Byron was prepared to risk sending his boat with the kedge into range of the American's long guns aft was not to be known. Shortly after 9 A.M. a light breeze came out of the south. Hull was quick to brace his yards around for what slight advantage he could wrest from it, and he had the boats hoisted in with their crews standing by oars, a wise precaution, for dead calm soon fell again and once more the small craft of both sides crawled over a glassy sea, hauling ships of war like helpless hulks. The *Shannon*, twelve boats on her towline, again closed the distance, and the alternatives confronting Hull loomed more urgently. He could submit the frigate he had commanded for six years to certain destruction by resisting attack, or he could surrender, with no loss of honor, to a vastly superior force. Yet he regarded the necessity of choice as still premature, and it would remain so while he could somehow lighten the *Constitution*. Setting the pumps to work, he sacrificed more than 2,000 gallons of precious water, nearly two weeks' supply for the ship's entire complement. And again the *Constitution* drew ahead.

The dreadful toil of towing and kedging went on accompanied, noted the *Constitution*'s surgeon, by "alternate elevation and depression of spirits." Whenever the breeze justified the additional labor, Hull sent his weary men to the yards with buckets of sea water to spill down the sails so that they might hold more of the wind. Dusk fell and the drudgery did not slacken. The British ships were being kept from two to four miles at bay. Close to 11 o'clock Hull trimmed his sails to snare a sudden breeze and hauled in his boats, affording his hard-working crew some moments' respite. But few slept on the *Constitution* that night, no one left his quarters, and long before dawn the boats were out again. Daylight brought a dismaying sight. The *Belvidera* was abeam to leeward, not yet within gunshot but coming about to close while the *Aeolus*, close-hauled, had gained on the *Constitution*'s weather quarter.

Thirty agonizing minutes passed, all the ships, canvas spread, creeping across a glistening, flat sea, the *Belvidera* and the *Constitution* on converging courses. When Hull could no longer postpone tacking, the maneuver brought him almost into cannon shot of the *Aeolus*. Even Hull's skill might have proved insufficient to extricate the *Constitution* now, but that which he had so far demonstrated was rewarded with luck. The captain of the *Aeolus*, Lord James Townshend (formerly of the *Halifax*), his faculties perhaps dulled by the long chase, may have overestimated the range. In any event, no broadsides thundered from his divisions, and then it was too late. Opportunity had flown. The apparently indefatigable American crew were working their ship ahead again.

It was another day of drudgery in a fragile breeze. But the British were slipping farther astern and to leeward. About 6:30 P.M. a violent rain squall bore down on the *Constitution*. Hull met it with light sails furled and heavy canvas reefed, and before the last gusts had swept beyond the frigate he was issuing fresh orders to make all sail and close-haul. The British officers lost sight of their quarry in the squall, and had their recovery been as shrewdly planned and smartly carried out as Hull's, it still would have availed them little. The *Constitution* had for a few lively minutes made eleven knots. Now she could hardly be picked out in the night glass. But all through that second night of pursuit the British persevered. When another day brightened, the *Constitution*'s sails were slowly vanishing below the horizon. The sky promised no change in wind or weather. The chase had lasted sixty-six and a half hours. Only now did the British abandon it. They stood about to the northeast, and words then penned or uttered aboard their ships formed the best of all tributes to Isaac Hull and a crew yet to be at sea a full week. Captain Broke's understatement was that "the *Constitution* sailed well and escaped." But his biographer tells of sharp recriminations among the British sailors and melancholy reflections shared by their officers in the *Shannon*'s great cabin. Captain Byron's feelings on the occasion are beyond doubt. The American's escape was extraordinary and "nothing can exceed my mortification."

Now Hull needed water. He put his ship about for Boston and entered harbor the following Sunday. He was anxious to meet the British again—an escape is not a victory—and, too, the longer he stayed in port, the greater the risk of becoming blockaded. He had received no orders from the Navy Department since those assigning him to John Rodgers' squadron, of whose whereabouts he learned nothing at Boston. To a hasty account of the pursuit written for John Bullus in New York he added an inquiry about the missing commodore. But the Navy agent was as completely in the dark as anybody else. It was still felt that Rodgers could not be far offshore. (The *President* was in fact somewhere between Madeira and the Azores.)

Just then Hull had something other than Commodore Rodgers' disappearance to worry about. He had cared financially for the widow and three children of a brother who had died in 1810, and now a second brother was gravely ill. This was bad enough. In addition Hull feared the damage his death might cause to their father's health. Writing from Boston he begged his father not to lose heart, but he could not conceal his own anxiety: "Indeed, my mind is in such a state I hardly know what I am writing." The next day, August 1, brought a fair wind, and the troubled captain put to sea, missing by a matter of hours a letter from Paul Hamilton confining him to port and transferring command of the *Constitution* to William Bainbridge.

Most of America's merchant vessels, Albert Gallatin's principal concern, had arrived safely in port, taking advantage of the uncertainty imposed upon the British captains by the knowledge that an American force was at sea. The salvation of the mercantile marine, however, did not alter the administration's naval policy, such as it was, of concentrating ships close to the seaboard. Nothing so far had occurred to remove the fear on which it was based, that for Americans to wander far from home was to tempt annihilation. Hence Hamilton's acute wish for the return of Rodgers' squadron and his efforts to confine what ships he could to home waters.

The *Constitution*, having escaped the Secretary of the Navy as decisively as she had earlier the British, for two weeks cruised the Bay of Fundy northeastward to the Gulf of St. Lawrence in the hope of disrupting the Canadian trade routes. News of the war declaration had already reduced sea traffic, and Hull's operation consisted mostly of scattering small ships of war and liberating their prizes. However, from freed captives he learned that British warships were close by in strength—his late pursuers, Hull may have surmised, having returned to Halifax for water and supplies. He changed course to the southward—a prudent move, for fortune was unlikely to favor his single frigate in a second encounter with a full British squadron. Also he had formed a plan to ravage the sea lanes around Bermuda.

Meanwhile the frigate *Guerrière* had detached herself from Broke's squadron and was making for Halifax with a damaged foremast and a weary crew. Formerly French—she was captured off the Faroes in 1806—the *Guerrière* had become the butt of some derision in the Royal Navy, perhaps because of her comparatively large displacement; and a defensive note can be detected in the pride which John Dacres, her captain, reportedly confessed in her. But Dacres, an admiral's son eleven years younger than Hull, was possessed of that ineffable confidence in Britain's naval supremacy which, by blinding her officers to defective ships and overwhelming odds, so often contributed to her victories at sea. The *Guerrière* carried 49 guns. When Dacres, on the afternoon of August 19, identified a sail to windward as a superior-gunned American frigate, he ran up four flags at once and cleared his decks for action.

At 4:05 P.M. he tested the distance with a shot, then he ordered a starboard broadside. Hull meanwhile, gratified that on this occasion a solitary British frigate and his own occupied an empty sea, had reefed topsails and beat his crew to quarters. The first British shots flew harmlessly above the *Constitution*'s tops, but the *Guerrière* yawed in a rising sea to bring her port batteries to bear, and this time two shots struck home. Hull chose this moment to hoist American colors. For the next forty-five minutes both vessels maneuvered warily, yawing to rake with a broadside or putting about to avoid one, maintaining always a generally parallel course. Hull set more sail to overhaul, quickening the heartbeats of his men as they divined his intention of coming alongside and perceived no reluctance on the foe's part to let him try.

The *Constitution's* bows closed on the *Guerrière's* port quarter, drawing abeam of her. Both ships now rose and plunged less than 200 yards apart. The *Guerrière* fired again. A single shot struck the *Constitution's* bulwarks and an explosion of splinters pierced some of her crew. Hull stood on an arms chest and would not be hurried. To Lieutenant Morris' pointed request for permission to order the guns into action he gently replied that they would fire when the captain thought fit. "So stand ready," he told his first lieutenant, "and see that not a shot is thrown away." And not until the range had closed to a hundred yards did he give the word.

There followed for fifteen deafening minutes an exchange of broadsides, the weight of each of the *Constitution's* exceeding the *Guerrière's* by more than a hundred pounds. The British gunners, firing at unflagging pace, hurled most of their metal into the *Constitution's* tops. British shot which did strike the American's hull fell into the sea, it was afterward said, inspiring one of Hull's men to shout, "Huzza! Her sides are made of iron!" The story gave her an affectionate and immortal title: Old Ironsides. The American fire was more effectively synchronized with each falling swell. Repeated storms of shot weighing more than 600 pounds crashed into the *Guerrière's* hull above and below the water line, and at 6:20 her mizzenmast toppled over her disengaged side, dragging in the rough sea and swinging her about. Now Hull decided to cross her bows and lay his port side upon her. But the *Constitution's* own damaged rigging slowed her responses—Hull's tendency to delay every next move until he had wrung all possible advantage from the immediate one may also have been a factor. Raking the *Guerrière* with a last broadside which wrought fearful injury on her gun deck, the *Constitution* crossed her bows too closely and the *Guerrière's* bowsprit, clear to her gilded figurehead, loomed above the American quarterdeck. It swung downward as the *Guerrière* pitched, the jib boom snapping off on the *Constitution's* taffrail and flying into the sea. Again the bowsprit rose, fouling the *Constitution's* mizzen rigging, and with the two ships thus locked their crews prepared to board.

Dacres could muster on the forecastle no more than forty men, immediate targets for the riflemen in the *Constitution*'s giddy tops and massed on her quarterdeck. Yet the British musketry was fierce enough to deny the Americans a boarding as well. Lieutenant Morris, displaying the alacrity which had thrust him ahead of Decatur on the *Philadelphia*, jumped to the taffrail. A musket ball struck him in the stomach. Lieutenant William Bush of the marines leaped in his place, sword in hand, and was shot at once through the brain. But casualties on the British deck were heavier, especially among the brightly clad officers, and included Captain Dacres, wounded in the back while exhorting his crew from a conspicuous position on top of netted hammocks in the *Guerrière*'s forecastle.

While the musket duel clattered and the *Guerrière*'s bowsprit soared and fell through the *Constitution*'s rigging, the stunned gunners on the former's gun deck rallied, resuming fire with bow guns directed at the *Constitution*'s stern. So close were the vessels that either burning wads or the flash of discharging guns set fire to Captain Hull's cabin. As members of the crew were beating out the flames, the *Constitution*'s sails suddenly filled and she surged ahead, wrenching herself free from the probing bowsprit. The ships drifted apart, captains surveying their damage, but the wounded Dacres, scarcely able to continue in command, had no time to order the hampering mizzenmast cut loose before his defective foremast with all its tattered rigging lurched against the mainmast and together they collapsed over the side. Now the *Guerrière* was a riddled hulk, fallen masts crashing against her sides, heavy seas flooding through gun ports and shot holes, seventy-eight men dead and wounded on decks awash with crimson foam. Yet her captain, with something of Isaac Hull's tenacity, refused defeat until a last desperate effort to manage the vessel by securing a spritsail to the bowsprit failed when almost at once the wind tore it away.

The *Constitution*, her own rigging repaired and her fourteen casualties attended to, had come about and was waiting for the *Guerrière* as she drifted back into cannon shot, a forlorn English jack fluttering from the stump of her mizzenmast. A single shot to leeward betokened her surrender, whereupon Dacres was helped aboard the *Constitution* for the face-to-face ritual of proffered sword rejected by magnanimous victor. Nothing could be done to save the sinking *Guerrière*. Her wounded were taken off—a harrowing task in darkness and a stormy sea—with whatever could be saved of personal possessions. Care was taken to retrieve Captain Dacres' family Bible for him. The *Constitution*'s surgeon assisted his English counterpart in dressing the British wounded—amputations, he recorded, were two arms, a leg, and a thigh. At 3 P.M. next day the *Guerrière* was set on fire and half an hour later she blew up. In the evening, the dead of both ships were consigned to the deep.

Isaac Hull might have continued his cruise. He had been out only three weeks, his stores and water were ample, his crew self-confident. But the ship carried more than 250 prisoners and wounded. And Hull had a natural desire to report his success. It was, as far as he knew, the first sea victory of the war. He was not likely to overlook its significance. In forty minutes he had shattered the reputation for naval invincibility which the British had taken over two centuries to create. Yet Hull was modest enough to view the victory as novel rather than unique. What he had done other Americans might repeat. "They [the British] are not now fighting Frenchmen or Spaniards," he wrote. Thoughts of his brother and father must also have weighed in his decision to press sail for home. But news of a third relative, his uncle, awaited him in Boston. And it is one of the saddest ironies of the day that during his triumphal absence at sea the name of Hull had become the most execrated in America since that of Benedict Arnold.

On July 12 General William Hull and 2,500 American soldiers had crossed the river from Detroit and entered Canada as self-proclaimed bearers of "civil, political and religious liberty, and their necessary results, individual and general prosperity." But intermittent pockets of resistance and false reports of strong enemy reinforcements so disrupted the advance that at the end of the first week Hull had ordered an inglorious withdrawal. The humiliating climax came at Detroit less than a fortnight later when, without firing a shot, Hull surrendered the well-stocked garrison and all his men to a motley force of militia and Indians less than half their number. Hull's officers variously ascribed his astonishing conduct to fear, incompetence, and senility. "Everybody pronounces him a traitor," wrote a traveler in Ohio, "and if he was to attempt to pass this way he would be hunted and shot like a mad dog."

In the midst of this stormy national emotion, Commodore Rodgers' squadron was at last sighted off Boston. But all that Rodgers had to show for his seventy days' cruise was the capture of two brigs. Like the *Belvidera*, a second English ship had escaped him (on the very day Isaac Hull was engaging the *Guerrière*) after carrying away his fore-topmast studding sail with an impertinent shot. And half the *President*'s crew were down with scurvy. Rodgers submitted his report as a communication "barren of benefit," although that first cruise was in fact the reason why so much of America's seagoing trade had made harbor unmolested. Rodgers might have felt better had he known of the complaint of an officer on the *Guerrière* (before her fateful meeting with the *Constitution*) that "we have been so completely occupied looking out for Commodore Rodgers's squadron that we have taken very few prizes." Paul Hamilton attempted consolation by correctly reminding Rodgers that his cruise had forced the enemy's single ships away from American ports. Rodgers eventually claimed that this was his intention from the start, but continued privately to regret that the squadron had "scoured the whole Atlantic Ocean and ran the coast of Europe from the British Channel to Cape St. Vincent without having more committed to history than merely that our commerce benefited by it."

August 30, the day after the downcast commodore had anchored off Boston, the victorious Captain Hull arrived, to be greeted deliriously by citizens and to receive from brother officers plaudits laced with envy. Decatur congratulated him upon being "first in the race for renown." The exultation spread beyond Boston, partly smothering Federalist opposition to "Mr. Madison's War" and banishing the gloom left by the news from Detroit. It could not be said that the Navy had completely atoned for the Army's ignominy, the main fleet having returned empty-handed. The glory belonged to a single ship, a loyal crew, and an expert captain. Rumors of Isaac Hull's questionable prewar business enterprises, like the possible ill-effects of his kinship to a dishonored general, were quietly forgotten. The *Constitution*'s victory was a national tonic and, wrote Hamilton to her captain, "We know not which most to applaud, your gallantry or your skill."

Yet the hour was not one that Hull could wholeheartedly enjoy. Following the private blow of his uncle's disgrace came news of his brother's death on the day he had arrived in port. The upkeep of a number of fatherless children now devolved upon himself. He requested immediate relief of his command and a furlough. The *Constitution*'s crew, after begging him to stay, gave him an emotional farewell. They greeted his successor without enthusiasm. Some who had sailed with William Bainbridge before stated to his face their reluctance to serve under him again. But Bainbridge, who once boasted of being a man of outspoken disposition, seems to have borne this unflattering display of frankness by his inferiors with no outward resentment. He was not in any event easily embarrassed. The most likely effect was to strengthen his determination that in the present conflict, unlike those against France or Tripoli, his name would not be associated with surrender.

Isaac Hull, after four months in command of the Brooklyn Navy Yard, was assigned to the yard at Boston. By then he was happier, the result of another conquest. He wrote John Bullus about it. "The last frigate I had the good fortune to capture is as right a little boat as I could wish and suits me to a marlinspike. I only wish you could have seen more of her before I took my departure. I am sure you would have liked her construction." But the *Constitution* had been Isaac Hull's last fighting command. The whimsical allusion was to Anne Hart, a noted beauty and his new bride.

A week after the *Constitution*'s homecoming it was the *Essex*'s turn to drop anchor. She had left port on July 3, David Porter commanding. A man of delicate physique and impetuous nature, Porter was among those fond of long, unaccompanied cruising, but one feels that in his case the partiality sprang less from an aversion to shared glory than an explorer's curiosity and a strange attraction to the special challenge of lonely and protracted command. "A man of war is a petty kingdom governed by a petty despot," he was to write. "The little tyrant, strutting his few fathoms of scoured plank, dare not unbend, lest he should lose that appearance of respect from his inferiors which their fears inspire. He has therefore no society, no smile, no courtesies for or from anyone. He stands alone, without the friendship or sympathy of one on board; a solitary being in the midst of the ocean." It would be hard to obtain a more poignant glimpse of a captain under sail.

On sailing, Porter ordered course for Bermuda, seeing nothing of the enemy en route until near the island, where he fell in with a British convoy of seven troopships. It is an indication of British naval deficiency in western waters then that their sole escort was the 36-gun *Minerva*, a frigate weaker than the *Essex*, which was powerfully armed with short-range carronades. Under cover of night Porter succeeded in making off with a vessel carrying 200 soldiers. He sent her in with a prize crew and during the next week captured nine more ships. On August 13 the *Essex* posed as a merchantman and lured the sloop *Alert* into a double broadside. Porter's laconic account of the episode can scarcely be improved upon. The *Alert* "ran down on our weather quarter, gave three cheers, and commenced an action (if so trifling a skirmish deserves the name) and after eight minutes, struck her colors, with but water in her hold, much cut to pieces, and three men wounded." He ordered her guns thrown overboard, transferred his prisoners to her, and sent them into Halifax with the signed agreement of the British captain to the parole of an equal number of Americans.

Porter's first cruise lasted sixty days. By the close of it Paul Hamilton was issuing orders reflecting a change in policy toward the separate offensive patrols. Ships of war were now to be divided into three small squadrons under Rodgers, Decatur, and Bainbridge, their task to "protect our trade and annoy the enemy." While Hamilton left the duration and course of each cruise to the commodores, he enjoined them to return home as quickly as possible, "consistent with the great objects in view," and to keep the Department frequently informed. On October 8 the *President, Congress, United States,* and *Argus* put out from Boston. Three days later the brig veered south for the Caribbean, the frigates holding course eastward. When they separated it was according to plan, but one can imagine with what relief Decatur on the *United States* set off alone. Almost immediately he brought to and boarded a Philadelphia-bound merchantman and, on the pretext that her cargo included British goods, sent her into Norfolk for inspection by his prize agents, Wheeler and Tazewell. It was a rather highhanded seizure, suggesting not so much an eagerness for prize money—it would have been trifling in this case—as for some positive action. But he did not have to wait long for the real thing. Early on October 25, off the Madeiras, his topmen descried a British warship twelve miles to windward and steadily approaching.

The commodore's impulse was to gain tactical advantage by wresting the weather gauge from her, that is, getting his own ship to windward of the foe. But the Englishman, no less determined to keep it, quickly hauled his ship by the wind. Decatur was not so blessed with measured self-control as Isaac Hull and he opened the action too soon. His first shots tumbled short. But when next he ordered fire, after impatiently waiting for suitable range, the *United States'* long twenty-fours thundered almost as one, and their shot tore the enemy ship's rigging to pieces and swept her mizzenmast into the sea.

Decatur could not know it, but he and his opponent had already met. In Norfolk early that same year Littleton Tazewell had presented to him Captain John Surnam Carden of the 38-gun frigate *Macedonian*, then at anchor in Hampton Roads. Samuel Leech of the *Macedonian*'s crew afterward recalled hearing the two jocularly wager the outcome of a sea fight between them should war happen. Carden, whom Leech remembered as a savage martinet (possibly confusing him with his predecessor, a captain cashiered for tyranny), had served without distinction against the French Navy and Irish rebels, and was brave but hardly astute. Through overanxiety to keep the weather gauge of the American ship, he lost his one opportunity to bring her under attack from his thirty-two-pound carronades. At 10 A.M., recovering from his foe's opening broadsides, he bore up and tried to close with the wind on his port quarter. Decatur backed his mizzen-topsail, allowed the lame *Macedonian* to crawl within a hundred yards of him, then raked her thoroughly once more.

The war was to confirm the excellence of American gunnery. Britain's officers, from motives of economy or delusions of infinite superiority, had long neglected the need for regular drill. Operating the great guns was a complicated business, from the ramming home of wad and shot to the application of a slow match to the touchhole. (In neither the American nor the British Navy was the more efficient friction primer yet in general use.) For effective fire all functions had to be performed with smooth rapidity and perfect timing. Amid gloom, clamor, and confusion, on a vessel which might be violently pitching and rolling, the cramped gun divisions often achieved an almost poetic fluidity of motion—but only after they had been frequently drilled over long periods at sea. Since the days of Preble and

Truxtun, exercise at the great guns had been, even in peacetime, an important essential of an American warship's routine. The deplorable helplessness of the *Chesapeake* before the *Leopard* (Barron's and Gordon's gunners had, after all, been on board for many days although it was their first at sea) proved the perils of neglecting it. Decatur, zealously supported by Lieutenant William Allen, had organized a vigorous program of gunnery practice on the *Chesapeake*: when, with many of her old crew and officers—including Allen, now first lieutenant—he transferred to the *United States*, the policy was continued.

Ships' guns bore affectionate nicknames. Those on the *United States* included Glory, Lion, Sally Mathews, Brother Jonathan, Torment, Jumping Billy, Bruiser, Nelson, Bulldog, Happy Jack, Long Nose Nancy. But there was nothing frivolous about the damage and slaughter they inflicted. "Grapeshot and canister poured through our portholes like leaden hail," writes Leech. "The large shot came against the ship's side, shaking her to the very keel, passing through her timbers and scattering terrible splinters." More than one-third of Carden's crew became casualties—forty-three dead and sixty-one wounded, including the first lieutenant. "Our men fought like tigers," says Leech. Yet their fire caused only a dozen American casualties, five fatal, and trivial injury to the spars and rigging. The *Macedonian*, however, was a pitiful sight. Her mizzenmast, foremast, and mainmast were gone, over a hundred shot had struck her hull, all her guns on the engaged side had been wrenched or shaken from their mounts, and those on the main deck were plunging under with each roll of the sea.

"My ship lay an unmanageable log on the ocean" was Carden's explanation of his surrender. Even had she been sinking, it is probable that Decatur would have tried to save her; having been beaten by Hull in "the race for renown," he was acutely alert to the special glory awaiting the first American to bring home intact a captured British frigate. "She is a beauty," he exulted to Bullus on his arrival at New London with her, "good for sore eyes." Indeed she was, and the many huge scars in her new oak had not obliterated the sharp, handsome lines or effaced all elegance from her figurehead bust of Alexander the Great.

Guided by the "two damn good Hell Gate pilots" whom he had

spurred the agent to send him, he sailed the *United States* with her prize down Long Island Sound and received a New York welcome as exhilarating as any ticker-tape effusion of our time. The celebrations continued into the new year. On January 8 more than 400 chilled but happy tars paraded along Wall Street behind their own officers and a French band liberated from the *Macedonian*. At the theater that night (where they were entertained by a transparency of the battle and a chorus of pretty actresses) Sam Leech, who had conveniently transferred his allegiance from the British flag to the American, was "much struck with the appearance of Decatur as he sat in full uniform, his pleasant face flushed." The commodore had been honored with the freedom of New York, and Thomas Sully would paint his portrait for the City Hall. His native Philadelphia was to present him with a second gold sword. A New York bank planned to issue dollar bills commemorating his victory. His three-twentieths share of the prize money was expected to total $30,000. Such tangibles of glory might have heightened the color even of men less infatuated with it.

The capital celebrated too. Decatur had hurried Lieutenant Archibald Hamilton, the Secretary's son, south with dispatches and a dramatic memento of the battle. The most notable event of the Washington social season as the year 1812 ended had promised to be nothing livelier than the marriage of Captain Thomas Tingey to a lady thirty-three years younger. Now naval developments more thrilling than the nuptials of the Navy Yard's gay commandant offered cause for festivity. With excellent timing, young Hamilton arrived on the date of a ball at Tomlinson's honoring Captains Charles Stewart, Isaac Hull, and the newly promoted Charles Morris. The lieutenant's news was the excuse for citywide illumination, and patriotic excitement rose to a delirious pitch when he appeared at the ball with the *Macedonian*'s colors and gallantly placed them at the feet of the President's wife.

Seven days prior to Decatur's victory the sloop *Wasp*, Master-Commandant Jacob Jones, had won an action off Albemarle Sound that has since occupied a relatively minor place in the chronicle of naval engagements but was as fiercely contested as any. Approximately equal in strength, the *Wasp* and the British sloop *Frolic* drenched each other with broadsides at close range and in rough seas until the *Wasp* was dismasted and more than half the *Frolic*'s crew of some 140 dead or wounded. Jones, almost immediately afterward, was forced to surrender his battered sloop to a British ship of the line. But the news of his victory heightened the exultation at home in the closing weeks of 1812, and thanks to a prisoner exchange in Bermuda he was enabled to participate with Decatur and Hull in the general celebrations. And then it was the turn of Captain William Bainbridge.

In its search for a profitable sea policy the administration had recovered somewhat from its summer floundering and decided on a raiding expedition in fertile waters. For this purpose a light squadron was formed under Bainbridge, consisting of his *Constitution*, the sloop *Hornet*, and the light frigate *Essex*, and ordered to the Indian Ocean. The ships were to meet in mid-Atlantic, but the *Constitution* and *Hornet*, missing the *Essex* at two prearranged rendezvous, continued southward. On December 14, the *Essex*, disguised as a merchantman and flying British colors, reached the second island meeting place, Fernando de Noronha, and there found a letter that Bainbridge, posing as British, had left addressed to Sir James Yeo of His Britannic Majesty's ship *Southampton*. Porter, also passing himself off as British, lulled the Portuguese governor with wine and cheese, then took the letter to his ship. He read: "My Dear Mediterranean Friend, probably you may stop here. Don't attempt to water; it is attended with too much difficulty. I learned before I left England that you were bound to the Brazil coast; if so, we may meet at Bahia or Rio de Janeiro. I should be happy to meet and converse on our old affairs of captivity. Recollect our secret in those times. Your friend of His Majesty's ship, *Acasta*, Kerr." Porter, familiar with Bainbridge's "secret," called for a lighted candle, and upon application of its heat the real message emerged. "I am bound off Bahia, thence off Cape Frio, where I intend to cruise until the 1st of January. Go off Cape Frio, to the northward of Rio de Janeiro, and keep a lookout for me. Your friend."

This latest employment of Bainbridge's favorite form of subterfuge had for its object the concentration of his little squadron for the East Indies. But David Porter's preference for cruising singly was undiminished even by the prospect of sailing with his old commander, and after dutifully calling at Cape Frio without finding him he searched farther for only a week before feeling free to pursue an independent course. The *Constitution* and *Hornet* meanwhile had arrived off Bahia and found an enemy sloop, *Bonne Citoyenne*, at anchorage. When the British captain, safeguarding the valuable specie he had just taken on board for England, refused to be drawn by a challenge from Master Commandant James Lawrence of the *Hornet*, Bainbridge left her to blockade him (provoking the usual irritability between the United States consul and a neutral government) and stood for sea. Late on December 29, some thirty miles from the Brazilian coast, the *Constitution* sighted the *Java*.

A refitted French prize, the *Java* was laden with stores for the British fleet off Bombay and also carried the newly appointed Governor of India and his staff. They were the guests of capable officers; few British captains were more distinguished for skill and gallantry than Henry Lambert, and he was suitably matched by his first lieutenant, Henry Ducie Chads. On the other hand, only a fraction of the *Java*'s crew had served on a man-of-war before. Many were impressed malcontents from the merchant service, some not averse, it was said, to sabotaging the guns. The *Java* mounted 47, and she was that many days out of Spithead on her passage to India when a shot hurtled across her bow from a vessel to leeward. Through his glass Lambert could see the American colors at the main-topgallant masthead and at the mizzen peak, with a commodore's broad pendant streaming from the main and a jack at the fore. He cleared his decks, hoisted his own colors, and replied with a broadside. The ships lay half a mile apart, the wind was a light northeaster, and the time 2 P.M.

Fifteen minutes later they were passing on opposite tacks trading heavy broadsides. Marksmen were firing from the tops too and an early musket ball struck Bainbridge in the hip. He was also wounded in the thigh by a copper bolt, a piece of langrage whose full force shattered the wheel. But far worse wounds could not have torn him from command now. He sent men rushing two decks below to work the tiller by tackles, and although the *Java* managed to cross the *Constitution*'s stern and swept her decks with shot, it was the only telling blow he allowed her to deliver. Goaded by memory, determined, it cannot be doubted, that never again under any circumstances would he submit without fighting, Bainbridge set the *Con-*

Escape of the *Constitution* from a British squadron, July 17-19, 1812. From a painting by Tuckerman, in possession of the Knickerbocker Club, New York City. *United States Navy*

After the fight between the *Java* and the *Constitution*, December 29, 1812. The *Java* completely dismasted. From a colored aquatint by R. and D. Havell, after N. Pocock. *Courtesy of the National Maritime Museum, London*

Two views of the engagement between the *United States* and the *Macedonian*, October 25, 1812. *(Above)* The opening shots. Oil painting by T. Whitcombe. *Courtesy of the National Maritime Museum, London. (Below)* The *Macedonian* crippled. Artist: Thomas Birch. *Henderson Collection, courtesy of the Philadelphia Maritime Museum*

stitution's fore and mainsail and closed rapidly with the *Java* until his starboard batteries could rake her fore and aft. Shot tore away her jib boom and bowsprit and left her rigging tattered, but scarcely bothering to survey the results of his gunnery, Bainbridge wore the *Constitution* cleverly behind a screen of smoke to a position two cable lengths off the foe's starboard bow and raked her again. At 3:05 the Englishman's foremast crashed through the forecastle. The vessels closed until the *Constitution*'s rigging snared the stump of the *Java*'s bowsprit. Lambert, desperate in a confusion of smoke, blood, and flying splinters, called for boarders. The attempt was never made. Almost simultaneously the *Java*'s main-topmast fell, her gaff and spanker went over the side, and a musket ball struck Lambert in the breast. The *Java*'s physician, probing his captain's wound under fire, deduced that splinters must have pierced the lung. Lieutenant Chads then took command and, though himself seriously wounded, maintained it until the last gun fired.

The *Constitution* clung relentlessly to the *Java*'s starboard quarter. Dead and dying seamen and boys clogged the British gun deck and only with difficulty now could a few batteries be brought to bear. The *Constitution*'s seemed never to rest. At 3:55 the *Java*'s mizzenmast fell and, hanging over the side, caught fire from gun flashes as the two ships lay side by side. At last the *Constitution*, having, in Chads's words, "effectively done her work," hauled away for Bainbridge to assess her damage. Some thirty of his crew were casualties. The *Java* meanwhile had begun to roll, gun muzzles plunging into the sea. But her dazed crew, under the lieutenant's firm control, hacked away the burning mizzenmast, cleared several gun divisions of their bloody debris, and endeavored to get before the wind by setting sails on jury masts. This had not been completed when the mainmast began to sway, threatening to fall inboard. Chads ordered it cut down. And at 5:25 the *Constitution* bore again on the ravaged *Java*. Now Chads's casualties were well above a hundred, half of them fatal. Some of his men had defiantly tacked colors to the stump of the mizzenmast. But the lieutenant was not a man to prolong useless slaughter, and he surrendered at 5:55.

After removing the British crew and passengers to his ship, Bainbridge ordered the *Java* burned. Victory must have tasted sweet to the commodore's long-embittered soul right then, but the cost in blood just as assuredly offended his humane instincts. And it was with genuine sorrow that he returned the vanquished's surrendered sword to Captain Lambert as the Englishman lay dying on a cot in the shade of an awning on the *Constitution*'s quarterdeck.

Ridding one's ship of prisoners at the earliest opportunity was, from standpoints of hygiene and victuals, more a necessity than a concession of war. Bainbridge paroled his at Bahia and decided, in view of the *Constitution*'s injuries, to postpone the eastern cruise. He was also, we may be sure, acutely eager to return home and accept the country's plaudits. But he had sailed before Decatur brought in the *Macedonian* and he was surprised, even dismayed, to discover on his arrival at Boston in February 1813 that his was the third, not the second, frigate victory. The inspiring novelty of naval coups was not likely to wear off so long as Army communiqués from Buffalo and Albany repeated each other in terms of misplanning and retreat. Thus, after a parade from Long Wharf to the Exchange Coffee House with an escort of the Boston Light Infantry, Bainbridge received his due quota of cheers, banquets, oratory, and congressional awards. Yet to his annoyance he frequently found himself sharing the public's acclaim with Isaac Hull, with Decatur—whose duty, he told a friend, had been to destroy the capture, not deplete his own ship with a prize crew for her—and even with John Rodgers, whose second cruise, of 11,000 miles, would have been almost a total embarrassment had not one of the two prizes taken by the *President* been carrying $200,000 in gold and silver. William Bainbridge knew he had fought bravely and brilliantly. He could feel confident of a worthy place in posterity. But he would have undoubtedly felt happier had there been no others to diffuse the aim and intensity of the applause of his countrymen, which, as he truthfully admitted, "has for me greater charms than all the gold that glitters."

CHAPTER SEVENTEEN

The Loss of the *Chesapeake*

ALTHOUGH THE FORMAL HOST was Captain Charles Stewart (who long afterward recalled spending three years' salary on preparations), the idea for a public ball on board the *Constellation*, moored in the Washington Navy Yard, had been conceived by Paul Hamilton to woo congressional sympathy for his naval expansion policies. Sad to say, on the decorated frigate in the presence of President and Mrs. Madison and some six hundred congressmen and other guests, the Secretary of the Navy was quite obviously drunk. And at a subsequent ball onshore to repay naval hospitality—the function enlivened by his son's appearance with the *Macedonian's* flag—Hamilton's inebriety was even more noticeable. His servility to the decanter was no secret in Washington (the French Minister wrote home that for two years Hamilton had been unable to perform any duties after each midday meal), and the service also knew of it. No energy could be expected from the present incumbent at the Department, David Porter told a friend, "while a pint of whisky can be purchased in the District of Columbia." The addicted Secretary was an affront to many high-minded congressmen and thereby a considerable obstacle to his own program. On December 29, 1812, a few weeks after the *Constellation* ball, the President had to inform him that the price Congress demanded for continued support of the Navy was a soberer grip on the Department's helm. He did not dispute Hamilton's claims to credit for rebuilt ships, retrenched expenses, even the frigate victories now exciting the nation. But he had to request his resignation. Quietly Hamilton retired to the seclusion of South Carolina plantation life and on January 8, 1813, the President nominated William Jones as fourth Secretary of the Navy.

Jones, a Philadelphia merchant who had served in youth on board a privateer commanded by Thomas Truxtun, brought a fresh attitude to the Department. He favored the concentration of naval power in fleets of ships of the line, evinced a keen interest in the problems of shipbuilders, and paid more attention than had any of his predecessors to scientific experiment. A handsome man who liked the company of intelligent women, he had extravagant personal habits and lived almost continuously above his means. Charles Goldsborough, chief clerk since Stoddert's day, resigned soon after Jones took office, probably because the new Secretary disapproved of his popularity with the older clique of officers and the self-importance he had acquired from running the Department during Hamilton's lengthy indispositions. Goldsborough was replaced by Benjamin Homans, a bureaucrat who never sought the same intimacy with professional men and who evidently believed, as Jones seems to have, that naval officers literally had no business off the quarterdeck.

Paul Hamilton, who had begun his office without a single vessel capable of a twelve months' voyage, left his successor a sturdy, seagoing naval force and by his unsung departure had cleared the way for a stronger one. On January 2 a bill passed Congress authorizing four 74-gun ships of the line and six more 44-gun frigates. Authority for six 22-gun sloops was added three months later. The national legislature's abrupt discovery of the naval facts of life was too much for the saltier of the country's pair of retired Presidents. "Oh! The wisdom!" taunted John Adams. "The foresight and the hindsight and the rightsight and the leftsight; the northsight and the westsight that appeared in that august assembly." Forsaking sarcasm for humility, Adams went on to confess a special pride in every naval achievement, and he could look upon the captains as "my sons, and enjoy every laurel they acquire as much as if it were obtained by my sons, by nature."

One of the "sons" was finding the laurels dismayingly elusive. So far John Rodgers had won no battle honors, nor was his record of merchant prizes outstanding. The total value of ships taken on the

President's and *Congress*' latest voyage in company did not exceed the record of the little brig *Argus*, Master-Commandant Arthur Sinclair, which reported into Boston three days after the frigates with five prizes worth $200,000. The prize-money partnership between Rodgers and Stephen Decatur was dissolved at the latter's request, and after Rodgers chased and lost an enemy sloop on the third cruise, it was Captain John Smith's turn to part company with him. On the fourth departure, Smith took his ship, the *Congress*, southward out of Boston, leaving the *President* to maintain the eastward course alone.

The British had assigned only the 38-gun frigate *Shannon* to patrol the approaches to Boston, on the wishful assumption that New England's antiwar sentiments did not afford a welcome harbor for the American Navy. But now, with American warships coming and going as they pleased, the blockade might be expected to tighten. It was therefore advisable to clear the harbor of those valuable vessels able to move. The *Constitution*'s battle damage was still unrepaired, but the *Chesapeake*, not long returned from a virtually uneventful cruise of 122 days, was ready for sea again. However, her captain, Samuel Evans, had gone blind in one eye and his other was failing. Therefore, in the first week of May 1813, the Secretary redirected the *Chesapeake*'s new sailing orders from Evans to Captain James Lawrence, who had wanted the *Constitution*, now the Navy's favorite. He had lately displayed vigorous qualities of command. After a British 74 had chased his brig *Hornet* from the mouth of Bahia Harbor, where she was blockading the *Bonne Citoyenne*, he had beat up the Brazilian coast and fallen in with the *Peacock*, an enemy brig spruced and gleaming as befitted her name. But the skill of her gunners proved less sparkling than her paint and polish, while Lawrence's guns fired so rapidly they required constant dousing to cool them. In fifteen minutes the proud *Peacock* was a sinking wreck, and she took twelve men including her captain to the bottom. After that, Lawrence was confident that he deserved the *Constitution*, and he might have had her if she had been fit, for Bainbridge was now supervising the building of a new 74. Certainly Lawrence did not want the *Chesapeake*. Nothing had occurred to free that vessel from her stigma of bad luck. Accidents, routine on other ships, when they befell the *Chesapeake* became proofs of the evil spell she sailed under. Even as she entered harbor from her latest voyage, a topmast fell into the sea, drowning the topmen who clung to it. Thus she still claimed her victims, and seamen shrank from service aboard her. Lawrence was without superstition—he had studied for the bar before joining the Navy—but he knew the difficulty of enlisting satisfactory men, and he appealed for some other command, even if it meant retention of the brig *Hornet*. The request was refused.

Shortly after midday on June 1 Lawrence mustered the *Chesapeake*'s new crew on her spar deck before putting out to meet the *Shannon*. The British ship waited motionless on the shimmering horizon about twenty miles east of Boston Light. In bright sunshine Lawrence ran up a flag bearing the motto "Free Trade and Sailors' Rights" which no more inspired the *Chesapeake*'s men than the short address he delivered, which they several times interrupted. Some of them chose this moment to demand prize money owed them from previous cruises. Morally and physically, few were combat-fit. Many were foreigners, to whom appeals for allegiance were meaningless. Even Lawrence's officers were a doubtful quantity. The first lieutenant was ashore dying of a lung ailment, the second also ashore and sick. To the third, Augustus Ludlow, aged twenty and untried at the business of breaking in new crews, fell the responsibility for running the ship under her captain. He was assisted by a midshipman hurriedly promoted to acting lieutenant. To develop the mutual understanding necessary for the establishment and maintenance of discipline on a sailing ship of war was a slow process requiring many days of cruising. The *Chesapeake* under Lawrence was allotted but hours. There was no time for gunnery exercise, no time for officers and men to get accustomed to each other, no time for either to become familiar with the ship. Little enough time even for the seamen sleeping off their eve-of-sailing drunkenness in odd corners of the ship to waken and stand erect.

It is possible to blame the unprepared state of Lawrence's *Chesapeake*—and James Barron's had scarcely been worse—on an administration which paid its seamen poor salaries and delayed authorization of their prize money. One feels bound also to question Lawrence's intelligence in taking the poorly manned frigate out in broad daylight—the *President* and *Congress* had sensibly escaped at night—to an early, inescapable contest. Was he so deluded by the American victories, especially his own easy conquest of the *Peacock*, that he believed the *Chesapeake*, notwithstanding her half-mutinous crew and the inadequacies of her lieutenants, a match for any British ship? This has been suggested by some historians. But it implies an unprofessional, puffed-up confidence nowhere to be found in a letter he had just written to Master-Commandant James Biddle, declaring his intention to sail "providing I have a chance of getting out clear of the *Shannon* and the *Tenedos*, who are on the lookout." Perhaps a decisive factor was the presence of spectators. The *Shannon* was visible from the shore. Crowds had thronged the wharf when he took leave of his two sons, and a host of pleasure craft followed in the *Chesapeake*'s wake. To have delayed sailing, or to have crept out furtively after dark, besides being odious to Lawrence's nature, would have shamed New England watchers who supported the war and would certainly have amused the majority, who were openly pro-British Federalists. Out of patriotism no less than vanity, Captain Lawrence had an audience to consider.

He ordered prize moneys issued to the most aggrieved complainants among his crew and looked anxiously for an improvement in their dependability. At roughly the same time, Captain Philip Bowes Vere Broke, on the *Shannon*'s quarterdeck, gestured at the American frigate coming out and exhorted his crew to "let them know there are Englishmen who still know how to fight. Fire into her quarters, main deck into main deck, quarterdeck into quarterdeck. Kill the men, and the ship is yours."

Long supremacy on the high seas had begun to breed in the British a dangerous complacency. Its manifestations ranged from inertia in the halls of the Admiralty to the abandonment of regular gun-division drill on the oceans. Philip Broke belonged to the diminishing band of Royal Navy captains who still upheld the highest standards of discipline and efficiency. Broke's uninterrupted command of the *Shannon* since 1806 had made her one of the best-managed vessels under any flag. Weather or warfare permitting, his men exercised her fifty-two guns daily, twice a week firing at targets—casks usually—thrown into the sea. Shortly before commencing her vigil off Boston, she was struck by a lightning bolt which split masts, melted chains, and set her tops afire. Broke's crew quickly recovered from their instinctive fear and extinguished the flames. The same discipline was in evidence now as the *Shannon* and *Chesapeake* closed off Cape Ann. At 4 P.M. the American ship, from a distance of seven miles, fired one of her forty-nine guns, signaling a readiness to engage. But the English gunners registered no haste. They waited, obedient to Broke's firm order not to fire while the enemy kept his bows toward them. Not until 5:45, with the *Chesapeake* now off the *Shannon*'s starboard beam, did Broke order fire. His tense divisions cheered, and the main deck guns thundered in quick succession.

A torrent of shot swept the *Chesapeake* and she vanished momentarily in a cloud of smoke and flying debris. Her gun deck rallied and fired back immediately. But her quarterdeck was grievously stricken. Captain Lawrence, Lieutenant Ludlow, the fourth lieutenant, sailing master, and boatswain were all killed instantly or mortally wounded. The second and third lieutenants were below at the guns. With a dazed midshipman commanding the quarterdeck, with dead men at her helm and her jib sheet cut, the *Chesapeake* came up into the wind and drifted into her adversary, her quarter grinding the *Shannon*'s side just forward of the starboard main chain. A British boatswain tried to lash the vessels together. An American cutlass descended and his right arm flew off.

But the *Chesapeake* had been struck fifty-seven times in repeated broadsides. All but ten of her forty-four marines were dead or wounded, her seamen leaderless and demoralized. When Lawrence, bleeding from knee and abdomen, gasped for boarders, his words, if heard, were virtually ignored. The confusion worsened when a munitions chest on the quarterdeck was struck by a grenade from the *Shannon*'s maintop and exploded. Lawrence, now in dreadful agony, was borne to the cockpit, where he implored his men to fire faster and not to give up the ship—brave words for posterity and naval tradition but of little avail as some fifty men of the *Shannon*, led by their captain, came swarming over the bulwarks to the American quarterdeck. There were valiant flashes of resistance. A pistol ball narrowly missed Broke's head and it cost the American chaplain who fired it an arm almost severed by the Englishman's broadsword. Second Lieutenant George Budd called all hands to repel boarders. Perhaps a dozen responded, but they were quickly scattered while Budd was knocked down the main hatch. Lieutenant Ludlow dragged his dying body up on deck and was further mutilated by saber blows. And all the while, high above the bloody tumult, men in the *Chesapeake*'s mizzentop and maintop exchanged musket fire with those in the *Shannon*'s foretop and maintop. The enmeshed rigging of the two vessels suddenly parted, leaving Broke's boarding party momentarily stranded on enemy decks, but the American crew were beyond noticing opportunities for recovery. Pursued forward to the forecastle, a few turned to fight at bay, and a cutlass stroke opened Captain Broke's skull almost to the brain. At the same time an inadvertent shot from his own ship decapitated the British first lieutenant in the act of hauling down the American ensign. But fifteen minutes after the boarding, all resistance ceased. Though the *Chesapeake* did not formally surrender—in her whole career she struck once, under Barron in peacetime—the British were undoubtedly in possession of her, even of her valuable signal book, shotted for casting overboard and left forgotten on the cabin table.

Sixty-one died on board the *Chesapeake*. The *Shannon*, whose fatalities were about half that number, towed her into Halifax, where Lawrence and Ludlow were buried with full military honors—their remains were returned to Boston under flag of truce six weeks later for reburial. Philip Broke, never to recover wholly from his wound, sailed home to a celebration whose fervid extravagance—including guns fired from the Tower of London and a knighthood for himself—attested to Britain's eagerness to reverse the humiliating series of American naval triumphs. The country's joyful relief got an additional fillip from news that an intensified blockade of the American coast had bottled up the *United States* and the prize frigate *Macedonian* in the Thames River, Connecticut. But exultation was brief: only two months after the *Chesapeake*'s defeat, the young lieutenant who, from her decks, had fired the first, forlorn shot at a British ship, the *Leopard*, was causing the utmost consternation in London's business and insurance houses.

The 18-gun brig *Argus*, Lieutenant William Henry Allen, had brought over William Crawford, the new American Minister to France, and Department orders next bade Allen to conduct an offensive in the enemy's coastal waters. By this means William Jones, the Secretary of the Navy, hoped to bring the war home decisively to the British. After landing the envoy at L'Orient, Allen spent the next thirty days beating up and down the Irish Sea, capturing or burning two and a half million dollars worth of ships and cargo. Had the cruise of the *Argus* continued, it might well have fulfilled Jones's stated expectations of a service to the country surpassing that ever performed by any other single vessel. But at 5 A.M. on August 14, off the Welsh coast, Lieutenant Allen sighted the 21-gun British brig *Pelican*.

She was of heavier tonnage than the *Argus* and it must have been obvious to Allen that his fast-sailing brig could easily outdistance her. For him to avoid engaging a superior ship would have been perfectly compatible with his important mission of crippling British trade. But instead he waited for the *Pelican* to come down. Perhaps he could do no other. The clue lies in the intensity of his privately expressed contempt for Commodore Barron's conduct on the *Chesapeake*. Allen was an officer in bondage to a pride so rigid, a code of honor so repressive, they allowed small latitude for decision. That his fiercely held principles should have obscured practical common sense and the promise of patriotic benefit at this moment was particularly disastrous, for only the previous day the *Argus* had taken a wine-laden brig out of Oporto, and before burning her many of the American crew had got at her cargo.

Five minutes after the opening fire a round shot from the *Pelican* carried off Allen's leg. He fainted and was taken below. Four minutes later his second in command was struck in the head by grapeshot. The *Pelican* outweighed the *Argus* by about seventy tons, but was not overwhelmingly superior in gun power. Yet the *Argus'* gunners did very little damage to her, whereas their ship was quickly rendered unmanageable and on the first sign of a British boarding party she surrendered. Considering the well-founded reports of Lieutenant Allen's zeal for gunnery drill, it is difficult to disregard the stories that some of his crew were too drunk to carry out their duties. It can be said that a highly profitable cruise had come to an unnecessary end. Allen did not survive to shed further light on the reasons. He died in Mill Prison Hospital, Plymouth, on August 18 after intense physical pain, which his British captors declared he endured without complaint, his consciousness fixed only upon the loss of his ship. Eight British captains acted as pallbearers at his funeral.

That same summer of 1813 the *President's* third cruise had ranged from the Grand Banks to the Azores, thence north to the Shetlands and eastward to the Norwegian coast. In the course of it Commodore Rodgers pursued another phantom Jamaica fleet for a week and was himself pursued for eighty hours by two sail which he took to be a British line-of-battle ship and a frigate, but which were in fact two far smaller craft. He lingered in Scandinavian waters for two weeks— now hoping to intercept the Archangel fleet—unaware that his former protégé was not far distant and by contrast busily engaged in fruitful seas. The commodore's apparent reluctance to enter them resists charitable explanation unless one bears in mind his concealed and hampering caution, and it is not much easier to visualize him as the object of an anxious and widespread British hunt. Yet this he was, according to confidential enemy documents taken from one of his twelve prizes, the modest score after a cruise lasting 147 days. "Rodgers has twice traversed over more than half the globe," a contemporary American journal noted, "without ever meeting a British frigate. He has sought them in their own seas, and along their own shores; but he has never yet had the good fortune to bring one to action. And with all this he suffers no diminution of reputation." The public, of course, was not to know how often the *President* had altered course to skirt rather than penetrate the very waters where the enemy's merchant ships, if not his frigates, might best be come upon.

In any case, the return of John Rodgers from his latest luckless cruise coincided with a renewed burst of acclaim for the Navy. On September 4 the little veteran *Enterprise* had engaged the brig *Boxer* off the Maine coast in an action more significant than might have been supposed from the comparatively few fatalities—though these were serious enough and included the two commanders, Lieutenant William Burrows of the *Enterprise* and Captain Blyth, six times wounded in sea fights with the French. The *Enterprise*'s deadly sustained fire crippled the *Boxer* in thirty minutes, and the shock forced upon the British for the first time some intense self-inquiry. The fact had to be faced that the *Boxer*'s loss was due to the enemy's better fire control. The London *Times* declared it to be only too true that "the Americans have some superior mode of firing; and we cannot be too anxiously employed in discerning to what circumstances that superiority is owing." No longer could the alarming truths be ignored. The Royal Navy, in vessels, guns, quality of strategy, and perhaps discipline, had deteriorated. The omniscience of the Lords of the Admiralty, the valor of the captains, the stoutness of British ships and of the hearts of those who manned them, were suddenly perceived as fallible or inadequate. It was eight years since Trafalgar. No guarantee existed that the naval supremacy achieved there would endure of its own right. Arrogance and too handy a recall of past glories were no substitutes for constant research in pursuit of improvements in gunnery, tactics, ship design, men, and matériel. On British acceptance of such distasteful verities was to be based the construction programs and organizational reforms which would influence her command of the waves for the next seventy-five years. By compelling her to this enlightenment, American warships and seamen made their contribution to her historic naval eminence. This was scarcely to be appreciated at the time, of course—certainly not by the British, who were shaken, hard upon the news of the *Boxer*'s defeat, by yet more incredible signs that their Navy could not even be counted upon for continued mastery of the North American Great Lakes.

CHAPTER EIGHTEEN

The Battle of Lake Erie

> The command of the lakes is obviously of the greatest importance.
>
> —James Madison, August 27, 1812

> The Government has at last awakened to its duty with respect to command of the lakes.
>
> —Governor Tompkins of New York, September 9, 1812

SINCE THE PRESIDENT was no fool, control of the vast waterways through which the British supplied their western armies and Indian auxiliaries was from the start among his principal objectives. At first he had calculated on gaining it by military invasion. Then, after Detroit, he felt that the government had been "misled" into relying upon land operations exclusively. At the emergency cabinet meeting to discuss General Hull's surrender, he authorized the creation of a Great Lakes naval force, not with its own powers of initiative, of course, but to support, as necessary, future land operations under Hull's successor, General William Harrison.

Daniel Dobbin, a veteran Great Lakes navigator who had brought the bad news from Detroit to Washington, was given the service rank of sailing master and sent back to Lake Erie with orders to begin building a flotilla. But Lake Ontario was expected to be the scene of greatest activity. To control it was to dominate all the western supply routes and hold the fate of militia, regulars, Indians, ships, and gar-

risons from the St. Lawrence to the upper lakes and the bivouacs of
the Michigan Territory. At the beginning of the war six British
vessels, mounting in all seventy-eight guns, were based on Kingston
while thirty-five miles across the water, off the bleak settlement of
Sackets Harbor, the Americans faced them with a single 16-gun brig,
the *Oneida*. The British had tried early to eliminate this vessel and
what facilities existed for adding more, but their attack had melted
away before the *Oneida*'s batteries, reinforced by an old thirty-two-
pound cannon that naval personnel had dug out of the mud.

Isaac Chauncey brought to over-all command of the Great Lakes
naval force managerial and organizational talents perfected during a
lengthy supervision of the Brooklyn Navy Yard. Within six weeks of
his appointment, this corpulent, touchy forty-one-year-old captain
had a hundred officers and seamen, forty carpenters, and quantities of
guns, munitions, and stores streaming over the wilderness route up
the Hudson and the Mohawk to Sackets Harbor. Before the onset of
winter, the lonely outpost was transformed into a busy shipping base.
There were numerous obstacles to overcome or live with, including
unsound communications and security—mail from Washington arrived only once a week and "the deputy postmaster is an ignorant
cobbler who suffers the letters to be examined by any person who
chooses to go into his shop." But the first keels were laid, and in the
meantime things had begun to move, on a more modest scale, in
Chauncey's other theater of command, Lake Erie, where, not yet
informed of the commission bestowed on Daniel Dobbin in Washington, he had entrusted the creation of a squadron to Lieutenant
Jesse Duncan Elliott.

It was as well for the founding of the Lake Erie flotilla that Dobbin, besides possessing an unshakable faith in his own judgment, was
still too much of a civilian to show instinctive deference to superior
rank. In his opinion the only rational site for a shipyard and harbor
was the bay formed by the crescent peninsula of Presque Isle and the
log-cabin village of Erie. A sandbar at the entrance rarely submerged
by more than six feet would discourage attackers from the lake, while
ways could be found for outgoing ships to clear it. This choice met
with Elliott's immediate opposition. The lieutenant had plumped
for Black Rock, a small inlet at the mouth of the Niagara River,
rejecting all other locations on Lake Erie as too shallow, or inde-

fensible against both weather and the enemy. The tone of his correspondence with Dobbin makes clear that he would brook no argument. But the sailing master was ready to match his knowledge of Lake Erie alongside that boasted by any man. He reported his preparations already under way and implicitly defied Elliott to stop them. Certainly Black Rock, no matter how convenient in Elliott's view, might at any moment become untenable. Opposite across the river stood the British garrison of Fort Erie. But proximity sometimes favors both sides. And it was under the guns of Fort Erie that Jesse Elliott displayed a notable enterprise.

On October 8 he led a force of fifty sailors—fatigued new arrivals from Sackets Harbor—with fifty volunteer artillerists commanded by Captain Nathan Towson on a cutting-out raid aginst two British vessels moored before the fort. They pushed off after midnight in two barges and some small boats, and were detected in midstream by a sentinel on the British brig *Caledonia*. Braving musket fire, Towson's men boarded her, crushed resistance on deck at a cost of two soldiers killed, and brought her safely to the American shore. Elliott's casualties on board the brig *Detroit* were equally light, but, fleeing with her downstream under round, grape, and canister fire, he ran aground on Squaw Island and ordered her burned. The American gains besides the *Caledonia* and her $150,000 cargo of pelts included the liberation of forty captives taken at Detroit. Towson, long afterward, complained that the Army's role in this lively action was underrated considering that his men had saved their prize intact. But the planning and command had been Elliott's, as were therefore the chief rewards. He received a congressional sword and promotion to master-commandant over the heads of thirty lieutenants.

The boldness of the act was greater than its material benefit. By adding one more vessel to the four schooners he had purchased locally, Elliott had simply increased the size of a little squadron which, through his dogged preference for Black Rock as an anchorage, was immobilized at birth. Nothing more apparently possible there, Elliott rejoined Chauncey at Sackets Harbor and took command of the 22-gun sloop *Madison*, newly completed by a high-speed Scottish shipbuilder named Henry Eckford. At Kingston meanwhile the British were forging ahead with their own construction program. All through winter the race continued, and when Chauncey, in the spring of 1813, put out with a flotilla of fourteen vessels mounting about ninety guns, the enemy's force was of equal size and slightly superior gun power.

Chauncey was left in no doubt of the scope and purpose of his command. "Whatever force the enemy may create we must surpass," William Jones told him. "Indeed, you are to consider the absolute superiority on all the lakes as the only limit to your authority." Not that the government had in mind an interminable and expensive shipbuilding contest. Mastery of Lake Ontario, after all, might be speedily won by a successful surprise attack on the enemy's main naval base. The War Department had in fact whipped up confidence for an infantry dash across the frozen lake to Kingston, but it melted even before the ice, and left a confusion of aims between the planners in Washington and the service chiefs on Lake Ontario. It was Isaac Chauncey's belief that the few gestures that the enemy was now making in the direction of Sackets Harbor were feints to conceal his real designs against General Harrison's troops based on the Sandusky River. He therefore proposed to meet bluff with bluff, simulating preparations for a raid on Kingston but actually carrying it to York (Toronto) and Fort George, comparatively weak outposts at the western end of Lake Ontario. Chauncey calculated that this move might force total British withdrawal from the Niagara peninsula, thus freeing the five Black Rock vessels for service at Presque Isle, whither the commodore himself, after detailing a token force to blockade Kingston, intended to transfer his flag. Chauncey's plan had the full approval of General Henry Dearborn, commanding the military in the area, who also favored the abandonment of Kingston as a principal objective, though for different reasons. Napoleon's Grand Army had perished in the winter snows of Russia, and as a result Britain had legions to spare for her war with America. The news provoked a rash of rumors that massive reinforcements were transforming Kingston into an unassailable stronghold of six or eight thousand men. Chauncey disbelieved such wild exaggerations, but General Dearborn swallowed them whole.

With the uneasy acquiescence of the War Department, the plans were put into operation. On April 25 Chauncey and twelve sail carried Colonel Zebulon Pike's brigade of 1,700 troops westward for the harbor and village of York, capital of Upper Canada. Dearborn, a passenger on Chauncey's flagship, was sick most of the time. After two days' sail, Pike's men landed under covering volleys of grape from Chauncey's inshore schooners. They met only slight resistance, but the explosion of a powder magazine, killing nearly a hundred men of both sides, including Pike, turned an insignificant raid into wasteful tragedy. The instant outbreak of American arson and looting (unchecked by Chauncey or Dearborn) accomplished nothing except to furnish the British with cause for still more senseless retaliation.

It was almost a month before the Chauncey-Dearborn expedition turned from York to its second westerly objective, Fort George, and while the ships were thus occupied at the head of the lake, disaster threatened their base at the other end. On May 29 Vice-Admiral Sir James Lucas Yeo, newly appointed to the command of Canada's inland seas, appeared off Sackets Harbor with a squadron and 750 soldiers. The Governor General of Canada himself, Sir George Prevost, was on board Yeo's flagship. It was he who, while his assault troops were ashore in the process of crushing the outnumbered American regulars, thought that the wind was about to shift and recalled them to their transports. The ships turned back into Kingston.

Prevost's nervousness was a stroke of good fortune which Chauncey and Dearborn perhaps ill deserved. Their westward excursion did nothing to impair British naval control of Lake Ontario and on July 6 Dearborn, an alert colonel in the Revolutionary War but a sickly general in this one, was relieved of his command. Chauncey suffered no decline in reputation. He had, after all, though at the risk of losing Sackets Harbor, fulfilled one of his primary hopes. The successful bombardment of Fort George caused the British to retire, temporarily, from other forts on the Niagara peninsula as well, thus permitting transfer of the ships at Black Rock to Presque Isle. This proved a feat of hazardous labor: two hundred men and as many yoke of oxen took a week to warp them against adverse winds and the Niagara rapids into Lake Erie. And it might very well have taken longer had there not been in charge a newcomer to the lakes who for all his youth and inexperience—he was only a twenty-seven-year-old master-commandant—combined stamina and resourcefulness in extraordinary amounts.

So far, little about Oliver Hazard Perry had impressed official circles. Mishap marred his first command when in February 1811 a pilot's error caused him to run the 12-gun schooner *Revenge* aground in a fog. The vessel was a total loss, and although his court of inquiry exonerated him the Department showed no hurry to give him another ship. But when it turned him down for command of the *Argus* in favor of William Henry Allen (junior in rank), he reinforced his formal applications with political weight. A Rhode Island senator's influence at least as much as Isaac Chauncey's recommendation secured his release from the unexacting command of a gunboat flotilla off his native Newport and his appointment to supervision of the fleet being built on Lake Erie.

He had not found things at a standstill. Noah Brown, the New York shipwright, was there and with Sailing Master Dobbin had laid the keels of two brigs, each to weigh 480 tons and mount twenty guns. Work was also proceeding on three schooners. To advance thus far, Brown's laborers had endured ill-health, poor food, Arctic weather, and the necessity of scavenging for materials. Yet, under Brown's indefatigable direction, they also built a blockhouse, guardhouse, men's quarters, offices for Perry, fourteen boats for the completed fleet, and all the gun carriages. The brigs were almost ready to be launched as Dearborn and Chauncey were mounting their assault against Fort George. Perry left Erie to join them, traveling first by rowboat, then on foot and horseback across the Niagara peninsula, in constant danger from British patrols. He reached Dearborn's headquarters on the eve of the attack and is said to have irritated Army officers with brash advice concerning the best means of landing units. And indeed, when the time came Chauncey found him "present at every point where he could be useful," guiding Dearborn's troops in under fire and, one imagines, performing functions which anticipated those of beachmaster in today's amphibious operations.

Though sturdily built, Perry suffered intermittent stomach disorder. He was stricken on the journey to Presque Isle with the Black Rock ships. But it never appeared to defeat him, and by July he was able to report the launching of the brigs *Niagara* and *Lawrence* (named for the *Chesapeake*'s slain captain). A total of 562 men would be required to man them. He could now count on less than a third, and the likelihood of ever getting the balance was becoming alarmingly slender because of Chauncey's apparent self-interest on the neighboring lake.

Yeo's move against Sackets Harbor while the flotilla was out had reversed Chauncey's order of priorities. He no longer talked of shifting his flag to Lake Erie. But neither did he give a great deal for his own chances on Lake Ontario. Yeo now had seven warships and six gunboats, 106 guns in all. Chauncey's fourteen vessels were less powerfully armed and he was frankly apprehensive about the outcome of a meeting—"I have not the temerity to believe that I can effect impossibilities." The commodore resisted Yeo's efforts to lure him into the lake. Even with the addition of a new corvette, the *General Pike*, adding twenty-six long guns to give him a comfortable margin of superiority over the mostly carronade-armed British ships, he still stayed clear of Kingston. In August he took a fleet of thirteen sail westward to raid little York a second time and on the seventh fell in with Yeo and a force half the American size for three further days of diffident sparring. Chauncey had more to fear from the weather— the *Hamilton*, 19, and *Scourge*, 10, foundered in a night squall with heavy loss of life. That no decisive engagement occurred was attributed by each commander to bad winds and the adversary's trepidity. Now it was clear that the odds favoring such an encounter loomed larger on Lake Erie—provided the protagonists there could man their ships. Yeo, like Chauncey, screened each new batch of recruits for Great Lakes service and kept the best men. He seems, in fact, to have starved the British squadron off Amherstburg, at the western end of Lake Erie under Robert Heriot Barclay, even more than Chauncey did Perry.

Barclay's true rank, in spite of an active service record—he had lost an arm at Trafalgar—was still only lieutenant. He was the same age as his foe across the lake, and as quick to protest unjust treatment. Almost every seaman doled to him, he informed Yeo, was "a poor devil not worth his salt," and unless reliable seamen were hurried to Amherstburg, "the great superiority of the enemy may prove fatal." He was forced to man his vessels with some of General Henry Proctor's 41st Regiment and Royal Newfoundland Fencibles before he could at last parade a fleet of six sail off Presque Isle. Then it was Oliver Perry's turn to couch his appeals in desperation. "Give me men, sir," he urged Chauncey, "and I will acquire both for you and myself honor and glory on this lake or perish in the attempt."

In truth, the overriding factor was not personal honor or glory but military requirement. West of Lake Erie, General Harrison's troops could not be thrown against Proctor's forces without the assurance of American naval superiority on the right. The Navy Department sent Perry a number of impatient letters that not only reflect the cabinet's anxiety but indicate a failure on William Jones's part to appreciate the problems of supply and man power at Presque Isle. Perry felt himself unjustly chided for inaction while deprived of men and taunted by the sight of an enemy fleet within striking distance. He confessed to biting his fingers with vexation and again he implored Chauncey, "For God's sake, send me men." On July 23 seventy marched in, too exhausted for immediate service, and the sixty who arrived one week later were "a motley set . . . blacks, soldiers, and boys." This latest grumble pricked the serenity with which Chauncey had borne previous agitations from Presque Isle and, ordering off a batch of abler men, he also wrote Perry a tart reproof. "I have yet to learn that the color of the skin, or the cut and trimmings of the coat, can affect a man's qualifications or usefulness." He went further, accusing Perry of going behind his back to seek a separate command.

On August 2 Barclay withdrew his ships from before Presque Isle for reasons still obscure. His departure gave Perry the chance to come out. Planning for this moment, Noah Brown had devised "camels"—flooded scows arranged to support a vessel by timbers passed through her ports. When the camels were plugged and pumped dry they rose, reducing her draft enough to float her across the bar. It was ideal in theory, but the depth of Lake Erie now proved below Perry's calculations. The *Niagara* and *Lawrence* grounded in turn going over and the whole process had to be repeated each time on top of the bar, the men pumping and hauling, very much aware of their exposed position should the British suddenly appear. While the *Niagara* was perched helplessly, some of Barclay's ships were indeed briefly sighted against the horizon. But without interruption the toil went on for four days. Then Commodore Perry's squadron stood for the open lake.

His ships were manned somehow. He had beaten the forests for recruits at $10 a month. General Harrison had sent him a hundred Kentucky sharpshooters. Master-Commandant Jesse Elliott, the bearer of Chauncey's caustic letter, had brought two lieutenants, eight midshipmen, and ninety seamen. Perry's effective strength of

490 men still fell short of his requirements and less than one-fourth of them were regular naval personnel. But more than anything else now it was that letter which rankled Perry, and no sooner were his ships safely across the sandbar than he wrote to Washington asking the Secretary to relieve him of the Lake Erie command. Jesse Elliott, who had taken the *Niagara*, was next in line for it and one is tempted to speculate on the course of events had William Jones not told Perry to remain in charge. Before the Secretary's letter (and a vaguely healing one from Chauncey) could reach him, Perry was moving up the lake. But the correspondence which awaited him at General Harrison's camp on the Sandusky included yet another complaint from Jones, this time alleging wasteful expenditures at Presque Isle. From no source could Perry derive encouragement. His relations with the Department were in poor shape. Those with his commander in chief were not much better. He was shivering in the grip of gastric fever again, and his ships were "neither well-officered or manned." Intolerable strain and worn patience had brought him to the point of resignation. But men with Perry's determination did not build fleets and deliberately cast adrift all promise of winning glory in them. It would not be surprising if he prayed after its dispatch for his request to quit not to be taken seriously. The Secretary did so react and the ships remained Perry's to command. Sick, bitter, and overworked, but with a heart set on battle, he took them into the lake and sailed boldly to and fro in full view of the anchored British squadron at Amherstburg.

Commander Barclay might now have regretted lifting his blockade of Presque Isle. On his control of Lake Erie depended provision of his crews, General Proctor's regular troops, and about 14,000 Indian auxiliaries. Supplies were already low; the Amherstburg store contained one day's reserves of flour. Time was no ally to the one-armed officer, yet he felt obliged to accept Perry's challenge only with the utmost confidence of victory. He would not risk disaster merely to test Sir George Prevost's flummery that he had "only to dare and the enemy is discomfited." To replace the armament intended for the new brig and destroyed at York, he commandeered an assortment of guns from the ramparts of Fort Malden. Still he hesitated, awaiting promised naval reinforcements from Kingston. They arrived September 9, a disheartening handful: two lieutenants, one master's mate, two gunners, and thirty-six seamen. Even Barclay could delay no longer. He ordered his fleet, "deplorably manned," to make sail.

Perry meanwhile had withdrawn his ships to Put-in-Bay, near the mouth of the Sandusky River, about thirty miles across from Amherstburg. Battle plans were drawn up. Barclay was to be forced into action by an attack on his ships at their anchorage. To match his superiority in long-range armament (about double Perry's fifteen long guns), the Americans could expect to hurl the greater weight of metal. "Engage each your designated adversary in close action," Perry's written orders began, and he quoted Nelson: "If you lay your enemy alongside, you cannot be out of place." The battle council, held in the *Lawrence*'s cabin, ended on a note of sentimental dedication, Perry displaying a blue flag specially made for him with Lawrence's last words sewn upon it in white muslin—"Don't Give up the Ship." It was flying from the flagship's main-royal masthead against a cloudless blue sky next morning, September 10, 1813, as the fleet of nine sail stood off in a light breeze. And there was no need to approach Amherstburg. The British fleet was out too, advancing from the northwest—four sturdy brigs, a sloop, and a schooner, one behind the other, or "in line ahead."

"Nothing equals the beautiful order of the English at sea," a Frenchman had observed during England's wars with Holland. "Never was a line drawn straighter than that formed by their ships; thus they bring all the fire to bear upon those who draw near them. They fight like a line of cavalry." The British line on Lake Erie, though too small to be imposing, was probably as straight as that in which Barclay had fought at Trafalgar. As for Perry, the emergence of the enemy faced him with unfamiliar problems. No previous American experience in fleet action existed from which he might draw guidance. He was aware that the powers of initiative conferred by possession of the windward position applied to squadrons no less than to single ships. But even with the best of crews, maneuvering several vessels as a unit to capture the weather gauge could mean sacrificing opportunities for effective engagement; on the other hand, allowing each captain to make his own way into action risked disorder. With time pressing, however, tactical advantages weighed less upon Perry than a determination that the squadrons should come to grips. "I don't care," he is reported to have exclaimed, "to windward or to leeward, they shall fight today."

He had assigned his commanders their adversaries: the *Lawrence*, assisted by the small brig *Caledonia* and schooners *Aerial* and *Scorpion*, would engage the *Detroit*, *Chippewa*, and *Hunter*. The brig *Niagara*, 22, would fight the brig *Queen Charlotte*, 17, in what was from the American standpoint the most favorable match, gun for gun. The *Somers, Porcupine, Tigress*, and *Trippe* would take on the *Little Belt* and *Lady Prevost* in a contest of sloops and schooners. So both fleets of little ships advanced into battle, obeying the rigid convention of "the line ahead": Barclay's because it was mandatory in the century-and-a-half-old Fighting Instructions of the Royal Navy, Perry's because no alternative tactic readily suggested itself.

Perry gave a last fleet order: commanders were to close up to their prescribed position of half a cable's length of each other and preserve their stations in line. Now the two columns were converging at about four knots, the British in a smart line pointing due south, the Americans bearing down perhaps less smartly from the northeast. Perry, in these final moments, may have spent some consideration of Barclay's possible maneuvers once under attack. It certainly could never have crossed his mind that, were he permitted the choice, it might be less of an urgency to read the enemy's thoughts than those of his own second in command on the quarterdeck of the brig *Niagara*.

The main impression one gets from Jesse Duncan Elliott's scandal-studded career is that every uproar was precisely to his liking. Had he become the lawyer he started out to be, we might have heard no more of him than of his father, a frontier colonel slain by Indians. But in 1804 he had abandoned his studies, which were being financed in part by the pension provided his widowed mother, and obtained a midshipman's warrant. He served most of his naval apprenticeship under James Barron, and after the *Chesapeake*'s peacetime surrender he showed a perverse unwillingness to side with the prevailing steerage sentiment against the disgraced commodore. At least on the evidence of Elliott's foray from Black Rock to cut out the British brigs, he ill deserves the imputations of cowardice raised during his lifetime and by some historians since. But whatever his motives—and greed, revenge, ambition, and jealousy can be detected at one time or another—it is certain that he relished every wrangle into which they pitchforked him. It is the one constant clue to his shadowy personality. Let other officers lust after glory and prize money. Jesse Elliott's predominant appetites fed on intrigue and controversy.

Now his brig followed dutifully in the wake of the slow *Caledonia*, Towson's prize at Fort Erie, and a galling reminder, if Elliott needed one, that he had once dreamed of commanding the assault to drive the British from the lake. That cutting-out expedition let it be known that Elliott meant action, even as his insistence upon Black Rock for naval operations had been a necessary assertion of his authority. What he had then declared to be impossible—the establishment of a naval base at Presque Isle—was an accomplished fact. Thus the very existence of Perry's squadron was an affront as objectionable to Elliott as when Stephen Decatur summoned a carpenter to belittle his testimony before the *Chesapeake* court. And since he had just been informed of his promotion to the same rank as Perry, master-commandant, it must have rankled all the more that he was following in the line of battle instead of leading it.

At 11:45 A.M. the *Detroit* tested range with a shot from a long twenty-four. Five minutes later she fired another which crashed through the *Lawrence*'s bulwarks. Immediately the *Scorpion* opened the American fire, and at meridian the flagship's own twelve-pounders flashed into action. Pinning his hopes on the *Lawrence*'s close-quarter carronades, Perry signaled his other vessels to follow and bore down on the *Detroit* with such rapidity that they were unable to keep up. Still the *Lawrence* plowed ahead and at 500 yards or less from the *Detroit* ran unaccompanied into heavy gusts of shot which might have speedily disabled her had not the makeshift guns on Barclay's new brig been improperly equipped. Firing locks and port fires were missing and the Englishmen had to discharge them by snapping pistols at the touchholes.

But in a very short time the *Lawrence* was contending with more than just the erratic fire of the *Detroit*. The *Caledonia* and behind her the *Niagara* had been in long-range action with the *Queen Charlotte*. At 12:45 P.M. the *Niagara* had exhausted her long-range ammunition and the moment was considerably overdue for Elliott to run her into carronade range. He made no such move. His failure to close promptly with the *Charlotte* or run ahead to the assistance of the *Lawrence* was to be blamed by some on the light and fluky wind.

Isaac Chauncey. From an oil painting by
John W. Jarvis. *United States Navy*

Oliver Hazard Perry. From a painting by
John W. Jarvis. *United States Navy*

Jesse Duncan Elliott, c. 1814. Engraved by
David Edwin. *United States Navy*

Thomas Macdonough as a midshipman. Artist unknown. *United States Navy*

David Porter. Artist unknown. *United States Navy*

Samuel Southard, Secretary of the Navy 1823-29. From a painting by S. Conrad. *United States Navy*

Elliott himself preferred to cite Perry's orders to maintain the line as the reason. Indeed, he shortened sail to stay astern of the *Caledonia*, and even so the *Niagara*'s jibboom was over her stern. The *Charlotte*, observing that her opponent showed no further disposition to fight, ran down and attached herself to the *Detroit* and *Hunter*, and the *Lady Prevost*, last but one in the British line, also closed up. As some forty guns were brought to bear on the *Lawrence*, her faithful little consorts did what they could to help. But their crews were exposed without bulwarks to storms of grape and canister, and guns were mishandled or overcharged by inexperienced gunners. The *Scorpion*'s single carronade burst. One of the *Aerial*'s twelve-pound pivot guns jumped its carriage and tumbled down the hatchway. And this left Oliver Perry's flagship alone to bear the brunt of Barclay's guns. They drenched her with metal three times heavier than the most she could hurl in reply.

Her masts, hull, and sails were quickly riddled. Carnage mounted with horrifying speed, the blood flowing faster than boys could scatter the sand designed to prevent the decks from becoming slippery. Death and destruction encompassed Perry, without claiming him. Lieutenant John Brooks, his close friend, was swept from his side by a cannonball. Blood ran over the pine planks and sprayed through seams into the wardroom, which, there being no safe cockpit below the water line of the shallow *Lawrence*, had to serve as surgeon's quarters. It was a ten-foot-square chamber of horrors where flying splinters and crashing cannonballs mutilated the already maimed and the surgeon, Usher Parsons, sponged wounds and performed six amputations. Such was the human havoc that every word of Commodore Perry's desperate shout through the wardroom hatch for men to right toppled guns has a ghastly ring of unconscious comedy: *"Can anyone down there pull a rope?"* Yet soon was heard a more terrible demand between the groans and sobs, the roar of guns, and the rumble of their carriage wheels as they ran in and out of the ports. A wrathful question, unanswered on the quarterdeck, gasped within Usher Parson's charnel house by those capable of sound, and said to have been the last utterance of the dying Lieutenant Brooks. *Where is the Niagara? Why does she not come up?*

Not a musket had been discharged on Jesse Elliott's ship, nor more than a single broadside of his carronades. And not until the *Law-*

rence's guns fell silent—the last carronade being manned by her several-times-wounded first lieutenant, John Yarnall—did Elliott cease to be a distant spectator. (He did not deny afterward that at this point he presumed Perry to be dead.) Hailing the *Caledonia* to put up her helm and make way, he pressed sail under a freshening breeze. He bore on for at least half a mile, to windward of the crippled flagship and ahead of her. To some of the British officers it appeared as if he were deserting the battle.

And now, about 2.30 P.M., Oliver Perry put out from his ship's port side in a boat manned by four oarsmen. It drew instant fire from the *Queen Charlotte*, but sought the cover of settling gunsmoke and reached the *Niagara* safely in a quarter of an hour. Elliott's thoughts as he watched his commanding officer coming on board can only be guessed at. Barclay's afterthoughts on this historic transfer of his adversary's flag are known. "The American commander, seeing that as yet the day was against him, made a noble and alas! too successful effort to regain it."

There is no doubt that Perry determined to continue the action from Elliott's undamaged brig, even though, according to witnesses, he despaired of the outcome, blaming his gunboats at the rear of the column. Elliott emerges in considerable testimony as an undaunted optimist volunteering to dash off on a perilous mission in Perry's boat to hurry up the laggard vessels. It is a somewhat more irascible Elliott we find at the end of the line, boarding the *Somers* and surprising her commander drunk at the bottom of the hatchway, and then beating a disrespectful gunner with his speaking trumpet. At any rate, Elliott did succeed in bringing the vessels into effective action—the sixty-ton sloop *Trippe* closed enough to pour grape and canister into the *Queen Charlotte*. The *Niagara* meanwhile, flying Perry's pendant, had made a right-angle turn and was aiming directly for the British line, just as Lieutenant Yarnall on the battered *Lawrence*—she was drifting helplessly between friend and foe—hauled down her colors. Perry's "unspeakable grief" at this moment was absorbed by immediate prospects of vengeance. And the cheers with which the exhausted Englishmen greeted the American flagship's surrender died away before the sight of the *Niagara* as she bore down on them with main-topsails backed and her men standing ready at her double-shotted guns.

Even before this, the action had not been altogether one-sided. The British had suffered much. The *Queen Charlotte*'s captain and lieutenant were dead, as was the first lieutenant of the *Detroit*. Commander Barclay, struck repeatedly in the shoulder, had lost the use of his remaining arm and was semiconscious below deck. The British ships tried to turn for their unengaged guns to meet the *Niagara*, but, leaderless and with stays and braces shot away, they reeled in disorder. The *Queen Charlotte* and *Detroit* collided, tossing hull to hull and facing opposite directions. The *Niagara* raked their decks with starboard broadsides. The *Lady Prevost* fell within half-pistol shot of the American's other side and took a terrible pounding from her port batteries—when the smoke lifted, the only living soul seen standing on the *Lady*'s grisly deck was her stunned and bleeding commander. Barclay's ships now bore no resemblance to the proud, straight column which had sailed out of Amherstburg. And all hopes of recovery were gone. The *Detroit* struck her colors. The *Chippewa* and *Little Belt*, the only vessels in any condition to attempt flight, were swiftly overtaken by the *Scorpion*, and it was that schooner's long thirty-two-pounder which fired the last shot of the battle, as it had the first.

The gunfire and killing had their usual sequel of chivalry. Barclay was particularly appreciative of the humanity shown by Commodore Perry to all ninety-four British wounded, regardless of rank. There were forty-one British killed. The American count of thirty killed and ninety-three wounded—almost all were on board the *Lawrence*—comprised one-third of Perry's total complement. These somber estimates were to intensify the bitterness of the controversy left in the battle's bloody wake. The first dark charges were being whispered even before the last deck was purged with hot vinegar of its shambles smell, and before the last of the dead, in sewn canvas shrouds with cannonballs at their feet, went sliding off the boards into the now peaceful lake.

"We have met the enemy and they are ours." On receipt of this penciled message from Perry, General Harrison sent his troops across the lake to capture Amherstburg and rout the British before they could retreat very far down the road back to Lower Canada. It was victory with a special meaning. The dissolution of Proctor's mixed force of regulars and Indians along the north bank of the Thames

did more than destroy the right division of British influence in the Great Lakes area. For the first time, it provided those responsible for the national defense with an excellent example of the necessity of naval support to certain military ventures. The lesson was not perceived right away. Of more immediate concern to an administration beset by increasing opposition to its prosecution of the war, the news from Lake Erie contained abundant political benefit. Gratitude, therefore, was unstinting: a captain's promotion for Perry with effect from the battle date (although he commanded a squadron, few had been able to call him "commodore" without mutual embarrassment), gold medals for himself and Elliott, silver medals for all other officers, and three months' extra pay for the people. The greater share of the $225,000 prize money for the capture of Barclay's flotilla went to Commodore Chauncey, an unfair allotment, many thought; but even greater injustice was seen in the award of equal amounts of $7,140 to Perry and Elliott. Neither did subsequent congressional approval of an extra $5,000 to the new captain satisfy the feelings of those who felt convinced that his second in command had done nothing to deserve a penny.

Oliver Perry had known Elliott but a few weeks, by no means long enough to grasp such a devious character. And he could not at first bring himself to endorse the shocking imputations then in circulation. "I did not know enough of human nature," he was to say, "to believe that anyone could be guilty of a determination to sacrifice me by keeping his vessel out of action." In his report to the Secretary he attributed the *Niagara*'s inaction to the lightness of the wind and, disregarding the advice of friends to deny Elliott even the smallest credit, he made positive reference to his gallantry. He refused Elliott's own demands that he revise the account to read more flatteringly of him, but nevertheless furnished him with a personal letter of approbation, and sent officers around the Put-in-Bay anchorage and to General Harrison's camp, quashing the rumors of Elliott's misconduct. Extraordinary lengths, one feels, even granting that Perry was then so flushed with victory that "there was not a person in the world whose feelings I would hurt." Later he was to offer different reasons: Elliott, sick with remorse at Put-in-Bay, had stirred his pity; and he was resolved not to besmirch the Navy's wartime reputation by disclosing cowardice within its ranks. In all likelihood, what hap-

pened was that Perry did initially give Elliott the benefit of doubt—
"I am aware of my weakness in being very credulous," he once said.
Upon gradual reflection, and influenced by every embittered survivor of the *Lawrence*, he grew to believe that Elliott, from some
diabolic motive, did try to "sacrifice" him on Lake Erie. By then, of
course, he repented his testimonial, and cursed himself for having
commended Elliott in his official report to the Department and
posterity.

Perry's apparent awakening was accelerated by the inability of
Jesse Elliott to let the matter drop even while he stood at least officially without blemish. To his peppery demands for an inquiry the
Department replied patiently that none was needed. And none
might ever have been held had not Robert Barclay, after Perry
paroled him, returned home to face a court-martial for losing his
ships. A proud but tragic figure before his peers—one arm gone, the
other in bandages, a portion of his thigh missing, five wounds elsewhere in his body—Barclay had described the *Niagara* as "making
away" from the battle. These words virtually guaranteed an inquiry
for Elliott, not so much to suit his object of confirming his spotless-
ness as from the necessity of defending the Navy's good name against
British insinuation. (Commander Barclay was honorably acquitted of
blame, but never went to sea again. There is a story, difficult to resist,
that in view of his mutilated condition he offered to release his fian-
cée from their engagement. She replied that if there was enough of
him left to contain his soul, she would marry him. And she did.)

Elliott's court of inquiry was presided over by Captain Alexander
Murray on the sloop *Ontario* in New York Harbor on April 16,
1815. Perry was then at Newport, Rhode Island, but the court
avoided the potential embarrassment of his appearance as witness by
choosing to regard his official account of the battle as his testimony.
Other important witnesses had died from war wounds or other causes
—the *Niagara*'s purser, the last person Elliott had consulted before
leaving the battle line, had committed suicide. Two former junior
officers of the *Lawrence*, supported by members of her crew, testified
that the *Niagara* could have been brought into closer action. The
point was not pursued by the half-deaf president of the court (one of
its two other members was half-blind and epileptic) and the proceedings consisted for the most part of negative answers to Jesse Elliott's

reiterated question: did the *Niagara* at any time try to make off from Barclay's ships? The court not only found the British implication to be false and malicious but concluded that indeed the only vessel to bear away from the battle that day had been the *Queen Charlotte*, dispatched by the long guns of Elliott's brig *Niagara*.

CHAPTER NINETEEN

Pacific Follies, Potomac Fireships

AT SEA in the War of 1812 there were no clashes of great fleets like those characterizing England's successive conflicts with the Spanish, the Dutch, again the Spanish, and the French. All the same, it was naval war on a global scale. Not for 130 years were American ships to wage duels in waters so far from home. And to thousands of American sailors the routine monotony of interminable voyages was broken not alone by prize-taking and bursts of conflict but also by the novelties and fascinations of exotic environments. Of all the wartime frigate cruises, this was especially true of that of the *Essex*, an episode often so isolated as to lose all bearing with the war and the mainstream of naval events, and containing so many of what we have come to accept as romantic clichés of the South Seas as even to lose semblance with reality.

It is fortunately well documented: we may chart its course with Midshipman William Feltus or Midshipman David Farragut as pilots —both left informative journals. Or we may employ Captain Porter's own account, in spite of the English reviewer who disdained it as pornography written in the style of a boatswain's mate.

From the start Porter had hoped to sail alone—his best chance of reaping great profit from the cruise—and while there is no reason to doubt the sincerity of the efforts he made to rendezvous with Commodore Bainbridge, it is certain that their failure was pretty much to his liking. In the first weeks of 1813 he ran the *Essex* down the Brazilian coast and by the close of February, after doubling Cape

Horn in furious hail squalls, the frigate lay west of Tierra del Fuego, her captain speculating on ways to injure the enemy and amass wealth, her people generally of good cheer notwithstanding fatigue, frostbite, and so great a distaste for their stale, weevily rations "that a rat was deemed a dainty, and pet monkeys were sacrificed to appease their longings." In the main, Porter kept the crew healthy.

On March 14, just a week before Perry arrived at Presque Isle, Porter put into Valparaiso. The Chileans, who were taking their own first steps to independence from Spain, England's ally, were disposed more to be cordial than neutral. Indeed Porter must have been tempted to linger, but he had his mind set on making the most of the enemy's failure, so far, to station a warship in the South Pacific. The chief British enterprise in these waters, whaling, was at his mercy. On the 23rd he got under way for the Galapagos Islands; and cruising in their neighborhood for the next five or six months, he captured about a dozen whalers.

Since the whale fishery did not constitute a vital part of the enemy's mercantile marine, breaking up the whaling fleet was less of a patriotic service than, say, the cruise of the *Argus* around Britain's coasts, which accounted for twenty prizes in thirty-one days. However, it guaranteed considerable wealth for Porter on his return home, and by drawing nourishment from the prizes it was a cruise that cannot be said to have strained the national Treasury: the captures provided Porter with all the cordage, sails, guns, food, and medicines he wished, even money to pay his seamen's salaries.

Two puncheons of rum discovered on board the *Sir Andrew Hammond*, captured on September 13, so affected his crew that "many were taken to their hammocks perfectly drunk." Porter's disapproval of intemperance in the Navy Department did not extend to his people at sea, where "no evil was likely to result from a little inebriety." Indeed, the men at this time gave him less trouble than his officers. His second lieutenant tried to shoot him in a fit of drunken madness, and thenceforth needed constant watching because of a remorseful tendency to suicide. And a duel on a lonely islet lost Porter his fourth lieutenant. "A practise which disgraces human nature"—this was his opinion of dueling. Nevertheless, he took no action against the surviving principal. Porter had few enough good officers: he was forced to make a sailing master lieutenant and to turn twelve- and fifteen-year-old midshipmen into prize-masters, with select veteran seamen at their elbows.

Now the *Essex* began to show the ravages of her twelve months at sea, and Porter decided to put in at the Marquesas for refitting—even though this meant a further 3,000-mile penetration of the Pacific. In the Marquesas, a Polynesian group discovered by the Spanish explorer Mendaña and since visited only by French and Indian missions, the Americans received an uninhibited welcome when their flotilla (the *Essex* and five prizes) anchored half a mile from the beach at Nuku Hiva, largest of the thirteen islands.

Porter was himself no sooner ashore, surrounded by hordes of tattooed natives, when "my attention was drawn to a handsome young woman of about eighteen, her complexion fairer than common, her bearing majestic, her glossy black hair and skin highly anointed with coconut oil." He learned that she was Pitanee, the chief's granddaughter, and he felt at once that it would be sensible to cultivate her interest. But "she received my advances with the coldness and hauteur of a princess and repelled everything like familiarity. Yet this lady, like the rest of the women on the island, soon followed the dictates of her own interest, and formed a connexion with one of the officers which lasted with but little fidelity on her part, showing herself to be, on the whole, a most notorious jilt."

Porter was met on his return to the *Essex* by such a clamor for shore leave that he immediately allowed the boats to be put out. On touching land, they were seized by throngs of females aged from ten to sixty, "some as remarkable for their beauty as others for their ugliness." By sheer weight of numbers the women commandeered the boats for use as a ferry service to the *Essex* and she was quickly swarming with them—four hundred, according to David Farragut's estimation, perforce a hasty one since he and other midshipmen of tender years were bundled off the frigate and confined, safe from temptation, aboard one of the prizes.

The *Essex* was also visited by Gattenewa, the native chief, a practically naked old man whose scaling skin and stupefied expression Porter attributed to overconsumption of the islanders' favorite beverage: the spittle juice of chewed *kava* root. Porter sought to impress him by ordering a gun fired, but all the effect this had on Gattenewa was to hurt his ears. Then the old chief threw himself on the settee in Porter's cabin and fell asleep. After waking, he honored the American with a ritual exchange of names, casually adding that the Happahs, a hostile tribe in the hills, had lately cursed the bones of his mother; and inasmuch as Porter now bore her name, he too was an insulted party and obliged to assist in the Happahs' conquest. Porter was beyond direct reply to "the old man's sophistry," but he promised to reflect on it.

For one thing, Porter was disturbed by a strong hint from the chief that his warriors were cannibal. In any event, his mission in the Marquesas was the refit of his ship, not involvement in tribal conflicts. Still, although there was much calking and painting to be done, and rigging to repair, Porter allowed a liberal work schedule, his crew quitting daily at 4 P.M. to devote the balance of the day to repose and amusement; one-fourth of them were permitted to spend each night on shore. Even the youngest midshipmen had opportunity to frolic with the natives—Farragut wrote admiringly of their plumage, their red and white cloaks, and their prowess with twelve-foot spears. And Porter revised his opinion: they were, after all, an honest people (the clothes of officers bathing in an island stream were never stolen) who "rank highly in the scale of human beings." He was beguiled by their amorality. "They attach no shame to a proceeding which is considered as natural, an innocent and harmless amusement. With the common sailors and their girls, all was helter-skelter and promiscuous intercourse, every girl the wife of every man in the mess and frequently of every man in the ship." Their only asking price was quantities of whale teeth; and no risk accompanied their favors for "that terrible disease which has proved so destructive to mankind is unknown to them, and they give free scope to the indulgence of their passions, living in the most pleasurable licentiousness."

Perhaps, after all, there was an enchantment to these islands. Within a week of his arrival Porter had donated a six-pound gun—hauled by Gattenewa's men into the hills—and had sent his first lieutenant, John Downes, with forty seamen to bolster an attack on the Happahs. After a feeble resistance with stones and spears, the hill people surrendered. But that still left the Typees, on the north side of Nuku Hiva, a tribe reputed to be unbeatable in battle and unquestionably ill-disposed to all strangers. When Porter dispatched a request for some sign of friendliness, they baffled and annoyed him with a reply that could be fairly interpreted as one word: *Why?* Moreover, they alluded to the alien visitors as "white lizards." But David Porter was now determined to put the whole island under his peaceful subjugation—"for our own security"—and after brandished American muskets had silenced those natives who saw fit to question his authority, he directed Gattenewa to begin war preparations. At the same time, he talked the tribe into declaring a pledge of loyalty to America, whose "pure republican policy so nearly approaches their own."

The attack on the Typees was about to start when Porter's whaling captives, whom he had placed on virtually the same footing as his own people, showed their gratitude by conspiring to escape. They planned to seize control of the guard vessel *Essex junior* (formerly the British letter of marque *Atlantic*) after drugging her crew with rum and laudanum. So angered was Porter that he clapped all prisoners in irons and shot a lax or conniving sentry in the thigh with his pistol. As he explains the incident, "Promptness and vigilance on my part were the only sure guarantees to the success of a cruise so highly important to the interests of my country." To further these interests Porter annexed for his country, without its knowledge, new citizens and overseas territory. (When the government did find out, it withheld ratification.) On November 9, 1813, Gattenewa's people saluted the American flag as it rose above Porter's four-cannon fort, his bakery, guardhouse, and six dwellings, comprising Fort Madison, and their own village, now Madisonville, on Madison Island, overlooking Massachusetts Bay. And they delightedly proclaimed themselves to be *Mellekees.*

Three weeks later Porter in the *Essex junior* led 5,000 of them, in five boats and twenty war canoes, around the island to the Typees' domain. But their vigorous blowing of conch shells to maintain boat formation alerted the Typees, who beat off the first landing party of thirty-five men with showers of stones. At this, Porter's new Americans lost faith in the assault and turned their craft for home. Next, Porter himself took two hundred men ashore, and they marched on the Typee mountain stronghold, leaving a trail of incendiarism along a valley of such natural charm that the captain was fleetingly distressed by the necessity of proving his invincibility. The pang scarcely slowed him, however, and with sword and musketry his men swept to the summit, where they set the Typee capital ablaze. Now Porter stopped "to contemplate that valley which, on the morning, we had viewed in all its beauty, the scene of abundance and happiness. A long line of smoking ruins marked our traces from one end to the other. Unhappy and heroic people," he lamented, "the victims of your own courage and mistaken pride." His less sublime regret when the Typees acknowledged defeat by bringing him hogs and fruit was that these propitiatory gifts were unaccompanied by salt with which he could have cured some of the pork for his sea stock.

It was now December. The *Essex junior*, after a visit to Valparaiso, brought Porter word that a superior British force was bound for the Chilean port. His ship was refitted, well provisioned, ready to sail. The state of his crew was doubtful. Actually, after their protracted idyll, it speaks volumes for their morale that any of them were on board at all when the moment came for departure. Nuku Hiva's relentless women had been lining the shore night and day, trying to subvert them with alternatively alluring and threatening gestures. Three seamen who capitulated and swam ashore were brought back and flogged at the gangway. Then rumor gripped the ship that, rather than weigh anchor, the men would mutiny. Porter summoned all hands to the port side of the frigate's quarterdeck, laid his cutlass on the capstan, and (he would have suited his stance to the word), looking every inch the terrible little martinet, announced that should any man disobey the order to weigh he would "put a match to the magazine and blow them all to hell." To set an example, he called forth a suspected malcontent, ignored the wretch's denials, and had him dumped over the side into a passing native canoe. The *Essex* and *Essex junior* made sail without further trouble. As for the women of the island, they were not entirely bereft of American consolation. Some of Porter's prizes remained, manned by a small party under Lieutenant John Gamble of the Marine Corps, whose orders were to make his way homeward if no word came from the *Essex* after five months.

Porter might have honorably returned to America with his prizes or, more profitably, continued as a commerce raider at large in new seas. Instead, he made for the Chilean coast again, anchored off Valparaiso on February 3, 1814, and repaid the city's earlier hospitality with a ball on board the *Essex*. Next morning a lookout on the *Essex junior* sighted two British ships coming over the horizon.

Captain Porter had no intention of taking on more than one ship at a time, and he had already planned with Lieutenant Downes, in command of the *Essex junior*, a fighting retreat if they found themselves outnumbered. He might have felt bolder on a different vessel. After all, he had not long ago considered the *Essex* as the worst frigate afloat. For one thing, the severely sharp lines designed to increase her speed caused her to become easily overweighted, thus making her a fickle sailer. But most of all, Porter nursed an "insuperable dislike" for carronades. The *Essex* mounted forty, her entire armament with the exception of six long twelve-pounders. Porter, before sailing, had been deeply disturbed by visions of the *Essex* becoming disabled early in an action. "A ship much inferior to her in sailing and in force," he had warned Paul Hamilton, "armed with long guns, could take a position beyond the reach of our carronades and cut us to pieces." But the Secretary had not agreed to the expense of the substantial alteration in the *Essex*'s guns that Porter proposed. The captain's hostility to carronades was based on an assumption that they had not left the experimental stage and therefore could not be relied upon. He evidently had forgotten or was unimpressed by the fact that short guns had played a principal role in every major British naval victory from the Glorious First to Trafalgar. But for a pair of bow chasers, the entire armament of some of the smaller British cruisers consisted of carronades. When the frigate *Phoebe*, Captain James Hilyer, with the 20-gun sloop *Cherub* sailed into Valparaiso, the *Essex* was in a position to have disabled both ships with broadsides from seventeen of the guns he despised. The temptation was strong, but promises made by both captains to respect Chilean neutrality limited their exchanges to threats and then polite reassurances issued through voice trumpet. But the vessels maneuvered about each other as if seeking tactical advantage, and now there began a whimsical war of nerves. An American seaman who thought a British counterpart was pulling faces at him through a port was only in the nick of time prevented from firing a musket burst into the British ship. The crew of the *Essex* hoisted a banner bearing the words "Free Trade and Sailors' Rights." The *Phoebe*'s people displayed the slogan "God and Sailors' Best Rights, Traitors

Offend Both," whereupon the *Essex* came back with "Our Country and Liberty—Tyrants Offend Them." Derisive shouts and satiric or sentimental songs wafted nightly from ship to ship. At last Hilyer, having watered and provisioned his ships, withdrew from harbor and waited for the Americans to come out. Porter tarried several weeks, aware that a victory, perhaps survival itself, was attainable only through the mouths of his carronades at close quarters. We do not know whether, during this hesitant prelude in Valparaiso Harbor, Porter regretted his decision to return—or how much longer he would have stayed there had not a black squall struck the roadstead on March 28, snapping one of the frigate's cables and driving her, with the other anchor dragging, out to sea.

Quickly the remaining cable was cut. With topsails set and reefed, Porter dashed for the western extremity of the bay, hoping to squeeze between it and the *Phoebe*. The English ship was making all sail for the same area. Another furious gust swept the bay and the American's main-topmast went flying over the side, five topmen clinging to it. Now it was touch and go for Porter, his alternatives seriously diminished. Yet he could still gamble on his ship's fast-sailing potential, could bear up and run before the wind, taking the enemy's fire but perhaps outsailing him sufficiently to replace the topmast in safety. Farragut, reviewing the episode long afterward, thought his captain should have taken this chance. But Porter, who, as we have seen, had a shaky confidence in his vessel, sought refuge instead in an inlet three miles from Valparaiso. Still he might have beached her, broadside on to prevent raking, and held Hilyer as long as possible, perhaps driving him off altogether. But within pistol shot of the beach, he anchored stern to the enemy. It can be said that Porter had no reason to fear an actual onslaught in view of Hilyer's promise—the *Essex* was not out of neutral waters. But even a gentleman's word is no stronger than his defenses against the temptation to break it. The situation of the American ship was an enticement bound to have quickened Hilyer's pulses. At 4 P.M. his two ships bore down on the *Essex* and while still at safe range, the *Phoebe* let loose a broadside from thirteen long eighteen-pounders.

Manning three long twelves which had been hastily shifted to cover the frigate's vulnerable stern, Porter's gunners replied, pounding the *Phoebe* for a full twenty minutes until she backed off farther for

The American recovery on Lake Erie, September 10, 1813. The *Niagara,* center, under Perry's command, is shown forcing her way through the British line, firing broadsides left and right. The disabled *Lawrence* can be seen at middle distance right. Line engraving by B. Tanner after T. T. Barralet. *Courtesy of the National Maritime Museum, London*

The Battle of Lake Champlain, September 11, 1814. The British frigate *Confiance* (middle right) is engaging the corvette *Saratoga* and brig *Eagle.* From a water color attributed to Warren, in the Mariners Museum, Newport News. *United States Navy*

Two drawings by Captain David Porter, later engraved by William Strickland, of Porter's experiences in the Pacific. *(Above)* In November 1813 his frigate *Essex* is anchored peacefully with her prizes off Nuku Hiva in the Marquesas. *United States Navy. (Below)* Four months later off Valparaiso she is trapped and at bay before the victorious guns of the *Phoebe* and the *Cherub*. *United States Navy*

immunity from which to hurl fresh broadsides. Then death and disorder took possession of the frigate *Essex*. Fifteen of her crew
perished in three attempts to man a single gun. A Scotsman, leg gone
at the groin, dragged himself to the sill of a gun port, loudly
lamented that he was of no further use, and flung himself into the
sea. A less self-sacrificial seaman fled his post and was grotesquely
pursued around the deck by an angry shipmate hobbling on a shattered leg and trying to shoot him. Belatedly Porter decided to run
the frigate ashore and burn her. But as she headed toward the bluffs,
the wind altered, took her flat aback, and paid her offshore into
another raking fire from the *Phoebe*. For one desperate moment
Porter tried to maneuver his riddled ship close enough to bring her
carronades to bear. Hilyer put his helm up at once, keeping his
distance, and just then the *Essex* caught fire below. Flames burst
through her hatchways. Powder exploded. Burning men ran up on
deck and jumped overboard. The *Phoebe*'s guns kept firing, and her
victim was a smoking, listing hulk when, at 6:20, Porter surrendered.
Fifty-eight of his crew were dead, thirty-one missing—many had
drowned over the side—and the cockpit, steerage, wardroom, and
berthdeck could take no more wounded.

The stormy months at sea, the campaign against the whalers, the
labor and dalliance in the Marquesas—it had all come to this, the loss
of a handsome ship of war with two-thirds of her crew casualties. Had
her captain stood for the China Sea or the Indian Ocean instead of
deliberately making for waters where he knew a strong enemy was
about to seek him, there could have been no more catastrophic
climax to the saga of the frigate *Essex*.

One hundred and thirty survivors of the *Essex* were paroled by
Captain Hilyer and most of them left Valparaiso for home with
Porter on board the *Essex junior*. At about the same time, the
Polynesian idyll earned its own melancholy footnote. Seamen on one
of the prize vessels that Porter had left behind mutinied, seized control, and stood out of the bay, where they put Lieutenant Gamble
and his midshipmen over the side in an open boat. They made shore
safely, only to be attacked by unexpectedly hostile natives. Two midshipmen were murdered. The rest of Gamble's party escaped to another prize ship, the former whaler *Sir Andrew Hammond*. Leaking
badly, manned under Gamble by seven wounded and scorbutic die-

hards, she held together somehow and managed to reach the Sandwich Islands. It seems rather anticlimatic that her reception was nothing more than a greeting from a solitary American trader named Harbottle.

When David Porter arrived home in July 1814 after an absence of nearly two years, British ships were hovering off the Atlantic seaboard as they had been throughout the previous winter. In the main, their commercial blockade was successful: American flour exports, for example, were in process of falling almost 90 per cent. The only part of the country to escape the worst effects was New England, whose merchants responded to Mr. Madison's periodic appeals to their patriotism by proclaiming business as usual and trading as much as they dared with the British. But so long as New England ports, however reluctantly, gave shelter to American warships, the British had perforce to patrol them also. They were not, however, as successful in confining America's fleet as they were inhibiting her commerce. The *Constitution*, the corvette *Adams*, and the three new sloops *Frolic*, *Peacock*, and *Wasp* had all slipped out under cover of mists and storms between January and May. But the *United States* and her prize *Macedonian* remained bottled up, as they had been since an unsuccessful attempt by Decatur to run out through Long Island Sound. Decatur had then been forced to retreat five miles up the Thames River and Admiral Sir Thomas Hardy's squadron had promptly concentrated along the Connecticut coast. "Here we are," Decatur wrote philosophically to a friend, "John Bull and us, all of a lump." His next try to run the blockade was abandoned following reports that traitorous Federalists were betraying his movements with blue light signals from Groton Long Point.

In March 1814 Decatur was offered a choice of commands: the new frigate *Guerrière*, about to be launched at Philadelphia, or the *President*, which had just put into New York, completing Commodore Rodgers' fourth and (one is no longer surprised to learn) largely uneventful war cruise. Since the *Guerrière* would not soon be ready for sea, Decatur asked for the *President*; but the blockade still deterred him from venturing out, so William Jones appointed him in charge of the New York Harbor defenses. We find Decatur prominent among the officers—they also included Oliver Perry, Lewis Warrington, and James Biddle—who advocated adoption of David Fulton's design for a steam-propelled battery of forty-four guns capable of driving British 74's from the American coast.

It was not Stephen Decatur's first contact with the inventor—earlier, sealed up in the Thames, he had discussed with him the feasibility of a submarine cannon to force a passage of escape. But the steam vessel was a more practicable idea, and also it had the support of William Jones. Congress was persuaded to authorize $120,000 for construction of the battery and it was launched later in the year, christened *Demologos*. But although the inventor felt convinced of its value beyond mere harbor defense—properly used, "it must produce a total revolution in maritime war"—even the most progressive among the naval officers were unable to imagine for it a broadly offensive role. For fifteen years the *Fulton* (as a name, *Demologos* never caught on), with its huge central paddle wheel and with scantlings so thick that none but the heaviest shot could have pierced them, was to sit uselessly in New York Harbor, the unheeded portent of a new age of steam ironclads.

The defenses of New York under Stephen Decatur were never put to the test. Elsewhere along the coast, the enemy's threats and thrusts strained the capacities of men who had rather fight him at sea. The problems of protecting shore installations and civilian personnel, and the necessity of sharing authority with civil and military officers, proved almost too much for sea captains accustomed to plain odds and absolute sway. The frustrations each man struggled with were compounded by his instinctive assumption that the zone in his custody was uppermost on the enemy's list of priorities. This was true of Isaac Hull and William Bainbridge, supervising the naval defenses of Portsmouth, New Hampshire, and Boston, including the construction of the two 74's at those places. Both had their minds set on launching and commanding the first ship of a line against the British, and by early summer, 1814, Bainbridge was obviously ahead. On June 2, anticipating the launch of his 74 within three weeks and concerned that the British were about to attack, he asked the Secretary to give the vessel a name and rush her guns to him.

Fifty-five miles up the coast Isaac Hull, too, looked anxiously for Department action. In hourly expectation of an enemy landing in the vicinity of Portsmouth, he could see no way of raising anything like an adequate defense—the state of New Hampshire had forbidden its militia to serve under any officer of the United States government or man a federal post. Hull was dependent solely upon a handful of marines and the crew of the *Congress*, moored upriver for safety, to protect the Navy Yard, harbor facilities, and the unfinished 74. He begged for reinforcements. Bainbridge worried about guns. Unfortunately for both captains on the northeastern seaboard, their uncertain peril had now lost importance to pressing exigencies in the interior.

Throughout the first half of 1814 the government's war (and peace) plans hinged upon the dramatic news from Europe of Bonaparte's military reverses, abdication, and exile, of the restoration of the Bourbons to the French throne, and, above all, of the summit of power and influence attained by victorious Britain. To Madison, each dispatch seemed to reduce the chances for the success of the hand-picked peace delegation (Albert Gallatin, late of the Treasury, was a leading member) that he had sent to Europe, as a result of Russian offers of mediation, in May of the preceding year. The President, although willing to talk peace, was then determined not to yield a fraction of his demand for an end to British impressment. This position had now become obsolete—the downfall of Napoleon, by rendering the Royal Navy's man-power needs less critical, had removed the chief pretext for impressment. Meanwhile, war expenditures had brought America to the brink of bankruptcy: the war might any day be ignominiously terminated by a collapse of the national Treasury. Of all this Madison's cabinet was distressingly aware, and when on June 27 he canvassed its views on a peace treaty omitting any mention of impressment (officially the main reason for going to war in the first place), he found it unanimously prepared to approve.

For a man so jealous of principle as we know Madison to have been, dropping the impressment issue entirely—not even demanding guarantees against revival of the practice—called for some sacrifice of pride. Yet the President issued appropriately modified peace instructions to his peace emissaries in no mood of abject submission. If America could not negotiate from superior strength, neither must she appear to do so out of desperation. And as much as anything it was to preserve America's image of an honorable equal at the bargaining table in the Flemish capital of Ghent that the campaign was pressed against the enemy in Canada. The new plans for the Canadian front required General Jacob Brown to capture Burlington Heights, clearing the Niagara peninsula and taking York. But as the President himself emphasized, Brown's success depended initially on Chauncey's gaining command of Lake Ontario. The commodore continued to show a reluctance (as did Yeo) to hazard his fleet in an engagement without overwhelming superiority. Indeed, there were grounds for belief that it was only Perry's brilliant example on Lake Erie that shamed Chauncey out of the harbor the following month to chase Yeo's ships up the lake. Even then, after a promising skirmish in Burlington Bay, Chauncey had broken off the engagement when enemy stern shots took away the *General Pike*'s maintop, killing or wounding twenty-seven of her crew. Thereafter, when ships of both sides ventured out and sighted each other, they promptly withdrew to their respective harbors.

If anything, this common reticence added to an atmosphere of tension in which the British and Americans on Lake Ontario were busily building ships faster than they could be armed. In Washington the Secretary of the Navy, convinced that "the moment is critical," ordered the guns manufactured for Bainbridge's 74 (launched on schedule at Boston with the name *Independence*) diverted to Chauncey's command. He also sent officers and men marching or riding stage to Sackets Harbor from the new sloop *Erie*, idled at Baltimore; from the *Macedonian*, embedded in the Thames mud at New London; and from the *Congress*, in Hull's charge. This caused immediate consternation at Portsmouth and Boston. But as the Secretary was quick to point out, seamen were primarily recruited for active naval service, not for the protection of ports—nor that of unfinished ships of the line. In fact, sooner than strip other vessels for the defense of these helpless hulks, Jones would have ordered them burned in their stocks.

There was enough on the Secretary's mind without having to explain or repeat his orders to qualmish officers on the New England coast. A flotilla of perhaps two dozen gunboats under Joshua Barney —an elderly Revolutionary War captain, more recently a successful privateersman—was all the water-borne force he could muster against increasing British raids along both shores of Chesapeake Bay. As for the naval situation on the Canadian front, it had him utterly baffled.

On May 5 Yeo had paraded a squadron before Oswego depot and landed 1,500 men under covering bombardment. Leaving the garrison in flames—outnumbered five to one, the Americans had abandoned it—the ships moved fifty miles along the shore and on May 19 had confronted Sackets Harbor. Yeo's blockade was brief: early in June, after the near annihilation of some two hundred British marines and seamen who had waded ashore near Sandy Creek, he retired his ships into the lake. But Commodore Chauncey made no attempt to follow, nor was the Secretary able to move him.

The most direct pressure on the dilatory commodore was coming from General Jacob Brown, encamped at Buffalo, completing plans for his push across the Niagara peninsula at the beginning of July, and anxiously wondering when he might expect the Navy "in the neighborhood of Fort George." Chauncey promised him that the fleet would sail the first week of the month "to offer the enemy battle" and, should Yeo not accept, to blockade him in Kingston or follow him up the lake. This was uselessly vague to Brown, who counted on the ships to bring him cannon for besieging Fort George and to provide support for an eastward advance along the shore of Lake Ontario. The general's confidence in his ability to drive beyond York, even to Kingston and perhaps as far eastward as Montreal, suggests that he overestimated the fleet's supportive powers. It was certainly unwise to stake so much on Commodore Chauncey. On July 3 he sent his infantry across the Niagara River to seize Queenston, saw no sign of an American warship, and again wrote to Sackets Harbor: "Meet me on the lake shore, north of Fort George, with your fleet. For God's sake, let me see you!" Chauncey's response makes it dramatically clear why he would not be seen. His fleet's sole purpose was the capture or destruction of the enemy's and "I shall not be diverted from my efforts to effectuate it by any sinister attempt to render us subordinate to, or an appendage of, the Army."

The commodore's jealous fear of military control was of course not known in Washington, where the Secretary of War found the silence and delay at Sackets Harbor "unaccountable" and the Secretary of the Navy suffered torments of embarrassment before the cabinet and the country. William Jones, while admitting to uncertainty regarding precisely what co-operation the military expected from the Navy, considered Chauncey's main tasks to be the destruction or blockade of Yeo and the prevention of the westward flow of British troops and supplies. That these aims could scarcely be achieved by idling in Sackets Harbor was made only too tragically clear when sizable enemy reinforcements suddenly confronted General Brown's army and forced it off Queenston Heights. Brown pulled back his lines to Chippewa Creek. On July 25 the enemy fell on him with 3,000 men and eight field pieces. The fighting was savage, particularly in the locality of Lundy's Lane, Brown was wounded and all his staff officers cut up.

In Washington, along with this dreadful news, came at last some word from Chauncey, but still no hint of a sailing date or plan of action. "I hourly expect to hear of your departure," Jones wrote back to the commodore. "The public anxiety is beginning to be extreme for the ultimate safety of the Army." According to the next information received, Chauncey's sailing had been held up by a shortage of gun blocks and ironworks, and now the commodore was ill with fever. After the acute mortification of laying this latest report before an obviously incredulous President, the Secretary of the Navy sent off a letter to New York ordering Stephen Decatur to Sackets Harbor at once.

A transfer of command—with the interesting possibility of Decatur winning a second fleet action on the Great Lakes—failed to materialize because Chauncey just then had himself carried on board his flagship and ordered all vessels to make sail. Again Yeo avoided a fight by beating back into harbor. And Commodore Chauncey, after destroying an empty troop transport and making an unnecessary appearance off Fort George on August 5, did likewise. But Sackets Harbor offered no refuge from the volleys of criticism now being fired at him. He tried to counter it with public excuses of material shortages and work stoppage caused by illness. In his private correspondence with General Brown he accused him of attempting to pin blame for the military reverse on a fleet which "you well know, sir, could not have rendered you the least service during your late incursion upon Upper Canada."

This marked an end to military developments of any importance in the Great Lakes area. In any event it would have been impossible, as August wore on, for the government to give the Canadian fiasco undivided attention. A British invasion fleet of thirty-eight sail had entered Chesapeake Bay, and by the third week of the month five thousand redcoats were marching on the federal city.

Among the few redeeming features of a peculiarly shameful episode in America's political and military history must be counted the brave showing of some of her Navy men. When Joshua Barney failed to stop the invaders on water, he burned his gunboat flotilla in the mouth of the Patuxent River and marched four hundred men overland to meet the foe at Bladensburg. They stood their ground with twelve- and eighteen-pound cannon until deserting militia left their right flank exposed and Barney was felled by a musket ball.

Captain Thomas Tingey, through his command of the Washington Navy Yard, was the one naval officer to share in the politicians' ignominy. At an extraordinary cabinet session within the Yard at dawn on August 24, it was decided to destroy it rather than leave it to the enemy. Tingey, after directing the emplacement of combustibles, put off firing the powder train as long as he reasonably could, until receipt of advice from the War Department that the Yard could no longer be protected. Still he delayed, suffering the importunities of local citizenry and some naval officers, most notably Captain John Orde Creighton, to refrain from the deed. It was nearly 8:30 at night before he ordered the matches applied, and by then the British, having entered Washington unopposed, were thrusting pikes tipped with fireballs through the windows of the Capitol. As Tingey went down the Eastern Branch in the gig to Alexandria, the flames from his burning Navy Yard merged with those of the enemy's superior incendiarism. Vengeance rather than permanent occupation was the purpose of the British visitation, and the invaders' prompt withdrawal allowed Tingey to return next morning and see with what thoroughness he had discharged his melancholy duty. Except for the commandant's house (which still stands) and the paymaster's office, all the buildings were in charred ruins. So were the ships. They included not only the *Boston, New York,* and *General Greene*—those rotting hulks were no great loss—but the new 18-gun sloop *Argus* and the frigate *Columbia,* on her stocks and only ten days short of her launching date.

The British briefly occupied Alexandria, and were then given a hot descent of the Potomac by American naval men without ships. Oliver Perry and David Porter, with remnants of the *Essex's* crew, had come south in time to man the batteries along the river bank. After running a gauntlet of eighteen-pound shot, the British squadron was also endangered by a flotilla of fireships sent floating into its midst. And one feels that had their employment been supervised by anybody else but Commodore John Rodgers, the British would not have found it so easy to tow them all safely off. The enemy's threat then shifted to Baltimore. Here Rodgers, in a prominent defensive role, had far better luck than with his Potomac fireships. He blocked the mouth of the Patapsco with more than a score of sunken craft, put gunboats into effective position, and set up naval cannon on the northern heights. Unable to attack the port frontally, the British disembarked at a headland, lost their commander in chief to a sniper's bullet along the march—lost, too, when they beheld the city's stout defenses, what lingered of their hopes for victory. Their last flourish in Chesapeake Bay was to stage a long and colorful bombardment which failed in its object of turning the defenders' flank because the range was too great but achieved memorability by leaving them with the inspirational stanzas of a future national anthem.

Meanwhile the three new sloops getting to sea that year had met varying fortune. The *Frolic*, commanded by Master-Commandant Joseph Bainbridge, was chased sixty miles by a 36-gun frigate and surrendered without a shot. A week later the *Peacock*, Captain Lewis Warrington, encountered the 18-gun British brig *Epervier* five days out of Havana. An hour's hot fire left the *Epervier* riddled, with five feet of water in her hold, her main-topmast gone, and twenty-three men killed or wounded. The third sloop, *Wasp*, Captain Johnston Blakely, following the example of Allen and the *Argus*, dodged patrolling frigates to the mouth of the English Channel and for several weeks burned and scuttled the enemy's commerce. On June 28, in smooth waters west of the Bay of Biscay, she engaged an inferior brig, the *Reindeer*, as the vessels lay abreast of each other less than twenty yards apart. So close were they that men hacked and thrust at each other through open ports. Captain William Manners of the *Reindeer*, both thighs shattered by grapeshot, was dragging himself to the rigging in an impossible effort to lead a boarding party when two balls from the *Wasp*'s maintop pierced his skull. The *Reindeer*'s casualties stood at seventy-seven—more than half her crew—when she surrendered.

On August 27 the *Wasp*, in a thirty-minute night action near the spot where she had defeated the *Reindeer*, reduced the 11-gun *Avon* to an unmanageable wreck. Then she ranged south and west, falling in with the Swedish brig *Adonis*, bound for Europe from South America. Two American passengers, Lieutenant Stephen Decatur McKnight (the commodore's nephew) and a midshipman, survivors from the *Essex*, paid off to the Swedish captain and transferred aboard the *Wasp*, no doubt agog to tell their countrymen of their late ship's cruise and fate in the South Pacific. But the strange tale would never be heard ashore from them or any of the *Wasp*'s company. She made sail, "standing for the Spanish Main," and was never seen again.

CHAPTER TWENTY

Lake Champlain

THE *Adams* was a 28-gun frigate cut down to a flush-decked corvette and mounting twenty-six eighteen-pound columbiads: lightweight, large-bore cannon intended as improvements over the carronades. In the middle of August 1814, returning from a prize-hunting cruise of the Irish coast with a scurvy-ridden crew, she ran into thick fog off Maine and grounded on a reef south of Bangor. Lightened by the sacrifice of provisions and spars, she was brought half sinking by Captain Charles Morris twenty miles up the Penobscot River, at whose mouth, on September 1, a British force of two line-of-battle ships, three frigates, and ten troop transports took station. Seven companies of British soldiers swarmed upstream and ran into a surprise barrage from Morris' columbiads, mounted onshore and manned by survivors of the scurvy outbreak, a small unit of Army regulars, and some diversely armed militia. The defenders checked successive enemy thrusts until, outnumbered eight to one, they were obliged to burn the corvette and retreat into the forest. After a 200-mile march through wilderness—without a single desertion, it was Morris' proud boast—his crew stumbled exhausted into Portsmouth.

Isaac Hull received their news of a British penetration into Maine with dismay. He feared a speedy attack on Portsmouth and the inevitable collapse of his force, only slightly augmented by Morris' weary band, in defense of his still unlaunched 74. He wrote hastily to William Jones, "I cannot but prepare your mind for the worst."

But Hull was himself unprepared for what happened next. William Bainbridge, without Department authority, issued orders for the survivors of the *Adams* to continue southward and assist him in defense of Boston. It would be hard to decide which was the greater, the commodore's peremptoriness or the palpitating rage it generated in the captain. Was not the *Independence* launched and able to defend herself? Arguing thus, Hull was evidently unaware that the *Independence* had not received her guns. Did not ten to fifteen thousand well-armed men surround her? And in a harbor difficult for the foe to enter? "Will you take another view?" he implored the commodore. "Let me hear from you, and for God's sake, leave the men." Bainbridge was certainly in a more tenable position than Hull. While New Hampshire still balked at handing over its militia to the command of a United States Navy captain, the neighboring state of Massachusetts thought the risk of admitting increased federal control worth taking to keep the British out, and had not only placed its militia at Commodore Bainbridge's disposal but six thirty-two-pound guns as well.

But Bainbridge was not to have the *Adams* men, for Secretary Jones, responding to Hull's distraught appeals, reminded him that the *Adams* was outside his command and he must therefore "correct the error." Bainbridge did so, without apology. The incident left an acrimony smoldering between Bainbridge and Hull which would one day culminate in another squalid quarrel.

Earnestly Hull began to solicit political support for the abolition of a commodore's ambiguous authority and the establishment of an admiral's rank. The ease and frequency with which captains claimed eligibility to the courtesy title undoubtedly bred absurdity and friction. Three broad pendants flying over as few as four ships together— with all the tripartite rivalry that the scene implied—were not uncommon. "We have now so many commodores," Hull observed caustically at the close of 1814, "that to be a plain captain is rather of the two most honorable." Even a master-commandant could acquire the title (as in Perry's case). And it was a master-commandant in charge of a squadron who, while Hull and Bainbridge waged their tawdry contest under a coastal threat which failed to materialize, won on an inland sea the war's most influential naval victory.

The suggestion that troops be transferred from Lake Champlain to Lake Ontario and thence to the assistance of Jacob Brown's embattled forces on the Niagara peninsula had made sense when General George Izard first addressed it on July 19, 1814, to the Secretary of War. But during the following week secret dispatches were reaching the Canadian government from London containing plans for strategy revisions permitted by the reduction of military requirements in Europe. Pressure was to be maintained against America's naval bases on the Great Lakes. So were simultaneous diversionary operations along her east coast. These would also assist in the destruction of her elements on Lake Champlain, an enterprise which was left to Sir George Prevost's discretion. It could hardly have failed to attract him. Lake Champlain, 107 miles long, formed the first quarter length of an almost unbroken line of navigable waterway—river and lake—connecting Montreal with New York. Prevost could dream of marching his divisions down that same route which Burgoyne had attempted. Thus the focus of strategic discussion in Canada now shifted eastward. Nothing was planned for the Niagara peninsula beyond, perhaps, a strengthening of existing positions. On Lake Ontario, Admiral Yeo's fleet would be built up to unconquerable size—the American side of that lake would in any case become outflanked by British possession of Lake Champlain.

In Quebec preparations began for an offensive against the first objective, a garrison town on Lake Champlain's northwest shore: Plattsburg. In the first weeks of August reports smuggled across the border by scouts and friendly Indians told of massive troop concentrations in the area above the lake, and the Plattsburg officers were in the midst of intensive defense planning when a letter came in from Secretary of War John Armstrong detaching two whole brigades for service on Lake Ontario.

At the first rumors of offensive movements in the north General Izard had sensibly written to Armstrong that since to weaken Plattsburg now would hasten its fall, his July 19 proposal should be considered no longer militarily prudent. Whether his letter would have changed Armstrong's mind can only be guessed at, but in any event it reached him after he had decided that Izard should "carry the war as far westward as possible while we have ascendency on the Lakes." The general had no choice but to obey. On August 29 he marched out of Plattsburg with 4,000 men.

There is some resemblance in this situation to that which William

Jones faced earlier in the summer, when he was under occasionally frantic pressure to strengthen the naval defenses of Portsmouth and Boston at the expense of his forces on the Great Lakes. Jones had resisted; and had Commodore Chauncey fulfilled the Secretary's hopes by winning supremacy on Lake Ontario and vigorously supporting General Brown's troops, this latest crisis could hardly have arisen. A different Secretary of War might yet have saved the situation by turning Izard back to Plattsburg as speedily as communications allowed. In addition to acknowledging the sudden importance of those brigades to the defense of Lake Champlain, he might well have foreseen that their presence on Lake Ontario could only multiply burdens of liaison that the naval commander there had already shown himself unable to bear. And indeed, very soon after General Izard reached the Niagara peninsula to co-operate with Jacob Brown's men, he too had found cause to complain about Commodore Chauncey's unmistakable preference for the safety of Sackets Harbor.

Izard's departure had left Plattsburg manned by not much more than 2,000 regulars and what militia the garrison commander, General Alexander Macomb, might borrow from the states of Vermont and New York. On Lake Champlain itself things looked a little better. At first, in 1813, America's modest naval strength there had vanished in a single summer afternoon when Lieutenant Sidney Smith (Commodore Barron's hostile witness on the *Chesapeake*) rashly pursued enemy gunboats into the Canadian narrows. Fluky winds and shore artillery had driven him to surrender two sloops and 110 men. William Jones, seeing "no end to this roar of broad axes," had then opposed further shipbuilding on Lake Champlain—"God knows where the money is coming from"—but the President farsightedly overruled him. Thanks to the brothers Adam and Noah Brown, who launched the 26-gun corvette *Saratoga* forty days after her timber was cut and built the 20-gun *Eagle* in under three weeks, the naval balance on Lake Champlain swung back to the Americans.

Yeo had done little to redress it for the British and, even as General Prevost assembled an invasion force in Montreal which included the Duke of Wellington's seasoned infantrymen, he continued to preoccupy himself with the three-decker he was building at Kingston. Prevost's impatience to advance while he had good campaigning weather stirred the naval commander in chief to pay Lake Champlain somewhat greater attention, and on August 25 a 36-gun frigate, the *Confiance,* was launched at the British base of Ile aux Noix. Prevost, refusing to wait three weeks until she was ready for service, sent 12,000 troops surging over the border and they forced an American withdrawal to the eastern bank of the Saranac River. But that was as far as Prevost would allow them to go until his ships came up the lake. Now he firmly geared his advance to naval support, even though the garrison confronting his columns was considerably less than a stronghold. Prevost did not think it sufficiently vulnerable so long as its defenders could draw inspiration and support from the presence of an American flotilla in Plattsburg Bay. Not until those ships were attacked would he attack. He sent a series of urgent and even insulting letters to Captain George Downie, only recently placed in command at Ile aux Noix, harassing him into action.

Downie, his mind still uneasy about the condition of his squadron, got under way on September 9, and after a passage slowed by headwinds his vessels hove to off Cumberland Head at dawn on the eleventh. After a brief reconnaissance he decided to attack that same morning. Along the western side of the Saranac, British infantrymen and artillery waited. The news that the American flotilla had been destroyed at anchor would be their signal to storm across the river. To Wellington's old campaigners it bid fair to be one more battle, hardly different from any in their fighting experience. But victory at Plattsburg would constitute, in today's parlance, a major British breakthrough. Rapid advances on Albany and New York would surely follow. Before winter set in, Prevost might politically as well as geographically sever industrial New England from the main body of the republic. It was not unthinkable that he might penetrate into the agricultural southland for a triumphant connection with British forces even then about to embark from Bermuda for an invasion of Louisiana. So much was at stake. So much depended on the depleted Plattsburg garrison and behind it, in the bay, the American squadron of a corvette, a brig, two sloops, and ten gunboats, under command of Master-Commandant Thomas Macdonough.

This tall physician's son from Delaware, one of that stellar company of midshipmen under Preble in the Mediterranean, had become at thirty an efficient and sternly religious ship commander who liked to pepper his speech with marine allusions from the Scriptures. "He that wavereth," he quoted to a visitor on board his flagship *Saratoga* on the Sunday before Downie's squadron came up the lake, "is like a wave of the sea, driven with the wind and tossed." And he added, "Behold the ships, which though they be so great, yet are they turned about with a very small helm." Problems of turning about now weighed on Macdonough's mind. He had spring cables rigged to his vessels, enabling them to turn in a wide arc without setting sail, and he also went to the trouble of laying out kedge anchors attached to each quarter of the *Saratoga* so that if necessary she could be warped in a full circle and use all her guns. By keeping his squadron at anchor between the harbor headlands instead of offering battle in the open lake, he secured for himself a distinct advantage. Downie could only approach it with his forward guns brought to bear. Macdonough proposed to meet him with his four ships broadside on.

It was a brilliant fall morning. The sun had cleared the Green Mountains to sparkle off the lake and spread a warm glow over the rolling Adirondacks. Shortly before 9 o'clock on September 11, 1814, Downie's squadron doubled the Head: the *Chubb, Linnet, Confiance,* and *Finch* abreast, and twelve galleys to leeward. As the British ships bore down steadily on the American line, Macdonough summoned his officers to the quarterdeck and they knelt in prayer. A few minutes later the first British guns spoke, their shot splashing short except for one that wrecked a hen coop on the *Saratoga* and released a gamecock. Fluttering to a gun slide, the bird crowed lustily, provoking cheers and laughter from Macdonough's crew. In this atmosphere of piety and mirth the Americans opened their fire, and Macdonough himself discharged the first of the *Saratoga*'s long twenty-five pounders.

The shot flew the length of the *Confiance*'s deck, carpeting the holystoned planks with dead and wounded. Yet as every American long gun began to roar and the galleys' armament bellowed their contribution, the *Confiance* stood on through smoke and shot as if under royal review at Spithead. Not until within 500 yards of the *Saratoga*'s beam did Downie anchor, first swinging slightly to fire his bow guns at the *Eagle* while giving the *Saratoga* full benefit of his sixteen double-shotted long twenty-fours. At the same time, the 16-

gun brig *Linnet* closed on the *Saratoga*'s bows with a raking fire. The American flagship's first lieutenant, kneeling to sight a bow gun, was killed instantly by a shot through the port. Macdonough, working alongside his gunners, was momentarily stunned by a grisly accident when a gunner's severed head hit him like a boulder in the face. It was during this early violent cannonade that the *Saratoga* sustained most of her damage and casualties: fifty-five shot holes in her hull, fifty-seven men killed and wounded. One by one her guns fell silent, knocked out by shot or crippled from mishandling. The last of her carronades sheered a bolt on firing, flew off the carriage, and plunged down the main hatch. Still, the sum of Macdonough's troubles just then hardly equaled the disastrous state of affairs on the *Confiance*. A shot from the *Saratoga* had struck one of her long twenty-four-pounders and knocked a quoin into Captain Downie's abdomen, mortally wounding him. And now too the British flagship came under renewed fire from the *Saratoga*. Macdonough's foresight had served him well. His crew, working amid flying shot at the kedge anchors, slowly, skillfully hauled the loftily sparred corvette about until all her undamaged port guns were brought to bear on the mauled and leaderless *Confiance*.

Sharp fighting raged meanwhile between schooners, sloops, and gunboats all down the line. At the foot of it the British *Finch* was badly cut up by the *Ticonderoga*'s long guns and carronades and she crawled along the line, half her crew dead or disabled, to run aground on Crab Island, where a six-pound shore gun finished her off. Vengeful British gunboats swarmed about the *Ticonderoga*— some even tried to board—and were beaten off by bursts of canister. Galleys drifted out of the fight with dead men at their oars. The *Chubb* was hammered into surrender by the new American *Eagle*. And now, at the head of the line, the sole surviving lieutenant of the *Confiance* was trying valiantly to turn her about for effective reply to the *Saratoga*'s relentless broadsides.

But her sails were in ribbons, her masts sundered, three-quarters of her crew casualties. More than a hundred shot holes riddled her hull. She was fast filling with water and her wounded were in danger of drowning. The lieutenant hauled down her colors. Macdonough then turned his guns on the *Linnet* and pounded her also into a sinking hulk. The battle was over before noon. With shattering emphasis Thomas Macdonough had asserted American naval supremacy on Lake Champlain. Sir George Prevost's advance troops had already started to cross the river when the shocking news reached him. The British infantrymen, many of whom had stormed more formidable forts on the Iberian Peninsula, might still have carried the Plattsburg garrison. But they needed different leadership, for Prevost was no Wellington. Having staked all on naval support—Admiral Yeo charged afterward that he had "goaded [Downie] on to his fate"—the general could now see but one recourse. At nightfall he withdrew his forward detachments, and before another sunrise above the Vermont peaks his entire army was marching back across the Canadian border.

"The Almighty has been pleased to grant us a signal victory," Macdonough reported—prompting a British newspaper comment that "Much as we admire the laconic in letter-writing, we should have been better pleased with Commodore Macdonough had he informed us by whose earthly means exclusive of his own he was allowed to achieve a victory so contrary to expectations and all human probability."

By all accounts it did not go to his head: humility and modesty remained prominent among his characteristics. But its effects upon other persons and events were profound. For one thing, Madison was inspired to draft an even more ambitious shipbuilding program on Lake Ontario, possibly with the hope that now Chauncey would be emboldened to crown the successes of his junior officers on the lakes with a third great victory. He ordered the commodore to build two 94-gun ships of the line and a 44-gun frigate. He also expressed an interest in using Fulton's steam frigate in the Canadian theater until it was explained to him that the vessel lacked sufficient engine power to withstand the Great Lakes storms. William Jones again raised doubts about the wisdom of more building on the lakes: it was expensive and meant stripping the ocean-going fleet of guns and men. Now, at the close of 1814, he had 10,617 men on the naval roster and less than a thousand were at sea. The great majority were on the lakes or listed as in "harbor defense," which meant for the most part under blockade with their ships.

But Madison had plans for the oceans too, where Britain, for all her vaunted naval might, remained extremely vulnerable. American privateers had seized more than 1,500 merchant vessels and, through continued harassment of her sea lanes, were imposing a heavy strain upon her convoy system. Late in November the President ordered six light and swift squadrons prepared under Rodgers, Decatur, Stewart, Morris, Porter, and Perry to sail as soon as they could get out on a commerce-raiding cruise from the coast of England to the China Sea. It is clear that Madison's increasing initiative in naval affairs was not entirely to William Jones's liking, particularly since the Secretary thought that public funds were being wastefully employed on them. Jones's own financial situation was in sad shape and he now found himself unable to carry on his duties. "My life is at the service of my country," he told a friend, "but not my reputation and peace." He left office on December 19 after drafting a reform program which, though not adopted at once in its entirety, was to influence naval organization for many years to come.

One proposal immediately acted upon was the establishment of a senior board of naval officers to give the Secretary expert professional guidance. The idea had long been advocated by naval men, including William Bainbridge, whose preference for the term "commissioners" over that of "inspectors" was adopted, and who had abundant confidence in his qualifications for a member's seat if not the board president's chair. One or the other would certainly have been his had John Rodgers accepted President Madison's invitation to the post of Secretary of the Navy. But Rodgers, influenced by brightening prospects that Congress would enact a law for the creation of admirals, asked if he might retain his service rank while occupying the cabinet office. This Madison could not accede to. Passing over Robert Fulton, who aspired to the post with eager plans for converting the sailing navy to steam, he selected Benjamin Crowninshield, a Salem marine merchant. Crowninshield at first declined on grounds of health and domestic duties, but changed his mind two days later. And Rodgers became first president of the Board of Naval Commissioners.

Meanwhile the news of Downie's defeat on Lake Champlain, following so soon upon the British repulse at Baltimore, heartened the American emissaries around the Ghent peace table while vexing the British. "If we had either burned Baltimore or held Plattsburg," one of the latter wrote to his War Minister in London, "I believe we should have had a peace on the terms you sent us"—terms which would have drastically altered the Canadian-American boundary, created an Indian buffer state between the two countries, parceled out much of Maine to the British, and left them in absolute control of the Great Lakes. The American retreat from the impressment issue had been an open invitation to these humiliating demands. But now the British could see no hope of furthering them without quick military recovery on the American front under more energetic leadership. Wellington was offered the command only to turn it down. ("The question," he told his government, "is whether we can obtain this naval superiority on the lakes. If we cannot, I shall do you but little good in America.") No further attempts to humble the republic across the ocean, however much she deserved it, appeared to be profitable. Christmas Eve saw the signing of a treaty of peace.

But it would take seven weeks before H.M.S. *Favourite* spanned the Atlantic with the document, and in the meantime the naval war continued. There is a creditable naval aspect even to Andrew Jackson's gory defeat of the British at New Orleans on January 8, 1815. Five of the derided "Jeffs" under Lieutenant Thomas ap Catesby Jones harassed the invaders in the middle of Lake Borgne—winning precious time for Jackson to receive reinforcements and set up extra batteries—until they were overwhelmed by an enemy force of small craft nine times their number. And while Americans anxiously awaited word from either the battlefield at New Orleans or the palace at Ghent, their warships still put to sea. On December 14 the *Constitution*, Captain Stewart, had taken advantage of a westerly gale and slipped out of Boston. One month later the *President*, Commodore Decatur, left her anchorage off Staten Island at nightfall and plowed into the gray murk of a snowstorm. On January 22 the splendid sloops *Peacock* and *Hornet* crossed the bar at daylight under storm canvas and pierced the British cordon unmolested. Carrying orders to rendezvous with the *President* at Tristan da Cunha, they accordingly set course for the South Atlantic. Their captains were unaware of the improbable fate which had swiftly overtaken the nation's most exalted commodore.

The *President*'s misfortunes stemmed from a pilot's error or misplaced marker boats which caused her to run aground in snow squalls at about 10 P.M. on January 14. For ninety minutes she was pounded by waves, losing much of her copper, straining the keel, and twisting her masts. She was sorely damaged, but once heavy seas had forced her over the bar Decatur could do no other than keep going; westerly winds made it impossible to attempt putting back. The British blockading squadron meanwhile, blown off the coast by the same gale, had tacked northward on moderating winds, seeking to intercept any American bold enough to have put out in rough weather. Throughout the night Decatur had been creeping up the Long Island shore. At 3 A.M. he altered course to southeast, and in the first wintry daylight of January 15 he found himself surrounded on three sides by the 56-gun frigate *Majestic*, 24-gun frigate *Endymion*, and the two light frigates *Pomone* and *Tenedos*.

Had the *President* not grounded, she would easily have been at sea beyond visual range of British telescopes. She was now to leeward, still in a favorable situation for escape—had she not been injured. Now she could only crawl through the rough seas, and she was taking water steadily. Decatur, ordering boats and provisions overboard, was enabled to keep the enemy at a distance during the hours of bleak light. But as dusk gathered, the *Endymion*, Captain David Hope, aided by a shift in wind, gained the American's starboard quarter. Night enveloped the ships. Decatur changed course to due south. The *Endymion* did the same and ran abreast of the *President*'s starboard side, discharging main-deck twenty-four pounders. The boarding party which Decatur mustered with typical prematurity stood idle. Even to bring the *President*'s guns to bear was denied him, for Hope cleverly hauled his faster ship off each time she closed. Now the wind dropped further, and Decatur was being pursued as Hull had once been. But this was January, not July, and the pursuers had their quarry within gunshot. Even as the commodore's desperately stern orders sent men swarming into the freezing tops with buckets to wet the fully spread canvas, the *Endymion*'s broadsides tore through sails and rigging, and left his decks strewn with casualties. Archibald Hamilton (the lieutenant who had borne the *Macedonian*'s colors to Washington) was cut in two by a twenty-four-pound shot. Another knocked Lieutenant Fitz Henry Babbitt—the talkative midshipman at Barron's trial—down the after hatch and in half an hour he died of a fractured skull. Twenty more were killed during a punishment so intolerable that Decatur decided to stake all chance of escape on the opportunity of hitting back. He put up his helm, and as the *President* swung to starboard her broadside guns roared at last. Side by side and rolling heavily, the two ships fought a running battle for two hours before the *Endymion*'s fire flickered out. With her sails stripped from her yards she fell astern and bore off into the night. But the *Pomone* and *Tenedos* had come up, guided by the furious concentration of gun flashes. And although the firing had ceased, a clearing sky betrayed the *President* in fitful moonlight. The *Pomone* luffed to port, letting loose a broadside, and with the *Tenedos* astern prepared to rake.

Splinters had opened Decatur's forehead and torn his chest. Oblivious to the wounds, he had managed his ship with exceptional coolness. It need not be assumed that personal pain and exhaustion weighed much in his calculations now. It was enough that the continued ability of his ship and people to endure had fallen into grave doubt. The light English vessels, their crews in fresh condition—the Americans had scarcely rested in thirty-six hours—might cripple the *President* with their eighteen-pounders even before the *Majestic* and repaired *Endymion* came up to turn the inevitable defeat into unnecessary annihilation. To intensify the ordeal of his men would avail nothing. We may conjecture with what anguish Decatur searched his soul at this point—he seldom committed his innermost thoughts to paper—but concern for his people and a realistic assessment of the odds molded his final decision. "Thus situated, with about one-fifth of my crew killed or wounded," wrote the commodore who so often had appeared to equate capitulation with cowardice, "all that was left for me to do was to receive the fire of the nearest ship and surrender."

Five weeks after Decatur's departure for Bermuda as a captive of the British, Charles Stewart, captain of the *Constitution*, sighted the enemy sloops *Cyane* and *Levant* northeast of Madeira. On the *Constellation* under blockade and on his present ship bottled up in Boston Harbor, Stewart must long have abandoned hopes for glory in this war. Unaware that officially no further chances existed for it, he opened fire, and the ships traded shots under a clear moon. Stewart's advantage of long twenty-four-pounders would have been diminished without his corresponding seamanship, so skillful and threatening were the thrusts of his lightweight adversaries. But first the *Levant*, then the *Cyane*, struck. Hounded by three 50-gun British frigates, Stewart managed to run home with the *Cyane*. The other prize separated from him and was retaken by the British.

The winter weeks passed. Neither Captain James Biddle on the *Hornet* nor Lewis Warrington on the *Peacock* knew that the commodore with whom they expected to rendezvous had been taken, interned in Bermuda, paroled back to America. The *Hornet* fell in with the British *Penguin* and shot flew high and low as the ships rose and fell in turbulent seas. The *Hornet*'s first broadside cut the enemy captain's body in half. The vessels closed and the *Penguin*'s bowsprit sawed through the *Hornet*'s mizzen shrouds while Biddle's musketry swept back an enraged British boarding party. The *Penguin* was soon shipping water fast and, with one-third of her crew casualties, she struck. Three more weeks at Tristan da Cunha without sign of the *President*, and the sloops set course eastward, doubling the Cape of Good Hope and sighting, on May 27, a strange sail which they took at first for a large Indiaman. Almost too late they discovered that she was an enemy line-of-battle ship and they hauled at once upon the wind, pursued by "the grim, towering stranger." At 8 P.M. the *Penguin* got clear away, but the enemy—the 74-gun *Cornwallis*—weathered upon the *Hornet* fast.

Biddle cast away a sheet anchor, some cable, rigging, and spars. Half an hour later, the *Cornwallis* still gaining, his crew chopped through the wardroom deck to get at the ballast, and they heaved some ninety pieces overboard. This lost the *Hornet* a good fifty tons of weight and at 2 A.M., as Biddle tacked to the southward, she had a fair chance to escape. But at daybreak the *Cornwallis* was still there, on the *Hornet*'s lee quarter, and now her bow guns flashed. Over the American's side went more kentledge, more spars, then guns, shot, provisions, spare sails, and all the rigging. The chase continued into the afternoon, the *Hornet*'s crew cutting up her launch under heavy fire of round and grape shot, and with it over the side went all Biddle's muskets and cutlasses. It is impossible not to marvel at Biddle's dogged resolve to escape. At 3 P.M. the ship's bell and armorer's forge had been hove overboard, men were breaking up the topgallant forecastle, and others were placed as human ballast to trim the ship. And at 4:30 the *Cornwallis* began to drop astern. At 6 she was hull down in the *Hornet*'s wake. And next morning she had vanished.

After the extraordinary chase—it had lasted forty-two hours—Biddle put back to the Cape of Good Hope. The *Peacock* continued her cruise alone across the Indian Ocean to Sumatra. Far behind, on the other side of the world, Bonaparte had escaped from Elba, raised an army on French soil, and shattered it against Wellington's stubborn squares on the field at Waterloo. America had naught to fear in consequence: Congress had ratified peace with Britain four months before and gone on to authorize another war against a former, less significant foe. Of all this Lewis Warrington knew nothing. He steered his ship through the Straits of Sunda and sighted a small brig of the East India Company. When her captain hailed with news of peace, Warrington, skeptical, insisted on her colors coming down. This was refused, and the *Peacock* brought them down with a broadside that left seven casualties. It was June 30, 1815, three years to the fortnight since the first American naval vessel had surrendered. And Lewis Warrington's prize in those far distant waters, the last ship to strike in the War of 1812, bore the same name: *Nautilus*.

CHAPTER TWENTY-ONE

Again the Mediterranean

The importance of a permanent naval establishment appears
to be sanctioned by the voice of the nation.

— Preamble to a report of the Secretary
of the Navy, 1815

ON FEBRUARY 4, 1815, torchlight processions through the streets of
Washington celebrated the triumphant news from General Jackson's
headquarters in New Orleans. That same day, orders sped forth from
the new Secretary of the Navy to Commodore Chauncey, suspend-
ing the emergency measures on Lake Ontario and transferring
batches of men from his command to New London, Boston, and
Baltimore for service on ocean-going vessels. Peace with Britain had
yet to be ratified by Congress, but Mr. Madison, encouraged by the
Navy's unprecedented strength and prestige, was already contemplating its use in a new war against an old enemy. Despite America's
payment of tribute, the depredations committed on her shipping by
Algerian corsairs had never entirely ceased. Now seemed the ideal
time for suppressing them once and for all. Since 1812 the number of
American warships had more than doubled and now included the
new line-of-battle ships. Thirty captains were on the Naval Register
compared with twelve at the outbreak of the war; there were twice as
many lieutenants as then; and the number of able seamen, ordinary
seamen, and boys had grown from 5,000 or so to almost 12,000.

Predominant in the popular mind were the victories of the naval war, not the defeats and misfired plans, and certainly not the lessons, of which there was no lack. An examination of the frigate record, for instance, would have raised serious doubts whether they had proved worthy of their investment. Throughout one war year, 1813, three had been bottled up in harbor; the *Essex* was afar on her long and ultimately disastrous Pacific adventure; the *Chesapeake* failed to survive the summer; the rest—*Constitution, President, Congress*—took fewer prizes than the sloops of war *Hornet* and *Argus*. In 1814 frigates captured no more than twenty enemy merchant vessels and, far from destroying any of Britain's naval force, supplemented it with the *Essex*. All in all, America's warships had done less harm to British commerce than her privateers, a comparison sure to have been reversed had the moneys originally spent on frigate construction gone instead to the creation of a fleet of nimble brigs and sloops. The unrelated duels on the oceans had negligible influence on the war's outcome. However bravely won, the American victories could not materially compensate for the miscarriage of attempts to get a squadron into fertile East Indian waters, nor for the occasional breach rather than total dissolution of the British blockade.

Yet the frustrations of the war, the absence of clear causes and conclusive designs, its exposure of gross military deficiencies, its crippling costs and negative gains, all counted for little against the phenomenal enrichment of America's identity as a sovereign power by the glowing deeds of her Navy. Hence there was no serious postwar disposition to probe the Navy's own defects—many of which, in any case, the newly appointed Naval Commissioners were expected to remedy. The three-man board would be responsible for all naval construction and repair. It would possess absolute authority over navy yards, constructors, and purchasing agents, and no shipbuilding or major repair would begin without its approval. The principal gain was foreseen as a uniformity of vessels, equipment, and modes of refitting, achieved through the imposition of standardization upon a technical branch long bedeviled by confusion and delays in rigging, sparring, and gun installation. The Board of Commissioners was warmly welcomed by Department officials and naval officers alike as a long-overdue innovation. And the frictions that almost immediately ensued might have been averted had the Act of Congress on which the Board was founded defined with greater clarity the division of powers between Commissioners and Navy Department.

Meanwhile, in the general enthusiasm for the Navy, the citizens of New London overlooked Commodore Decatur's recent surrender and gave him a hero's welcome on his return from Bermuda. But his wife's joy and relief—night after night during his absence she had paced the floor sleeplessly—were annulled by the fear of his going off again. On the eve of President Madison's request to Congress for a declaration of war against Algiers, she wrote a pathetic letter to the Secretary of the Navy begging him to exclude her husband from plans for the Mediterranean expedition. Susan Decatur was evidently unaware of the prevailing assumption among naval officers that her husband was by no means the leading candidate for command of the war fleet to Algiers; that this distinction belonged almost by divine right as much as seniority and professional qualification to one man, William Bainbridge. And the commodore himself, on board the *Independence*, expressed gratification with only modest surprise when Department orders reached him near the end of February alerting his precious new ship of the line for the Mediterranean. About the same time, his repatriated fellow commodore was writing a letter of consolation to the retired old officer Richard Dale on the loss of his son's leg during the battle with the *Endymion*. (Midshipman Dale was to die of the wound in Bermuda.) In light of the upsetting developments in store for Bainbridge, there is an ominous ring to a certain portion of Decatur's letter. "I have lost a noble ship, sir," he wrote, "but I hope it will be considered there has been no loss of honor." Before sealing the letter for dispatch he scored through the words "it will be considered" and above the deletion wrote boldly, "I shall satisfy the world."

That the aspersions of a Bermuda newspaper on the *President*'s surrender had been recanted a few days after publication was not calculated to remove them from common gossip or prevent their widespread currency. And for all Decatur could know during his brief internment, the news of his defeat had already lowered him in the estimation of his countrymen. Thus he had come home beset by fears of a tarnished reputation and bent on prompt vindication before a court of inquiry. He craved some arresting exploit to secure his glory before it had a chance to dim; he needed a public gesture of undiminished confidence in him and an opportunity to justify it dramatically. Nothing else mattered, including his wife's emotions; these had got the better of her judgment, he informed the Secretary, requesting that the Department ignore any further distaff attempts to interfere with his official duties. This was part of Decatur's reply to an unusual private communication from Benjamin Crowninshield disclosing plans for two Mediterranean squadrons and offering him command of either one or a post ashore in charge of the Boston Navy Yard. "In short, my dear sir," the Secretary's letter had concluded, "your wishes are to be consulted. Any service or any station that is at the disposal of this Department, rely upon it, you may command."

It was an uncommonly generous token to an officer from whom the taint of surrender had yet to be removed by formal court. But Decatur's glittering reputation, more inviolable than he himself believed, was scarcely dulled by the loss of his ship. And Crowninshield, a weak and indecisive administrator, regarded Decatur as the officer best able to get things done to the Department's credit.

Decatur had shown the Secretary's letter to Washington Irving, a friend and fellow guest at Bradish's, the favorite naval boardinghouse opposite the New York Battery, during recuperation from his chest wound. Irving (by his own account) had immediately advised him to seize the chance for a brilliant dash from under the cloud lately flung over his celebrity, to get smartly ahead of Bainbridge, to "whip the cream off the enterprise." Decatur needed little urging and on March 20 had sent his reply: he would take the first squadron to the Mediterranean provided that he was allowed to avoid a subordinate appearance by leaving that sea for home the instant Commodore Bainbridge arrived with the second squadron. To this there was no objection. The ports of assembly for the squadrons were New York and Boston. Decatur was appointed to command of the New York force, given the new frigate *Guerrière* for a flagship, and ordered to prepare for departure at one hour's notice.

It would be the largest American naval squadron yet to sail. The *Guerrière*, 44, named for Hull's victim, was joined by Decatur's prize, the freshly repaired *Macedonian*, 38, and there were the 18-gun brig *Epervier*, 14-gun brigs *Firefly*, *Spark*, and *Flambeau*, and the 12-gun schooners *Torch* and *Spitfire*. Up from Norfolk sailed the *Constellation*, 38, a specially designed sofa in her great cabin to accommodate the physical infirmity of her captain, Charles Gordon, who still clung to a hope of restored health.

Jesse Elliott arrived with the 18-gun sloop *Ontario* and a sickly crew after a storm-tossed passage from Baltimore. It was now that Elliott's application for a court of inquiry to dispel insinuations of perfidy on Lake Erie was granted; and never satisfied, he reacted to the favorable verdict with a request for additional testimonial from the Department to his "high character." This was turned down. The same court, Murray, Evans, and Isaac Hull (on his way to Washington and a seat on the Board of Commissioners), inquired into the loss of the *President*. Crowninshield was not yet in possession of its finding that Decatur was wholly blameless when he officially appointed him commander in chief of the Mediterranean squadron, empowered to destroy the forces of Algiers or negotiate an honorable peace.

Of all this, even of the decision to form two squadrons, William Bainbridge was completely in the dark. Moreover, he was in agonies of concern over the *Independence*'s armament. The lightweight type of thirty-two-pound guns originally cast for her lower-deck battery and diverted to Chauncey during the crisis on Lake Ontario were still at Sackets Harbor. The thirty-two-pounders at the Washington Navy Yard now earmarked for the *Independence* each weighed seven hundredweight heavier, potentially hazardous to a vessel whose ports were already low in the water. Also, they were the wrong fit for the carriages that Bainbridge had arranged to be specially made of the best seasoned wood at a cost of $3,500. New carriages would have to be constructed, he reminded Crowninshield, or extensive alterations made to those in hand. Surely the guns could be transported from Sackets Harbor to Boston? But this the Secretary decided would take too long and cost too much. The commodore would have to ship the heavier guns—they were on their way up in the schooner *Lynx*.

The gunnery delay on the *Independence* gave Crowninshield enough justification for allotting the New York squadron priority in men and matériel. The *Macedonian*, for instance, at first assigned to Bainbridge's command, was detoured into New York on Decatur's prompt suggestion that she could be got ready for sea much sooner under his supervision. Decatur also interpreted the government's stated wish for speedy preparation as carte blanche for the appropriation of men and supplies ordered elsewhere. He intercepted and kept thirty seamen detailed for the *Congress* (at Boston), whose captain,

Charles Morris, thereupon demanded Department guarantees against censure arising from possible detention of his ship. And now, slowly and painfully, the light began to dawn on Commodore Bainbridge.

Officially uninformed of Decatur's appointment, he had refused to heed the rumors of it. Nevertheless, their mere circulation was mortifying, as "my friends and the public have believed that I was to command in chief the forces designated for that sea." When he could no longer ignore the fact that his orders were being countermanded by a junior, he committed the error of directing his protests to him. Decatur merely acknowledged them, while confiding to the Secretary that highhandedness was a necessity of "imperative duty"; and neither man forwarded Bainbridge explanation or apology. Now too he belatedly learned, in connection with another source of frustration— the search for competent seamen—that while his authority to offer two months' advance salary and no bounty was unchanged, other captains had received permission to pay three months' wages and $20 bounty. Once, before the war, Isaac Hull had sympathized with Bainbridge for apparently being so often and viciously singled out by "that damned jade misfortune." If the commodore did not consider Hull's reference all too apt in the present circumstance, it was only because of a growing awareness that he now contended less with the gods of chance than the guile of men.

Late in April Madison's preparations for naval war were interrupted by the startling news that Bonaparte had escaped from Elba and recaptured the French throne. The President thought it best now to await the trend of European developments. During this suspension there occurred the first serious collision between the professional and civilian branches in American naval history. At issue, as a result of the Board's forced reliance upon "common report" for guidance in the fitting out of the squadrons, was whether it had a right to be officially informed of their destinations. The Board's president claimed in fact the power to *dictate* ship movements. John Rodgers, in an astonishing letter to President Madison, argued that the Secretary of the Navy held no authority under legal statute but that of appointing his own clerks and convening courts-martial. Under the Act of Congress which established the office in 1798, additional functions relating to construction, armament, equipment, and employment of vessels were delegated to him at the President's pleasure. Since the Act of Congress creating a Board of Commissioners empowered it to discharge these same functions, the President ought now to transfer all the ministerial powers of the Secretary to the Board. Rodgers was unquestionably serious. One can only wonder whether he expected the President to give equally serious consideration to what was in effect a plea for the abolition of the office of Secretary of the Navy and the establishment of Commodore John Rodgers as administrative overlord.

Madison endorsed his Secretary's stand in the dispute, and, thus fortified, Crowninshield explained it for the Board's benefit: "The control and direction of the naval forces of the United States belongs to the Secretary of the Navy, acting under the authority of the President of the United States. It is for him alone to judge, therefore, whether it is proper to communicate to the Board of Commissioners the objects and destination of any squadron."

By then the delay resulting from Napoleon's last bid for European supremacy had ended. After William Shaler, Madison's new envoy to the Barbary States, had taken up quarters on the *Guerrière*, the squadron of ten sail in New York Harbor got under way on May 20 with a fair wind. Morale on board all the ships was high. Peter M. Potter, a musician on the *Spitfire*, wrote in his diary that no sooner were they in blue water when the men flung out mackerel lines, pieces of colored bunting with a sixpence on the hook for bait. A week later, as the ships were rearing and nodding in heavy mid-ocean weather, all hands, piped on deck to splice the main brace, received an extra allowance of grog. On July 12 the squadron arrived off Gibraltar, where Decatur learned that the ships of Algiers, at last report in the Atlantic, had beat back into the Mediterranean. He continued eastward, on sharp lookout for them.

In Boston meanwhile a bewildered Bainbridge, deploring the discourtesy of silence from the Navy Department, went ahead with the equipment of his 74, and the infusion of discipline, through a time-consuming series of courts-martial, into his far from satisfactory recruits. Not until the end of May—Decatur had been at sea ten days—did Bainbridge receive any official intimation of the existence of two squadrons and then only through oblique reference in the Secretary's letter. The commodore, infuriated, reacted with a vow to command neither, and although of course he had no alternative but to obey when sailing orders finally got to him, he barbed their acknowledgment with pointed resentment against having been kept in ignorance.

His pride was still intact. He retained considerable distinction as commander of the first American ship of the line ordered into war. The government now empowered him (as it already had Decatur) to destroy the Dey's fleet if peace was refused, and to show the flag before Tunis and Tripoli. It is easy to imagine what all this meant to him: the opportunity of wresting surrender from vanquished Barbary in waters once witness to his unforgettable humiliations. Yet right to the last minute, his departure was impeded. He had ordered William Crane to stand out in Boston Bay a few leagues and try the ship. When the flag captain did so, her tenderness under sail was obvious, even though her boats and spare spars were not yet on board. The commodore was taken out to her on June 27 and saw for himself how badly she had settled. But he can never in his life have been more ferociously determined than now. Ordering every overweight thirty-two-pound gun taken off the lower deck, he replaced them with medium guns of the same caliber, each twelve hundredweight lighter, from the main deck. Then he hustled his weary crew into dismantling the twenty-four-pounders from the *Constitution* (awaiting repair in the Navy Yard following her long cruise under Stewart) and had these mounted on the 74's main deck. His stolid regard for propriety, however, impelled him to notify the Commissioners in detail of the alterations, affording their president, smarting from the late encounter with the Secretary, an opportunity for asserting the Board's incontestable authority in at least the technical area. Bainbridge had expressed the assumption that his experience and judgment would not be called to question. Instead he was informed that the very particulars he had conscientiously submitted were evidence that as a 74 the *Independence* was unfit for sea, and it was recommended that she be razeed—cut down to a two-decker. One feels that afterthoughts on the wisdom of telling the Board all must have accelerated Bainbridge's steps for departure. Certainly, when Benjamin Crowninshield's order confining the *Independence* to harbor on the advice of the Board of Commissioners reached Boston, the commodore and his squadron, eight ships in all, were safely at sea, bound for the Mediterranean.

Much of the outward passage Bainbridge devoted to the drafting of lengthy proposals for improvements in ship design and armament, fairer distribution of prize money, better pay for officers, and harsher modifications to certain naval laws—a hundred lashes, for instance, was too mild a maximum penalty for displaying contempt or a mutinous spirit before a superior officer. The offense deserved death. Not unexpectedly, he also proposed changes in Article 30 relating to the subject of last-minute transfers of petty officers and seamen from their assigned vessel to another.

In mid-ocean the *Independence*, like the *Guerrière* before her, ran into rough weather. Often the sills of her lower-deck ports disappeared under the swell. But if we are to judge from Bainbridge's reports and letters at this time, her speed and ease of sailing were better than anyone could have wished for. Certainly the first ship of the line weathered her maiden transatlantic crossing successfully, and with the rest of the squadron—the *Congress*; sloop of war *Erie*; brigs *Chippewa, Saranac, Boxer,* and *Enterprise,* and schooner *Lynx*—she passed through the Straits of Gibraltar on the last day of July. At half-past two next afternoon she spoke a schooner whose captain relayed the incredible rumor that Commodore Decatur had shattered a powerful Algerian force and settled the Mediterranean war. And one could almost wager that it was the shock of sober corroboration next day from an English brig out of Alicante, and not the attack of measles recorded in the surgeon's log on the *Independence*, which prostrated Commodore Bainbridge for the remainder of the week.

Looking back, there is a ruthlessness about Stephen Decatur's audacity at this period which clearly stems from his determination to "satisfy the world" of his untarnished renown. To his self-vow can be traced the manipulation of a pliant Secretary, the brazen confiscation of personnel and equipment ordered for other commands, the calculated indifference to fellow officers, and the embarrassing confusion thus brought upon a senior commodore. Little of any of this was known outside the service. At home the public prints carried proud applause for the two majestic squadrons marching one by one across the Atlantic, and no hint intrigued their readers that in command were commodores deeply entrapped in rivalry, the one pitiless and confident, the other sullen and embittered as he trailed far behind Decatur's wake with the consolation prize of the second squadron.

In the familiar waters of the Mediterranean, Decatur's personal course took on even greater momentum. "Bringing to and boarding everything on sight," wrote Peter Potter. "Every five minutes from the masthead came 'sail-ho.' " On June 17—the day Crowninshield signed Commodore Bainbridge's sailing orders—the first squadron was proceeding about twenty miles off the Spanish coast when the *Constellation*, the headmost ship, sighted a large frigate under topsails. Battle honors at last lay within Charles Gordon's reach: the stranger, lowering her false English colors and flaunting in their place the red Algerian ensign, was the 44-gun *Mashouda*, flagship of Reis Hammida, who had left his native mountains as a youth to become one of Barbary's most notable admirals. On the *Constellation*, all was astir. Gordon brought the enemy into action with a broadside. But before he could order his guns run out a second time, the *Guerrière* bore up, plunged between the two ships, and poured heavy shot and musket fire across the Algerian's decks. Following the commodore's example, the rest of the squadron closed on her and, such was their eagerness, all but fired into one another. A gun burst on Decatur's main deck, killing five men and wounding thirty, insignificant casualties compared with the bloodshed on the *Mashouda*, where a forty-two-pound carronade shot from the *Guerrière* had butchered Hammida as he sat in his quarterdeck chair. After two hours the vessel was rolling like a log, with more than 160 dead and wounded stretched about her seesawing decks. The *Guerrière*, from "her favorable position," brought the enemy into close action and obtained her surrender with two broadsides—so ran the commodore's official report. No mention was made of the *Constellation*.

Two days later the 22-gun brig *Estedio*, sighted off Cape Palos, fled close inshore where the big ships dared not hazard, and ran aground. Decatur sent his small vessels racing in after her; and of two enemy boatloads that tried to put out in flight, one foundered under the *Epervier*'s heavy fire. An American boarding party found twenty of the brig's crew dead and a number of survivors hiding below. There was a flurry of pillaging—a disapproving Potter saw one shipmate rob the dead of ten cutlasses to wear about his waist—then the brig was floated off and sent with the *Mashouda* into Cartagena. The squadron continued eastward. Seven days further cruising brought it into Algiers Bay, a white flag at the *Guerrière*'s foremast, Swedish colors at the main, signifying a wish to negotiate through the mediation of the Swedish consul.

An emissary for the Dey who came out with the diplomat was handed a copy of President Madison's war declaration and a peace treaty, drafted by Shaler and Decatur, whose terms called for abolition of tribute, release of captives, and compensation for seized American property. The Dey could take his choice: accept the terms or suffer attack. And any argument must be heard on the *Guerrière*, for the Americans refused to go ashore. This was at Decatur's insistence, and if the commodore rather than the consul—each invested with equal powers of negotiation—seems to have taken the initiative, it is not so remarkable. Formal diplomacy as represented by William Shaler was contingent upon the effect produced on shore by the show of naval strength. That this had already been swiftly employed off Spain served to emphasize the point; it was evident from the consternation with which the Algerians received the news. Even so, the Dey's spokesman doubted whether the American terms would be acceptable without some assurance of the return of the captured vessels. Shaler at first hedged. But nothing could prevail against his fellow negotiator's overweening drive to force a settlement before the second squadron hove in sight. Decatur gave verbal guarantees, omitted from the treaty, and after three hours' deliberation at the royal palace the Dey's emissary, accompanied as before by the Swedish envoy, came out under flag of truce with the document signed and sealed. Peace, Decatur wrote home exultantly, had been dictated at the mouths of his cannon.

On his ships it was the signal for general rejoicing. The crews forgot the scurvy that had lately affected many of them, and on July 4 was held what Potter recorded as "a regular blow-out." It was a memory doubtless treasured by men of the brig *Epervier* as she stood for home that week with the treaty of peace—her captain, William Lewis, whom Decatur had considerately transferred from the *Guerrière* with a lieutenant to permit both an early reunion with the two sisters they had married on the eve of coming out. It never took place. Last seen west of Gibraltar on July 14, the *Epervier* vanished forever.

On July 26 Decatur's squadron anchored off Tunis, where he exacted $46,000 from the Bey in compensation for British prizes retaken from American ships. Ten days later the squadron hoisted all colors in view of Tripoli. Now the commodore collected a further $25,000 and secured the release of several captive Scandinavians. And on the same day, nearly a thousand miles to the west, the *Independence* stood in for Cartagena.

To cure his measles Commodore Bainbridge had been severely bled and heavily dosed with salts. And his cough, an old complaint, had returned to bother him. But harder to bear than the infirmities of the flesh was an oppressive sense of outrage. There can be no mistake about it: Bainbridge felt himself to be victim of a fraud hatched at home which deprived him of unique rights to glory in the Mediterranean. Nothing was left to him—not fighting, negotiation, not even the clear-cut satisfaction of showing the flag along the Barbary Coast. Harassed by problems of ship's discipline—on August 15, for example, his crew were mustered to witness the flogging of ten seamen and marines for drunkenness and sleeping on watch—he set course for Algiers, where he did not wait long enough to see William Shaler, newly installed as consul, before pressing on eastward. He showed the flag before Tripoli for a few hours from four miles out, then sailed for Tunis, where again he made only fleeting appearance. At each port of call he learned with what emphasis he had been preceded by Stephen Decatur. And now his disgust and resentment broke through in one letter after another, to Porter, Shaler, Rodgers, even in reports to the Department. He had brought out the nation's first 74 into waters of painful personal memory, and anticlimax was his only portion. Without bothering to pay Algiers a second visit, he crowded sail for Gibraltar and on September 29 stood into the bay.

William Shaler meanwhile stormed against the Navy for having abandoned him in "the most dreary residence on earth" to face the unpleasant consequences of Commodore Decatur's hasty peace settlement. Following on his promises to return the captured ships, Decatur had ordered the *Mashouda* handed over to an Algerian captain. But the *Estedio*, driven by the Americans into neutral Spanish waters, was not permitted to leave them and the commodore had gone to no great exertions to obtain her release. The Dey of Algiers charged America with bad faith and threatened to resume the war. To all this Decatur showed indifference—his reply to a protesting letter from Shaler scoffed that surely the consul had not expected his new office to be a bed of roses. Then, turning his back on Algiers, he sent his squadron on ahead to Gibraltar, following alone and leisurely in the *Guerrière* down the coast of Spain.

So far, his and Bainbridge's courses in the Mediterranean had not crossed. At the beginning of October Bainbridge, off Gibraltar, prepared to sail home, in a worse mood than ever. As if he were not exacerbated enough by recent events, the Department correspondence ruling his ship of the line unseaworthy now caught up with him. He wrote back tartly to Crowninshield that not a soul on board the *Independence* would have preferred serving on another vessel.

On October 3 the *Constellation, Macedonian, Ontario, Flambeau,* and *Torch* doubled Europa Point. Just then, too, the *United States* arrived, three weeks out of Boston. Commodore Bainbridge, for this brief interval in Gibraltar Bay, held command in chief of seventeen ships of war, the largest assembly of American fighting sail yet seen. He could hardly have felt less like celebrating it. Detaching the *United States, Constellation,* and two sloops for continued station in the Mediterranean, he gathered the remainder of his force and on October 7 was making sail out of harbor when, with the timing of a guest who deliberately delays his entrance at a party for maximum effect, the *Guerrière* rounded the point and amid cheers from every ship hove to astern of the *Independence.* There now occurred in full view of the fleet a remarkable attempt to snub. As Decatur put out in the *Guerrière*'s gig, his broad pendant fluttering from the bow, Bainbridge kept under rapid way. He was clearly bent on avoiding a meeting. But Decatur would not grant him even this much. "Determined to be courteous," he quickened the pursuit and finally got aboard. Bainbridge greeted him with glacial formality, and Decatur quickly returned to his gig.

Commodore Bainbridge put his fleet through complicated maneuvers until far into the Atlantic, when bad weather repeatedly scattered it. Much time was lost reassembling the ships. Decatur, who had allowed twenty-four hours to elapse before following Bainbridge out of Gibraltar on the *Guerrière,* reached home well ahead of him and received all the credit for settling America's problems in the Mediterranean. President Madison praised him warmly, he took a vacant seat on the Board of Commissioners (Isaac Hull having been granted permission to reassume command of the Boston Navy Yard), and Congress lost no time in approving payment of $100,000 to indemnify the commodore and his men for prizes restored to Algiers. What, above all, had won Decatur the national reaffirmation he had so determinedly pursued was the sweeping display of diplomacy at gunpoint, acclaimed on all sides as a long-overdue departure from the policy of bribing Barbary into good behavior and a stirring example to European powers committed to the same craven tradition.

By contrast, on the scene of his achievement, opinion of Commodore Decatur had sunk decidedly low. To have rushed off home before ensuring safe delivery of both prize vessels to the Dey was denounced equally by diplomats and Navy men, American and foreign, and also, of course, Barbary's rulers. Consul Shaler deemed Bainbridge as much to blame as Decatur and in a confidential letter to James Monroe, Secretary of State, charged both with failing their duty as peace commissioners, ruining America's prestige east of Gibraltar, and misleading their own government with false assurances. Shaler got no satisfaction from Washington, but by March 1816, when Commodore Oliver Perry arrived off Algiers in the new frigate *Java* with United States ratification of the treaty, the Dey had disavowed it.

The threat of a new war provoked impolite allusions in consulates and ships' cabins to the absent officer held most responsible. The Swedish consul's jeer was of "Bashaw Decatur . . . that spoiled hero . . . swaggering about with his Order of Cincinnati." The American agent in Gibraltar thought that Decatur would sacrifice his best friend to glorify himself—"Had Bainbridge not been close at his heels, be assured that reasons for continuing the war would not have been found wanting." This was in a letter to Commodore John Rodgers, who also received one from Charles Gordon denouncing Decatur for failure to keep his word. Considering how the *Guerrière* had robbed him of the *Mashouda*'s surrender, it is not surprising to find the captain of the *Constellation* among Decatur's latest detractors. Now he could blame him for the renewed war exertions forced upon a reduced squadron and his own debilitated physique. The Americans had decided to strike first; Gordon was to direct a night attack by 1,200 men in boats against the Dey's batteries and ships in harbor.

Close to the appointed time they learned that the crew of a French frigate had observed their preparations and informed the Dey. Surprise no longer possible, the idea was abandoned. In any case, Gordon had no strength left for further effort. The old duel wound had finally won. He died ashore at Messina, Sicily, on September 6. He was, in a sense, the last victim of the frigate *Chesapeake*.

At home Americans were scarcely aware of the new threat in the Mediterranean and Mr. Madison, unwilling on the eve of retirement from public office to disturb a growing national euphoria for which Decatur's swift success was in part responsible, reacted to the Dey's protestations with studied offhandedness. Fortunately, Spain at last surrendered the brig. And that summer the British and Dutch, themselves unable to settle with the Dey peacefully, combined fleets and almost leveled his port with a heavy bombardment. Before the end of the year William Shaler had secured the signature of a vastly subdued Dey to a new treaty, which did not, however, signal the conclusion of American involvement in the Mediterranean. Thereafter until 1830 every annual message of a United States President was to contain some reference to the need for maintaining warships in that quarter.

Once the latest war crisis had blown over, the Mediterranean squadron turned its attention inward to affairs of personality. The fall of 1816 had seen the acquittal of Captain John Orde Creighton at his court-martial for bullying on board the ship of the line *Washington*. The acquittal caused fifty-one midshipmen on various vessels to petition Congress for protection against tyrannical commanding officers. Creighton was a great believer in the lash and said to be such a fanatic for ceremony that he sent his midshipmen to their stations in full uniform complete with cocked hat and dirk. Congress sided with the senior officers, who condemned the petition as insubordination, and took no action. But another was soon on its way. This time the focus of trouble was the *Java*. That her marines were a more than usually unruly set was, in Commodore Perry's view, the fault of their captain, John Heath, whose own unmilitary bearing was insolence itself. In arbitrary fashion Perry removed him from command of the marines—and then ignored him. Or perhaps, having gone thus far, he was uncertain of further action. At any rate, Heath sent the commodore a polite note asking what next? The innocence of its wording seemed to goad Perry further and at a late hour (after, it was believed, some drinking ashore) he summoned the captain to his cabin, where "passion became predominant and I gave him a blow." Subsequently, his apology spurned, Perry asked to be tried by court-martial and he brought countercharges against Heath. A court identical with that which had tried Captain Creighton, except that he now occupied Perry's seat on it, delivered guilty verdicts but handed down sentences of a reprimand. Coming on the heels of Captain Creighton's acquittal, this further light treatment inspired a memorial from fifty lieutenants, midshipmen, and marines to Congress protesting the gross partiality of Mediterranean courts-martial.

Shortly after Perry's return home early in 1817, he was appointed to a survey on the *Independence*, the latest in a seemingly endless series of affronts to Commodore William Bainbridge that, one feels, cannot have been entirely unrelated to the Navy Department's private opinion of him as an officer of "high and assuming notions." Among these was a possessive attitude toward the Boston Navy Yard, whose transformation from a muddy desolation in 1812 to its present well-ordered state was a favorite Bainbridge boast. Already in extreme ill-humor after his frustrations in the Mediterranean, Bainbridge found Isaac Hull ensconced in his old quarters and tried at once to remove him. But Hull had strong pecuniary reasons for remaining at the Boston Navy Yard, including the need to keep a close eye on his heavy property investments adjacent to it. Determined not to be pushed out, he advised the Secretary of the Navy that he would consider any attempt to evict him a slur upon his reputation. The matter was even discussed in cabinet session, but as Bainbridge had not been expected back from the Mediterranean quite so soon, and his successor's appointment to the Yard was in any event not conditional upon his return, the administration's verdict went in favor of Hull. On the heels of that rebuff Bainbridge had received harsh words from both the Board of Commissioners and the Secretary of the Navy for an alleged peremptoriness in the appointment of certain officers. It was just after this that he had unwittingly invited the Board to find serious fault with the *Independence*.

All he did actually was test her lower-deck guns by tapping them with a maul, but the method differed from that prescribed by the Commissioners. Their president, Commodore Rodgers, reproached him in terms more suited for a delinquent midshipman, and "inasmuch as the Commissioners have lost their confidence in the guns subjected to a trial so severe as that by which you have tested those on the *Independence*," the entire lower-deck armament would have to be replaced. Up in arms, Bainbridge had then taken the unprecedented step of challenging the Board's judgment and refusing to obey its "informal and unnecessary order." He hammered away at his ship's other guns to prove that no maul blow could result in measurable damage. But the order to remove the guns was repeated, and, in what was his last arbitration in naval affairs, Mr. Madison himself intervened to advise the commodore that it had better be obeyed.

Bainbridge, once warm advocate of a controlling board of naval officers, now as fervently wished that it would follow Mr. Madison into retirement, for not withstanding his earnestly defensive praise of the 74 in letters to David Porter, the only commissioner he felt he could trust, the Board reviewed its manifold doubts about her and ordered a complete survey. His appointment as one of the surveyors was evidently the final cruelty—Bainbridge begged to be excused and it was his replacement, Oliver Perry, who obtained a reprieve for the Navy's first ship of the line by recommending reduction of her masts, ballast, and stores rather than cutting away her spar deck.

After the survey Bainbridge renewed his attempts to oust Isaac Hull from the Boston Navy Yard, pinning his hopes now on a new President, to whom he appealed in person. But James Monroe would not reverse his predecessor's decision and in the spring of 1817 Bainbridge admitted defeat. For the next three years, his command restricted to the *Independence* at anchorage within sight of the establishment of which he considered himself usurped, he brooded beneath his broad pendant at the 74's masthead—the single token of his superiority in title over the usurper onshore.

The doldrums of peace were encouraging mischief-making passions to stir. We may wonder if those of Jesse Duncan Elliott ever slept. In May 1818 he reopened the Battle of Lake Erie with accusations of slander directed at Oliver Perry, who promptly replied that they could have been conceived only by a base and vulgar mind. "The reputation you have lost is not to be recovered by such artifices; it was tarnished by your own behavior on Lake Erie." Perry, now finding himself under fire on two flanks, adopted the attitude that neither of his assailants was worthy of notice. Captain Heath, bothering him for a duel, was "an impertinent and insolent blackguard." And to Elliott's call to the field early in July, Perry's response was a curt notification that official charges were being filed against him with the Secretary of the Navy. Only when Elliott had exculpated himself before court-martial could his challenge be regarded as issuing from a man of honor.

The charges against Jesse Elliott ranged from spreading falsehoods to cowardice, negligence, or disaffection under fire; and it remains a mystery to this day precisely what became of them. Certainly they were mailed as Perry had promised. They arrived in Washington after the Secretary had gone north to escape the sickly weeks of August in the capital—hence Elliott's scoffing letter to Perry saying that he had met Crowninshield at Fall River, Massachusetts, and found him unaware of any charges. On October 3 the Secretary, back in Washington, acknowledged their receipt and transmitted them to the President. At this date, during a period of relative national calm, Monroe would hardly have been willing to countenance the risk of repudiating all the approbation of Elliott that had proceeded from Perry's own report of the action on Lake Erie. Other reputations besides Elliott's—indeed Perry's and the Navy's—might be discredited by such belated publicity. This no doubt explains why Monroe declined to authorize the requested court-martial, though it leaves unclear the fate of the charges. If the document was returned to the Navy Department, it has since disappeared. The important point is that the original or a copy came into the possession of Commodore Decatur.

There is no evidence that Perry protested the government's inaction on his charges. Very likely Decatur explained the government's position and discussed alternative ways of employing them during his journey with Perry to the dueling field above Hoboken where, in the gloom of an October morning, Captain Heath and the commodore finally confronted each other. There was a prearranged avoidance of bloodletting: Heath fired wide and Perry would not even raise his pistol.

The outward calm continued. A small squadron based with Spanish permission at Port Mahon, Minorca, was all the safeguard required now for America's commerce in the Mediterranean. And Europe's new peace gave signs of permanence. Permanence with growth was much in evidence at home too. Indiana, Mississippi, Illinois, and Alabama increased the number of states to twenty-two.

The American and Canadian governments agreed to demilitarize the Great Lakes, and a boundary was fixed stretching westward to the Rockies. Indeed the most important sailing cruise at this stage was related to westward expansion: the sloop *Ontario* rounded Cape Horn and sailed up the Pacific to Cape Disappointment, where on August 19, 1818, Captain James Biddle proclaimed the Oregon country an American possession. Benjamin Crowninshield and the Board of Commissioners pushed ahead in uneasy partnership with an ambitious building program. Not yet sufficient thought was applied to problems of organization, strategy, personnel training, and discipline. But in ships at least the Navy seemed certain to grow from strength to strength. In April 1816 Congress approved an annual expenditure of a million dollars for the next six years to construct nine 74-gun ships of the line, a dozen 44-gun frigates, ten sloops, and three experimental steam batteries "for defense of ports and harbors."

The funds were not always readily available when most needed. The rate of construction was slow. By 1820 few of the 74's were advanced beyond keel laying, still less progress had been made on the frigates, and nothing at all was done about the steam batteries. The far-reaching squadrons envisaged by this positive legislation were not to appear until well into the century's fourth decade. Now all sense of urgency was absent. In Washington the atmosphere was peaceful and domestic.

The Navy Commissioners met regularly in a Department office surrounded by war trophies, ship models, and flags of captured vessels. Rich with prize money, they built palatial homes. Porter's splendid castle, set in 151 acres which he struggled in vain to farm, overlooked the city and the Potomac. John Rodgers lived in high style on Greenleaf Point near the Washington Navy Yard and owned extensive property and a large retinue of slaves. The Decaturs settled into the somewhat somber mansion Benjamin Latrobe had constructed for them close to the White House. (It still stands.) And the couple quickly won a reputation for parties every bit as elegantly gay as those Thomas Tingey continued to give at his Navy Yard. Decatur had outgrown his youthful bravura and seemed content to let his wife enjoy the social limelight. He was quiet-spoken now and of temperate habits, although, unlike his neighbors around the square that was to become Lafayette Park, he shunned churchgoing. "I shall feel ashamed to die in my bed," he told a friend; but if indeed he was secretly bored with the quiet life, it showed only in flashes of irritation with the other Commissioners, particularly Rodgers. His domestic scene was untroubled except perhaps for regret over his childlessness, when he could be heard to envy the Benjamin Crowninshields their daughter, who wore a dimpled resemblance to Susan Decatur. Altogether, it was a rather touchingly contented existence that the commodore now led, betraying no hint of approaching tragedy.

CHAPTER TWENTY-TWO

Pistols at Bladensburg

In 1819, one might have thought, tranquillity ruled everywhere. It was the beginning of Mr. Monroe's "Era of Good Feelings." But however apt a phrase to describe the national mood or the political honeymoon, it could not be safely applied to the Navy. Beneath the surface calm ran too many currents of mischief, and it is as if they had awaited the right agent or medium through which to influence the tides of men. Fate could have produced few more haplessly suited to this function than Commodore James Barron.

The man who ordered the *Chesapeake's* colors lowered under the guns of the *Leopard* in June 1807 had been largely forgotten during the war for which that encounter off the Virginia capes had so ominously set the stage. Barron lived miserably in Danish exile for the duration, subsisting on the charity of other American *émigrés* and the United States consul in Copenhagen. His several inventions while abroad, including a lock cutter and a spinning machine, failed to bring him the profits he had hoped would finance his return home with his head up. In despairing letters to his family in Hampton, Virginia, he wrote of an "unconquerable reluctance" to expose his penury before foes. It kept him in Europe long after peace had restored passage facilities to America. His term of separation from the Navy had expired early in 1813. His letter to the Navy Department in July of that year, stating that he could be reached, if his services were required, in Copenhagen or St. Petersburg, had gone unanswered. He made no further report and not until the close of 1818 was he back in America. Six years almost to the day after the expiry of his suspension from the service, he applied in person at the Navy Department for restoration to active duty.

He received a shock. The price of his rehabilitation as imposed by Smith Thompson, President Monroe's Secretary of the Navy, was not solely an explanation for his prolonged absence in Europe but an answer to charges contained in a letter that had gathered dust in the Department for seven or eight years. Signed by Captain William Lewis, it quoted a Baltimore merchant who swore to having heard Barron revile his own government during an 1809 conversation in Pernambuco with the British consul. This was the first Barron had heard of the letter and he vehemently denounced it as a lie. But denials were unacceptable. The condition was that Barron request a court of inquiry before which to disprove the charge. It was asking a lot. Captain Lewis could not be called to account, having vanished on the *Epervier* in 1815. And while Barron, at home in Hampton, agonized over his next move, the Baltimore merchant named in Lewis' letter also died.

Smith Thompson's firm opposition to giving the commodore a command was supported or (as Barron had no doubt) inspired by the Board of Naval Commissioners. It is therefore easy to imagine the feelings of this already harrowed officer on being informed that one of the Commissioners, Stephen Decatur, while visiting Norfolk to inspect plans for a naval dock, had publicly boasted that he could insult him with impunity. Barron had no alternative but to do what was expected of him, namely, demand of Decatur whether the reports were true. Yet the impression one gets is that what he most yearned for now was peace of mind. When Decatur responded that he could not have been so egotistical whatever he may have said in the "very frequent and free conversations I have had respecting your conduct," Barron disregarded the taunting candor and accepted the denial. And though Decatur then wrote unnecessarily that his disclaimer applied only to the specific remark attributed to him, this closer approach to contempt drew only silence from Barron. Unhappily, things were not to end there.

In Washington Decatur had just bidden farewell to his friend Commodore Oliver Hazard Perry. President Monroe, continuing the practice of giving naval officers diplomatic assignments, had ordered

Perry to Venezuela to win Bolívar's co-operation in the suppression of piracy. Perry sailed with little enthusiasm and a heart full of foreboding. Outward bound on the *John Adams*, he was soon pining for home—he wrote of counting the hours until he saw it again. His wife too was beset by premonitions. "I have a thousand fears for your safety and have a dark cloud over my reflections." She penned these words to him on September 2, and by then the worst had already happened.

Perry, leaving the *John Adams* at Trinidad, had gone up the Orinoco in the schooner *Nonesuch* to Angostura (now Ciudad Bolívar) and started talks with the Venezuelan government. They were interrupted by an outbreak of yellow fever among Perry's crew. Quickly he returned to the ship and on August 15 weighed anchor. Just beyond the river mouth five days later—the commodore's thirty-fourth birthday—the *Nonesuch* shipped a heavy sea which drenched him severely and brought on a chill. Then he developed yellow fever. On the 23rd, while still forty miles from Port of Spain, he summoned his officers to witness the signing of his will. Perry died at half-past three in the afternoon, and when the *John Adams*, after a month's slow passage, anchored in Hampton Roads with the sad news, all ships' flags fluttered to half-mast, a solemn salute repeated from port to port up the Atlantic coast to grieving New England.

It was to be Susan Decatur's affirmation, when none lived who might have corroborated it, that Perry sailed for South America with her husband's promise, should he not return, to publish his charges of misconduct against Jesse Elliott. While this fitted a prevalent theory that with Perry's death Elliott had transferred his hate to Decatur, there is in fact no evidence that Elliott was aware of such a private arrangement. It may be no more than coincidence that the news of Perry's death was followed within less than a month by a tortured letter from James Barron to Decatur. All the same, around Norfolk at least, little doubt existed that the instigator of the fatal phase of the Barron-Decatur correspondence was Jesse Duncan Elliott.

If so, secondary troublemakers assisted, informers traveling between Norfolk and Washington, telling Decatur that Barron was determined to call him out, telling Barron that Decatur expressed himself willing to fight if at last he had decided to act like a man. It was this latter slur that set the pens once more in motion. Barron announced that he considered it a challenge, which he accepted. Decatur, evidently surprised by the letter after four months' silence, denied that one was intended. But again he ran on with unnecessary cruelty. Since the *Chesapeake* affair Barron's conduct had been such as should forever bar his reinstatement in the service. He would continue officially to oppose it. Regarding a duel, although he was not obliged to deal with someone too degraded for notice, he had "incautiously" pledged himself to come out if called. As for Barron's apparent determination to fight someone, it was an object better achieved had he taken up arms in the late war.

So letter follows letter. As scorn from Washington wrings impassioned retort from Hampton, the correspondence itself becomes a duel fought with diatribes. Reading Barron's letters, one visualizes a man obsessed by the notion of being at bay before a remorseless persecutor. In a different perspective they appear as an epistolary exercise in the extraction of a challenge and the avoidance of being maneuvered into issuing one. Little zeal in fact is exhibited by either side for the initiative of replacing pens with pistols. Barron, after all, had never developed a taste for duels and Decatur made clear that he had long outgrown his. They were not adolescent midshipmen pursuing absurd affairs of honor to a gory, tragicomic climax but middleaged senior officers—Decatur was forty, Barron eleven years older—with loved ones to consider. It was to keep them from worrying that the commodores wrote in furtive secrecy, the one in his lonely home on the Hampton shore, the other from the elegant heart of Washington society.

In December an emotional missive from Barron which nevertheless stopped short of a challenge brought in reply a letter full of devastating broadsides against every argument he had mustered to defend his past conduct. Still the call was unissued. "Your jeopardising your life," Decatur wrote, "depends upon yourself and is done with a view of fighting your character up." He would ignore all further communications from Barron except a direct summons to the field.

Had one come just then, Decatur would have been embarrassed for want of a second. His fellow Commissioners, Rodgers and Porter, refused to become involved. Commodore Thomas Macdonough, also on hand, had his own troubles: Commodore Charles Stewart had sent him home from the Mediterranean for an alleged infraction of court-martial regulations. (Macdonough was also unwell—within five years he would die at sea of tuberculosis.) Captain Charles Morris, passing through Washington on his way to resume the diplomatic negotiations in Latin America begun by Perry, not only declined to serve but took the occasion to remind Decatur how perfectly simple it was for a man of his unquestionable courage and national esteem to disengage from the dispute with Barron without harm to his reputation. Privately Morris thought him unduly apprehensive lest he give the appearance of deliberately avoiding a duel. In other words, Decatur was under similar compulsions to those dictating his ruthless course in 1815. Only now, while preserving his reputation, they reinforced the trap into which he had talked or written himself.

At least two members of James Monroe's cabinet knew what was developing. So probably did the President, who would not, surely, have wanted anything to mar the felicity of a social season whose main event was the wedding of his daughter. Decatur's inability to find a second provided the Secretary of the Navy or the other Commissioners with every opportunity to intercede. Decatur himself gave them grounds to effect a settlement by making it known that in the event of a duel he would fire into the air. But no peacemaker came forth. To deny Decatur a second was, it seems, to give him all the loophole he needed and was going to get.

An ambiguity creeps into the closing exchanges between Barron and Decatur as if both men are spent of venom and accusation. "Whenever you will consent to meet me on fair and equal grounds, you are at liberty to view this as that call." Thus the message from Hampton dated January 16, 1820, and when Decatur professes himself at a loss to its meaning—*if* a challenge, he accepts it—Barron merely responds with a terse announcement that he is suffering from bilious fever. On this undramatic note their personal correspondence ended. The dispute was taken over by more efficient management.

President Monroe's recently announced hopes for trade and diplomatic relations with the Ottoman Empire had stirred William Bainbridge's ambitions, never fully quiescent, of showing the flag before Constantinople in vastly different circumstances from those which humiliated him in 1800. He furnished the government with strong arguments for sending the first Minister to Turkey on board a 74-gun ship of the line and volunteered himself for the command. The *Independence* was still blacklisted by the Navy Commissioners and due to be laid up in ordinary. The *Columbus*, launched by Doughty, was under completion at the Washington Navy Yard. Late in November 1819 Bainbridge handed over the *Independence* to Captain John Shaw and departed south to take command of the new ship of the line.

He arrived in Washington already aware of simmering strife between Barron and Decatur—Captain Shaw had passed on a few details. Still, there was every reason to pay it no heed. For one thing, supervising the fitting out of a ship of the line for a long cruise required his maximum attention. And what had he to do with the disputants? Friendly to Barron in the Tripolitan War, he was now more likely to be neutral toward him with perhaps private sympathies. It is what he felt for the other man that arouses speculation. His biographer and close friend describes Bainbridge as a man of acute, even morbid, susceptibilities. Certainly he stalked or sailed through life with a pervading sense of grievance. The chilling animus toward Decatur manifest in his attempt to snub him off Gibraltar in 1815 had scarcely been melted by his recurrent difficulties with the Board of Navy Commissioners—of which Decatur formed an influential third. Since that Mediterranean cruise Bainbridge had avoided any contact with him. What, then, are we to make of the scene on Pennsylvania Avenue at about Christmas Eve 1819 when Bainbridge leaped from a carriage, ran to Decatur, and grasped his hands with fervid protestations of friendship? To Susan Decatur's astonishment, he came home with her husband—whose own reaction, as far as can be gleaned, was a kind of bemused resignation—and on December 27 moved in as a house guest. With this strange encounter fate had played all its cards. The rest of the affair takes on a semblance of human conspiracy.

At the start of the new year Bainbridge (unknown, of course, to Susan) agreed to act as Decatur's second. His duties kept him traveling between Washington and Saint Marys, lower down the Potomac, whence the *Columbus* had been towed by steamboat to escape the ice. But, as he told Decatur, personal inconvenience would not be allowed to affect his services to such an esteemed friend. This was February 20. He had not yet heard from the other side. When he did, it was a brisk request from Barron's second, Jesse Elliott, in Norfolk, to meet him in order to make arrangements for the protagonists to close. The *Columbus* was ideally situated for the seconds' rendezvous, her anchorage off Saint Marys lying roughly halfway between Washington and Norfolk. Not so felicitous a choice was the date, March 8—the Decaturs' fourteenth wedding anniversary. And while the couple quietly celebrated in Washington, the other two, closeted privately on board the new 74, settled upon terms tending significantly to favor Commodore James Barron.

William Bainbridge's explanation for what looked like soft compliance on his part was so worded that any question Decatur felt disposed to raise must have died on his lips. Pressed by Elliott, Bainbridge had consented, against his original intentions, to fix the final details now instead of on the field, in order to avoid "unfavorable suspicions against you [Decatur] by not doing so," and had then agreed to a distance between the duelists shorter than the customary ten or twelve paces. But Decatur must not consider this to be surrender of a privilege. "Captain Elliott dwelt much on Commodore Barron's defective sight, but that had no influence on my mind, for I had resolved, a month since, that the distance should be eight paces."

Bainbridge's true motives can only be surmised. One cannot even be sure that he knew of Decatur's stated intention not to aim at his adversary. At any rate, the terms he had hatched with Elliott on the *Columbus* hardly encouraged humane gallantry from the man he was supposed to represent. Now Decatur modified his decision to one of disabling Barron by wounding him in the hip. He would still avoid taking the other's life even at risk of losing his own. Thus the door remained open for an accommodation, had the seconds been seeking one—as indeed was their duty. The duel was set for March 22. There was even time to alert appropriate authorities to an impending breach of civil law. Still no one took action.

The capital's festivities celebrating the White House wedding commenced with a large party at the Decaturs' mansion. The commodore's duel was now three days away. Some of the guests thought he looked abstracted, except when he fixed his stare upon his carefree wife as she played the harp before a semicircle. On Pennsylvania

Avenue the day preceding the duel he appeared ill and dispirited. That evening it was the John Quincy Adamses' turn for lavish hospitality—about a hundred persons danced cotillions until nearly midnight. Six hours later, on the opposite side of what is now Lafayette Park, the door of Decatur's house opened and the commodore, alone and heavily cloaked, crept out. In the bleak hush of dawn he passed the White House and walked the poplar-flanked length of the avenue. Skirting the unfinished Capitol in its scaffolding, he entered Beale's Hotel to breakfast with Bainbridge and Samuel Hambleton, the *Columbus'* purser. He was wanly cheerful, Hambleton thought, and showed no desire to take anyone's life. He drew up his will, but deferred signing it in the absence of a third witness. Gathering up pistols and brandy, they departed in a hired coach along the road toward Bladensburg.

The chosen site was a shallow ravine between the Washington-Baltimore highway and the Eastern Branch, now called the Anacostia River. Safely outside the legal jurisdiction of Washington and masked from the road by trees, it was close enough to city limits for a quick escape should any Maryland law officer try to arrest them. Barron's party approached from the north—they had spent the night at the Indian Queen tavern in Bladensburg. Shortly before 9 the principals were standing widely apart from each other, their seconds occupied with formal preliminaries. Besides Hambleton the only witnesses were Barron's nephew and two doctors.

Bainbridge measured eight paces. He tended to stammer when excited, so Barron asked him for a test utterance of the command he intended to give. Bainbridge obliged, then loaded a pistol for Commodore Decatur. Barron received his from Elliott. And then, quite unexpectedly, the principals addressed each other. Barron, by all accounts, spoke first. "I hope, Commodore Decatur, that when we meet in another world, we shall be better friends than we have been in this." To which Decatur replied: "I have never been your enemy, sir."

Among the theories spawned in the wake of this duel is one describing Barron as a man persuaded to it as a means of removing all doubts concerning his courage and safeguarded by Elliott's secret assurance of a last-minute adjustment on the field. If so, now was the time. Just as propitious was the occasion for Bainbridge to step in with honorable words of conciliation. The ice was broken for anyone to take advantage of it. Indeed, the voluntary exchange between Barron and Decatur constituted an unheard-of-violation of the dueling code forbidding principals, once the challenge has been given and accepted, to notice each other except with pistols aimed. But this perfect opportunity to decide on the bloodless solution for which the duelists' words may actually have been a disguised plea was allowed to pass unnoticed. All that the seconds did was alert their friends for firing.

At the call *Present!* each man aimed for the other's hip, Barron a trifle unsteadily—not, at eight paces, on account of his myopia but because the stiff surtout buttoned to his adversary's neck concealed the figure's true outline. At Bainbridge's "two" both men fired simultaneously. Barron received the bullet in his fleshy thigh. That which tore into Decatur glanced upward through the groin and he sank to the grass with a cry, "Oh, Lord, I am a dead man!"

The crack of pistol shots brought Commodore Rodgers and Captain Porter rushing to the field on horseback. They had been waiting for no obvious reason half a mile away at the Indian Queen. Now they found the doctors probing wounds in the fallen duelists and the seconds nowhere in sight. Elliott had fled in the carriage reserved for Barron. Bainbridge was making all speed to the Washington Navy Yard, where a tender waited to carry him back to the *Columbus*. Porter galloped off the field again, overtook Elliott, and recovered the carriage, reportedly by threat of force. In all these bizarre arrivals and departures, the wounded officers were beyond interest. Sprawled on the grass beneath gold-braided coats, they persevered over pain in a dialogue recalled afterward by one of the doctors as reminiscent of the dying words between Hamlet and Laertes. Actually the commodores' last conversation, ending with Decatur borne away still gasping the other's name, was a barely coherent echo of the senseless arguments that had protracted and inflamed their correspondence.

Decatur died at his home after a dozen hours of extreme suffering. Eulogies issued from the obscure as well as the notable. One grief-stricken seaman was heard to lament that "the Navy has lost its mainmast." Capital society canceled its White House wedding events. Naval officers were ordered to wear crepe for thirty days. Ships' guns off Washington and Norfolk fired every thirty minutes, and Congress adjourned for the funeral, the cortege drums, throbbing across the city, clearly audible to the commodore who nursed his own wound on a cot in Beale's Hotel. Elliott had reappeared at Barron's side. When Barron had sufficiently recovered to travel, they returned to Norfolk and were greeted with the assurances of friends that after Bladensburg the world could no longer consider James Barron a coward.

Later on Susan Decatur claimed to have secured President Monroe's promise never, so long as he was in the White House, to give Barron a command. But it was the seconds at the duel whom she most bitterly blamed for her premature widowhood. She made public Perry's charges against Elliott and then, rather than risk facing one or other of "my husband's murderers," she forsook Washington society for seclusion in Georgetown, where she died a destitute recluse in her eighty-fourth year.

Commodore Bainbridge mourned with stoicism. While regretting Decatur's death, "the vicissitudes of my life [he informed the Secretary of the Navy] have fortified my mind for trying events." Before sailing in the *Columbus* for Turkey he had the duel letters published with the stated purpose of correcting reports adverse to his late friend's memory. Their appearance had exactly the opposite effect. Typical of a virtually unanimous newspaper reaction was the comment of the *American Watchman*, Wilmington, that Decatur's "stinging sarcasm, sneering hauteur, and vindictive accusation were enough to drive any man in Barron's circumstances to desperation."

The *Columbus* weighed anchor April 28—Bainbridge's sailing orders including a directive to employ the sternest measures to put down dueling in his command. Four times Bainbridge had entered the Mediterranean, and each had turned into a cruise of frustration. Now he sailed without fear of shame or rivalry. True, no war existed from which to derive glory. But the maintenance of peace depended a great deal upon his experience in these waters. Unhappily, he still had an attraction for that "damned jade misfortune." The chief object of the first cruise of the *Columbus* was to show the flag off Constantinople and sound the disposition of the Ottoman government to receive a United States Minister. The Turks refused to allow Bainbridge east of the Dardenelles.

As for Commodore Barron, neither had his woes ceased with Decatur's death. The court of inquiry he asked for failed to grant him a clean bill: it declared the Pernambuco charges unproven but judged his extended stay in Europe was absence without leave. The reason no court-martial ensued was that the commodore's claim to full reinstatement in the Navy had become Mr. Monroe's dilemma. Smith Thompson, reflecting the views of the Navy Department and Board of Commissioners, as well as officers with important connections in Congress, wanted to continue treating Barron as a pariah. On the other hand, prominent Virginians to whom Monroe was politically indebted (with the significant exception of Littleton Tazewell) were anxious to cleanse Barron's clouded past with a presidential pardon. In addition to these pressures Monroe may also have had to bear in mind the promise, if one was indeed made, to Decatur's widow.

Uncertain what to do, he sought advice from Thomas Jefferson. But impartial consideration of Barron's case was apparently impossible even in the tranquillity of Monticello. Had he not, according to the late Captain Lewis' letter, told an Englishman that the unprepared state of the *Chesapeake* in 1807 was all part of a plot by Jefferson to provoke war? That was enough for the former President. "Barron is a most unprincipled man," he wrote back to Monroe, "unworthy of any military trust."

Not until 1824, at the close of James Monroe's administration, did Commodore Barron get his first command in seventeen years, that of the Philadelphia Navy Yard.

CHAPTER TWENTY-THREE

Obsolescence

Resolved: That the Committee on Naval Affairs be instructed to inquire into the expediency of constructing steam ships for the naval service of the United States.

—House of Representatives,
December 31, 1838

THE SAILING NAVY survived the death of Decatur by scarcely two decades. Considering the internal dissensions on every level of rank and the contempt shown by the Board of Navy Commissioners toward new ideas, one is surprised that the Navy itself lasted that long. As an editorial in a contemporary issue of *Niles' Weekly Register* warned, the proliferation of feuds alone was almost enough to sink it. (No one fished in the troubled waters more zestfully than Jesse Duncan Elliott. When Commodore John Shaw drew a sentence of six months' suspension for slandering Captain Isaac Hull, who had disputed Shaw's right to fly the broad pendant, Elliott wrote to him hopefully, "Your case could be a second Barron's.") The rash of quarrels was hardly an example of idleness begetting mischief. Although Smith Thompson was too much of an absentee Secretary to supervise his senior officers stringently, those at home were supposed to be busy surveying sites for naval depots, shipyards, lighthouses, and coastal fortifications. Overseas, enough convulsive changes were occurring to occupy the most restless temperament.

The coasts of South America demanded constant attention. Blockades and seizures accompanying the overthrow of Spanish sovereignty had made it brutally plain that the United States flag, unsupported by naval force, offered no sure protection for American commerce. When the *Macedonian*, Captain John Downes, patrolled the coasts of Chile and Peru from 1818 to 1821, it was the first peacetime watch on foreign shores by a United States naval vessel. In 1822, another consequence of Madrid's steadily crumbling control in the Western Hemisphere brought the *Macedonian* out of Boston again. Picaroon activity had revived, and since Spain could no longer adequately police West Indian sea lanes the task fell to the United States. At first the *Hornet, Enterprise, Spark, Porpoise, Grampus,* and *Alligator* sailed the Gulf of Mexico and the Caribbean at will, sinking or burning freebooters on sight. When it became clear that this haphazard method was producing inconclusive results, decisions were made in Washington to organize the ships into a squadron augmented by a frigate and to solicit closer co-operation from the civil authorities in Cuba. In accordance with these plans the *Macedonian*, Captain James Biddle, arrived off Havana late in April.

The *Macedonian*'s crew were a sickly collection at best and Havana was notorious as the hemisphere's most fever-ridden port. Biddle would have been wise to take leave when the Spanish governor refused his request for permission to pursue pirates, if necessary, across the Cuban mainland. Instead the ship lay off Havana for several weeks, Biddle foolishly taking on water and neglecting to warp her broadside into the wind for cross-ventilation. The people were exercised at the great guns to the point of fatigue and as punishment for some infraction were confined for a number of nights on the berth deck with the ports tightly closed. Thus was pestilence invited. By the middle of June the *Macedonian* was again at sea, thirty of her men dead, and the captain and his officers cursing the Boston Navy Yard for not having broken open the ship's hold following her Pacific cruise.

The sickening stench of bilge filth issuing from the ship's depths and the initial hesitation of the ship's surgeon, John Cadle, to diagnose the malady as the familiar yellow jack strengthened suspicions that the frigate herself, not Havana, was the real source of contagion. Before Doctor Cadle could develop his theories, it had destroyed him also. His assistant surgeon carried on, treating the sufferers with calomel and jalap, until he too took to his cot, whereupon, with results that harrow the imagination, these purgatives were administered to the stricken by their own messmates.

July brought little wind and no relief from heat. The frigate crept homeward, now a ship of horror, the newly infected crawling about her decks with swollen faces and painful extremities, those in their second or third day contorted by abdominal cramps and fits of vomiting. The babble and mutter of delirium rose ceaselessly to the tops. Each appearance of the black vomit wrought panic and despair. Thirty-five more died. People as yet uninfected stood their watches in mortal terror and slept where they might, "some in the chains, some in the tops, some in the boats and on the booms, and but few in their hammocks." On August 4 the *Macedonian* entered Hampton Roads with the seventy-sixth death recorded in her log, and when she anchored in quarantine off Craney Island her dead numbered 101 officers, seamen, and marines.

A court of inquiry consisting of Commodores Rodgers, Chauncey, and Charles Morris had just expunged a persistent taint of graft and jobbery from Captain Hull's command of the Boston Navy Yard. The same court found that under Hull's direction the *Macedonian* had been thoroughly purified before her catastrophic cruise. By implication the blame fell on Biddle, but the Secretary of the Navy took no further action.

The tragedy did not bring about any improvement in naval hygiene. Ships' ventilation in the United States Navy continued to depend on a captain's concern and the blowing of a breeze. Since the middle of the eighteenth century British warships had been ventilated by an apparatus of pipes and a furnace or, less commonly, an arrangement of fans operated by windmills. A bellows-type ventilator designed by James Barron and installed experimentally on a few American ships reportedly kept their crews in excellent health; but whether because of official indifference or bias toward its inventor, it never was adopted by the Navy as standard equipment.

The offensive that Biddle had failed to launch against the picaroons was vigorously pressed by his successor in command of the West Indies squadron, Commodore David Porter. But unlike Biddle, whose naval career survived the plague-ship scandal to last another twenty-five years, Porter's headstrong nature brought his to an abrupt end. In November 1824 one of his lieutenants, chasing thieves into Puerto Rican territory, fell into the hands of local authorities and was briefly jailed. Porter immediately sent 200 sailors and marines storming ashore at Fajardo to spike the harbor guns and deliver such a frightening ultimatum that the *alcayde* himself came rushing from the city full of apologies. Porter's action received no more official backing from Washington than had his ceremonious annexations in the Marquesas during the war. A little later on he might have behaved similarly with proper authorization (thus establishing the precedent for naval application of the Monroe Doctrine proclaimed in December 1823) since Monroe's cabinet was in fact contemplating a tougher Caribbean policy, including the hot pursuit of pirates into their island sanctuaries and, if circumstances required, a blockade of Cuba. The commodore's precipitancy threw these plans into some confusion and an irritated cabinet voted in December to order him home.

The appointment of Commodore James Barron, whose own rehabilitation had only just begun, to preside over Porter's court-martial stood to his advantage, or so it was thought, for what tribunal with Barron as its head would dare censure a naval officer for redressing an insult to the service? But Porter persisted in making matters worse for himself by openly criticizing government policy and writing offensive letters to the President and the Secretaries of State and the Navy. The court found him unco-operative as well as guilty of violating Spanish sovereign territory and sentenced him to six months' suspension. This stung him into resigning the following year, and soon after he went to Mexico, was hired to build the new republic's first navy, and after an unsuccessful attempt to entice former colleagues in the United States Navy from their allegiance, "metamorphosized" native Indians into sea officers. For the next three years Porter's Mexican Navy kept Cuba in periodic fear of invasion, and plagued Spanish shipping, until an embarrassed government in Washington was asked by Spain to do something about him. Before Washington acted, however, Porter left Mexican service and returned home, disillusioned by assassination attempts, nonpayment of his salary, and political intrigue. When Andrew Jackson, a kindred spirit, became President, he invited him to rejoin the Navy. Porter would not, but he accepted the post of Chargé d'Affaires in

Constantinople, where he served from 1831 until his death twelve years later.

Samuel Southard, who had taken over the Navy Department from Smith Thompson in 1823, held office for six years and proved to be the postwar sailing Navy's most competent Secretary. By no means always successful, he at least tried hard to introduce long-overdue procedures and reforms. High on his targets for overhaul was the obsolete promotion system. Midshipmen were known to gain middle age before a lieutenant's commission, and in the absence of any retirement plan captains who had held their post a quarter of a century hung on in the service, some with the sublime status of commodore, age rooting them to old ways and fortifying their distrust of new views and practices.

The most pernicious effects of this conservatism upon the Navy's advancement were felt through the decisions of the Board of Navy Commissioners, a peremptory triumvirate which never lost an opportunity of overruling the opinions of even the most skilled and experienced constructors. Slow rotation of membership kept the Board loaded with officers of prewar vintage (though never including Barron or Elliott) and Commodore John Rodgers was its president for an almost uninterrupted twenty-two years. The Commissioners, each salaried at $3,500 a year, dictated ship design, material procurement, and construction in a way that all too often betrayed their apparent determination to insulate themselves from new developments in merchant-ship design and particularly steam propulsion. Between this self-centered Board and a generally lukewarm Congress, the best that Samuel Southard could do was plant seeds for future improvement.

His perception of the Navy's value in scientific exploration led to the ship sloop *Vincennes'* four-year global cruise beginning in 1826 and her subsequent Pacific and polar expeditions. He infused life into the scientific survey of the United States coastline—approved by Congress in 1807 and since then an unwanted burden shuttled between the Treasury and the Navy Department. He also began a renovation of the navy yards and managed to install a few steam-powered saws (introduced into British dockyards in 1798), but it took another fifteen years before these were in general use by American naval carpenters. And despite Southard's forceful version of requests made periodically since Benjamin Stoddert's time for dry docks, none were in operation for American warships until 1833. Southard was especially concerned with founding a naval school "which shall unite a practical with a scientific education." But Congress failed to act on this, too, and naval education continued as before to be the responsibility of schoolmasters and chaplains going to sea, dedicated souls who spent the interminable cruises teaching midshipmen mathematics and guiding them through the mysteries of the quadrant and Bowditch's *Navigator*, the basic equipment each youth was required by the Navy Department to bring to his appointment.

It was beyond even Southard's powers to check what seems to have approached a national disenchantment with the Navy, expressed in occasional newspaper derision and diminishing appropriations in Congress. In 1826 naval strength had fallen to 272 captains, master-commandants, and lieutenants, with about 5,000 seamen and boys. The only frigates at sea were the *Constitution, Constellation, United States,* and what a popular steerage song called the "roaring *Brandywine."* Most of the eighteen serviceable schooners, brigs, and sloops were in port. The Great Lakes were the graveyard of seventeen sunk or moldering vessels. Two unfinished ships designed for 74 and 130 guns drooped in their stocks at Sackets Harbor, never to be launched. In the Atlantic-coast navy yards work advanced slowly if at all on five 74-gun ships of the line and five frigates. Of the seven ships of the line launched, all but one rotted in ordinary. The *Ohio*, ultimately to prove the finest of Henry Eckford's many designs, did not sail out until eighteen years after her launch in 1820. Throughout that period, to the professional consternation of visiting British naval men, she stood alone at Brooklyn, unhoused, weatherbeaten, and neglected. And at Philadelphia things moved only fitfully toward completion of the largest sailing man-of-war ever to be built for the United States Navy: a four-decker, rated at 120 guns but pierced for 132 exclusive of bow chasers and stern guns.

The *Pennsylvania* was intended for coastal defense rather than high-seas cruising—only painful memories of the British blockade could have justified such extravagance—and had been designed by Samuel Humphreys, Joshua's son, after he had studied the plans of the two big ships that had fought at Trafalgar: the *Royal Sovereign* and the Spanish *Santissima Trinidad*, then the largest ship in the world. Work began on the *Pennsylvania* in 1822 and for the next fifteen years of slow growth to immensity, sheltered by a soaring roof, she was a conspicuous Philadelphia attraction.

If anything, Andrew Jackson's frontier background and the political program he professed for liquidating the national debt boded yet more ill for the Navy when in March 1829 he became President. John Branch, his choice to head the Department, was a plantation-owning politician who possessed no discernible qualifications for naval administration and probably left a weaker impression upon the service than did Jackson's fourth auditor of the Treasury, Amos Kendall, a political strategist with a sharp eye for fiscal mismanagement. Actually, the Navy's bookkeeping had been in worse shape—in 1818, for instance, when an earlier fourth auditor had estimated that the accumulated public debts left by two deceased navy agents (one of them Doctor John Bullus, the missing witness at Commodore Barron's trial) exceeded a quarter of a million dollars each. Since then, at least one worthy performance of the Board of Navy Commissioners had been the exertion of tighter control over expenditures. Ships were no longer equipped at the pleasure or caprice of their captains, stores and timber were kept under strict inspection, and new specifications for proof and testing had diminished the danger of costly gun bursts. In addition, Commodore Rodgers had submitted a plan calling for the establishment of a navy yard at Newport, Rhode Island, which, with that at Norfolk, would permit the reduction of the yards at Washington and Boston to an auxiliary status while those at Portsmouth, New Hampshire, and Brooklyn, New York, would be, in today's parlance, "phased out."

Even though all of this conformed with the Jackson policy of fiscal retrenchment, Kendall thought he detected, through the fading luster surrounding the sea war's old heroes, some of them busy at fraud—as a gossip said, he "discovered the knavery of the Navy." Rodgers himself fell under suspicion, but when Kendall showed up at the Navy Department to investigate in person, the commodore threatened to kick him through the door. William Bainbridge's reaction when Kendall withheld approval of a contingent allowance due him was to write John Branch a furious letter abusing Kendall and demanding that the President overrule him. It only showed how little Bainbridge knew of the fourth auditor's standing at the White House. When Jackson saw the commodore's letter, he ordered him removed at once from his command of the Philadelphia Navy Yard.

For Bainbridge it was the final mortification. He had long been depressed and now his health collapsed. A new Secretary of the Navy, Levi Woodbury, gave him command of the Boston Navy Yard, but the opium Bainbridge had begun to take was affecting his mind. This was 1833, the year of the decision to rebuild the *Constitution*, upon whose shot-swept quarterdeck Bainbridge had gained his one indisputable victory. Popular opinion fired by the sentimental poetry of a law student named Oliver Wendell Holmes had reversed the joint recommendation of the Navy Department and Commissioners that the unseaworthy frigate be broken up and sold. A ship may achieve material perpetuity through constant restoration. But captains must live on only in reputation. On July 27 Bainbridge struggled upright on the bed where he had lain helpless for weeks, demanded his sword and pistols, and called aloud on all hands to repel boarders. Then he fell back and two hours later expired.

The ship that Bainbridge had most proudly and jealously identified himself with was the *Independence*, and the commodore's period of decline had coincided with her deterioration in ordinary. No symbolism need be read in this since so many vessels were also experiencing sad neglect. But the officially maligned three-decker had a strange rebirth. Razeed, cut down at last, she reappeared as a 54-gun frigate of excellent seaworthiness. On her first time out, four years after Bainbridge's death, she made full requital for her long abjection with a transatlantic sailing record, clearing Boston Light on May 20, 1837, and only three weeks later beating up the English Channel in time to honor Victoria's accession to the British throne with a forty-one-gun salute off Spithead.

By then steam blemished the horizon. Five years earlier, when tension arose with France over what looked like her hedging on the payment of American spoliation claims dating from the Napoleonic Wars, the predominating bluff in Andrew Jackson's threats of stern action was embarrassingly obvious. France had eighteen steam-propelled ships of war. No United States war steamer was even on the drawing boards. Levi Woodbury deemed it "imprudent" to overlook the "probable importance" of steam to maritime warfare, but neither the Commissioners nor Congress showed a scintilla of enthusiasm for his suggestion that two floating steam batteries be built.

The Board's trouble was a refusal to envisage the possibility of steam totally supplanting sail, while Congress, like the country at large, had forgotten the value of a Navy over the past relatively peaceful decade, and had therefore lost interest in its growth. Woodbury's eloquent reminder in the annual report of the Secretary to Congress in November 1833 is worth quoting from. "It may be well to reflect how safely the Navy enables us not only to send to new and most distant markets, and thus to give increased value to the surplus proceeds of our agriculture, manufactories, and fisheries, and to obtain on return whatever may conduce to our comfort, improvement or wealth, but what protection and enhanced worth it confers on most of our immense coasting trade; and how much our national reputation abroad is known by it, the respect it inspires, the security it yields; and how justly it may be apprehended that new perils will, ere long, await a portion of our trade and the tranquillity of our maritime frontier, and against which the Navy, from the insular situation of our country as to most of the world, must always be regarded as our great safeguard."

But accounts of the Navy's conduct overseas hardly stimulated pride at home. Mothers with sons of tender years on the Mediterranean station lost sleep over the sinful stories told about Port Mahon, where, through the courtesy of Spain, American warships wintered and took on supplies. Vice and insubordination apparently flourished. Rare was the ship's divine service, it was said, that was not followed by the muster of all hands around the capstan to witness punishment. And the officers could not be relied upon to set a good example. Captain Daniel Patterson, for one, regularly visited his constant mistress in Mahon even when his wife shared his quarters on the cruise. Lieutenants and midshipmen were to be found at Mahon's gaming tables or playing host at masquerade balls. And there was considerable indulgence in the ultimate vice of dueling.

Efficiency in the Mediterranean was, understandably, not at a peak. Early in 1834, when the *United States* fired twenty-one guns off Toulon in honor of Louis Philippe's birthday, three that the crew had failed to unshot hit a French shore battery and the ship of war *Suffren*, killing three French sailors. News of American shot striking more legitimate targets was just then beginning to offset the Navy's bad publicity. In 1831 a Salem merchantman in the pepper trade had been plundered by Malay pirates off Sumatra. Andrew Jackson, responding to New England's demand for vengeance and future protection of commerce, changed the sailing orders of the frigate *Potomac* at the last minute; instead of transporting Martin Van Buren to an Ambassador's post in Great Britain, she left New York that August bound for Sumatra. In February 1832 Captain John Downes sent a force of the *Potomac*'s marines ashore at Kuala Batu and they slew 150 natives, guilty or not, an exercise in ruthlessness which fell short of establishing Jackson as a hero among New Englanders and drew criticism from his own party for having so heavy-handedly striven to appease them.

But the political repercussions of Kuala Batu were transitory. Its most notable relevance is to the expansion of American sea power, for the effect on the domestic considerations of the Navy was a shift in emphasis from frivolities at Port Mahon to responsibilities around the world. One year after the *United States* fired blunderingly upon the French at Toulon, the first American naval squadron was on regular patrol in southeast Asian waters.

It was dispatched by Mahlon Dickerson, since July 1, 1834, the eleventh Secretary of the Navy. Dickerson, a theater-loving bachelor from Succasunna, New Jersey, drew periodic fire for the liberal favors he dispensed to officers with imposing congressional connections. This and a sense of frustration based on genuine concern for the Navy's future in a world of technical change developed in him a chronic distaste for his job. He had inherited a fleet badly in need of funds and zeal for its repair and completion: thirteen ships of the line and frigates in their stocks; five ships of the line, two frigates, and six sloops of war in ordinary; one ship of the line, four frigates, and fourteen sloops and schooners in commission; and a far from elite strength of about 6,000 officers and seamen. Dickerson therefore was seemingly whistling in a desert when he declared, "No nation whose fleets may come in contact with ours should be in advance of us in the science or application of steam power." Yet it was under his administration that the sailing Navy took its final steps to dissolution.

Conservative prejudices had isolated many officers from what now can be seen as a national trend toward brisker decisions, scientific inquiry, a zealous girding for revolutionary challenges. Throughout America the once tremendous past was relinquishing its hold on the popular imagination to influences of modernity, industrial innovation, and national growth. This was the decade 1830–40, when the population expanded by one-third, the Midwest opened up rapidly, and the ouster of Indian tribes in the Southeast released tens of millions of acres to land speculators. Americans were journeying to and fro in vaster numbers, steam getting more and more of them to their destinations. In 1834 five hundred steam vessels were plying inland and coastal waters. The Camden and Amboy Railroad was two years old. Yet new American war vessels were essentially the same as in the days of Truxtun and Barry: two or three decks, massive wooden walls, smooth-bore armament, and the majestic pyramid cloud of canvas. Their best speeds hardly exceeded those of medieval Venetian galleasses. Fulton's old war steamer, a barnacled receiving ship at Brooklyn, had accidentally blown up in 1829 with considerable loss of life. Now the Board of Navy Commissioners would not even sanction construction of small steamers for haulage tasks in the navy yards. Commodore Rodgers finally approved the Navy's purchase of a small steam tug to tow warships in and out of New York, but only because the cost of hiring private steamers threatened to become a scandal.

There were admirals in the British Navy every bit as conservative as their American counterparts. Moreover, they could base opposition to steam on firsthand experience. Gun power on the five steam sloops commissioned for the British fleet in 1830 was seriously impaired by their huge side paddles. (The screw propeller did not appear until the 1840's.) Still, by 1836 steam-driven vessels in the British and French navies respectively numbered twenty-one and twenty-three. That same year a group of young American naval officers led by Matthew Calbraith Perry, brother to the late hero of Lake Erie, campaigned for the construction of war steamers with sails for auxiliary power—sheer blasphemy to a naval establishment which had to force itself even to contemplate steam propulsion as a useful auxiliary to sail in such exigent circumstances as calms, through ice, and over sandbars.

Not all the older American officers opposed steam. Commodore Jesse Elliott, during the indemnity crisis with France, had tried to get President Jackson interested in building a steam fleet. Elliott probably got his ideas from Commodore James Barron, whose inventive bent placed him naturally in the front rank of steam visionaries. Barron furnished the Board of Navy Commissioners with unsolicited memoranda on the application of steam to war vessels and devoted much of the period 1833–44 trying vainly to win interest in his steam-powered armored ram, which would have been the first of the ironclads. These still belonged to the future. But steam propulsion was now a matter of practical fact, and, as it happened, authorization for construction of steam batteries for the American Navy already existed, a long-forgotten item in the Act of April 29, 1816, laying down the postwar naval shipbuilding program. Mahlon Dickerson drew the Board's attention to it and on June 26, 1835, directed that an experimental steam war vessel be designed and built. Commodore Rodgers' reply, that the Board knew nothing about steam and should not be trusted by itself to seek contracts for furnishing steam engines, set the tone for an exchange of notes on the subject that leaves one with the impression of a Board of Navy Commissioners adrift and dragging its anchor in despised and uncharted waters.

But the Board was now to lose its central personality. Alfred Mahan says of Commodore John Rodgers that no one better understood the principles of naval strategy. Rodgers himself was only too bitterly aware that his war record would give historians no reason for rating him in a bolder context. Glory had passed him by. High office might have been his—twice he lost the chance of becoming Secretary of the Navy because he would not surrender his naval rank and commission. To have paid this price would have disqualified him from the honor of becoming the nation's first admiral. And this was another hope unrealized, for in session after session Congress resisted the pressure to pass the necessary law. (The rank was not created until 1862.) Rodgers never recovered from cholera he contracted while nursing the dying son of Tobias Lear, the late diplomat and friend of his Tripoli days. He resigned from the Board of Commissioners on May 1, 1837, and was thus spared by two weeks the necessity of applauding the launch of the experimental steam battery *Fulton the Second*. He died in August 1838.

That same summer Mahlon Dickerson, fatigued by the problems of a Navy in transition and the endless disputation over the fitting out of a long-delayed expedition to explore the South Seas, resigned from the Department and hurried back to Succasunna. "I am *steamed* to death," wrote his successor, James K. Paulding, in the face of growing agitation for war steamers. Never would he "consent to see our grand old ships supplanted by these new and ugly sea monsters." History, giving Paulding the reputation of a minor literary lion, has quite overlooked his reputation for mulishness as last Secretary of the Navy in the age of sail and the least progressive of any who ever held the office. He even opposed a shore academy, convinced it would turn out scholars instead of seamen. In March 1839, when Congress, having responded to public demand with provision for three war steamers, directed him to furnish copies of Department correspondence dealing with steam engineering, the Secretary was proud to reply that none existed. He convened two naval boards with an engineer on hand to discuss steamers, comforting himself with the delusion that he was keeping the zealots quiet "by warily administering to the humor of the times." Meanwhile he encouraged the Board of Navy Commissioners to build more and more sailing ships.

But the Commissioners now shaped an uneasy course. Their shipbuilding program had aroused controversy, especially after their designs for the South Seas Exploring Expedition produced three sluggish vessels useless for anything more than salvage work. Following this fiasco, Pennsylvanians blamed the Board for the embarrassment that surrounded completion of the massive four-decker named for their state. The *Pennsylvania* was launched on July 18, 1837, without her bottom coppered and as soon as she was equipped had to be towed to Norfolk, where dry-dock facilities existed for finishing the job. The *Pennsylvania* was now the world's biggest line-of-battle ship, displacing more than 3,000 tons and armed with 104 thirty-two-pounders and 16 of the new French eight-inch-shell guns. From her Hercules figurehead to her ornate quarter galleries she was beautiful and mammoth, an awesome seagoing gun carrier. But to the government, forced by recent economies to reassess the enormous cost of maintaining her complement of 1,100 officers and men, the *Pennsylvania* had become a floating white elephant. She made only that one short cruise, from Philadelphia to Hampton Roads, and thereafter she served as receiving ship for the Norfolk Navy Yard.

The Practical Shipbuilder, the first American textbook on the subject, came out in 1839 with charges that the stultifying influence of the Commissioners had retarded progress in American warship design for two decades. Young officers accused them openly of sending "a nest of tubs" to sea instead of sturdy men-of-war. Congress took up the cry, demanding the Board's abolition. As if to weather the storm of criticism with a yet greater spread of sail, it authorized construction of seven more ship sloops. The Commissioners had no doubt derived confidence from the presence of an arch-conservative in the most strategic position to resist winds of change. But in 1841 this protection vanished with Paulding's resignation from the Navy Department. And in August the following year Congress voted the Board of Navy Commissioners out of existence.

In the structure of separate bureaus which replaced it, provision was made for an office of naval engineering. Only the stubborn could deny now that the sailing Navy belonged to history. The war steamers *Mississippi* and *Missouri* were at sea, and in the fall of 1842 Congress authorized construction of the first ironclad. The revolution took place with no dramatic suddenness. In wind, a smart sloop or frigate could easily outrun the first paddle wheelers. And although sail was assuming a secondary function, it continued for a long while to dominate the scene physically. Indeed, it must have lifted the hearts of diehard officers to observe that on each of the new steamers the boilers, paddle wheels, and three furnaces were overshadowed by some 19,000 square feet of white canvas.

New sailing ships appeared even after the advent of steam. For one thing, there prevailed a policy of restoring rotting frigates, first begun under Samuel Southard in 1829, and often the ship's deterioration was so advanced, her overhaul carried out so thoroughly, that what came off the ways was a wholly new vessel. The *Congress*, broken up at Norfolk in 1836, was redesigned as a frigate of the first class and rebuilt to larger dimensions at Portsmouth, New Hampshire. Launched on August 16, 1841—forty-two years and a day after the launching of the original *Congress*—she was the last and probably the finest sailing frigate designed for the United States Navy. She was not the last frigate *launched*. Work on half a dozen of the 44-gun vessels approved by Congress in 1816, their keels laid about 1820, had proceeded so slowly that they left their stocks in the 1840's and 1850's: the *Cumberland, Savannah, Raritan, St. Lawrence, Sabine,* and finally, on February 16, 1855, the *Santee*—splendid frigates launched into immediate obsolescence.

The frigate *Constellation*'s long and valuable career included a circumnavigation of the world during which she sailed by log more than 58,000 miles in 492 days at sea. From time to time she was extensively repaired and at last, in the Norfolk Navy Yard, she was broken up and entirely rebuilt as a 22-gun sloop of war. The new *Constellation* that cleared Hampton Roads on August 10, 1855, while bearing the name of the first of the federal government frigates to put out, was not of the same model, dimensions, appearance, or gun rate. Still in existence today after further periods of "restoration," she was the last sailing man-of-war designed and built for the United States Navy.

One by one, the old commodores vanished with the sails they had fought under. Some, like Charles Morris, Jacob Jones, and Charles Stewart (who lived until he was ninety-one), served out their years without ostentation. Others flaunted their self-importance to the end. In 1839 Isaac Hull, no longer attacking the broad pendant since command of a squadron off South America had won him the privilege of flying it, provoked close to a wardroom officers' mutiny on the *Ohio*'s first cruise. The Secretary of the Navy, James Paulding, had allowed the commodore's wife to accompany him as far as Italy, but he learned too late that one, perhaps two, of Mrs. Hull's sisters were also on board. "This was certainly not my intention," Paulding wrote to the commodore, only to hear next that, far from getting off at Italy, Mrs. Hull "has in fact assumed command of the ship." Protest petitions trailed each other from Port Mahon to Washington, and in their wake appeared three officers sent home by Hull for disrespect. Paulding could think of nothing better to do than send them back out. Fortunately for his dilemma, a groundless report that Britain planned to bottle up the American squadron in the Mediterranean resulted in the *Ohio*'s immediate recall. Two years later Hull, his business sense alert even in the face of approaching death, summoned the undertaker to discuss what effects his now extreme fatness would have upon the dimensions and cost of his casket. He died February 13, 1843, with, it was said, the declaration, "I strike my flag."

Jesse Duncan Elliott charmed and blustered on foreign station with considerable benefit to his country. When Spain in 1829 tried to regain control over Mexico, it was a squadron under Elliott that neutralized the Old World threat while safeguarding American interests endangered by the new republic's internal strife. Andrew Jackson considered Elliott the right man for touchy domestic situations as well. Although the commodore acted off his own bat by sending seamen and marines to assist the suppression of Nat Turner's slave revolt along the James in 1831, when the President got to hear about it he warmly approved, and the next year, during the nullification crisis, Elliott was his choice for the naval intimidation of South Carolina. The commodore confronted Charleston with the sloop of war *Natchez* and made a significant show of exercising her eighteen guns.

Out of appreciation for Jackson's faith in him, when Elliott took command of the Boston Navy Yard during the *Constitution*'s reconstruction there, he resolved to "put the General on the bow." But Boston detested Jackson while revering Old Ironsides, and in the summer of 1834 during a stormy night a young merchant captain named Samuel Dewey stole on board the *Constitution* with a saw, auger, and cordage and removed the head "very neatly sawed immediately below the nose and ears."

The *Constitution* was fitted with another Jackson head off Sandy Hook, a safe distance from Boston, and for the next three years she patrolled the Mediterranean, Elliott showing the flag—off Lisbon, for example, when Portugal struck him as becoming "somewhat lukewarm on the subject of our affairs"—and winning compliments from kings, queens, and various potentates. He also piled his decks with gifts, booty, and livestock, and sowed such a harvest of grievances among the frigate's people that scandalous reports about "Old Bruin" soon drifted back to America. (After the War of 1812 "Old Bruin" seems to have been in common use as a people's epithet for overbearing officers. It was frequently applied to Elliott in the closing days of sail, even by newspapers.) When the *Constitution* anchored at Norfolk in August 1838, her crew, their furloughs delayed, were made to unload a remarkable cargo including horses, jackasses, animal feed, rare coins, marble columns, slabs and busts, and two massive sarcophagi from Beirut.

And Elliott now found himself the cause of widespread denunciation from every quarter over his sacrifice of the crew's comfort and ship's efficiency for the convenience of jackasses. The Battle of Lake Erie was raked over and Elliott's willingness to shed American blood contrasted with his diffidence before the British. The duel at Bladensburg was rehashed and Elliott forced to solicit privately a letter from Barron to the Baltimore *Sun* testifying that he had taken no part in the duel correspondence. No such letter appeared.

In May 1840 Commodore Elliott faced trial on thirteen charges of misconduct in the Mediterranean, ranging from oppression and immorality to wastage of public funds. Part of his defense was that by bringing jackasses home he only meant to improve the American breed. A court consisting almost entirely of his juniors judged him guilty on five counts. He was sentenced to four years' suspension from the service. After the first two he sought permission to use up the balance by serving in the French Navy. Perhaps fortunately for then improving Franco-American relations, political friends returned to power with the new administration of John Tyler, and what remained of Elliott's sentence was remitted. His Mediterranean relics were distributed among universities and scientific institutes. He offered one of the sarcophagi to an ailing Andrew Jackson as a roomy and "noble receptacle" for his mortal remains. The former President graciously refused it as too imperial for a republican to spend eternity in and Elliott donated it to the Smithsonian Institution, where it still rests.

Jesse Elliott had thrived on controversy. A long speech that he delivered in the courthouse of his Maryland birthplace, Hagerstown, reviewing his disheveled career without apology, was afterward published by him as a book-sized pamphlet, and relish can be read in almost every line. It was his valedictory. In December 1845 he died peacefully, aged sixty-three.

James Barron outlived his sometimes indistinguishable friends and foes. In March 1846 Commodore William Crane, last survivor of the lieutenants who testified against him at the *Chesapeake* court-martial, cut his throat in the Navy Department. As death overtook Barron's contemporaries, their pasts were recounted in charitable terms. Obituary writers recalled defeats as triumphs and turned lapses into virtues. Commodore Isaac Chauncey was eulogized for avoiding

"Very neatly sawed between the nose and the ears." The Andrew Jackson figurehead installed by Commodore Elliott's orders on the *Constitution* after removal at night by an offended Bostonian. *United States Navy*

The new Jackson figurehead for "Old Ironsides," restored by Elliott at a safe distance from Boston. Now at the U.S. Naval Academy. *United States Navy*

Original sailmaker's plan of the *Independence*, the U.S. Navy's first ship of the line. *United States Navy*

The Mediterranean squadron off Port Mahon, 1825. From left to right: ship of the line *North Carolina*, frigates *Constitution* and *Brandywine*, sloops *Erie* and *Ontario*. Painted by A. Carlotta. *Courtesy of the Naval Historical Foundation*

bloodshed on the Great Lakes, his campaign against Yeo being described as "a war of tactics between two inland admirals [with] several beautiful chases and some elegant maneuvering." As if to ensure a measure of approbation when Barron's time came and repair his record for posterity, a son-in-law in 1843 petitioned the government to nullify the sentence of the *Chesapeake* court-martial on grounds that witnesses should have been sworn in by its Judge Advocate, not by its president. But (replied the government) a request to set aside a judicial sentence, approved by the President of the United States, on a minor technicality and after the passage of a generation, was to expect too much.

Barron, since the death of John Rodgers, had borne his inerasable stain in the conspicuous position of senior officer of the United States Navy. Despite command of navy yards (Philadelphia, then Norfolk), the sense of being ostracized accompanied him to his grave. Records of the United States Patent Office show thirteen inventions in Barron's name. No one could have convinced him that the indifference with which they were received was anything but willful.

Given the conservatism of the naval establishment, it is questionable whether the products of an inventor less stigmatized would have aroused any greater interest. To what degree those of Commodore Barron could have assisted the Navy's improvement can never be known. What can be gathered from private correspondence is the dolefulness of his last years. There is no evidence of final satisfaction as to the wisdom of his life's decisions. All his unhappiness had flowed from the apprehensions that he allowed to govern his conduct on that fateful afternoon in June 1807, and yielding to them, he seems to have felt, was his one big mistake. The impression is strengthened by a remark in a letter advising his grandson to "guard against too great a degree of anxiety on all occasions, for it often leads men into ruinous difficulties." This was probably the last piece of moral counsel the commodore issued to anybody. He died in April 1851 in his eighty-third year and was mourned in the South as a brave and ill-requited patriot.

The generous sentimentality which the nation in the mid-nineteenth century accorded departing naval veterans (the few black sheep excepted) was, in a way, a fond farewell to its own recent past.

Due in part to population growth and scientific modernization, Americans very suddenly lost contemporaneity with the generation of the founding fathers. That generation included the War of 1812, a conflict which was, in fact, popularly regarded, outside New England at least, as a continuance of the struggle for independence. So its naval heroes were viewed in the same affectionate perspective as those of the Revolutionary War and their memory began immediately to undergo a unique romanticizing process. This has led to a comparative scarcity of intelligent literature about the Navy under sail and, what seems even more of an injustice to the captains and commodores, a perversion of the subject into patriotic juvenilia and superpatriotic myth.

The Navy meanwhile has kept their memory alive in the traditional fashion of naming ships after them. The rush of destroyers down the launching ways from World War I through World War II caused an intensive search for personalities meriting historic distinction, and the result has been a warships' register peppered with obscure names that baffle even naval historians. The shortage of suitable candidates, however, has never been so acute that the names of Barron, Gordon, or Jesse Duncan Elliott have had to be considered. Stephen Decatur has had at least five ships named for him. Captain Thomas Tingey, who ruled the Washington Navy Yard for twenty-seven years, has not been overlooked. The Secretaries of the Navy have been well represented, even including a 1918 destroyer commemorating Andrew Jackson's uninspired appointee John Branch. Today, the memory of several notables of the United States Navy under sail is enshrined in the nomenclature of vessels whose class, armament, motive power, and operational function their imaginations could never have conceived. Guided-missile destroyers that form part of America's antisubmarine warfare fleet carry the names *Benjamin Stoddert, Decatur, Macdonough, Preble, Sterrett, Biddle*. A fleet of nuclear-powered frigates is in process of creation, and the first two ever to be launched were christened *Bainbridge* and *Truxtun*.

CHAPTER TWENTY-FOUR

Epilogue

THE STEAM SLOOP *Pawnee* was racing against time. After dropping down the Potomac from Washington, she anchored off Fort Monroe just long enough to augment her force of a hundred men with a regiment of Massachusetts volunteers. Then she labored on for the Norfolk Navy Yard, Commodore Hiram Paulding, whose flag she flew, chafing with anxiety lest he arrive too late. The federal government's largest naval installation—ninety acres of ship houses, workshops, guns, armories, and a granite dry dock—was in the hands of an irresolute old man at close quarters with treason. It was April 20, 1861.

An insurrectionist attempt to capture the Navy Yard was believed certain to coincide with the outbreak of general fighting. Subversion within the Yard and clamorous hostility at its gates ruled out the practicability of trying to keep it in operation. Paulding's orders were to relieve the commandant and save the guns, ships, and shipbuilding material from rebel seizure, by successful defense or, if necessary, by destruction. Hence the *Pawnee*'s cargo: forty barrels of gunpowder, eleven tanks of turpentine, twelve barrels of cotton waste, and 181 portfires for igniting them. Paulding hoped to get the steam frigate *Merrimac* out if, as he expected, she was stoked up and ready. The other vessels at Norfolk were much less important, derelict even, their worth scarcely measurable in other than sentimental terms.

No larger or more representative collection of relics from the bygone Navy was assembled at any other yard. Except for the sloop of war *Cumberland* (cut down from a frigate), anchored 200 yards off shore, they lay fairly close together, rather like variously sized creatures of a species facing extinction herded for last futile comfort: the brig *Dolphin*, the first-class ship sloops *Plymouth* and *Germantown*; the first frigate launched, *United States*, and two from a later period, the *Raritan* and *Columbia*; the unfinished ship of the line *New York*, forty-three years in her stocks; the veteran 74-gun liners *Columbus* and *Delaware*; and finally, rooted in the mud since 1842 as a receiving ship, the enormous *Pennsylvania*.

Commodore Charles Stewart McCauley, commandant of the Navy Yard, was in a desperate state. Trains rumbled into Norfolk's waterfront railroad station daily, unloading columns of taunting rebel troops. His masthead lookouts on the *Cumberland* reported rebel batteries being mounted beyond the trees facing the Yard entrance. More than half of his officers boasted rebel sympathies and down to the lowliest watchman he could trust no one. He looked in vain for the Union reinforcements promised him by the government in Washington, and now, at about 4 P.M., the shouting at the gates grew louder and sudden panic dictated what was to be his last act of command. He ordered the *Merrimac, Germantown, Plymouth,* and *Dolphin* scuttled where they lay and the Navy Yard guns spiked. When the *Pawnee* made fast alongside the Yard at 8 P.M., Commodore Paulding found four ships settling.

Then the fear of imminent attack gripped him too. He sent out the Massachusetts volunteers and the *Pawnee*'s marines to plug the Yard buildings with inflammables, to set explosives at the dry dock, and to disable 300 modern Dahlgren guns with eighteen-pound sledgehammers. And he ordered Lieutenant Henry Wise to take a boat party among the ships and lay powder trains.

The lieutenant worked from a penciled list of the ships to be destroyed. His men first boarded the *Merrimac* and then attended to the sailing ships. Despite the intimidating uproar from the Yard gates, Wise labored with methodical coolness. Scuttled ships can be raised. It was essential that these burn before they could sink. Thus he had them thoroughly prepared. On each vessel two lines of combustibles formed a V by meeting at the foot of the mainmast, their turpentine-soaked rope ends protruding through ports. Turpentine ran over the decks fore and aft. The *United States* was so

Destruction of the sailing warships at Norfolk, April 20, 1861. The *Pennsylvania* in the center. *Smithsonian Institution, Washington, D.C.*

"Largest ship in the world." The 120-gun line-of-battle ship *Pennsylvania*. Her sailing career consisted solely of a cruise from her place of launch, Philadelphia, to dry dock and retirement at Norfolk. From a sketch by C. C. Barton, USN. Lithograph by A. Hoffy. *Courtesy of the Franklin D. Roosevelt Library*

Three veteran ships photographed. Training vessels for U.S. Naval Academy midshipmen, seen here moored for safety at Newport, Rhode Island, during the Civil War. Left to right: the *Constitution,* the *Santee,* and (rebuilt as a first-class ship sloop) the *Macedonian. Courtesy of the U.S. Naval Academy*

decayed it was decided not to waste combustibles on her. No trains were laid on the *Pennsylvania* either, it being calculated that she would take fire from the vessels on both her quarters. By 2 A.M. all was ready. The noise from beyond the gates had subsided. The night was calm, starlit.

Commodore McCauley's command of the Norfolk Navy Yard had foundered in a crisis of divided loyalties. The planned annihilation of revered ships snapped what remained of his self-control. He had served fifty-two years in the Navy, almost entirely under sail. Paulding disregarded his emotional refusals to leave the Navy Yard and ordered him forced on board the *Pawnee*. About now the marines and volunteers marched back to the steam sloop, having failed to break a single trunnion on the Dahlgrens. The Yard's marine barracks prematurely burst into flames as the *Pawnee* shoved off with the *Cumberland* in tow. At 4:20 A.M. Paulding ordered a rocket fired, and on this signal the party remaining behind ignited powder trains and applied portfires. Then they put off hurriedly in boats after the *Pawnee*.

Within thirty minutes, wrote a *New York Times* correspondent, the conflagration was roaring like a hurricane. The escaping boats ran through tumbling flakes of fire. Flames from a ship house reached the *Pennsylvania* and leaped up her vast sides. Slowly settling ships burned to the water line, except for the *Delaware* and *Plymouth*, which cheated the fire by sinking out of sight. The gunpowder at the dry dock failed to ignite, but workshops and two huge ship houses burst into crackling infernos. And "in all this magnificent scene the old *Pennsylvania* was the center piece. She was a very giant in death as she had been in life. From every porthole of every deck spouted torrents and cataracts of fire, that to the mind of Milton would have represented her as a frigate of hell pouring out unremitting broadsides of infernal fire." The great ship burned for five and a half hours, some of her guns discharging, and at daybreak her mainmast tottered and came crashing down in a swirling cloud of sparks.

One could hardly wish for a more vivid spectacle to symbolize the end of the sailing Navy. Few scenes provide dramatic fulfillment more satisfyingly than a funeral pyre. And, with perfect coincidence, the ships were set afire on the sixty-fifth anniversary of the Act of April 20, 1796, which, by authorizing completion of the *United*

States, Constitution, and *Constellation,* ensured the genesis of the Navy. However, the holocaust at Norfolk was but one dramatic scene in the closing act. The other awaited the salvaging of the half-burned *Merrimac* and her conversion into an iron ramship. On March 2, 1862, with a full head of steam she descended into Hampton Roads, where the *Cumberland* and the handsome frigate *Congress* were blockading the mouth of the James. Both sailing ships deluged her with full broadsides, but the balls clanged uselessly off her sloping iron. She rammed the *Cumberland* amidships, withdrew to fire her bow pivot gun, and rammed the sloop of war again. The *Cumberland* sank with her Stars and Stripes still flying from the gaff. The *Congress* ceased her futile fire, slipped cables, ran aground, and blew up under the ironclad's bombardment.

A month after the tragic end of that last sailing frigate, the first was attacked by Confederate axmen trying to sink her as a blockship in the Elizabeth River. But the decayed hulk of the *United States* showed astonishing resistance. A whole box of axes was destroyed, it was said, without even piercing her sides. She had to be bored from within, and not until 1866 was she finally broken up.

The most notable warship of the early sailing Navy to survive into the twentieth century was the razeed *Independence.* After her successful career as a frigate, she served as receiving ship at Mare Island, California, until 1912, when she was condemned as unfit for human habitation and the following year scrapped. Today, the only substantial accumulation of original timber from a vessel of the early sailing Navy is preserved at an out-of-the-way village in Hampshire, England. When in 1820 the frigate *Chesapeake,* following a last ignominious service as a Devon prison ship, was broken up and sold, some of her timbers were used to build houses in Portsmouth. But far the greater amount went into construction of a red brick mill ten miles distant in Wickham. German bombs in World War II destroyed the houses. The mill is still in operation, nestling near a riverbank, with its joists and floor beams, portions of deck once paced by Barron, Decatur, and Lawrence, easily visible from within. Under the British Town and Country Planning Act the Chesapeake Mill was designated in 1954 as a building of historic interest. It is seldom visited by Americans.

Sources

The principal research for this book concentrated upon the Naval Records Collection, Record Group 45, maintained by the Naval History Division, Department of the Navy, and housed in the United States National Archives, Washington, D.C. While the main wealth of RG 45 consists of the bound correspondence between each Secretary of the Navy and his officers, the collection also includes a number of ships' logs, journals, and private diaries. Valuable material was found in the section of RG 45 entitled "Area File, 1775–1910," officially designed to preserve unbound miscellany in eight different geographical categories. The contents are generally unsorted and cover a broad range of subject matter from squadron deployment and prize-money claims to naval discipline and duels.

Also in the National Archives, the Records of the Judge Advocate General (Navy), RG 125, are essential to the study of court-martial and court-of-inquiry hearings; and there is considerable material relating to naval affairs scattered among the General Records of the Department of State, RG 59.

Headway throughout the task of preparation demanded such habitual employment of these official records that a detailed chapter-by-chapter explanation of sources would tax the reader with repetition. The following selected references, approximating in order the chronology of the book, are for the most part other than the aforementioned official records:

For the exchange of views between John Adams and Thomas Jefferson regarding the use and cost of a navy, we consulted *The Adams-Jefferson Letters* edited by Lester J. Cappon (2 vols., Chapel Hill, University of North Carolina Press, 1959). Alexander Hamilton's doodled minutes at the private caucus to plan for a navy are in possession of the Charleston (South Carolina) Library Society. The primary source for our study of the early naval debates and measures in Congress was, of course, the *Annals of Congress, 1789–1824* (Washington, D.C., 1834–56), but one can ask for no better guides to the legislative foundation of the United States Navy than *The Congress Founds a Navy, 1787–1798* by Marshall Smelser (Notre Dame, University of Notre Dame, 1959) and *The Rise of American Naval Power* by Harold and Margaret Sprout (Princeton, Princeton University Press, 1939). As for the technicalities and development of early sailing warship design, they are affectionately and exhaustively detailed by Howard Chapelle in *The History of the American Sailing Navy* (New York, Norton, 1949).

The Thomas Truxtun letterbooks in the Historical Society of Pennsylvania threw valuable light on the commodore's personality and experiences. In addition to these and the official records, the Adams Family Private Papers (microfilm copies in the Library of Congress, Manuscript Division) were drawn upon for material concerning the quasi war with France and Benjamin Stoddert's varied difficulties with the infant Navy. The unusual agreement between Great Britain and the United States regarding private signals is fully disclosed in "Miscellaneous Letters, Department of State, January 5–December 31, 1798" (National Archives).

The formidable task of researching the quasi war has been greatly facilitated since publication of *Naval Documents Related to the Quasi-War between the United States and France: Naval Operations from February 1797 to December 1801* (U.S. Office of Naval Records and Library, Government Printing Office, 1935–38, 7 vols.). The same holds true with respect to the Tripoli War: *Naval Documents Related to the United States Wars with the Barbary Powers: Naval Operations Including Diplomatic Background from 1785 through 1807* (U.S. Office of Naval Records and Library, Government Printing Office, 1939–44, 6 vols.), which, while replete with information, serves also as a multiple signpost to primary sources as far apart as the Edward Preble Papers in the Library of Congress and the Log of the *George Washington* in the Henry E. Huntington Library and Art Gallery, San Marino, California.

The description of the loss of the *Philadelphia* is derived from the Edward Preble Papers; *Horrors of Slavery: or, The American Tars in Tripoli* by William Ray (Troy, New York, 1808); and the report to the Secretary of the Navy of the court of inquiry into the loss. William Bainbridge's letters of torment from prison appear in the Preble Papers and *The Life and Services of Commodore William Bainbridge* by Thomas Harris, M.D. (Philadelphia, Lea and Blanchard, 1837).

A biographical note on Stephen Decatur in the Wilmington *Commercial*, December 22, 1874, attributing his entrance into the Navy to a local scandal, would be entitled to no serious consideration but for the naming, after a period of some eight decades, of two lawyers allegedly involved. Investigation shows them to have existed and been active in the Philadelphia area, and one was a member of a family on close terms with the Decaturs. A recollection of Decatur as describing (in 1804) James Barron as "more than a father" to him is contained in a letter from Captain Arthur Sinclair to Caesar Rodney, April 17, 1820, among the Caesar Rodney Collection in the Delaware Historical Society, Wilmington, Delaware. For the campaign against Tripoli under the successive commands of Samuel Barron and John Rodgers we studied the Barron Family Papers in the Library of the College of William and Mary, Williamsburg, Virginia; the Rodgers Family Papers in the Library of Congress, Manuscript Division; and the microfilmed collection of John Rodgers Papers in the Navy Department Library, Washington, D.C. The genesis of the John Rodgers–James Barron enmity is revealed in a letter dated July 10, 1805, from Captain William Bainbridge to Lieutenant David Porter, in the U.S. Navy Collection, New-York Historical Society.

Lieutenant William Henry Allen's disclosure that "more than half the seamen in the United States Navy are foreigners" was made to Senator William

Plumer, his traveling companion in a northbound stage, March 1807 (Plumer Papers, Library of Congress, Manuscript Division). The significant link between Captain Charles Gordon and the Nicholsons and Gallatins was verified among the genealogical holdings of the Hall of Records, Annapolis, Maryland, and strengthened by the discovery of several references to Gordon in the Albert Gallatin Family Papers, New-York Historical Society, and the collection of Joseph Hopper Nicholson correspondence in the Library of Congress. The nature of his father's shame, which he felt obliged to live down, is described in "Charles Gordon: Jacobite and Loyalist," an article by Herbert Baird Stimpson in the *South Atlantic Quarterly*, Vol. 27, No. 4, October 1928. The increasingly agitated spring-summer 1807 correspondence, concerning deserters, that went on between the British envoys, the Mayor of Norfolk, and Admiral George Berkeley, was traced in the photostat collection of the British Public Records Office, Admiralty Papers, in the Library of Congress, Manuscript Division; and the Admiral George Berkeley Letters, Toronto Public Library, Toronto, Ontario. The key omission that contributed to the *Chesapeake* affair, namely, David Erskine's failure to apply for the restoration of Jenkin Ratford, was detected in a letter James Madison wrote to Erskine on October 9, 1807, among the documentary collection entitled "Department of State, Notes to Great Britain, 1807" (National Archives).

For the *Leopard*'s attack we consulted "Occurrences and Remarks Aboard the United States Frigate *Chesapeake*," a journal kept by Lieutenant William H. Allen (Huntington Library and Art Gallery); a journal aboard the same ship kept by Midshipman Alexander Wadsworth (Maine Historical Society); the Log of the *Chesapeake* (Library of Congress); a small but revealing collection of Lieutenant Allen's letters also in the Library of Congress; which of course Commodore Barron's official report to the Secretary of the Navy, and his private observations (Barron Papers, William and Mary College).

The most impressive evidence of the feelings of the *Chesapeake*'s officers toward Barron appears in the handwritten minutes of the court of inquiry into the frigate's surrender, long believed "lost" but which turned up at the National Archives under the impetus of our research. A request by Decatur's widow in 1821 for a copy of the hearings of the court-martial led to the publication, at the behest of President Monroe, of *Proceedings of a General Court Martial Convened for the Trial of Commodore James Barron, Captain Charles Gordon, Mr. William Hook, and Captain John Hall of the United States Ship Chesapeake, January 1808* (Published by Order of the Navy Department, Washington, 1822. In a pamphlet published as *Notes to the Trial of Commodore Barron, 1808* (New-York Historical Society) Barron cites Captain Hall's confession that his and Captain Charles Gordon's defenses were composed for them by the Judge Advocate, Littleton Tazewell.

A number of personal glimpses by participants in the War of 1812 were gathered from their letters to John Bullus (U.S. Navy Box and Miscellaneous Papers, New York Public Library). For operations on the Great Lakes we drew in part from the extensive number of documents, issued by both sides, contained in *Documentary History of the Campaigns on the Niagara Frontier, 1812–14*, edited by Lieutenant-Colonel E. Cruikshank, F.R.S.C., for the Lundy's Lane Historical Society (Welland, Ontario, 1908). In general, our account of the conflict is based upon the official records in the National Archives.

Benjamin Crowninshield's private letter to Decatur, March 14, 1815, offering him a choice of commands, is described by Alexander Slidell Mackenzie in *The Life of Stephen Decatur, a Commodore in the Navy of the United States* (Boston, Little, Brown, 1846). The commodore's reply, March 20, 1815, and his wife's attempted intervention, in the preceding month, to keep him at home, are among the Benjamin Crowninshield Papers in the Peabody Museum, Salem, Massachusetts. The measure of Decatur's fallen stock with Mediterranean diplomats following his "peace" with Algiers, and Consul Shaler's opinion of the rival commodores and his complaints to the government, are all to be found in the William Shaler Papers (Historical Society of Pennsylvania), which also contain some self-revealing correspondence from Decatur, including his own observation on Bainbridge's attempt to snub him off Gibraltar.

According to an unsigned note accompanying a slim folder of William Bainbridge material in the New-York Historical Society, letters dealing with the Barron-Decatur duel were, at his death, burned in the backyard of his daughter's home. Purser Samuel Hambleton's account of the duel is to be found in the Commodore David Porter Papers, Library of Congress, Manuscript Division. Commodore Barron's version is in William and Mary College. The duel correspondence furnished by Bainbridge was published in the Norfolk *Beacon* on April 8, 1820, subsequently in other newspapers, and in Mackenzie's *Decatur*. Barron sent his copies to the Richmond *Enquirer*. Since there was talk, supposedly emanating from Barron's side, of suppressed letters, the following may be of interest: Near the close of the correspondence, Decatur had been obliged to write Barron two letters announcing his authorization of Bainbridge as his friend, the first letter having gone unacknowledged. The second letter, still in existence and apparently of no dark significance, was omitted from the published texts. The text of the duel correspondence appearing in the appendix to Mackenzie's *Decatur* includes an acknowledgment by Decatur of a letter from Bainbridge dated February 6, 1820. Nothing in Decatur's words gives any indication of the nature of this letter from his second, which, since it has never come to light, may be entitled to classification as "missing."

The extent to which Commodore David Porter embarrassed the United States Government in 1825 by his activities in Mexico is thoroughly conveyed in Volumes 6 and 7 of *The Memoirs of John Quincy Adams*, edited by Charles Francis Adams (Philadelphia, J. B. Lippincott, 1874–77, 12 vols.). Andrew Jackson's partiality for Jesse Duncan Elliott as a naval officer is attested to in the Levi Woodbury Papers, Library of Congress, in which collection we also found considerable evidence of the Navy's declining popularity during the first half of Jackson's administration. The extreme conservatism of the last Secretary of the Navy under sail is self-displayed in *James Kirke Paulding: Letters* (Madison, University of Wisconsin Press, 1962).

In addition to the sources mentioned above, the following were seen or consulted.

Adams, Henry. *The Life of Albert Gallatin*. Philadelphia: J. B. Lippincott, 1879.

Allen, Gardner W. *Our Navy and the Barbary Corsairs*. Boston: Houghton Mifflin, 1905.

———. *Our Naval War with France*. Boston: Houghton Mifflin, 1909.

————. *Our Navy and the West Indian Pirates.* Salem: Essex Institute, 1929.

————, ed. *Commodore Hull; Papers of Isaac Hull, Commodore, United States Navy.* Boston: Boston Atheneum, 1929.

American State Papers (Naval Affairs). Washington, D.C.: Gales and Seaton, 1834.

Baltimore *Patriot.*

Baltimore *Sun.*

Brant, Irving. *James Madison* (6 vols.). Indianapolis: Bobbs-Merrill, 1941–61.

Cooper, James Fenimore. *History of the Navy of the United States* (2 vols.). Philadelphia: Lea and Blanchard, 1839.

Cowdery, Jonathan. *American Captives in Tripoli.* Boston, 1806.

Dickerson, Mahlon. Papers. New Jersey Historical Society.

Emmerson, John C. (compiler). *The Chesapeake Affair of 1807.* Portsmouth, Virginia: privately printed, 1954.

Ferguson, Eugene S. *Truxtun of the Constellation.* Baltimore: Johns Hopkins Press, 1956.

Irving, Pierre M., ed. *Life and Letters of Washington Irving* (4 vols.). New York: G. Putnam, 1863–64.

Lewis, Charles Lee. *The Romantic Decatur.* Philadelphia: University of Pennsylvania Press, 1937.

Macdonough, Rodney. *The Life of Commodore Thomas Macdonough of the United States Navy.* Boston: Fort Hill Press, 1909.

Mackenzie, Alexander Slidell. *The Life of Commodore Oliver Hazard Perry* (2 vols.). New York: Harper & Brothers, 1843.

Maclay, Edgar. *A History of the United States Navy* (3 vols.). New York: D. Appleton, 1917.

Mahan, Alfred T. *Sea Power in Its Relation to the War of 1812* (2 vols.). Boston: Little, Brown, 1905.

Morris, Charles. *Autobiography of Commodore Charles Morris.* Boston: A. Williams, 1880.

National Intelligencer.

National Manuscript Collection, National Archives & Records, Franklin Delano Roosevelt Library, Hyde Park, N.Y.

Niles' Weekly Register.

Norfolk and Portsmouth *Herald.*

Paullin, Charles O. *Commodore John Rodgers.* Cleveland: Arthur Clarke Co., 1910.

————. *Battle of Lake Erie.* Cleveland: Arthur Clarke Co., 1918.

————. "Early Naval Administration Under the Constitution." *Naval Institute Proceedings,* Annapolis, Vol. XXXII, 1906.

Philadelphia *Gazette.*

Pinckney, Pauline A. *American Figureheads and Their Carvers.* New York: Norton, 1940.

Porter, Commodore David. *Journal of a Cruise Made to the Pacific Ocean* (2 vols.). New York: Wiley and Halstead, 1822.

Porter, David D. *Memoir of Commodore David Porter.* Albany: J. Munsell, 1875.

Roosevelt, Theodore. *The Naval War of 1812.* New York: Putnam, 1882.

Roos, Hon. Frederick Fitzgerald (R.N.). *Travels in the United States and Canada.* London: W. H. Ainsworth, 1827.

Southard, Samuel. Papers. Library, Princeton University.

Trial of John Wilson Alias Jenkin Ratford. Boston: Snelling and Simons, 1807, from a pamphlet published in Halifax, N.S.

United States Naval Academy Museum: The Zabriskie, Rosenbach and Miscellaneous Manuscript Collections.

United States Navy Department: *Annual Reports* of the Secretary of the Navy, 1824–40.

War of 1812 Collection of Manuscripts. Bloomington, Lilly Library, University of Indiana.

War of 1812 Collection of Manuscripts. Ann Arbor, William L. Clements Library, University of Michigan.

Index

About the Authors

Fascination with naval history and historical mysteries (in this case the Decatur-Barron feud), and an opportunity to comb through previously uncatalogued naval documents in the National Archives, prompted the collaboration of Leonard F. Guttridge and Jay D. Smith that resulted in this book. A native of Cardiff, Wales, Mr. Guttridge moved to Washington, D.C., in 1947, where he worked as Librarian to the Embassy of India. He lives in Alexandria, Virginia, with his wife and two children and now writes full time. Mr. Smith was born in Harrisburg, Pennsylvania, attended the University of Pittsburgh, and served as a career officer in the United States Air Force for twenty-one years. He lives in Spain and has contributed articles to *Saturday Review*, *Jazz Review*, and *Overseas Weekly*.

ABOUT THE EDITOR

JAMES C. BRADFORD was born in Michigan in 1945, attended Michigan State University where he earned his B.A. and M.A. in History, and studied early American history at the University of Virginia, from which he received his Ph.D. He taught at the U.S. Naval Academy for eight years before joining the faculty of Texas A&M University, where he teaches courses in naval and early American history. His principal research interests are navies in the Age of Sail and the lives of naval officers. He is currently editing the first comprehensive collection of the papers of John Paul Jones. Recent publications include *Anne Arundel County, Maryland: A Bicentennial History, Makers of the American Naval Tradition: Command under Sail*, and articles on John Paul Jones. In addition, he serves as the book review editor of *The Journal of the Early Republic*.